War in The Gulf

WAR IN THE GULF, 1990–91

The Iraq–Kuwait Conflict and Its Implications

Majid Khadduri
Edmund Ghareeb

New York • Oxford • OXFORD UNIVERSITY PRESS • 1997

Oxford University Press

Oxford   New York
Athens   Auckland   Bangkok   Bogotá   Bombay
Buenos Aires   Calcutta   Cape Town   Dar es Salaam
Delhi   Florence   Hong Kong   Istanbul   Karachi
Kuala Lumpur   Madras   Madrid   Melbourne
Mexico City   Nairobi   Paris   Singapore
Taipei   Tokyo   Toronto

and associated companies in
Berlin   Ibadan

Copyright © 1997 by Oxford University Press, Inc.

Published by Oxford University Press, Inc.
198 Madison Avenue, New York, New York 10016

Library of Congress Cataloging-in-Publication Data
Khadduri, Majid, 1908–
War in the Gulf, 1990–91:
the Iraq-Kuwait conflict and its implications /
Majid Khadduri and Edmund Ghareeb.
p.   cm.   Includes bibliographical references and index.
ISBN 0-19-508384-9
1. Persian Gulf War, 1991.
I. Ghareeb, Edmund.   II. Title.
DS79.72.K397   1997
956.7044'2—dc20   96-33658

1 2 3 4 5 6 7 8 9

Printed in the United States of America
on acid-free paper

Dedicated
to
Shirin and Faris

Preface

E ver since the Gulf crisis ensued in 1990, an increasing number of authors have commented on the subject, but almost all have viewed the crisis created by Iraq's invasion of Kuwait as an act of aggression and a threat to international peace and security. For this reason, the Western powers, under the aegis of the United Nations, have been portrayed as intervening not only to compel Iraq to withdraw from Kuwait, but also to reestablish peace and security in the world.

This view, however, is one-sided. True, Iraq had violated the Charter of the United Nations which prohibits aggression and calls for the settlement of disputes by peaceful means. But Western intervention to restore the status quo—instead of dealing with a crisis whose roots and cumulative differences between two neighbors over frontier, territory, and sovereignty—is not an answer to longstanding disputes that have lasted over three-quarters of a century. Nor is the settlement of a crisis reached under pressure a guarantee for future peace and security.

The purpose of this work is to provide readers with "views from the other side." But this does not mean that we intend to provide an uncritical summary of these views. Our intention is rather to analyze the events and differences that culminated in the invasion of Kuwait and subsequently to examine Western intervention and its consequences. This work, dealing essentially with the political and legal aspects of the subject, is not a study in military strategy.

Apart from published official and unofficial documents, we have made use of personal contacts with men in high authority, some formed during our previous travels to the Arab world, some during their visits to the United States. We have also sought the advice of Arab scholars and writers who provided us with information and counsel. We should like to acknowledge the kindness extended to us by all from whom we had the privilege of seeking advice and assistance. No one, however, is responsible for any error or for our personal views in this work.

M.K. and E.G.

Contents

PART IV   RESPONSIBILITIES FOR THE GULF WAR

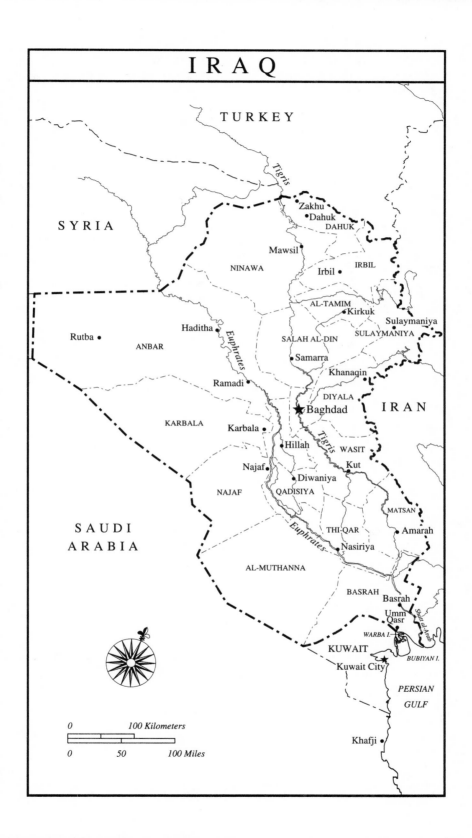

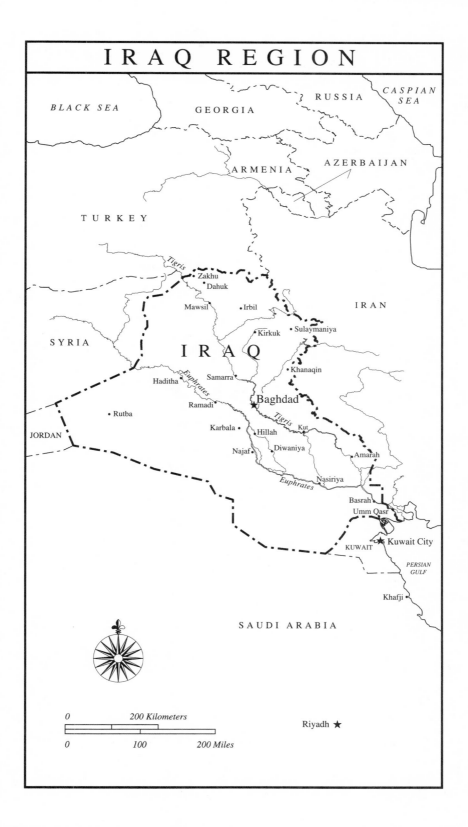

IRAQ REGION

BLACK SEA

GEORGIA

RUSSIA

CASPIAN SEA

ARMENIA

AZERBAIJAN

TURKEY

Tigris

Zakhu

Dahuk

IRAN

Mawsil

• Irbil

• Kirkuk

Sulaymaniya

I R A Q

Khanaqin

SYRIA

Samarra

Euphrates

Haditha

Baghdad

• Rutba

Ramadi

Tigris

JORDAN

Karbala

Hillah

Kut

Najaf

Diwaniya

Amarah

Nasiriya

Euphrates

Basrah
Umm Qasr

★ Kuwait City

KUWAIT

PERSIAN GULF

SAUDI ARABIA

Khafji

0   200 Kilometers

0   100   200 Miles

Riyadh ★

Part I

ORIGINS OF
THE GULF WAR

This work not only discusses the Gulf crisis, leading to war, which was created by Iraq's invasion of Kuwait, but also examines the cumulating differences and disputes between the two countries that led eventually to the invasion. These differences and the attempts at resolving them are the theme of the first part of this work.

In the first of five chapters in part one, we identify and define in broad terms the nature and elements of Iraq's variety of claims. In the next two chapters, we discuss in detail Iraq's so-called historical and legal claims; we also discuss the validity of these claims. In the final two chapters of part one, we examine the impossible attempts at bringing some form of unity between the two countries.

Part one will be helpful for an understanding of the lingering differences between the two Gulf neighbors.

Chapter 1

Introduction

On August 2, 1990, Iraq invaded Kuwait. To the outside world, the news came as a complete surprise. Two years earlier Iraq and Kuwait had stood together as allies against the rising tide of the Islamic Revolution in Iran, which threatened both countries as well as the region as a whole. During the eight-year war with Iran, Kuwait—indeed, along with several other Arab neighbors—supported Iraq not only politically in international councils, but also financially when its income from the export of oil was reduced by Iran's raids, which destroyed most of its oil fields. Small wonder that the invasion of Kuwait aroused concerns in international circles about Iraq's intentions, and the Western media, already disenchanted with Iraqi policy, launched an outrageous campaign against its leadership.

Iraq's differences with Kuwait, however, were not new nor were they unknown to other Arab countries. Those differences have intermittently been recurring with increasing complexity ever since Iraq and Kuwait were separated from the Ottoman Empire after World War I. The differences began about the question of frontiers when both countries were still under British control, but, after independence, the disputes over territorial sovereignty, security, and oil prices rendered the settlement of those differences increasingly more difficult leading eventually not only to the invasion of Kuwait, but also to a war in which over thirty countries were directly or indirectly involved. As the war is now over and Iraq has finally recognized Kuwait's sovereign independence and demarcated borders, will Iraq and Kuwait put aside their longstanding differences and conduct their relationships as good neighbors? Before an answer to such a question is attempted, an inquiry into the origins and development of those differences is necessary and will be dealt with in the pages to follow. Three sets of underlying forces can be identified to have considerably affected the course and depth of the differences between the two neighbors.

In the first place, the historical claim to sovereignty and territory has almost always been raised directly or indirectly by Iraq whenever men in official or unofficial capacities met to discuss political, economic, or social problems. This claim is based on the fact that Kuwait was but a part of Basra (a southern province of Iraq) under Ottoman rule and that only after Iraq came under British control did that area split into two countries. But in the relationship among states, history has never been regarded under the law of nations as valid evidence for legal rights. With regard to Iraq's claim to the sovereignty of Kuwait, an answer to the question of differences would depend on where Kuwait's sovereignty had rested following the dismemberment of the Ottoman Empire with which we shall deal later.

Second, in any territorial arrangement made between Iraq and Kuwait, whether to achieve unity or make territorial adjustment, the wishes of the people in each country were not taken into consideration. The claim of Iraq to Kuwait's sovereignty on the grounds that Kuwait was once a district in the province of Basra under the Ottoman administrative system may have established only a precedent for some form of unity between the two countries. But any scheme of unity should be validated either by a plebiscite or by an assembly representing the people in each country to express their wishes on the subject. Such an arrangement would be in accordance with the Wilsonian principle of self-determination that has become today an acceptable norm in the relationship among nations. The prevailing opinion in Iraq seems to have been in favor of unity with Kuwait, but the wishes of the Kuwaiti people have not yet been expressed in the call for unity save once in the mid-thirties.

Third, there were underlying social forces which deeply affected the relationship between the two neighbors. Both the populations of Kuwait and southern Iraq, composed of tribesmen who have been constantly on the move for livelihood, could not possibly have established permanent borders, as tribesmen owed loyalty to their chiefs and recognized no lines drawn in the desert. As Kuwait was sparsely populated, no need was felt to draw a line that would separate it from Iraq. Consequently, immigration, intermarriage, and other forms of socialization profoundly affected the demographic structure of both sides. True, these underlying factors may also be found operating in several other Arab countries. In the case of southern Iraq and Kuwait, however, there was and still is a greater degree of social mobility than in other Arab provinces, not to mention the common cultural heritage and historical memory which the Arabs of this area share. Even after Kuwait's administrative breakaway from Basra had taken place following World War I, socialization between the two neighbors continued and many well-to-do Kuwaiti citizens often used to pass their weekends in Basra City, as it was considered a more open society than the Kuwaiti capital.[1]

Underlying social forces can always play an important role in cementing the relationship between one society and another. Before the discovery of oil in Kuwait, there was a strong current of opinion in favor of unity with Iraq, especially in the mid-thirties, following Iraq's independence and the relative prosperity it had achieved by its income from oil. This situation, however, began to change when oil became the source of even greater prosperity in Kuwait; the differences between the two countries were accentuated and became exceedingly more difficult to resolve.

In an inquiry into the causes of any major question, Muslim scholars make a distinction between the category called "*sabab*" (reason) and another labeled "*'illa.*" The latter is defined as the immediate factor that precipitates an action; the former is the remote factor which creates or initiates an act before it becomes an enormous and more complicated issue. Western writers have often used the equivalent expressions of the original or deeper causes implying the "*sabab,*" and immediate causes implying the "*'illa.*"[2]

Part One of this work is devoted to an inquiry into the original causes and the differences that had arisen before Iraq and Kuwait had become independent states. Part Two is an inquiry into the immediate causes. Part Three deals with the crisis created by Iraq's resort to force. Part Four is a summary of the consequences and responsibilities of the parties concerned for their involvement in the Gulf crisis.

Chapter 2

Iraq's Historical Claims to Kuwait

E ver since Iraq became a nation-state, almost three-quarters of a century ago, it has on more than one occasion asserted territorial claims to Kuwait. The claims have varied considerably from a relatively modest request, to modify de facto borders, to a demand for full territorial sovereignty. These claims, however, have never been formulated in a completely coherent and documented *prima-facie* evidence. Taken together, they fall into three categories: historical, legal, and strategic. In this chapter, discussion will focus mainly on the so-called "historical claim," which Iraq has often presented as justification for its claims. Even in unofficial circles, whether in the press or in private conversations, the Iraqi people (the elderly often cite personal experiences) firmly maintain that Kuwait was but a part of southern Iraq and should rejoin the mainland.

Iraq's historical claim rests on the grounds that both countries, well before they became independent, were part and parcel of the Ottoman Empire. Since Kuwait was merely a district in the Basra province under the Ottoman administrative system, Iraq maintained, Kuwait would *ipso facto* become part of Iraq when the three former Ottoman provinces (Mawsil, Baghdad, and Basra) were reconstituted as a nation-state following World War I. Kuwait retorted, however, that it had already become fully autonomous when it passed under British protection in 1899, long before the Ottoman Empire had vanished; thus when British protection was withdrawn in 1961, it emerged fully sovereign, recognized by many countries, including Iraq in 1963.

Before analyzing the arguments of each side, historical or otherwise, perhaps a brief sketch is in order about how Kuwait came into existence and passed under Ottoman rule before it became an entity under British protection.

EMERGENCE OF KUWAIT AND ITS STATUS UNDER THE OTTOMAN EMPIRE

When Kuwait came into existence as a city-state early in the eighteenth century, the Ottoman Empire had shown no great interest in the Arabian peninsula, although the entire northern Arab world had already fallen under its control early in the sixteenth century. The tribesmen in central and eastern Arabia had for long been constantly on the move, but had not yet been developed into political communities. When the Saudi, the Khalifa, and other tribal chiefs were finally able to establish tribal political communities in the eighteenth century, the Sabah family followed suit and established a small political community in northeastern Arabia. Like other Arabian tribal chiefs, the Sabah 'Utub clan (like other tribesmen of the 'Anza confederation) started to move from central to eastern Arabia, and finally settled in the area of Kuwait Bay. It is not easy to determine when exactly the Sabah clan settled, but it is widely held today that they arrived early in the eighteenth century.[1]

Most of the tribesmen who settled in Kuwait formed a kind of merchant class engaged in fishing, pearling, ship-building, and exporting ghee and horses. They formed the nucleus of a closely knit political community. In a tacit social contract, it was agreed that Shaykh Sabah, assisted by his brother 'Abd-Allah, would become the head of a government with specific functions relating to the local administration and protection of the residents from tribal raids. In lieu of these services, the merchant community agreed to pay him voluntarily a financial contribution which later became a tax. Among the Sabah achievements, a wall around the town of Kuwait was built to protect it from tribal raids.[2]

Not only did Shaykh Sabah and his descendants succeed in creating a city-state but, perhaps no less important, they also consolidated and defended it against more powerful neighbors. To achieve these ends, they followed a policy of alliances with powers that could protect the regime from threats. First, they depended on the Ottoman Empire by accepting its nominal authority against foreign claims. But when the Ottoman government sought to bring Kuwait more closely into its administrative system, the Sabah Shaykhs turned to Great Britain, and through the British Raj in India, they were promised protection against Ottoman pressures without breaking off the Ottoman connection. The Sabah family also cooperated with the Saudi family and with Shaykh Khaz'al, ruler of Arabistan, situated to the northeast, on the opposite side of the Gulf. In pursuing a policy of alliances, which became the basis of Kuwait's foreign policy, the Sabah family succeeded not only in consolidating its rule but also in protecting Kuwait's independence, although not without hazards and bitter experiences.[3]

KUWAIT'S STATUS UNDER THE OTTOMAN EMPIRE

The rationale often given by the Ottoman authorities for their claim to Arabia was the right of conquest when their forces occupied Arab lands in the sixteenth century.[4] While it is true that Iraq and other northern Arab countries became part of the Ottoman Empire by conquest, most of central and eastern Arabia had not directly or indirectly been brought under Ottoman control until the nineteenth century. On the whole, however, Ottoman rule remained nominal in central and eastern Arabia because most of the inhabitants were tribesmen who owed allegiance to their chiefs, recognizing no authority above them. Even in certain localities such as Kuwait and other areas, where permanent settlements had been established, Ottoman rule was not always recognized by tribal chiefs, who often challenged the Ottoman authorities.[5]

In the latter part of the nineteenth century the Ottoman government maintained that its claim to Arab territory was not only based on the principle of conquest, but also on the Sultan's assumption of the title of Caliph. According to Islamic law, believers throughout the Islamic world were required to owe allegiance to the Caliph. For centuries, however, the historic title of Caliph had been held either by descendants from the Prophet Muhammad or from his tribe. The Sultan, therefore, needed validation for the transfer of the Caliphate from Arab to Ottoman hands.

The title of Caliphate, according to Ottoman authorities, passed from Arab to Ottoman hands as early as 1517, when Sultan Salim conquered Egypt and al-Mutawakkil, the last ʿAbbasid Caliph (who had been in exile in Cairo) formally surrendered his right to the Caliphate when both met in Cairo. Modern scholarship has demonstrated that such an event never took place.[6] Ottoman scholars, however, have argued that the transfer of the title was implicit when Sultan and Caliph met and the Caliph welcomed Sultan Salim upon his entry into Egypt. Moreover, while he was still in Cairo, Sultan Salim received the son of the Sharif of Makka, custodian of the two sanctuaries of Makka and Madina who delivered to him the keys of the two sanctuaries as a gesture of gratitude for his becoming ruler of Islamic lands. Although the Sharif of Makka claimed no right to the title of Caliph, Sultan Salim's acceptance of the symbolic honor of holding the keys of the two sanctuaries was later construed to carry with it not only the spiritual but also political authority on the grounds that the two were inseparable under Islamic law.

The Ottoman Sultan was only gradually and tacitly acknowledged as Caliph throughout the Islamic world, save in Persia and some other areas where the Shiʿi creed prevailed, whose followers owe allegiance not to the Caliph but to the Imam (a descendant from the Prophet's family who assumes the title by designation). The Ottoman Sultan's assumption of the title of Caliph was not constitutionally confirmed until Sultan ʿAbd al-Hamid II was acclaimed as Caliph in accordance with the newly proclaimed Ottoman Constitution in 1876.[7]

Not only did the Ottoman Sultan receive his subject's allegiance as a constitutional right, foreign governments also recognized him as Caliph. The first instance of such recognition by a foreign power came in 1774 under the Treaty of Kuchuk Kaynarja. According to this treaty (Article 3), the Sultan retained his spiritual authority over Muslims in the Crimea, which he had just ceded to the Tsar of Russia.[8] This precedent, perhaps based on the European doctrine of the separation of powers—a doctrine infeasible under Islamic law—was confirmed under subsequent treaties between the Ottoman Empire and other powers that recognized the Sultan as Caliph on the international plane. Thus, when ʿAbd al-Hamid II was proclaimed Sultan-Caliph under the Constitution of 1876, he had already been recognized as Caliph under the Treaty of Paris (1856) by virtue of which he was "admitted to participate in the advantages of the public law and system (concert) of Europe" (Article 7).[9] Needless to say, when Sultan ʿAbd al-Hamid was constitutionally proclaimed as Caliph in 1876, his European peers had already recognized him not only as head of the Ottoman Empire but also as head of an Islamic state.

In northern Arab countries from Iraq to Egypt, the Ottoman conquest was on the whole welcomed by the local inhabitants, as they were governed by foreign rulers, such as Mongols and Mamluks; but in central and eastern Arabia (the Arab Gulf region), where the tribesmen were governed by their own native tribal chiefs, the Ottoman authority had either been nominal or not acknowledged at all. In the Gulf region, where Great Britain's main objective was the pursuit of trade and influence, several Arab rulers began to enter into agreements with its representatives in order to assert their own authority and to resist first the Ottoman influence and later the claims of other countries that inherited the Ottoman dominion when the Ottoman Empire vanished.[10]

KUWAIT'S POLICY OF ALLIANCES

It is in order here to discuss briefly how the Sabah Shaykhs formulated and applied their policy of alliances, and what steps each took to carry out his policy.

The first three rulers—Sabah, ʿAbd-Allah (brother of Sabah), and his son Jabir—sought to protect their regimes by an alliance with the Ottoman Sultan. The Kuwaiti Shaykh paid an annual tribute to the Ottoman treasury and received an honorary dress from the Sultan. The Shaykh also hoisted the Ottoman flag over government offices and on his boats in the Gulf. In addition, he was on good terms with the Ottoman governors of Baghdad and Basra, and cooperated with them against Iranian attacks on Gulf coastal areas.

Cooperation with the Ottoman Sultan reached a climax under Shaykh ʿAbd-Allah II. In 1871, Midhat Pasha, governor of Baghdad and the future premier of the Ottoman Empire, decided to send an expedition to al-Hasa and al-Qatif, seeking to establish Ottoman control in that western littoral of the Gulf. Shaykh ʿAbd-Allah offered his cooperation by supplying some 300 boats and crews for the expedition. For his effort, ʿAbd-Allah was awarded with the title of Qaim-Maqam (subgovernor) of Kuwait.[11]

Apart from ʿAbd-Allah's enhanced position in the Ottoman Court, Kuwait became a district (*qada*) in the province (*wilayat*) of Basra. This arrangement, bringing Kuwait as a unit under the Ottoman administrative system, lasted nominally until the end of the Ottoman Empire. It was on the basis of this arrangement that Iraq laid its historical claim to Kuwait as a district in the province of Basra, forming part of the country after the fall of the Ottoman Empire. This action was but a formal recognition of the underlying social and economic factors operating among the people of the upper Gulf region as noted earlier.

The accession of Shaykh Mubarak to the Kuwait throne in 1896 marked a significant change in the direction of the policy of alliances. Mubarak proved to be a master diplomat who knew not only how to manipulate the forces under his control to consolidate the regime, but also to seek an alliance with an alternate power—Great Britain—to counterbalance the increasing Ottoman influence in his country, although the method he used to become Kuwait's ruler was brutal. Shaykh Mubarak cast an envious eye on his neighbors, the Shaykhs of Bahrain and the Trucial Coast, who were able to reduce Ottoman influence by entering into alliances with Britain. Were he to attain prototypical British support, he contemplated, his country would be immune to Ottoman pressure and possible threats from other quarters. As the Ottoman government continued to claim Kuwait as part of its territory, Shaykh Mubarak sought to preserve his independence by playing the Ottoman Empire off Great Britain following his entry into an agreement with the British without breaking the Ottoman connection in 1899. By pursuing such a policy he was able eventually not only to obtain a promise of independence shortly before his death in 1915 (when Britain was at war with the Ottoman Empire), but also he had virtually become more powerful than his Arab neighbors, who often denounced Ottoman authorities.[12]

Not all the elements of Mubarak's foreign policy, however, were the product of calculation; the immediate reason for seeking British protection was fear from opponents because of his arbitrary seizure of power. Mubarak did not assume power by succession. He assassinated his half-brother Shaykh Muhammad, who succeeded Shaykh ʿAbd-Allah early in 1886, presumably on the grounds that Muhammad (also his brother Jarrah, in charge of financial affairs, who was also murdered) had become too dependent on Ottoman authorities and had antagonized the merchant community by personal rule and excessive taxation. Moreover, Yusuf al-Ibrahim, Muhammad's uncle, and two nephews who had left Kuwait for Basra (where the Ottoman governor was ready to offer assistance), were very actively trying to unseat Mubarak and reinstate Muhammad's line of the Sabah family. Although Ibrahim's plots never succeeded, Mubarak sought British support, because he realized that the Ottoman authorities were opposed to him. Mubarak's feeling of insecurity was the immediate cause for seeking British protection, as Husayn Khalaf Khaz'al and Briton C. Busch pointed out, because Great Britain was quite reluctant at the outset to enter into an agreement with Mubarak.[13] British policy in the Gulf was to avoid meddling in an area where the Ottoman government was active and Britain had tacitly recognized its authority. But Mubarak continued to send messages to the British authorities in the Gulf that he was ready to enter into agreement with them.

The British Raj, concerned about the appearance of rival powers in that region, was in favor of bringing Kuwait under some form of British control as in other Arab Gulf areas. In 1898, the rumor of Russian intentions to establish a railway terminal in Kuwait may have influenced the British government to reconsider its position toward Mubarak. The specter of a Russian terminal (later another attempt was made to establish a German railway terminal) brought about far-reaching cooperation between Britain and Kuwait. In London, the formula of "protection," short of a full-fledged status of a "protectorate," was approved when Shaykh Mubarak had again asked for cooperation with Britain. Shaykh Mubarak, prompted by his own immediate security requirements, acted independently of the Ottoman authority. In taking such a step he opened a new chapter in the long controversy concerning the status of Kuwait, first between Britain and the Ottoman Empire, and later between Iraq and Kuwait.

THE AGREEMENT OF 1898

The agreement between the British Raj and Shaykh Mubarak followed the pattern of other agreements with Arab Gulf principalities. Shaykh Mubarak pledged not to enter into negotiation with any other foreign power without prior consent of the British government. The Shaykh and his successors were offered the "good offices" of the British government provided that he and his successors would "scrupulously and faithfully observe the conditions" provided in the agreement. The text of the agreement (called "bond"), embodied in an exchange of letters, follows:

> The object of . . . this bond is that it is . . . agreed between Malcolm John Meade, on behalf of the British government and the Sheikh Mubarak, Sheikh of Koweit, on the other part, . . . pledge and bind himself, his heirs and successors not to receive the Agent of Representative of any power or Government at Koweit, or any other place within limits of his territory, without the previous sanction of the British government; and further binds himself . . . not to cede, sell, lease, mortgage, or give for occupation or for any other purpose any portion of his territory to the Government. . . . [14]

On the same day, Shaykh Mubarak, in a letter from Malcolm John Meade, received the British assurance of "good offices" and British financial assistance. It was stated that the agreement should be kept "absolutely secret." The text of the letter, in part, follows:

> In view of the signing today of the agreement . . . I now assure you . . . of the good offices of the British government towards you . . . and successors, as long as you, your heirs, and successors, scrupulously and faithfully observe the conditions of the said bond. . . .

> The three copies of the bond will be sent to India to be ratified by Lord Curzon of Kedleston, Her Imperial Majesty's Viceroy and Governor-General in Council, and, on their return, one copy, duly ratified, will be conveyed to you, when I will take measures to send you, as agreed, a sum of Rs. 15,000 from the Bushire Treasury. A most important condition of the execution of this agreement is that it is to be kept absolutely secret. . . . [15]

The agreement, ratified in February 1899, contains no specific provision about "British protection," in order to avoid diplomatic complications with the Ottoman government, but there was an understanding, reiterated in a subsequent exchange of letters, that a form of "protection" would be extended to Shaykh Mubarak. The Ottoman government, however, was not unaware of the secret agreement and often protested on the grounds that Kuwait was an Ottoman territory and that any matter relating to it should be addressed directly to the Ottoman government.

Matters came to a head in 1901, when Shaykh Mubarak, threatened by Ibn al-Rashid (an Ottoman protégé, who had driven the Saudi ruling family from Riyad in 1891 when the exiled Saudis were offered protection by Mubarak), asked for British assistance against Ibn al-Rashid. The Ottoman government had already dispatched an infantry force to Basra and Ottoman troops were sent aboard a war vessel to Kuwait. The British captain, who had already arrived on board the British warship *Perseus*, warned the Ottoman captain that no Ottoman troops would be permitted to land. This incident, an evidence that "British protection" was implied in the secret agreement of 1898, prompted the Ottoman government to protest the British action and reiterated its claim that Kuwait was an integral part of Ottoman territory. The German government, considering the British action as a sign that Kuwait might become a British protectorate, informed the British government that its action was a violation of the Treaty of Berlin (1978). The Anglo-Ottoman controversy over Kuwait's status ended in a compromise. The British and Ottoman governments agreed that the Ottoman government would not send troops to Kuwait and the British would not occupy Kuwait or establish a protectorate in it. This compromise, called simply the "*status que*," implied that Britain, though tacitly acknowledging the Ottoman claim to Kuwait, would continue to deal with the Shaykh Mubarak in accordance with the agreement of 1899.

But the Ottoman authorities did not let matters stand at that stage. Alerted by British support of Shaykh Mubarak's intent to assert his authority, the Ottoman government sought to dismiss Mubarak. They instructed the Naqib of Basra—dean of the *sayyid*'s (descendants from the Prophets) community—to pay a visit to Mubarak and invite him to serve as a member of the Sultan's High Council in Istanbul. Mubarak, anticipating trouble from the Naqib's mission, appealed to the British to prevent the mission. Concerned about the possible threat to Basra, the Ottoman government sent a garrison to the province, including the port of Umm Qasr. From this port, a few men crossed to Bubiyan Island in order to build a guardhouse as authoritative evidence that Bubiyan was an Ottoman territory. Despite British protest, the guardhouse was never removed until war broke out in 1914. Although Mubarak claimed that the island was part of his territory, the British authorities were not quite sure that Mubarak's claim was valid, as no evidence was available to support it.

Under the vague but tacit agreement of the *status que*, Britain went beyond the "protection" of Kuwait to expand the area of the privileges granted under the agreement of 1898. On May 24, 1900, even before the *status que* compromise was agreed upon, Shaykh Mubarak in an exchange of letters promised the British to prohibit importing weapons into his country or exporting them from the country. In another communication (February 28, 1904), he promised not to allow the establishment of a post office in his country by any other power. In June 1904, he authorized the appointment of a British political agent to represent his country. Further promises not to grant concessions to foreign powers including pearling, sponge fishing, oil, and concessions to erect telegraphic stations were agreed upon during 1911–12. These actions, beyond anything under the agreement of 1898 or the *status que* of 1901, aroused the protest of the Ottoman government, but neither the British nor the Ottoman authorities were then prepared to indulge in a military confrontation.[16]

THE ANGLO-OTTOMAN CONVENTION OF 1913

Against this background, it became clear that both the British and the Ottoman governments had come to the conclusion that it was in their own interest to settle not only the controversy over the status of Kuwait, but also other pending issues in which Germany was involved. It was tacitly agreed that Britain could not completely ignore the Ottoman claim to Kuwait's sovereignty nor could the Ottoman government deny Britain's increasing interests in Kuwait. True, the immediate reason that prompted Britain to seek an overall agreement with the Ottoman government was German insistence on its plan to extend the Baghdad Railway to the Gulf. But there were also other reasons, such as the demarcation of frontiers between the province of Basra and Kuwait and Shaykh Mubarak's claim to the islands adjacent to Kuwait, that compelled both the British and Ottoman governments to reach an agreement.

Negotiations between Britain and the Ottoman government began shortly after the British secret agreement with Shaykh Mubarak was concluded. But it was not until the *status que* compromise was tacitly accepted that broad Anglo-Ottoman negotiations actually started. As the German government agreed to share the construction of the Gulf section of the Baghdad Railway with Britain, the controversy about the establishment of the Baghdad Railway terminal in Kuwait was settled. Meanwhile, the Ottoman government, in dire need of British good offices to end the Balkan war of 1912–13, was ready to concede both Britain's increasing interests in Kuwait and Kuwait's proposals about its frontiers with the Basra province. In these circumstances, the Ottoman government was bound to accept the draft of the Anglo-Ottoman Convention of July 29, 1913, although it had reservations about the British proposals concerning Kuwait's frontiers to include the adjacent islands.

The Convention, composed of several documents dealing with major Gulf questions, addressed itself for the first time to settle the questions of Kuwait's status and its frontiers. Although it remained unratified (and therefore not binding), it became the basis for future attempts to settle the frontier's issue in subsequent negotiations. The text of the relevant articles follows:

> Article 1: The territory of Kuwait constitutes an autonomous kaza (qada) of the Ottoman Empire.
>
> Article 2: The Shaykh of Kuwait will hoist, as in the past, the Ottoman flag, together with the word, "Kuwait" inscribed in the corner if he so wishes it, and he will enjoy complete administrative autonomy in the territorial zone defined in Article 5 of this Convention. The Ottoman Imperial Government, will refrain from interference in the affairs of Kuwait, including the question of succession, and from any administrative act as well as any occupation or military act, in the territories belonging to it. In the event of vacancy, the Ottoman Imperial Government will appoint by Imperial *ferman* a kaimakam to succeed the deceased Shaykh. It will also have the power to appoint a Commissioner to protect the interest of the Shaykh and the natives of other parts of the Empire.

Article 3: The Ottoman Imperial Government recognizes the validity of the conventions with the Shaykh of Kuwait previously concluded with the government of His Britannic Majesty, dated 23 January 1898, 24 May 1900, and 28 February 1904. . . . It also recognizes the validity of land concessions made by the said Shaykh to the Government of his Britannic Majesty and to British subjects. . . .

Article 4: The autonomy of the Shaykh of Kuwait is exercised by him in the territories the limit of which forms a semi-circle with the town of Kuwait in the center, the Khawr al-Zubayr at the northern extremity and al-Qurayyin in the southern extremity. . . . The islands of al-Warba, Bu-biyan, Mashjan, Faylaka, Awha, al-Kubr, Qaru, al-Maqta, and Umm al-Maradin, together with the adjacent islets and waters, are included in this zone.[17]

The Convention dealt with three basic issues: 1. it defined the status of Kuwait and implicitly acknowledged Ottoman sovereignty; 2. it laid down a broad sketch for Kuwait's borders which had never been spelled out before; and 3. it spelled the powers and the limitations of the Ottoman Sultan and the Shaykh of Kuwait.

As to the first issue, the British government indirectly acknowledged Ottoman sovereignty over Kuwait, implied in the formula that Kuwait was but a "gaza" (qada), a district within the Ottoman administrative system. As evidence of Ottoman sovereignty, the Shaykh of Kuwait would hoist the Ottoman flag (with the name of Kuwait inserted in the corner) and pay an annual tribute to the Ottoman treasury.

By considering Kuwait an Ottoman administrative unit, its status may be defined either as suzerainty or a dependent state. Such a status was not unique in the case of Kuwait, as the Ottoman Sultan had already given the Khedive of Egypt and the Beys of Algeria and Tunisia almost full powers of jurisdiction over domestic affairs as well as to grant concessions to foreign powers provided they were ratified by the Sultan.[18] On the basis of these precedents, the Sultan recognized not only the validity of the agreement which Shaykh Mubarak had entered into with Britain but also the validity of all other concessions he had granted.

Second, as to the proposal concerning Kuwait's borders with the Basra province (under which Kuwait was a district), the British extended Kuwait's territory by supporting Shaykh Mubarak's claim to a coastal area of the province of Basra as well as the islands of Bubiyan, Warba, and several other smaller islands. For this extended area to the north of Kuwait, a map (and a line marked in green) was attached to the draft Convention, which would indicate the extent of the frontier line; but no demarcation on land had been made. The Ottoman government reluctantly agreed to cede the extended area of the islands, although it had previously rejected Kuwait's claim to them on the grounds that they were uninhabited territories and that an Ottoman garrison had already been stationed to defend them. In a secret declaration, however, the Ottoman government promised to withdraw its forces from the islands; but, even after it signed the Convention, it was hesitant to do so in view of the negotiation on other agreements relating to Gulf affairs.

Third, with regard to the constraints on the power of the Ottoman Sultan, the Shaykh of Kuwait, not unlike the governors of the North African dependencies, was to "enjoy complete administrative autonomy" and the "Ottoman government will refrain from interference in the affairs of Kuwait, including the question of succession." But in reality, the Shaykh of Kuwait, not unlike the independent rulers of Algeria, Tunisia, and Egypt, acted as an independent ruler, although in speech he always paid high tribute to the Sultan and on almost every ceremonial occasion he sent substantial gifts to the Sultan. Concurrently, the Convention also imposed constraints on the Shaykh of Kuwait, such as the requirement of the Sultan's Imperial *firman* (decree) to validate the appointment of the Shaykh as a Qaim-Maqam to succeed his predecessor and the appointment of a commissioner to represent the Sultan in Kuwait.

Apart from the enlarged territory of Kuwait, the draft Convention sought to validate situations that had already been tacitly accepted in principle. The Convention may even be regarded as a declaratory statement of the *status que*. Nevertheless, it was not ratified because the Ottoman authorities were not quite satisfied with some of its provisions, although article 18 called for exchange of ratification within three months, a period that was extended several times. Nor was Shaykh Mubarak happy with the Convention, as he considered the appointment of an Ottoman Commissioner a serious limitation on his powers as a ruler, and he grudgingly accepted it.[19] Because it was not ratified, the significance of the Convention as a binding instrument is academic. The outbreak of war in 1914 put to the test the *modus operandi* that had been tacitly accepted by the British and Ottoman governments. As each side found itself on opposite sides during hostilities, each sought to take advantage of the two inconsistent principles stated in the Convention: 1. the principle that Kuwait's sovereignty was vested in the Ottoman Empire; 2. the principle that the "protection" of Kuwait was a British responsibility. When Britain declared war on the Ottoman Empire (November 6, 1914), an expeditionary force was dispatched to occupy Basra. Reassuring the Shaykh of Kuwait of protection, it invited him to participate in the defence of the region.

To assert its sovereignty, the Ottoman government dispatched forces to defend Basra and Kuwait from foreign attack even before Britain had declared war on the Ottoman Empire. On November 23, 1914, seventeen days after Britain had declared war on the Ottoman Empire, the Ottoman Sultan-Caliph declared a *jihad* (often called "holy war") in which he appealed to believers throughout the Islamic world to rise in arms against the enemies of Islam who had persecuted them and exploited the resources of their countries. "With the aid of

God and the intercession of the Prophet," the Caliph's declaration concluded, "you will defeat and crush the enemies of [our] religion."[20]

While the reaction to the Sultan-Caliph's appeal varied from region to region, it aroused on the whole a widespread sympathy with the Ottoman Caliphate, especially in regions where Islam had not yet been challenged by nationalist leaders in eastern Arabia and several other regions. In Kuwait and the Basra province, where there was an active anti-British propaganda, the British authorities informed Shaykh Mubarak to counteract its instigators. Although Shaykh Mubarak denied that there were anti-British activities in his country, a feeling of resentment against the British seems to have existed under the surface.[21] Nor did Shaykh Mubarak formally sever his connection with the Ottoman Sultan. It was perhaps owing to these difficult circumstances that Shaykh Mubarak did not take part in the British military operations in the Basra province, although he welcomed the offer to participate in it. Politically and militarily, Britain virtually dominated the entire Gulf region during the war years.

In 1915 Shaykh Mubarak died. He was succeeded by his eldest son Shaykh Jabir. Jabir was assured by the viceroy of India of British support so long as he acted in accordance with his father's commitments. Shaykh Jabir had no hesitation to continue his father's policy of cooperation with the British, but he suddenly died in 1917. He was succeeded by his brother, Shaykh Salim, who had shown greater dependence on, and sympathy with, the Ottoman Caliphate than on British protection. Shaykh Salim's sympathy with the Ottoman Caliphate stemmed partly from his personal inclination as a strict believer and partly from conservative elements who condemned cooperation with the British against fellow Muslims in the Ottoman Empire. Because of Shaykh Salim's increasing cooperation with the Ottoman authorities, the British government blockaded Kuwait during the last year of the war. The strained relations between Britain and Kuwait continued until 1921 when it ended with Shaykh Salim's death.

Following World War I, when the Ottoman Empire vanished, British-Kuwait cooperation became more intimate, as British political and economic interests had been expanded considerably. Britain virtually assumed all the privileges claimed previously by the Ottoman Sultan, although Kuwait was promised independence before the war. A brief analysis of the legal status of Kuwait before World War I might be illuminating for an understanding of the problems that arose between Iraq and Kuwait after World War I.

THE JURIDICAL STATUS OF KUWAIT

In reviewing the instruments relevant to the triangular relationship among Kuwait, Britain, and the Ottoman Empire, it is to be noted that the status of Kuwait was never clearly defined under International Law. The Ottoman government insisted that Kuwait was an integral part of its dominion and had no separate international status. But in 1898 the Shaykh of Kuwait entered into a secret agreement with Britain by virtue of which he was promised British protection. In other words, Ottoman sovereignty over Kuwait and the concomitant British protection were considered compatible and acceptable to the parties concerned, as Britain did not consider Kuwait a protectorate.

The British preference for the concept of protection over the concept of protectorate was at the outset to avoid complications with the Ottoman authorities, although Shaykh Mubarak seems to have preferred his country to become a British protectorate. Later, however, the British authorities found it in their own interest to deal with Kuwait as a principality under "British protection" rather than as a "protectorate," because they gradually began to render advice to the Shaykh of Kuwait not only on foreign but also on domestic affairs, a practice not feasible under a protectorate.

As the anomalous status of Kuwait was tacitly acceptable to Muslim rulers in other Arab Gulf principalities, British jurists sought to define it in terms recognized under modern International Law. They made a distinction between two types of protectorates: a Western "protectorate" and an Eastern or "colonial protectorate." In the former the protecting state assumed the right of protecting the smaller or weaker state by exercising the power of conducting its foreign relations, provided the attributes of its internal sovereignty were left intact. In the case of an Eastern or "colonial protectorate" the protecting power was entitled not only to the right to control foreign relations but also to the right of administering justice over subjects of civilized states, as stated in the acts of the Berlin Conference of 1884–85, and, under the General Act of the Brussels Conference of 1890, the right of organizing "the administration of judicial, religious and military services in the African territories was placed under the sovereignty of protectorate of civilized nations."[22]

Under the foreign jurisdiction of the British Crown the "protected states" were considered Eastern protectorates, and they were treated as coming under "tutelage," from the British constitutional standpoint. The Western concept of tutelage, however, was unacceptable to Muslim jurists, because it meant foreign domination without the prospect of emancipation. After World War I, the Arab countries ceded by the Ottoman Empire (as well as the colonies ceded by Germany) were placed under the League of Nations Mandates. In retrospect, the Mandates' system seems to have been tacitly acceptable to Arab nationalists in principle but not without reservations, because its law promised ultimate independence (Article 22 of the League Covenant). However the nationalists were constantly pressing for a quick emancipation from foreign control. Consequently, Iraq was able to achieve independence, in the early 1930s, in accordance with the League Mandate well before Kuwait could influence Britain to withdraw its "protection" and recognize its independence in 1961, although it had nominally been considered an independent state long before Iraq had come under the Mandate system.[23]

Chapter 3

Disputes over Status, Territory, and Frontiers

POLITICAL AND LEGAL STATUS OF IRAQ

Before World War I, Iraq was but a geographical expression. It existed only in the form of three provinces; each was integrated and dealt with as a unit within the overall Ottoman administrative system. Lacking an international status, each unit could not possibly deal directly with foreign governments.[1] True, in ancient and medieval times, Iraq was the seat of great empires; but, after four centuries of Ottoman rule, only historical memory and Arab traditions inspired the people with a sense of identity that they belong to one political community. It was to that historical memory, General Stanley Maude, commander of the British expeditionary force, referred in his address to the people, upon his entry to Baghdad, when he said that the British force had come not to dominate, but to liberate the country from Ottoman rule and to assist in the revival of its illustrious place in the history of mankind.[2]

Against this background, the Iraqi people were expecting to establish not a political entity under British "occupation," in accordance with the armistice of Mudros (October 30, 1918), but an independent state at the earliest possible moment. For three years, from 1918 to 1921, Iraq languished under British military control, and there was no sign that Britain was prepared to grant it independence. Syria, another former Ottoman territory, moved faster than Iraq to establish a national regime when Amir Faysal, son of Sharif Husayn (King of Hijaz and an ally of Britain) was proclaimed King by a Syrian National Congress in 1920. Iraqi nationalists, stirred partly by the events in Damascus, but mainly by continuing British rule over their country, became restless and demanded independence. Their agitation throughout the country in 1920, culminating in a revolt in the southern part of the country, prompted the British government to reconsider its policy in Iraq. It is outside the scope of this study to outline the political events in Iraq from 1918 to 1921; there are, however, a number of able studies to which readers may be referred.[3]

Until 1921, the British government had not yet made up its mind as to what policy it would pursue in Iraq. The opinion of the experts at the Colonial and Foreign Offices was divided on the matter. Some, under pressure of public opinion, demanded withdrawal; others, stressing imperial defence requirements, advocated the continuation of British control. The upshot of the debate was a compromise between nationalist demand for independence and British imperial interests. Instead of withdrawal, the British government decided to establish an "Arab regime," which would govern the country under British guidance provided it would be within the general framework of the League of Nations Mandate which Britain had already accepted in principle.[4]

For the implementation of this policy a Conference was held in Cairo in March, 1921. The Conference, presided over by Winston Churchill, Colonial Secretary, was attended by a team of experts from London, Cairo, Jerusalem, and Baghdad, and each was expected to present the views of the country it had represented. Percy Cox, British high commissioner in Baghdad, led the Iraqi delegation.

With regard to Iraq, Amir Faysal, who had just lost his throne in Syria in a conflict with the French, was nominated for the throne of Iraq. Faysal accepted the Iraqi throne on two conditions: first, nomination should be agreeable to the Iraqi people; second, the League of Nations Mandate (which had been opposed by the Arabs) would be replaced by a treaty of alliance with Britain. Churchill, in a conversation with Faysal (then in England), accepted these conditions in principle. The implementation of Faysal's nomination was entrusted to Percy Cox, who, as British high commissioner, returned to Baghdad to carry out the new British policy.[5]

Before discussing Iraq's status under the monarchy, perhaps a few words about the international status of Iraq is in order. Under the Treaty of Sèvres (1920), Ottoman sovereignty over Arab lands was relinquished; but because this treaty was never ratified, Iraq remained an Ottoman territory. Not until the Treaty of Lausanne, concluded between the new Turkey and the Allied powers in 1923 (ratified in 1924), did Ottoman sovereignty vanish. Turkey, the mother country, renounced all claims to the former Ottoman territories in favor of "the parties concerned" (Article 16 of the Treaty of Lausanne).[6] But the Treaty of Lausanne made no reference as to who exactly constituted the parties concerned.

As Turkey renounced all claims (except the provinces of Mawsil and Alexandretta which were subject to negotiations), the "parties concerned," with regard to Iraq and Syria might either be the people of the country in question or the occupying powers (or perhaps both). Under the Mandates system, the task of Britain and France, as mandatory powers over Iraq and Syria, was specifically stated not to act as occupying Powers, but merely to render "administrative advice." Article 22 of the League Covenant states:

> Certain *communities* formerly belonging to the Turkish (Ottoman) Empire where their existence *as independent nations can be provisionally recognized* subject to the rendering of administrative advice . . . until such time as they are able to stand alone (Article 22:4) [emphasis added].[7]

Under this article, the independence of Iraq as one of the former Ottoman "communities," was "provisionally recognized." As independence is an attribute of sovereignty, it follows that sovereignty must be considered to lie in each of the potentially independent "communities." Nor was the "administrative advice," the primary task of the mandatory power, regarded as permanent. Such a task, needless to say, would obviously come to an end whenever each "community" had become "able to stand alone."

At San Remo, the Iraq Mandate was entrusted to Great Britain, as the selection of mandatory powers was the privilege of the principal Allied Powers. Kuwait and other countries in the Arabian peninsula, which were also former Ottoman communities, were not brought before the San Remo Conference, perhaps because most of them, such as Najd and Hijaz (both united later as Saudi Arabia), Yaman, and Uman (Oman) had already been recognized as independent states. Bahrayn and the Trucial Coast principalities had already been under British protection, a status almost equivalent to that of Kuwait.[8]

In Iraq, a nationalist regime presided over by Amir Faysal was established on August 23, 1921, following a plebiscite, as proposed by the Cairo Conference. Faysal's primary objective was to replace the League Mandate by a treaty of alliance with Britain which would satisfy the aspirations of Iraqi nationalists and meet British commitments under the League Covenant. No sooner had negotiations for the treaty begun, however, than Faysal and his ministers found that everything in the Mandate, such as the "rendering of administrative advice" and other requirements were included in the British proposals for the treaty. "This is not the sort of treaty Mr. Churchill promised me in London," complained Faysal in a moment of despair.[9] After protracted negotiations (during which the King had to undergo surgery and Percy Cox, assuming supreme powers, dealt harshly with opponents to the treaty, including banishing their leaders to Hinjam, an island in the Gulf), the treaty was finally signed on October 10, 1922, with minor changes in which the word Mandate was never mentioned.[10]

Under the treaty, the King was obliged to accept the advice of the British high commissioner (and the advisers in the various departments were to render administrative advice to cabinet ministers) on all important matters before they were carried out in accordance with the League Covenant (Article 22), although no reference to that Article was ever made. In other words, Britain assumed a double role in its relationship with Iraq. On the one hand, it acted as a mandatory power responsible to the League of Nations under Article 22 of the League Covenant. On the other, it acted as an ally of Iraq in accordance with the treaty with Britain. The King and his ministers were not unaware of this abnormal situation; but Britain, under nationalist pressure, promised that the terms of the treaty might be reconsidered later to shorten the period of the Mandate.

In 1929, Britain informed Iraq that it was ready to support Iraq's candidacy for admission to the League of Nations which would terminate the Mandate and recognize Iraq's independence. To achieve this goal, a new treaty was concluded in 1930 by virtue of which Iraq would become an independent state within two years. True, the new treaty granted Britain two air bases, but Britain promised to recognize Iraq's independence and to defend it against foreign threat or aggression. Thus Iraq was at last able to become a member of the community of nations with full international status. In its dealings with Kuwait, however, Iraq's relations with Britain were often strained, particularly because of Iraq's claim to territorial sovereignty, which Iraq had often put forth to Kuwait after independence.

THE POLITICAL AND LEGAL STATUS OF KUWAIT

Unlike Iraq, which was a geographical expression until the end of World War I, Kuwait achieved the status of suzerainty (an autonomous *qada*) and a British promise of independence in 1914. World War I, however, resulting in the defeat of Germany and the destruction of the Ottoman Empire, proved to advance Iraq's status, notwithstanding that Iraq had to endure British mandatory control for nearly a decade and a half before it achieved full international status. By contrast, Kuwait's status which was expected to be elevated soon to independence, suffered a reduction after World War I, and the British-promised independence was almost forgotten. Sir Percy Cox and several other experts at the Colonial Office went so far as to propose a formal declaration of protectorate over Kuwait as a step to its being incorporated into the British Empire.

The reason for Britain's changed attitude vis-à-vis Kuwait under the new conditions created by World War I is not difficult to see. After the defeat of Germany and the destruction of the Ottoman Empire, Britain emerged as the supreme and uncontested great power in the Gulf. Kuwait's two Arab neighbors—Iraq and Najd (later Saudi Arabia)—that replaced the Ottoman Empire as Gulf states could not possibly play the Ottoman role as rival powers to Britain. Iraq passed under British control, and Saudi Arabia became an ally, not an opponent, of Britain. Small wonder that Kuwait as a buffer state in Anglo-Ottoman relations lost much of its significance, although it remained an important link in the overall British strategic system.

Nor did the rulers who sat on Kuwait's throne during the interwar years possess the leadership qualities of Shaykh Mubarak. The craftsmanship of Shaykh Mubarak created a meaningful role for Kuwait to play in the struggle for power in the Gulf. But none of his successors possessed enough foresight to create a new role for the country under the changed conditions created by World War I. Lacking the charisma and the ability to inspire popular support, they failed to assert Kuwait's full international status as a national demand—a weapon used by other Arab countries to assert independence. Furthermore, each of the three Shaykhs who succeeded Mubarak—Jabir (1915–17), Salim (1917–21) and Ahmad (1921–50)—were faulted on one policy or another which undermined the country's position in Gulf affairs. Jabir, who hardly ruled two years, offered to cooperate with Britain in the war, but he could not actively take the field before the British forces had arrived and dominated the Gulf militarily. Salim was a deeply religious man. It was often suspected that inwardly his sympathies were not with Britain but with the Ottoman Caliphate. His failure to stop underground support to the Ottoman side through smuggling and other surreptitious activities prompted the British to impose a blockade on Kuwait during the last year of the war. Ahmad, though in good standing with the British, became involved in a controversy with the newly established Consultative Council on domestic affairs which undermined his position in the country. He became entirely dependent on British support not only against threats from neighbors but also from opponents within the country. Under these circumstances, Kuwait's ruling family had become increasingly more concerned about the shaky position of the regime than about the international status of the country.[11]

In Britain there was also concern as to what the future of Kuwait would be in the aftermath of the destruction of the Ottoman Empire. The experts in Middle Eastern affairs held divergent views about British commitments not only to Kuwait, but also to other countries in the Middle East that emerged following World War I. For instance, T.E. Lawrence and Gertrude Bell, great admirers of Amir Faysal (who they supported for the throne of Iraq) held that he would be a reliable ally of Britain; Shakespeare and Philby (and possibly Percy Cox) were in favor of reliance on Sultan Ibn Sa'ud (later King of Saudi Arabia). Cox and More as well as others who asserted the viewpoint of the British Raj in India, were in favor of British commitments to protect Kuwait from more powerful neighbors. They argued that British commitment to Kuwait was longstanding under an agreement which was entirely unrelated to the annual subsidies for other countries. Still others, however (before oil was discovered), saw no future for Kuwait's survival and held that Britain might as well let one of its neighbors (Iraq or Saudi Arabia) absorb it.[12]

The British government, however, took no formal action to abandon its commitments to Kuwait. Even the viewpoint that a neighbor such as Iraq, were it to annex Kuwait, would become an obliging ally of Britain was faulted on the grounds that the other neighbor might become very unfriendly. For all these reasons, a threat to the Shaykh or to his regime whether from outside or inside the country was a serious matter to which Britain could not remain indifferent. The involvement of a foreign power in the affairs of another state is considered an intervention in domestic affairs and prohibited under International Law unless the victim is a dependent state or a colonial protectorate (as defined in British constitutional law). In the case of Kuwait, Britain considered its commitments under the Mubarak-Meade exchange of letters (1898) and the *status que* agreement (1901) would justify intervention. Since 1898, the Shaykh of Kuwait was in the habit of taking the initiative to grant Britain privileges which he considered necessary to protect the regime from foreign and domestic threats.[13]

Under Shaykh Ahmad's regime, the trend in the Anglo-Kuwaiti relationship was not to enhance Kuwait's international status but to protect the regime by granting Britain jurisdiction over Kuwait's domestic affairs. For example, Shaykh Ahmad granted Britain judicial jurisdiction not only over its subjects but also over all foreigners in Kuwait, and an order in Council to this effect was issued in 1925. Before World War I, foreigners enjoyed judicial privileges under the Ottoman capitulation provisions by virtue of which aliens were permitted to resort to their own consulates and not to local courts for litigation with Ottoman nationals. As an Ottoman *qada*, Kuwait was bound to grant foreigners the right to resort to their consulates in accordance with Ottoman capitulations, unless the powers signatory to the capitulation agreements had given up their rights which would allow the Shaykh of Kuwait to issue a decree to abolish them. Because there were no foreign consulates in Kuwait in 1925 (foreign consulates were established after 1950), Britain decided to assume judicial jurisdiction over aliens in Kuwait, to protect the interest of British subjects and also the interests of other aliens. For, were Kuwait to follow the example of Turkey and abolish the capitulations, the litigation of aliens with natives would necessarily come under local judicial jurisdiction.[14]

These and other actions seem to have given Britain the responsibility under the commitment "British protection" both to defend Kuwait against foreign threats, and also to protect the regime from any possible domestic threat. Kuwait's status, defined as a "colonial protectorate" by British jurists, was at no other time more true than during the interwar years. But this situation gradually began to change when Britain decided to reduce its military presence in the Gulf following World War II.

IRAQ-KUWAIT FRONTIER DISPUTES

Ever since it came into existence as a Gulf state, Iraq inherited unresolved frontier problems with two Gulf neighbors: Iran and Kuwait.
Although the Iraq-Iran frontier dispute took a long while before it was
defined and determined, the differences were finally reduced to a
choice between the *thalweg* (midstream) and the eastern bank of the
River Shatt al-Arab. As to the Iraq- Kuwait frontier disputes, they proved
more intricate and complex, since Iraq had often mixed the frontier
dispute with a claim to the adjacent islands of Warba and Bubiyan and
even to the sovereignty of Kuwait. Nor were the circumstances under
which the dispute came under discussion always favorable. The first
time the question was raised, Iraq was under British control and had
little or no power to negotiate freely or indirectly with Kuwait.

The Iraq-Kuwait frontier disputes may be dealt with under five periods: 1. the dispute under British control (1922–32);   2. the dispute
under the monarchy, (1932–58);   3. the dispute under the Qasim regime (1958–63);   4. the dispute under the 'Arif regime (1963–68);   5.
the dispute under the Ba'th regime (1968–90). In this chapter, the first
category will be discussed; others will be dealt with in the chapters to
follow.

THE DISPUTE UNDER BRITISH CONTROL

At the San Remo Conference (April 5, 1920) the Mandate over Iraq
was entrusted to Britain. It was also decided that the Iraq frontiers
should be determined. As both Iraq and Kuwait came under British
control, Britain was in the unique position to play a constructive role
as an honest broker and encourage them to reach an agreement to
their satisfaction, which might have spared them many a crisis and confrontation. Peace between the two neighbors would in the long run
have not been only in Arab interest but also in the interest of other
nations beyond the Gulf.

Britain, however, was after all pursuing its own Imperial interests
which were not always in accord with the interests of every Gulf country.
Nor were the conflicting interests of Gulf countries always easy to reconcile. For example, King Ibn Sa'ud and Shaykh Ahmad were not always on good terms. Differences arising from the shifting loyalty of
tribal chiefs (the 'Ajman tribes, though loyal to Kuwait under Shaykh
Mubarak, switched their loyalty to Ibn Sa'ud after Mubarak's death)
and the spread of the Wahhabi teachings in the eastern Gulf area
aroused fears in Kuwait that Ibn Sa'ud might overrun the country and
annex it for his kingdom. Nor did the Shaykhs of Kuwait always feel
secure from possible Iraqi attempts to annex the country, as no barriers

between the two neighbors had existed before World War I and travel was free from restrictions.

One of the primary tasks that Cox carried out before he retired in 1923 was to determine the frontiers among the three Arab Gulf countries: Iraq, Najd (Saudi Arabia), and Kuwait. It was no easy task to establish borders in a desert area divided among three states not always on good terms with one another. Cox, however, maintained that the establishment of permanent frontiers was in the interest of all, Arab and British. Britain was a friend and ally of the three Gulf rulers and one of them—King Faysal—owed his throne to the British. The Sabah family too owed its survival to British support; for, without British protection, the Ottoman government would have had no difficulty in replacing the Shaykh of Kuwait with an Ottoman governor from Istanbul. Ibn Saʿud, who established his throne against a pro-Ottoman tribal chief (Ibn al-Rashid), earned the respect of the British Government. As Britain sought to maintain friendship with all Arab rulers, Cox hoped that settlement of border disputes might create harmony and good neighborly relations to overcome at least the historic enmity between the Saudi and Sharifian families, as three members of the latter family had become heads of states surrounding Ibn Saʿud's kingdom: the Hijaz, Transjordan, and Iraq. Lack of fixed borders among the three neighbors, Cox held, was a primary source of misunderstanding. For without settled borders the nomadic tribes, in search of water and fodder, often got involved in pitched battles leading ultimately to suspicion and mistrust in the courts of these dynasts.[15]

Before he proceeded to act, Cox seems to have envisaged three steps, each he considered a necessary step for the settlement of the other. In the first place, he arranged to hold a conference to be hosted by Ibn Saʿud where the representatives from Iraq and Kuwait would meet. The conference, held at ʿUqayr (a town in eastern Saudi Arabia) on November 21, 1922, was attended by Ibn Saʿud, head of the Saudi delegation, Sabih Nashʾat, head of the Iraqi delegation, and More (a British agent) representing the Shaykh of Kuwait. Cox, representing the British government, was the dominating figure, although Ibn Saʿud, head of the hosting state, should have been the presiding officer, according to diplomatic practice. As Cox's knowledge of Arabic was insufficient for conducting the business of the conference, Colonel H.R.P. Dickson acted as a translator. Ibn Saʿud, like Cox, had his own translator, ʿAbd-Allah al-Damluchi, who also acted as a political adviser; but, as Amin al-Rihani (then Ibn Saʿud's guest) remarked, neither ʿAbd-Allah's English nor Dickson's Arabic were good enough for a translator.[16] Whenever Ibn Saʿud requested a private meeting with Cox, Rihani acted as his translator. It was in these private meetings that the crucial Saudi-Iraq differences were ironed out. In formal meetings that attended by the Saudi and Iraqi delegations, the proposals of each side were presented and the head of each delegation made a long rhetorical speech to justify his country's proposals.

For almost five days, speeches and wrangling went on and no agreement seemed to be in sight. Cox, tired and weary, intervened, according to Dickson, to tell the delegates that they were arguing like children, he decided to determine the borders himself. At the outset, Ibn Saʿud demanded the River Euphrates to be the border line between his kingdom and Iraq, and Sabih Nashʾat demanded a border some 200 miles to the south of the Euphrates. Cox proposed a border of some 150 miles of desert to the south of the Euphrates as a compromise. The Iraqi delegate, arguing that such an area was necessary as a home for the Iraqi tribes, accepted Cox's proposal. Cox with a red pencil drew a line on the map which Ibn Saʿud finally accepted. Cox also drew another line on the map which defined the border between Saudi Arabia and Kuwait by virtue of which Ibn Saʿud was compensated for the territory he conceded to Iraq at the expense of Kuwait. In addition, two neutral zones were established, one on the Saudi-Iraq frontier and the other on the Saudi-Kuwait frontier. They were designed by Cox, states Dickson, to permit "the free movents of nomadic tribes across borders, and the use by both countries of wells near the frontier."[17] As the treaty specifying the names of the tribes belonging to Iraqi and Saudi territories had already been dealt with earlier at Muhammara (May 5, 1922), the agreement specifying the territory belonging to each side that had just been concluded at ʿUqayr (December 2, 1911) was called a protocol supplementing to the Muhammara treaty. Ibn Saʿud, on behalf of Najd, and Faysal, on behalf of Iraq, ratified the treaty of Muhammara and the protocol of ʿUqayr shortly afterward.[18]

At ʿUqayr, the Iraq-Kuwait borders were not dealt with, only the Saudi-Iraq and the Saudi-Kuwait borders were determined. Major More, who attended the conference on behalf of Shaykh Ahmad, did not raise the question of the Iraq-Kuwait border. He might have, however, informally talked about it with Cox only to learn that the Iraq-Kuwait frontier was consciously postponed to be dealt with later.

On his way back to Baghdad, Cox stopped at Kuwait to disclose the bad news about Kuwait's borders with Saudi Arabia to Shaykh Ahmad. Colonel Dickson, acting as an interpreter, has provided us with an account of the conversation that went between Cox and Shaykh Ahmad. Upon learning that nearly two-thirds of his territory had just be assigned to Ibn Saʿud, Shaykh Ahmad's pitiful reaction, as described by Dickson, was as follows:

> Shaykh Ahmad pathetically asked why he had done this without even consulting him. Sir Percy replied that, on this unfortunate occasion, the sword had been mightier than the pen, and that had he not conceded the territory, Ibn Saʿud would certainly have soon picked a quarrel and taken it, if not more, by force of arms. . . . [19]

Shaykh Ahmad, who had no choice but to accept the verdict of 'Uqayr, was deeply disturbed and continued to complain about the unjust treatment. Cox, however, may have thought differently about the matter; for, as when the frontier with Iraq was finally determined, he demonstrated that he did not forget Britain's friend. For 'Uqayr was only the second step (next to Muhammara) in Cox's equation to settle the triple-pronged Gulf-frontier question.

The third step, the Iraq-Kuwait frontier, had yet to be scrutinized. In 1919, Shaykh Salim, predecessor of Shaykh Ahmad, had been informed through Lt. Colonel Howell, political agent in Kuwait, that Britain recognized the "green line" (the northern borders of Kuwait under the Anglo-Ottoman Convention of 1913) as the Iraq-Kuwait frontier. In 1920, Major More, who succeeded Howell as political agent in Kuwait, reported in a dispatch (September 17, 1920) to the political resident in the Gulf that Shaykh Salim considered the green line to be his country's frontier with Iraq. Major More, who represented Shaykh Ahmad at 'Uqayr, may have reported Shaykh Salim's position as to his country's borders with Iraq to Cox. Cox, however, was not unaware of the situation. But without instructions from the Colonial Office, he did not think it was proper to bring the Iraq-Kuwait frontier before the 'Uqayr Conference.

No sooner had he returned to Baghdad than Cox began to tackle the complex Iraq-Kuwait border sisuation, and he was determined to resolve it before he retired six months later. He had already asked Winston Churchill (when he was in Cairo) to deal directly with the political agent of Kuwait rather than through the political resident (perhaps to avoid bureaucratic red tape), and his request was approved by Churchill's successor, the Duke of Devonshire. In an exchange of letters (December 20, 1922), he proposed to the Colonial Office the green line as the frontier between Iraq and Kuwait. In further dispatches (prepared by B.H. Bourdillion, Cox's secretary in Baghdad), the green line was finally approved by the Colonial Office (February 2, 1923) exactly as proposed by Cox.[20]

Cox had already known More, political agent in Kuwait, and he must have had full confidence in him (confirmed during the meetings of the 'Uqayr Conference) when he requested that the colonial secretary to deal directly with Kuwait through the political agent. Both Cox and More were the product of the school of the British Raj, and both were in favor of the assertion of Kuwait's status under British protection. They found in Shaykh Ahmad's actions a readiness for cooperation, particularly in his ratification (though reluctantly) of the 'Uqayr Protocol, which prompted Cox to proceed with the third round to determine the Iraq-Kuwait frontier in Kuwait's favor.

Since the Anglo-Ottoman Convention had never been ratified, Cox and More seem to have agreed that the initiative to claim the green line, as Kuwait's border with Iraq, should be taken by Shaykh Ahmad.

More, accordingly, informed the Shaykh to prepare a memorandum in which the borderline would be as follows:

> From the intersection of the Wadi el-Audja with the Batin and thence northwards along the Batin to a point just south of the Latitude of Safwan wells, Jebel Sanam and Um Qasr, leaving them to Iraq and soon to the junction of the Khor Zobeir with Khor Abdulla.[21]

Shaykh Ahmad also claimed the islands of Warba, Bubiyan, Maskan (Mashjan), Fulayka, Awha, Qaru, and Umm al-Maradin to be included within Kuwait's boundaries, as these islands had already been offered to Shaykh Mubarak in a note dated November 3, 1914, sent to him by Cox, then British political resident in the Gulf. But Shaykh Mubarak was unable to occupy the islands nor was the Anglo-Ottoman Convention ratified to empower the British government to offer them to Kuwait.

On the basis of Shaykh Ahmad's memorandum, Cox sent a note (April 4, 1923) to More in which he approved of the memorandum that delineated the Iraq-Kuwait frontiers including the islands. In his dispatch to More, Cox proposed that the Shaykh "can be informed that his claim to the frontier and islands above indicated is recognized in so far as His Majesty's Government are concerned." But Cox pointed out that since the Shaykh's claim to the frontier were identical with the green line of the Anglo-Ottoman Convention, he saw "no necessity to make allusion to that document."

An exchange of notes between heads of state (or heads of government), may be regarded, under International Law, as an agreement binding on the two states concerned. But the exchange of notes between Cox and More were not between two heads of state (or government) nor were they formally acknowledged by Iraq. True, More may have been deputized to represent the Shaykh of Kuwait and Cox's dispatch to More was approved by the Shaykh, but Cox was not deputized by Iraq, nor were his notes to More approved by an Iraqi authority. In his dispatch to the Colonial Office (December 20, 1922), in which Cox proposed the green line, he stated that King Faysal would, "almost certainly," not object to his proposals. But we have no hard evidence that King Faysal had ever given his prior approval or that he ratified Cox's notes. Nevertheless, the Colonial Office endorsed Cox's proposals in a dispatch to Cox on February 2, 1923.[22]

Cox, who left Baghdad for England on May 1, 1923, to retire, probably felt that he had served to the best of his abilities the interests of all parties concerned. But Cox, reared in the tradition of the British Raj, had the British Empire uppermost in his mind. From this perspective, the "task of maintaining Pax Britannica" (in Cox's words)[23] prompted him to settle the Iraq-Kuwait frontier in Kuwait's favor. For the Gulf, considered in the eyes of the British Raj an appendage to the

Indian subcontinent, the green line (which defined Kuwait's border as a subdistrict within the province of Basra under the Anglo-Ottoman Convention of 1913) should be rather the border for a small Gulf political entity dependent on British support than for a potentially more powerful neighbor that might constitute a threat to British Imperial interest in the Gulf.

For almost a decade, the Colonial Office was unaware that the Cox-More dispatches concerning the Iraq-Kuwait frontier could not possibly be considered a substitute for a formal agreement between two states, notwithstanding that Iraq had not even been formally informed about it. For, as high commissioner, Cox's task was merely to "render administrative advice" (Article 22 of the League of Nations Covenant) on behalf of the British government, but not to act on behalf of Iraq without formal authorization or approval by the King, as head of state.[24]

Not until Britain had decided to nominate Iraq for membership in the League of Nations did Iraq's frontier with Kuwait come under reconsideration in the Colonial Office. As sponsor of Iraq's nomination, the British government began to prepare the necessary documentation to provide evidence of Iraq's readiness for independence. Before the Council of the League of Nations would recommend the admission of Iraq to the League General Assembly, a British representative had to attend the meetings of the Permanent Mandates Commission (an advisory body to the League Council dealing with all matters relevant to Mandates) to answer questions relevant to Iraq's readiness for independence. Among other things, one of the primary qualifications was that Iraq should have "a stable government and well-defined frontiers."

The British Foreign and Colonial Offices in London held an interdepartmental meeting (April 15, 1932) to provide the necessary documentation. With regard to frontiers, only the Iraq-Kuwait frontier, to their surprise, appeared as unsatisfactory in the documentation. The Colonial and Foreign Offices were agreed that approval of Iraq was necessary for the validation of the Cox-More exchange of letters. The Colonial office, considering that there would be no difficulty to obtain the approval of General Nuri al-Saʿid, prime minister of Iraq, insisted that an exchange of letters between Iraq and Kuwait should be completed through the British high commissioner in Iraq and the British political agent in Kuwait rather than directly between Iraq and Kuwait as the latter was under British protection.

In accordance with this procedure, General Nuri, prime minister of Iraq, sent a note to Sir Francis Humphrys, then British high commissioner to Iraq and later British ambassador to Iraq after its independence on October 3, 1932, in which he stated:

> I think . . . that the time has come when it is desirable to reaffirm the existing frontier between Iraq and Kuwait.

I therefore request that the necessary action may be taken to obtain the agreement of the competent authority or authorities in Kuwait to the following description of the existing frontier between the two countries:—

From the intersection of Wadi el-Audja with the Batin to a point just south of the Safwan Wells, Jebel Sanam and Um Qasr leaving them to Iraq and so on to the junction of the Khor Zobeir with the Khor Abdalla. The islands of Warbah, Bubiyan, Maskan (Masjan), Failakah, Auhah, Kubbar, Qaru, Umm el-Maradin appertain to Kuwait.[25]

The Shaykh of Kuwait, in his approval of the Iraqi premier's note, stated in a letter to the then Political Agent Dickson (August 10, 1932) that "the frontier proposed by the Iraqi prime minister is approved by His Majesty's Government" and agreed to "reaffirm the existing frontier between Iraq and Kuwait as described in the Iraq prime minister's letter."[26]

General Nuri's exchange of letters with the Shaykh of Kuwait in 1932 was considered satisfactory by the Colonial and Foreign offices to validate the Cox-More exchange of letters in 1923. This documentation, among others, was passed on to the British delegation at Geneva as evidence that the Iraq-Kuwait frontier was determined, should a question about frontiers be put to the British representative. British assertion at Geneva that Iraq's frontiers with neighbors were determined was taken for granted by the members of the Permanent Mandates Commission and the League Council. Before Iraq was admitted to membership in the League of Nations, the burning questions of immediate concern at Geneva (apart from Iraq's political, economic, and judicial organizations) was not about Iraq's frontiers, but about its readiness to protect ethnic and religious minorities (Kurds, Assyrians, Turkomans, Baha' is, and others) as there were a number of petitions submitted on their behalf by various organizations that had serious reservations about Iraq's readiness to protect minorities after it had become independent.[27]

Hardly three weeks after Iraq's admission to the League of Nations (October 3, 1932), Premier Nuri resigned on October 27, 1932. While the initial step he had taken to settle the frontier question was agreeable to Shaykh Ahmad on behalf of Kuwait, it was not necessarily binding for Iraq. There were, in addition, several matters which General Nuri had overlooked (whether he did or did not deliberately overlook them is difficult to determine) before he resigned.

First of all, General Nuri's exchange of letters with the Shaykh of Kuwait, were they to be binding, had to be ratified by Iraq. According to the Iraqi Constitution under the monarchy, any treaty or agreement with a foreign country must be approved by Parliament before it was ratified by the King. But Nuri's successors took no such step, and the agreement could not be considered binding on Iraq.

It might be argued that Nuri's exchange of letters, although considered an agreement, was not, strictly speaking, a treaty that would require ratification in accordance with the Iraqi Constitution. The distinction between a "treaty" and an "agreement" was clarified on September 7, 1927, when the Iraqi Cabinet passed a resolution to the effect that "international agreements of minor importance or of a scientific nature and not concluded between the heads of state, need not of themselves be submitted to Parliament." Obviously, an agreement about frontiers could hardly be considered of minor importance.[28] But it is not only in modern written constitutions that treaties, in order to be binding, must be ratified by the head of state. It is a tradition in Islam going back to the Prophet Muhammad and the Caliphs who succeeded him that treaties must be ratified by the head of state were they to be binding.[29]

No sooner had Iraq achieved independence than disputes resulting from lack of ratification led to a variety of conflicts ranging from the inability to establish permanent signs on the ground to occasional violations of frontiers consciously or unconsciously carried out. For instance, in the 1930s, even before the termination of the Mandate, the signboard that Major More had placed to indicate where the border line stood south of Safwan had been removed. Because the date gardens of Iraq owners covered the whole area to the south of Safwan, it became exceedingly difficult to know exactly where the border line of 1923 had existed. Lack of demarcation also led to disputes over police jurisdiction in areas claimed by both sides. These and other related matters were problems which prompted Iraq to deal directly with Kuwait after it achieved independence.

Chapter 4

Kuwait's Attempt at Unity with Iraq

B efore independence, when Iraq was still under British control, Iraq's borders with Kuwait were never contested whenever the question came under discussion with the British authorities. Iraq's main concern in dealing with the British was not about frontiers, but about when the British Mandate over Iraq would be brought to an end at the earliest possible moment. After winning its independence, Iraq began first to pay attention to the Syrian and Palestinian struggle against French and British domination, before it was drawn into Kuwaiti affairs when conditions in Kuwait were favorable for Iraqi intervention.

CONDITIONS IN KUWAIT AFTER WORLD WAR I

When Shaykh Salim suddenly died in 1921, the internal conditions in Kuwait following World War I were in disarray and there were no signs that they were expected to improve. The country was still suffering from the continuing Saudi embargo on Kuwaiti transit trade since World War I, because Kuwait refused to allow a Saudi representative at Kuwait Port to collect custom duties on Saudi imported goods on the grounds of interference in domestic affairs. No less important was a decline in the pearl trade, owing to Japanese competition in the artificial pearl industry, and last, but not least, the general world depression which affected the region as a whole, including Kuwait.[1]

But there were also political unrest and ideological stirrings to which Shaykh Ahmad al-Jabir, who succeeded Shaykh Salim, paid no attention. When Shaykh Ahmad returned from the Saudi Kingdom where he was negotiating a frontier dispute (March 24, 1921), he was confirmed as ruler on the understanding that he would consult the notables of the country on all matters of common concern. The leading notables who proclaimed his assumption of power formed a Council of twelve members, headed by Hamad ʿAbd-Allah al-Saqr, based on nomination (not on election) by the merchant community, which was agreeable to Shaykh Ahmad. But the Council was neither fully acceptable to the merchant community, nor did it operate as an organ capable of sharing power with the Shaykh. Its members often disagreed among themselves which allowed Shaykh Ahmad to disregard the Council. As a result, the Council died a natural death, and the Shaykh governed by decree as an authoritarian ruler without consultation.[2]

But there were other political and ideological factors which rendered the internal conditions more complicated. Following independence, Iraq appeared to many Kuwaiti citizens as the model of a progressive Arab country that they aspired to emulate. Not only did Iraq begin to use its income from oil (before the oil industry was under way in Kuwait) to improve economic conditions, but it also emerged in the thirties as an attractive pan-Arab center that could play the role of leader—indeed, some Arab writers referred to it as the Arab Prussia—in the drive to achieve Arab nationalist aims. Like pan-Arabs in other Arab countries, many an Arab in Kuwait also looked up to Iraq as the most promising country that might enhance Kuwait's status were it to join Iraq in an Arab federal or confederal union.

When King Ghazi ascended the throne in 1933, pan-Arab activities became more active in Iraq owing to the King's own ideological interest in the pan-Arab movement. He had violently denounced in no uncertain terms French control over Syria and Zionist claims to Palestine, and demanded, in defiance of British protests, the annexation of Kuwait. To counteract pan-Arab propaganda, Shaykh Ahmad paid two visits to Baghdad in 1935 and 1936, seeking to cultivate a personal friendship with King Ghazi, and the two seemed to have gotten along rather well. Ghazi was ready to visit Kuwait, but such a visit did not materialize. Shaykh Ahmad was advised against it, as the visit might turn out to be more advantageous to a popular pan-Arab king than to Shaykh Ahmad's regime. Thus, the attempt at establishing a friendly relationship between the two rulers that might have diffused the tension between the two governments came to naught. King Ghazi's pan-Arab propaganda in Kuwait coincided with the conflict between Shaykh Ahmad and the leaders of the merchant community which demanded the establishment of an elected legislative assembly to share power with him.

THE MERCHANT MOVEMENT

The ineffectiveness and final disappearance of the first Council encouraged Shaykh Ahmad to indulge in his autocratic rule paying no attention to the welfare of his people. This situation gave the opportunity to several merchants who often visited Iraq for their own business (some had already owned date farms in the Basra province) to voice criticism against Shaykh Ahmad's corrupt administration. They witnessed the social and economic development in Iraq, which was made possible by its income from oil, and reproached Shaykh Ahmad for his failure to pursue a policy of reconstruction and reform. By contrast, when the income from oil in Kuwait was expected to improve conditions in the country, Shaykh Ahmad instead raised the allowances of the ruling family and allegedly began to invest privately abroad. The merchants demanded that the income from oil be devoted to reconstruction and development, such as the construction of roads, hospitals, and public schools, and the provision of fresh water. But Shaykh Ahmad would have nothing to do with such projects; he persisted in his arbitrary rule and paid little or no attention to complaints about conditions in the country.[3]

The merchants, believing that Shaykh Ahmad's promise of consultation was not honored, were set to act as an opposition party. Since the role of public opinion in politics had not yet existed in Kuwait, the merchants resorted to other means of political opposition, such as the Municipal and Educational Councils which were established on the basis of consensus. The opposition was partly composed of members of the merchant community and partly notables, including dissident members of the ruling family, particularly Shaykh 'Abd-Allah al-Salim, future successor to Shaykh Ahmad. But there was restlessness in the country as a whole as well as among Kuwaiti citizens in Iraq.

Matters came to a head when a certain Muhammad al-Barrak, inspired by a few merchants, was secretly agitating against the regime. He was arrested in February, 1938, on charges of "writing anonymous graffiti," aimed at undermining the regime.[4] On orders from high authorities, Barrak was publicly flogged, and compelled to give the names of three prominent leaders of the merchant community who had encouraged him to indulge in political agitation. Barrak, not unlike other young men inspired by pan-Arab propaganda against the regime, held that the Shaykh and his ruling family were neglecting their duties to serve the community. Other opposition leaders, supported by the merchant community, were able to defend themselves with arms. Some who had business interests abroad, fled the country; others sought protection by the British in Kuwait.[5]

The merchants, as an opposition front to the regime, became active both internally and outside the country. Because of repressive measures, the opposition inside Kuwait formed a secret organization that distributed critical propaganda literature. In Iraq, the Kuwaiti opposition leaders found the press on the whole sympathetic, especially papers advocating pan-Arab ideas, such as *al-Istiqlal* and *al-Zaman*, which were highly critical of British policy in Arab lands. For example, *al-*

Istiqlal, in an article entitled, "The Movement in Kuwait: Iraqi Sympathy" (April 26, 1938) in which it called for unity between Kuwait and Iraq, stated:

> It pains Iraq to behold on her borders an Arab territory with an excellent geographical position and yet in a backward state, lacking modern systems of education, health, and economic organizations. Iraq, unable to conceal her strong feelings, is anxious that the sister people of Kuwait should join in the general awakening movement which has taken place in the majority of Arab countries . . .
>
> The new movement in Kuwait gives pleasure and gratification to every Arab, because it will yield results most beneficial to the inhabitants of Kuwait themselves. Perhaps they realize the happy future awaiting them if the present movement is directed towards cooperation with Iraq, with whom certain Arab countries are desirous of union. . . . The demands presented by the inhabitants of Kuwait to their ruler are sound and legitimate and it is hoped that they will be met with broad-mindedness and with a sincere desire for reform and reconstruction.[6]

Not only did the press in Iraq criticize the Shaykh of Kuwait and his corrupt regime, but also Kuwaiti citizens in Baghdad who were in contact with high Iraqi authorities, persuaded King Ghazi to use his private broadcasting station through which he himself began to criticize Shaykh Ahmad's regime and to call on the Kuwaiti people to overthrow their ruling family.[7]

The Shaykh of Kuwait was naturally offended by the attack of the Iraqi press. In an open letter, published in the Baghdad paper *al-Zaman*, he denounced the press campaign as an unfriendly act and interference in the internal affairs of his country. As the press did not stop, the Shaykh took it for granted that the campaign must have been inspired by the Iraqi government. But the Shaykh must have also known that the Kuwaiti opposition leaders in Baghdad were responsible for the agitation against him in the press and in broadcasts from King Ghazi's private station where they participated in the preparation of the programs. True, the continuing references to the Shaykh of Kuwait in broadcasts from King Ghazi's private station may have encouraged the press to criticize his regime, but both Iraqi Premiers Jamil al-Midfaʿi and General Nuri al-Saʿid tried in vain to stop the King's broadcasting campaign while they were in office in 1937 and 1938.[8]

The British authorities in Kuwait took a more constructive view of the impact of the merchant movement, although they were just as concerned as the Shaykh about its effect on the Kuwaiti public. Shaykh Ahmad was advised to express readiness to listen to complaints and to introduce reforms as part of his own program rather than to oppose them. However he was at the outset critical of British advice, considering it an interference in his administration.

THE LEGISLATIVE ASSEMBLY

On June 29, 1938, three leaders of the merchant community petitioned Shaykh Ahmad to call an elected assembly in which no members of his family were to be included. On the same day, the heads of 150 leading families met in the evening and elected an Assembly of fourteen members. The Assembly, which may be considered the first elected branch of the regime, chose Shaykh 'Abd-Allah al-Salim, as its speaker. A week later, despite attempts by members of the ruling family to undermine the Assembly, the elected members met with the Shaykh on July 4 and demanded in writing a formal approval of the election for a legislative assembly. On July 6, 1938, after two days of hesitation, he finally signed the document that recognized the existence of a legislative organ in his Government.

The first business of the Assembly was to prepare a draft organic law composed of five articles. Article 1 stated that the people were the source of authority and the Assembly, on behalf of the people, would enact laws for the country. Article 2 provided that the Assembly shall enact laws dealing with the budget, security, justice, education, and public construction. Article 3 dealt with the approval of all treaties, concessions, monopolies, and agreements that would be entered into, both domestic and foreign, by the Assembly. Article 4 stipulated that the Assembly shall act as a Court of Appeal until the establishment of such a court. Article 5 stated that the speaker of the house shall exercise executive authority in the foreign affairs of the state.[9]

The British authorities were quite concerned about the Assembly's assumption of the control of foreign affairs, although they were in favor of the role of the legislative power in principle. In an exchange of notes with the Shaykh, it was agreed that the relationship with Britain would be continued as it had existed in the past between the British government and the Ruler of Kuwait. As to the power of the Legislative Assembly with regard to foreign affairs, it was agreed at a meeting (October 15, 1938) attended by the British political resident in the Gulf, the political agent in Kuwait, the Shaykh, and some members representing the Legislative Assembly that two Council members in the Shaykh's Cabinet would exercise on behalf of the Legislative Assembly the authority to communicate with the British government. It was also agreed that the Shaykh, as head of state, would negotiate and sign all agreements provided that they would be approved by the Legislative Assembly. With regard to domestic affairs, the British saw the need for a legislative assembly to provide popular participation, a step in political development which had become popular in Arab lands. Realizing that his position had virtually been reduced to a figurehead, Shaykh Ahmad at first refused to sign. When the Assembly insisted on taking a firm stand, he reluctantly signed the first Constitution in the history of the country.

In its session from July to December, 1938, the Assembly passed laws that were primarily aimed at improving social and economic conditions. It abrogated export duties and taxes on fruits, vegetables and goods for sale to nomads and villagers. It reduced rents and abolished monopolies. It also passed laws for the construction of public buildings and works (schools, police stations, roads, and others) and measures to deal with corruption. No less important, it provided rules restricting the powers and privileges of all members of the ruling family, including Shaykh Ahmad, especially the income from the family's monopolies on shop buildings, forced labor, and other private privileges. In the past, the Shaykh controlled custom revenues, but the Assembly established a council to collect and distribute the revenue under its own control, and paid the Shaykh and other members of the ruling family their allowances. It also sought to control the state income from custom duties, taxes on the pearl industry, and income from oil. When Shaykh Ahmad realized that the forthcoming income from oil would be under the control of the Assembly he came to the conclusion that he was about to be stripped of all powers. On December 17, 1938, he took the drastic step of issuing a decree dissolving the Assembly. The Assembly, refusing to submit, took a firm stand. Shaykh 'Abd-Allah al-Salim, speaker of the house, tried in vain to negotiate a peaceful settlement. Neither side was ready to compromise. Shaykh Ahmad, calling on supporters from loyal tribes and elements affected adversely by the Assembly's reform measures, was able to overpower the Assembly and force it to surrender. But this was not the end of the opposition.

Shaykh Ahmad, in the guise of pursuing the principle of an elected Assembly, ordered new elections to be held on December 24, 1938. The new Assembly, chosen from an electorate of some 400, was composed of twenty members, including twelve of the dissolved Assembly, in accordance with a new draft Constitution which reserved most powers, including a veto, which virtually rendered the Assembly into an advisory council. Upon convening, the new Assembly rejected the draft Constitution, which prompted Shaykh Ahmad to issue an order (March 7, 1939) to dissolve it. But some members, encouraged by broadcasts from Iraq to oppose Shaykh Ahmad, continued to consider the Assembly undissolved.

Matters came to a head three days later when Muhammad al-Munayis, an opposition leader who had just returned from Iraq, distributed a propaganda leaflet against Shaykh Ahmad and made a fiery speech to the people in which he called publicly for the overthrow of the Sabah family and announced that the Iraq Army was ready to move. A former member of the Council, Sulayman al-'Adasani, held a petition signed by several other former members, addressed to King Ghazi, requesting the annexation of Kuwait. Munayis was immediately arrested. Two former members of the Council, Yusuf al-Marzuq and Muhammad al-Qitami, came to his rescue. In the course of the quarrel, Qitami was killed by a guard and Marzuq was wounded. Shaykh Ahmad, with a few supporters, arrived just in time to maintain order and retain Munayis. In an exemplary trial, Munayis was executed and ʿAdasani was thrown into prison. On the following day, several former members of the Council were arrested, but all other leaders, led by ʿAbd-Allah al-Saqr, fled either to Iraq or to India. With the disappearance of its leaders, the uprising subsided, but the idea of joining Iraq remained alive almost to the end of Shaykh Ahmad's unpopular rule in 1950.[10]

On March 11, Shaykh Ahmad appointed a new consultative Council of fourteen members. It began its first meeting on the following day, presided over by Shaykh ʿAbd-Allah, speaker of the house. It included nine prominent members of the merchant community (including two former members of the dissolved Assembly) and five members from the ruling Sabah family. This Council, meeting twice a week, lasted only two years when it suddenly stopped meeting. The incident that led to the Council's suspended meetings was the subject of investigation into the irregularity of the treasury accounts. There were differences of opinion as to the causes of the irregularity. Shaykh Ahmad, finding the members of the Consultative Council were constantly quarrelling about personal differences, stopped calling it to meet. Small wonder that he found the last decade of his career without a Council most satisfying.

The reasons for the failure of the merchant movement to establish a Legislative Assembly may be summarized as follows:

First, the initial British sympathy with the merchant reform movement was half-hearted. Since the movement turned violently against the regime, the British were not prepared to support a movement that could expose Kuwait to foreign intervention, least of one all calling for a union with Iraq. Nor was it in British interest to let down the ruling Sabah family.

Second, the leaders of the opposition, having lost faith with the British, became increasingly dependent on King Ghazi. But although King Ghazi was ready to lend support, his ministers, under British pressure, were not prepared to act. Without full Iraqi support, the merchant opposition movement had little or no chance to succeed, while Shaykh Ahmad could with full freedom crush the movement without much difficulty.

KING GHAZI'S RELATIONS WITH THE MERCHANT MOVEMENT

Long before the members of the Consultative Council came into conflict with Shaykh Ahmad, King Ghazi had already been attacking Shaykh Ahmad's regime from his private broadcasting station as corrupt, feudal, and unworthy of survival. As King Ghazi's attack on Shaykh Ahmad's regime was an interference in the domestic affairs of another country, particularly a country under the protection of Britain, the British Ambassador to Iraq, Sir Maurice Peterson, took up the matter with prime minister Midfa'i, who was on good standing with the King, and sought to persuade him to stop. The King, however, only temporarily stopped. When General Nuri al-Sa'id, a great friend of Britain, returned to power (December 24, 1938), he was expected to exercise greater control over the King. But owing to Nuri's return to power through the army's intervention (which Peterson seems to have deplored owing to the increasing influence of pan-Arab officers on King Ghazi), Peterson's efforts to limit Ghazi's meddling in foreign intrigues through Premier Nuri proved ineffective. Indeed, King Ghazi became even more violent in his attacks on Shaykh Ahmad and went so far as to promise the Kuwaiti merchant leaders to intervene militarily.

In his *Diaries* (February 19, 1939), General Tasha al-Hashimi, Iraq's minister of defence, complains that "King Ghazi has become very active in Kuwaiti affairs. . . .[He] has gone so far as to order the chief of staff to put the army on the alert."[11] General Taha, though a pan-Arab at heart, was a protégé of Premier Nuri and was bound to pursue Nuri's friendly foreign policy toward Britain. Perhaps for this very reason that King Ghazi ordered the chief of staff to put the army on the alert rather than the minister of defence. But the chief of staff, realized he could not possibly put the army on the alert without first receiving an order from the minister of defence, to whom he was directly responsible. He told General Taha about the matter and he was instructed to wait until the King's order would be communicated to him through the proper channel—Naji Shawkat, minister of the interior, who was then acting prime minister, as Premier Nuri was then in London (he was attending the Round Table Conference on Palestine). In his *Memoirs*, Shawkat states that a day after King Ghazi had issued an order to put the army on alert (February 19, 1939), he was summoned for an audience with the King.[12]

Upon his arrival at the Royal Court, Shawkat first met with General Taha al-Hashimi, who had already arrived at the Royal Court, in order to brief him on what he had to do as minister of defence. "The King had not only ordered the chief of staff to occupy Kuwait," General Taha told Shawkat, "he had also ordered the governor of Basra to provide all the necessary requirements for the occupation [of Kuwait]. . . . But he [as minister of defence] did not allow the chief of staff to carry out the order, as it was issued when the King was enjoying his happy hours. . . . It is now up to you to find a way out of this [messy] situation." In his *Memoirs*, Shawkat relates the conversation that went between him and the King as follows:

"What have you done," the King inquired, "about the occupation of Kuwait?" To which Shawkat replied:

> Sir you have not ordered me; you have ordered the chief of staff and the governor of Basra. Your Majesty, as you know, the King is secure and not

responsible. . . . [A]s long as the prime minister is in London, I cannot possibly do anything in his absence, since he is the person more directly responsible to act on this important matter. If you insist to pursue the matter . . . I shall at once send a cable to London in order that he [prime minister Nuri] might return to Baghdad. It is, however, my duty to bring two important matters to your attention: First, it is not in our interest to call Nuri to return from London, as he is undertaking a very important task; Second, Your Majesty, it is very easy to occupy Kuwait within twenty-four hours, but do you think that Britain, Iran, and Saudi Arabia will welcome such an action? Surely, they will turn against us. . . . Will Your Majesty be prepared to go to war against three states at the same time?

"His Majesty" says Shawkat, "at once replied: All right we shall wait until Nuri had returned."[13]

There seems to have been relief in higher political circles that the King had agreed to wait until Premier Nuri had returned to deal with the matter. It was taken for granted that Nuri, a great friend of Britain, would never attack a country under British "protection" without Britain's approval. In all matters relating to foreign affairs, in accordance with the Anglo-Iraqi treaty of 1930, Iraq was under obligation to consult with the British authorities on all important matters.

Even before Premier Nuri had returned, Sir Basil Newton, British ambassador to Iraq (who had succeeded Peterson), made an appointment to see Shawkat. Newton had several matters on his mind; above all he wished to present the British government's protest to the King for his calling on the Kuwaiti people from his private broadcasting station to overthrow the Kuwaiti ruling family. He also wanted to inquire whether King Ghazi was determined to occupy Kuwait. Shawkat, in reply, pointed out that he could not possibly interfere in the private affairs of the King. "After Premier Nuri's return," Shawkat added, "the King's broadcasting and other matters might be raised with him. . . . As to King Ghazi's intention to occupy Kuwait, nothing of this sort will ever happen."[14] Shawkat, aware of Iraq's obligations under the treaty of alliance with Britain, felt he could assure Newton that Iraq would never take an action against Kuwait without prior consultation with Britain.

Ghazi's broadcasts to the Kuwaiti people was the subject of British protest on more than one occasion, and Ghazi promised to stop. But after a short while he resumed his broadcasts on the grounds that he was responding to the appeal of Kuwaiti leaders to continue the broadcasts. Owing to his persisting involvement in Kuwaiti affairs and his private contacts with army officers, he was warned that these activities might undermine the position of the government. King Ghazi never completely stopped his broadcasts which alarmed both the Shaykh of Kuwait and the British, although his relations with the army officers, thanks to his premier's advice, were considerably restricted. Because the King's activities seemed to reveal anti-British feelings, they were exploited by Nazi propaganda which sought to fish in troubled waters.[15]

Following his return from London (February 27, 1939), Nuri began to talk about the need to remove Ghazi from the throne, on the grounds that his actions had compromised Iraq's national interests and undermined his own Cabinet. Nuri initially was toying with the idea of replacing Ghazi with another member of the royal family, but his political opponents were opposed to such a plan. Nor were the British in favor of Ghazi's removal. They maintained that such an action might lead to further difficulties and instability in the country. To his surprise, however, when Nuri was later on a visit to London, he found that the British were seriously discussing the possibility of replacing Ghazi with another member of the royal family, as he had become exceedingly difficult to bring under control.[16]

Ghazi's involvement in Kuwait was the principal reason that brought him into direct conflict with the British and provided Nuri with an excuse to replace him with another member of the royal family. It was contemplated that such a member should be agreeable to both the Iraqi leaders and the British. The most prominent candidates under consideration were three—Amir 'Abd Allah, ruler of Transjordan; Amir Zayd, Iraqi minister in Berlin, and Amir 'Abd al-Ilah, brother of Queen 'Aliya. Amir 'Abd-Allah, although agreeable to the British, was not popular in Iraq and dismissed as too busy in Transjordan. Amir Zayd, well-educated and an experienced diplomat (he had also served on more than one occasion as acting King) was highly regarded by the British, but he was unacceptable to the Iraqi leaders on the grounds that he was married to a Turkish divorcee. It was finally agreed that Amir 'Abd al-Ilah, uncle of Crown Prince Faysal, would be a more suitable candidate to serve as regent, since he was agreeable to the Iraqi leaders as well as he was close to his sister, the Queen Mother.[17]

While these various options were still under consideration, the problem was quickly resolved. On April 4, 1939, suddenly and unexpectedly, it was announced over the radio that King Ghazi was killed in a car accident. The event, as stated in the official communiqué, happened as follows. While King Ghazi, together with his personal servant and his supervisor of radio, was driving from the Zuhur Palace to the Harithiya Palace, on the evening of April 4th, when an accident occurred. The King was driving at an excessive speed while the two men were sitting in the back seat of the car.

> When the car had passed over the railway level-crossing between the two Palaces, [stated the communiqué] the vehicle got out of control owing to its high speed; it shot off the road on the rough ground, crashing into an electric standard before His Majesty could stop it. The crash broke the standard, which fell on His Majesty's head fracturing his skull and causing severe laceration of the brain. His Majesty was taken by police officers to Harithiya Palace, but died an hour later.[18]

Investigations were at once made by the police. "After examining carefully all aspects of the accident," stated the report of investigating magistrate, "it has been proved that the crash was purely accidental." The case was therefore closed, "as there was no suspicion of a criminal act."[19]

The government announcement of the accidental death was not taken at its face value. To the general public, there was no question that Premier Nuri and the British were responsible for the death of the King. To the better-informed political figures, the question was more complicated. Some of Nuri's friends and supporters may have blamed the British, but Nuri's opponents, who had deeper personal differences, blamed it all on Nuri and argued that Ghazi, owing to his popularity in the country, was labelled anti-British and pro-Axis.

More recently, several published studies about Ghazi's life and the events leading to his demise, based on both Iraqi and British archives that have become available to scholars, have thrown further light on the subject. The British documents provide details about Ghazi's personal life, his involvement in the Kuwaiti merchant movement, and his broadcasting station. But no documents seem to exist concerning the possible involvement of anybody in the car accident that caused Ghazi's death. More revealing, indeed, are the memoirs of Iraqi political figures, both opponents and friends of Nuri. For example, Naji Shawkat, minister of interior in Nuri's Cabinet in 1939, under whose signature the official announcements about the car accident and the funeral processing were issued, states in his *Memoirs* with candor that he had serious doubts about Ghazi's death being accidental, although he does not specifically accuse Nuri.[20]

Final judgment as to whether Ghazi's death was caused by a car accident or by design is indeed exceedingly difficult to determine. There is no hard evidence to prove either option. True, Nuri wanted to remove Ghazi from the throne, but he was opposed by political opponents, and initially discouraged by the British. When Ghazi remained determined to interfere in Kuwaiti affairs, the British seem to have given Nuri the green light to remove Ghazi from the throne, but not necessarily by illegal means. No evidence exists that the British authorities had discussed specific steps to be taken for the removal of Ghazi. It is likely that the British may have considered that any action taken should be a matter of domestic affairs. They might, however, be reproached for having given Nuri the green light, if they knew that he was likely to commit an illegal act. In such a situation, the British would bear moral responsibility which they cannot easily disclaim.

Almost all Arab writers have argued that the British bear the primary responsibility on the grounds that Nuri was their great friend and protégé. King Ghazi, in the eyes of his countrymen, was a pan-Arab who genuinely sought to serve his country's best interests according to his light. He was young and inexperienced when he came to the throne, and he suddenly found himself dealing with a set of politicians competing for power. He found comfort in his relationship with former cadets in the military who shared his pan-Arab views. But his friends in the army were no statesmen who could give him advice on how to conduct the business of state, least of all on foreign policy. On the contrary, their pan-Arab views induced him to make statements against the British which gave the impression that he was their enemy. Nuri, considering Britain an ally which would defend the country against foreign threat or attack, thought Ghazi unfit to rule. But Nuri's dependence on Britain was not shared by most political figures. Arab writers who became acquainted with the British documents, came to the conclusion that Britain, opposed to Ghazi's policy, must have been the principal culprit in their King's demise.[21]

It is, however, not unlikely that Ghazi was accidentally killed by his excessively fast driving as described in the official communiqué. The remarks made by his critics that the car was not the cause of death were neither conclusive nor entirely unrelated to the cause of death. The difficulty in examining this case is the lack of hard evidence proving that Nuri had directly been involved in it. No less important is the mixture of the emotional elements with the evidence provided by all concerned.

Finally, Nuri cannot be considered completely without responsibility, as he made life so difficult for Ghazi that his faults were not all necessarily good reasons for removing him from the throne. Nuri's role in Ghazi's demise carries with it not a little moral responsibility.

NEGOTIATIONS ON TERRITORIAL ISSUES UNDER GHAZI'S RULE

While King Ghazi was engaged personally in the Kuwaiti merchant movement to achieve unity with Iraq, Tawfiq al-Suwaydi, his foreign minister, was in the meantime conducting negotiations with the British government about several territorial issues, including the possibility of unity with Kuwait. Whether Suwaydi's negotiations with the British were prompted by an order of the King or by his own initiative is not clear. In his *Memoirs*, Suwaydi provides no clue for an answer; he only reports a brief summary of an aide-memoire he had submitted to the Foreign Office.[22]

Suwaydi, however, was not unaware of Ghazi's keen interest in Kuwait and he seemed to have searched for a legal or diplomatic precedent in the archives of the Iraqi Foreign Office to provide a basis for an Iraqi claim to Kuwait. While he was once calling on foreign minister Suwaydi, Maurice Peterson, British ambassador to Iraq, saw on Suwaydi's desk a copy of Aitchison's compilation of documents on the Gulf, to which we have referred earlier, in which he found a document referring to Kuwait as a district in the province of Basra before World War I. On the basis of that document, Suwaydi told Peterson, Kuwait

must belong to Iraq as a successor state following the destruction of
the Ottoman Empire. Upon reporting Suwaydi's argument to the British Foreign Office, it was undertaken to prepare a reply to Iraq stating
that the frontier separating Iraq from Kuwait had already been settled
before Iraq had become independent in 1932.

In September, 1938, while he was attending the League of Nations
meetings in Geneva, Suwaydi informed R.A. Butler, parliamentary undersecretary for foreign affairs (who was also attending the League's
meetings), that he intended to discuss a number of pending issues
relating to Kuwait with the British Foreign Office. Butler suggested that
an aide-memoire, consisting of the principal matters he intended to
discuss should be dispatched to the Foreign Office before his visit to
London.

In an able aide-memoire, Suwaydi raised for the first time the principle of Iraq's historical claim to Kuwait.[23] He made no mention of
Ghazi's dealings with Kuwait, perhaps because Ghazi's contacts were
not with the Kuwaiti government, but with a group of Kuwaiti political
leaders in their personal capacity. "The Iraqi Government," Suwaydi
argued, "as the successor to the Ottoman Government in the wilayat
[provinces] of Mawsil, Baghdad, and Basra, considers that Kuwait
should properly be incorporated in Iraq." The other two issues which
Suwaydi had raised were: a) smuggling and arms trafficking; b) an access to the sea. If unity with Iraq were to take place, Suwaydi pointed
out, the other two problems would be automatically resolved.

Suwaydi, however, was not insistent—indeed, he was quite flexible—in his proposal for the incorporation of Kuwait with Iraq. He had,
in fact, made it quite clear that if Britain were not in favor of the
incorporation of Kuwait within Iraq's frontiers, then a solution of the
other two problems, smuggling and access to the sea, must be found.
As to an Iraqi access to the sea, he proposed either the selection of a
suitable site for Iraq on the Kuwait Bay or the inclusion of an inland
extension of the Khawr 'Abd-Allah within Iraq's frontiers. If the first
proposal were agreeable, Suwaydi argued, it would be necessary for Iraq
to lease a site for a port on the Bay and a corridor for an Iraqi railway.
The second proposal, he went on to explain, calls for a rectification of
the frontier which would give Iraq a slice of territory and the whole of
the Khawr 'Abd-Allah to allow Iraq to operate.

No sooner had the aide-memoire reached the Foreign Office than
the Iraqi proposals became the subject of extensive examination not
only at the Foreign Office, but also at several other departments concerned with the British Empire. With regard to Iraq's historical claim
to Kuwait, although the claim was not initially taken very seriously, it
kept the Foreign Office Eastern Department busy for quite a while to
prove that Iraq's claim had no legal basis. As to Iraq's proposal for an
access to the sea, there was some sympathy with Iraq's need for a port
other than Basra through the Shatt al-Arab. Sir John Ward, director

general of the Basra port and the Iraqi railways, whose sympathy was with Iraq, informed the Foreign Office that the Basra port was no longer adequate for Iraqi needs. He suggested providing Iraq with an access to the Khawr Zubayr rather than a port on Kuwait Bay on the grounds that the former would be far less expensive. There were objections to the Iraqi demand for a port other than Basra from the Admiralty and the British Raj in India, but the Foreign Office saw some advantages in the proposal for a port on the Khawr Zubayr.

Upon Suwaydi's arrival in London, two meetings were held at the Foreign Office (October 4, 1938), one in the morning and the other later in the afternoon.[24] In the morning, Suwaydi met with Lord Halifax and the principal matters he proposed in the aide-memoire were discussed. With regard to the claim to Kuwait, Lord Halifax made it abundantly clear to Suwaydi that "His Majesty's government would find it difficult to admit any Iraqi claim, if the Iraqi government were ever to put forward such a claim, to sovereignty over Kuwait." Suwaydi at once agreed not to insist on discussing the sovereignty claim, although he did not necessarily mean that Iraq would give up its legal claim to Kuwait's sovereignty. As to the other proposals, such as Iraq's need for an access to the sea, Lord Halifax promised that those proposals would be scrutinized more fully with the Foreign Office experts.

In the afternoon session (at 6:00 P.M.), Suwaydi and C. J. Edmonds (British adviser to the Iraqi Ministry of Interior) met with C.W. Baxter, head of the Foreign Office Eastern Department, and P.M. Crosthwaite, another Foreign Office expert. At the request of Suwaydi, the proposals set forth in the aide-memoire were thoroughly examined. As head of the Eastern Department, Baxter took the lead in the discussion on behalf of the British government. On most of the issues, the conversation took the form of a contest between Suwaydi and Baxter; the former described the Iraqi problems and suggested proposals for solving them, while Baxter sought to protect Kuwaiti (and British) interests.

With regard to Iraq's claim to the sovereignty of Kuwait, Baxter, reiterating the statement made earlier by Lord Halifax, insisted that the British government would "find it difficult to admit any Iraqi claim." Suwaydi replied, as he told Lord Halifax, he had no intention to insist on discussing the matter. Suwaydi's purpose, it seems, was to bring to the attention of the British government that Iraq had a historical and legal claim to the sovereignty of Kuwait which might, perhaps, implicitly provide the rationale for King Ghazi's demand for unity between Kuwait and Iraq.

As to smuggling and arms trafficking, stressed in the aide-memoire as more urgent issues, Baxter sought at first to evade the issue by stating that "the British government had not received any evidence to show that any such smuggling of arms was, in fact, taking place." Not only did Suwaydi insist that the Iraq government had, in fact, at its disposal sufficient evidence, but he was also supported by Edmonds, who stated

that he personally had received evidence of smuggling and arms trafficking. At this point, Baxter conceded that the British government
"would certainly be prepared to give the whole question its attention
after the Iraqi government would produce all evidence in its possession."

Expressing Iraq's urgent need to control smuggling, Suwaydi suggested three proposals as possible solutions for the problem: 1) Custom
union between Iraq and Kuwait; 2) moving the northern frontier of
Kuwait further south in order to give Iraq jurisdiction to apply preventive measures; 3) combined preventive operations by the two countries.
Edmonds, in support of the Iraqi position, suggested the adoption of
some kind of control on the sale of arms in the Kuwait market such as
the control which the government of 'Uman (Oman) had pursued by
collecting all arms available for sale in one special warehouse and the
sale of arms came under some form of control by the authorities. Edmonds also suggested the possibility of an increase in the customs tariff
of Kuwait to the level of the Iraqi tariff by the Kuwaiti government.
Baxter said that such proposals would be examined further, but he had
shown no sign of sympathy with the Iraqi position on smuggling.

Only with Suwaydi's proposal concerning an access to the sea did
Baxter consider the matter worthy of discussion in favor of Iraq. He
maintained, however, that such an access should not be on the Kuwait
Bay, probably because such an access might give Iraq intimate relationships with the mainland area which might bring about eventual unity
between the two countries. He suggested instead a portion of Khawr
'Abd-Allah, on the side of the island of Warba, far from the mainland,
as a more suitable modern port near the Iraqi frontier. He gave suita-
bility and cost as his reasons for a preference of a port on Khawr 'Abd-
Allah than a port on Kuwait Bay. The city of Kuwait itself, he argued,
was not suitable as a modern port, and the establishment of a port
would be very expensive. At present, he added, ships do not anchor
nearer than three miles from the shore.

In reply, Suwaydi stated that the Iraq government would certainly
examine the Khawr 'Abd-Allah possibility, but the development of such
a port might require certain concessions on the part of Kuwait such as
an alteration in the existing frontiers. Baxter said that if the Shaykh of
Kuwait were asked to cede a part of territory such as Warba Island and
the navigable channel between the island and the open sea, Iraq would
have to compensate Kuwait elsewhere. "For this purpose," he added,
"it would be desirable that the Iraqi government's offer should be
made as attractive as possible." As to Suwaydi's inquiry that he might
approach the Shaykh of Kuwait (as he knew him personally), Baxter
made it clear that any official approach to the Shaykh of Kuwait should
be made through the British government.

In his *Memoirs*, Suwaydi states that before he returned to Baghdad,
he passed some twenty days in London and almost all of this time was

spent in conversations with high authorities about Iraqi affairs. However, he noted that there was no positive response to any of the issues
he had raised on the grounds that prior approval of the Shaykh of
Kuwait was necessary. But when he raised the question of ceding the
island of Warba to Iraq, he was bluntly told that Kuwait should be
compensated for ceding the island of Warba. To this Suwaydi retorted:
"But who had decided that the islands of Warba and Bubiyan were
Kuwaiti territory in the first place?"[25]

FURTHER NEGOTIATIONS UNDER GENERAL NURI'S GOVERNMENT

Shortly after Suwaydi's return to Baghdad, the premier under
whom he served as foreign minister resigned (December 24, 1938) before he had an opportunity to discuss Iraq's relationship with the
Shaykh of Kuwait. General Nuri, who formed a new government, instructed 'Ali Jawdat, his foreign minister, to pursue the negotiations
with the British about Kuwait where Suwaydi had left them. Jawdat,
however, did not pursue the negotiations until almost a year later. In
November, 1939, he informed the Foreign Office that Iraq was ready
to establish a port at the site south of Umm Qasr, considered within
Iraqi territory (the British Raj in India, however, considered it to fall
within Kuwaiti territory). Jawdat also demanded that Kuwait should
cede the islands of Warba and Bubiyan without compensation on the
grounds that those islands were barren and muddy and of no use to
Kuwait. The British Foreign Office saw no reason to influence the
Shaykh of Kuwait to cede part of his territory without compensation
and the matter dragged on until 1940.[26]

The negotiations during 1940–41, however, broke down on the procedural issue as to whether the demarcation of the frontiers should
first be settled, as demanded by Kuwait, or whether Kuwait should first
agree to surrender the islands of Warba and Bubiyan and to provide
Iraq with an access to the Gulf through the channel of Khawr 'Abd-
Allah. There was a possibility of compromise that Iraq might accept
only Warba before entering into negotiations with Kuwait. Because of
suspicion that Iraq might not accept demarcation in accordance with
the frontier set in the exchange of letters (1932) between the two countries, Kuwait refused to cede the islands that Iraq considered necessary
for its security requirements.

In mid-1941, when British forces landed in Basra for defence of
the Gulf, the British military authorities decided with the approval of
the Cabinet that Umm Qasr, which Iraq had decided to develop as a
port, had become important for the British Army as the Basra ports
was "liable to be closed by mines or other obstructions . . . for indefi-
nite period." Thus Umm Qasr suddenly became important not only

for Iraq but also for the British military authorities. Its construction was undertaken by Britain with the approval of both Iraq and Kuwait to operate under British control for the duration of the war. Iraq hoped that the port might be transferred to it after the war while the Shaykh of Kuwait suggested demolishing the port after the war to prevent Iraq from using it as an access to Khawr ʿAbd-Allah.

In the meantime, an unexpected controversy raged between the British Raj in India and the British Foreign Office in London as to whether Umm Qasr was indeed within Iraqi territory, as the British experts in India discovered evidence that Umm Qasr was within Kuwait's frontier. The Foreign Office argued, however, that Umm Qasr had already been approved as falling within Iraq's frontiers by the Shaykh of Kuwait before it was proposed by Iraq in 1940 to become a site for a port. No final decision had been made by the British government when the war was over, as the experts of the British Raj insisted that approval of the Shaykh of Kuwait was dependent on Iraq's acceptance of the 1940s arrangement. As Iraq had rejected such an arrangement, it could no longer remain binding on Kuwait. For this reason, the British military authorities demolished the construction of the port although the site was considered within Iraqi territory. In 1954, Iraq took the drastic step of constructing a port south of Umm Qasr. Meanwhile, Iraq continued to claim its right to the islands of Warba and Bubiyan (at times Iraq restricted its claim to Warba only) as necessary for its defence requirements, although Kuwait claimed the islands fell within its own territory under the agreements of 1923 and 1932.

Early in the 1950s, negotiations for the demarcation of borders appeared more prospective. There were several reasons for optimism.

First, the achievement of Indian independence following World War II seems to have considerably affected British policy in the Gulf region. The transfer of the British Raj from India to London put an end to the conflicting views that existed between the Foreign Office and the British Raj about the status of Kuwait and other matters. The British Raj sought to protect the interests of the Shaykh of Kuwait while the Foreign Office sought to protect the interests of Pax Britannica as a whole and tended to look at Iraqi interests more favorably than the British Raj.

Second, with the rise of India to statehood, Iraqi leaders friendly to Britain, such as General Nuri, Tawfiq al-Suwaydi, and others, sought to influence other leaders opposed to Britain to change their stand on the grounds that Anglo-Iraqi cooperation would be based on mutual interests and not only on protecting British imperial interests in India.

Third, Shaykh Ahmad, who had taken an antagonistic attitude toward Iraq (largely because King Ghazi supported the Kuwaiti merchant movement in 1938) died in January 1950. He was succeeded by his cousin Shaykh ʿAbd-Allah al-Salim, speaker of the Legislative Assembly, who was on the whole on good terms with Iraq. Upon his assumption of power, he visited Baghdad and was received with high respect and honor.

Because of these favorable conditions, Britain twice sought to offer its good offices to both sides in order to reach an agreement on demarcation of borders based on the 1923 and 1932 exchange of letters. The first offer of good offices was in 1950 when Iraq decided to construct its own port in Umm Qasr and sought to obtain Kuwait's approval for ceding the islands of Warba and Bubiyan in order to control navigation in the Khawrs of Zubayr and ʿAbd-Allah. Shayk ʿAbd-Allah was prepared to accept Umm Qasr as falling within Iraqi territory (a claim Shaykh Ahmad was opposed). Then, just as Britain was ready to offer a compromise plan, as both had agreed on the need for demarcation in principle, the Basra Oil Company (BOC) struck high-quality crude within twenty miles south of the town of Zubayr. On its part, the Kuwait Oil Company (KOC) had also been given permission to explore an area which came close to the BOC's area of interest (from Zubayr to Kuwait Bay) in 1951. Moreover, Kuwait continued to assert that the boundary line should run 1,000 meters south of Safwan while Iraq demanded one mile. These events caused both sides to put off negotiations.

In 1954, Britain again offered its good offices. It sought to encourage both sides to commit themselves on demarcation in accordance with the formula it had proposed consisting of a promise by Iraq to provide Kuwait with fresh water from the Shatt al-Arab, provided the costs of the pipeline were borne by Kuwait. Kuwait, however, did not want to become dependent on a source of water over which it had no control and decided instead to establish a desalination center under its own control. Iraq, on the other hand, insisted that demarcation should be one mile south of Safwan and rejected Kuwait's demand of 1,000 meters. The British government sought to commit Iraq and Kuwait to demarcation as a means to achieve settled frontiers embodied in a formal treaty binding on both sides. An atmosphere clouded with suspicion, often caused by territorial confilcts, specifically prospects of oil in disputed areas, and by incidents of smuggling and arms trafficking, prevented both sides from reaching a meeting of minds necessary for a formal agreement. Thus, when Britain finally proposed a draft agreement in 1955 in which all needs and security requirements of both sides were dealt with—the Umm Qasr port and the lease of Warba for security reasons, the demarcation line south of Safwan to 1,000 meters, and fresh water from the Shatt al-Arab for Kuwait—the draft agreement with minor changes was almost tacitly agreed upon before negotiations were disrupted by a chain of regional events over which the parties concerned had no control.

The most important event that postponed formal agreement was the nationalization of the Suez Canal Company in 1955, which precipitated the tripartite attack by Britain, France, and Israel on Egypt in

1956. In the wake of this disturbing event, a widespread anti-British feeling prompted President Nasir of Egypt to embark on a pan-Arab movement resulting in the establishment of the United Arab Republic in 1958. As a reaction, Iraq and Jordan formed the Arab Federal Union to which Kuwait was invited to join. These trends suddenly diverted Iraq's attention from the relatively small frontier dispute with Kuwait to the pressing regional need for an Arab union to protect countries friendly to the West, among which Kuwait might be included.

Chapter 5

Proposals for Unity by Means Short of War

In 1958, two pan-Arab unions were established: the United Arab Republic (UAR), composed of Egypt and Syria under the leadership of Nasir, president of Egypt, and the Arab Federal Union (AFU), composed of Iraq and Jordan, under the Hashimi family, the ruling dynasty in Iraq and Jordan. Because the UAR was an ally of the Soviet Union, the Hashimi family, a great friend of the West, received Western support in its endeavors to cooperate with other Arab countries friendly to the West (such as Saudi Arabia and Kuwait) in order to stand as a bulwark against the overwhelming appeal which Nasir's drive to achieve a grand pan-Arab union extending from the Atlantic to the Indian oceans had garnered. Approached to join the AFU, Saudi Arabia replied that it would support the Hashimi rulers in their cooperation with the West, but it did not want to abandon its traditional policy of non-interference in inter-Arab relationships. As Kuwait was then still under British protection, Iraq sought to deal with the question of joining the AFU through the British government. In 1938, twenty years before the AFU was established, King Ghazi tried in vain to bring about unity between Kuwait and Iraq by resort to violence. After the establishment of the AFU, Iraq made another attempt to draw Kuwait into the Hashimi camp by peaceful means. Kuwait was invited through the British government to join the AFU as an equal and independent partner. Nuri al-Saʿid, who headed the AFU government, was aware that if this new organization were ever to survive and become an active factor in regional peace and stability, it must include in its membership other Arab countries that would enhance the stature of the AFU politically and materially. Nuri maintained that Kuwait would be the most appropriate country to enlist, owing to its geopolitical location at the head of the Gulf, its potential in oil, and the fact that its Sabah ruling family advocated the same pro-Western outlook as the Hashimi ruling family in Iraq and Jordan.

But there was still another reason for Nuri's special interest in Kuwait. Conscious of the fact that his controversial frontier agreement with Kuwait (1932) had become the source of endless territorial and frontier differences between the two countries, he sought to resolve those issues which, in his old age, weighed heavily on his conscience. The opportunity to resolve them came sooner than he expected. In 1958, the United Arab Republic (UAR) was established which provided Nuri with a good reason that the frontier issue between the two countries might be resolved.

But what prompted Iraq and Jordan, it may be asked, to seek political unity in 1958?

The idea of an Arab union was not new, but in 1958 there were immediate as well as remote reasons that prompted Jordan and Iraq to form an Arab union. The immediate reasons were the new political alignments in the Arab world that had adversely affected Iraq's posture since World War II. In 1955, General Nuri, in an alliance with Turkey and in cooperation with Britain and the United States, formed the Baghdad Pact, which stood against Communist penetration into the Middle East.[1] Nasir, president of Egypt, led a campaign against Iraq because he considered the Baghdad Pact a Western tool designed to oppose the Soviet Union (a great power, he reasoned, that the Arabs had no reason to antagonize) while the Western powers were supporting Israel against Arab interests. In 1956, when Egypt was the object of the tripartite attack by Britain, France, and Israel (incited by its nationalization of the Suez Canal Company) a wave of pan-Arab sympathy swept the Arab world which inspired Nasir to ride the crest of the movement to achieve Arab unity. In his call to join the UAR, the first step in his grand Arab design, Nasir made a direct appeal to Arabs over the heads of their rulers to rise up and replace them by other rulers prepared to accept Nasir's leadership. Nasir's drive to achieve Arab unity was a confrontation to the current Hashimi rulers in Iraq and Jordan whose grandfather, Sharif Husayn of Makka, had called for Arab unity since World War I. Arab Gulf rulers, including the Shaykh of Kuwait, were concerned about Nasir's intentions on account of their rich oil resources.[2]

Before World War II, when Iraq achieved independence (1932), the idea of an Arab Prussia which would unify the Arab world by military action prevailed. Iraq, long before Egypt entered the field to provide leadership, was looked upon as the most promising country to play that role. Iraq began to pay attention to its military posture by enlarging the army and obtaining weaponry. It was during this period that the leaders of the merchant movement in Kuwait, disenchanted with Shaykh Ahmad's rule, appealed to King Ghazi for possible unity with Iraq. The movement failed, it will be recalled, not only because the

British were opposed to it, but also because Premier Nuri and his Cabinet stood against it. Only King Ghazi and a few opponents to Premier Nuri's regime showed an interest in the merchant movement, but they could not influence the military command to support it.

Following World War II, when the pan-Arab movement regained momentum in its drive to achieve Arab unity, President Nasir, who had defied Western pressures to be drawn into the Cold War, was considered the most likely leader to achieve pan-Arab ideals. Early in 1958, when Syria joined Egypt to form the UAR, pan-Arabs in several other Arab countries launched campaigns in favor of joining the UAR, campaigns that aimed at establishing a grand Arab union extending from the Atlantic to the Indian Ocean. Iraq and Jordan, alarmed by the celerity of Syria's action to merge with Egypt, moved quickly to forge an Arab union in order to counteract Nasir's pan-Arab drive.

THE ARAB FEDERAL UNION

Motivated by self-defence and British encouragement, the two branches of the ruling Hashimi family in Iraq and Jordan were ready to form their own Arab union. When the UAR was created, General Nuri was in England. He at once began to discuss the plan of a Hashimi Arab union with high authorities in London as a challenge to Nasir's UAR.[3]

Upon his return to Baghdad (February 7, 1958), Nuri conveyed Western concerns about the dangers of Nasir's threat to King Faysal and Crown Prince ʿAbd al-Ilah. After an exchange of views with King Husayn of Jordan on the subject, King Faysal with several members of the Cabinet and Parliament went to ʿAmman (February 11, 1958) to discuss how to meet the imminent threat to their countries. It did not take long to come to the conclusion that an Arab federal union between Iraq and Jordan should immediately be formed to meet the challenge of the UAR and also to realize the long-standing Arab aspirations to achieve unity under the leadership of the Hashimi family. Accordingly, the two Kings signed an agreement (February 14, 1958) to establish an Arab Federal Union (AFU) between the two countries based on the principles of equality, independence, and the integrity of internal regimes. The AFU, it was agreed, would be open to any other Arab country ready to join. The agreement was subject to the approval of the Cabinets and Parliaments of the two countries as well as to their peoples. It was decided to hold general elections in the two countries to ratify the AFU agreement and to amend their constitutions in order to establish a federal government to which all powers over foreign, defence, and financial affairs were transferred.[4]

It is outside the scope of this study to discuss in detail the constitutional structure and functions of the newly created federal system in the Arab world. Suffice it to say that it was composed of a Federal government, Federal Parliament, three Ministries—Foreign Affairs, Defence and Finance—and a Supreme Court. Any other Arab state prepared to join the AFU would be by means of an agreement with the federal government. Each member of the Union was free to preserve its own system of government and respect all agreements with foreign powers that it had entered into before joining the AFU, but any new agreement must be concluded with the AFU federal government. The federal Parliament, composed of an equal number of representatives from each participating state, would enact laws to regulate not only the relationship among the members of the AFU but also to ratify treaties entered into with foreign governments. Finally, it was agreed that the King of Iraq would be the head of the AFU with the King of Jordan as his deputy, but this arrangement would be reconsidered in the event another country wished to join the Union. It is to be noted that the powers of the federal government were confined to three principal functions; any other function entrusted to the federal government must be decided by the federal Parliament by a two-thirds majority.[5]

Following the establishment of the AFU, Shaykh ʿAbd-Allah al-Salim, ruler of Kuwait, visited Baghdad (May 10, 1958) and talked with General Nuri and other Iraqi leaders. His conversations, however, were noncommittal about Kuwait's relations with Iraq, and he tried to avoid any discussion about the possibility that Kuwait might join the AFU. When Nuri suggested the demarcation of the frontier and an offer to provide Kuwait with fresh water from the Iraqi rivers, Shaykh ʿAbd-Allah hinted that he was prepared to enter into an agreement with Iraq and Jordan without commitment to any specific terms. But he said not a word as to how and when it would be negotiated which left the impression that he had no intention of joining the AFU. His disclosure that he was planning to visit Cairo and meet with Nasir was very disappointing to the Iraqi leaders. Nevertheless, General Nuri was counting on British support to encourage Kuwait to join the AFU, as it was in their interests to enhance the position of the new Arab federation in its stand against Nasir's pan-Arab drive.[6]

General Nuri, who acted as premier of the provisional government of the AFU, was invited by the King of Iraq (head of the AFU) to form the first federal government on May 19, 1958. Nuri, pursuing the principle of equal representation, chose a Jordanian as deputy premier and three Iraqis and three Jordanians as Ministers and deputy ministers. The federal government began at once to discuss the implementation of the AFU Constitution and the preparation of a budget subject to approval by the federal Parliament.

With regard to the financial burden of each AFU member, Iraq was to bear eighty percent of the first annual budget and Jordan the remaining twenty percent. ʿAbd al-Karim al-Uzri, minister of finance of the AFU, approached the Iraqi and Jordanian ministers of finance to deliver their shares to the federal budget. The Jordanian minister of

finance, however, informed Uzri that Jordan could not possibly deliver
its share of the first annual budget before the American and British
grants to Jordan's defence, which had just been suspended, would be
resumed. Unless these grants were soon delivered, Uzri came to the
conclusion, the AFU would face a serious financial crisis.

To resolve the problem, Uzri sought the advice of Premier Nuri.
On June 9, 1958, Uzri met with Nuri. Both agreed that Iraq could not
possibly undertake the entire financial burden for the first year of the
Union budget. The Iraqi government, Uzri (a former Iraqi minister of
finance) pointed out, had difficulties in balancing its own budget and
could not possibly contribute large enough funds to cover all the AFU
expenses, unless some of Iraq's own projects of reconstruction and development were postponed. Nuri was counting on the possibility that
Kuwait would join the AFU and contribute its share as a member of
the Union. But the Shaykh of Kuwait had expressed no desire to join
the AFU. Nuri, according to Uzri, felt that Britain and the United States
should come to the rescue of the AFU, since it would serve Western
no less than Arab interest. Nuri reluctantly instructed Uzri to approach
Sir Michael Wright, British ambassador to Iraq, to inquire as to whether
the grant to Jordan might possibly be transferred to the AFU. But Nuri
was, above all, anxious to know whether Wright had received an answer
to the memorandum concerning the invitation to Kuwait to join the
AFU which had earlier been submitted to the British Foreign Office.
Nuri also asked Uzri to inquire whether Waldemar Gallman, American
ambassador to Iraq, had any idea as to when the American financial
assistance to Jordan would be delivered.[7]

Uzri, following an appointment made with Michael Wright, went
to see him on the same day at the British Embassy at 5:00 P.M. In his
conversation with Wright, Uzri made it quite clear that unless financial
assistance to the AFU were granted, the organization would suffer serious financial crisis. Wright promised to send a cable to London; but,
he warned, Harold McMillan, British prime minister, was in Washington and he did not expect a quick answer. Uzri also inquired whether
a reply from the Foreign Office concerning the memorandum about
Kuwait's adhesion to the AFU had arrived. Not having received a reply,
Wright tried to explain the delay on the grounds that he understood
the memorandum was exploratory in nature. From the British Embassy
Uzri went to the American Embassy. In his conversation with Ambassador Gallman, he found him to hold almost the same discouraging
views as the British ambassador. Disappointed by his talks with the two
ambassadors, Uzri came to the conclusion that both Britain and the
United States were neither ready to approve quick delivery of the financial assistance to Jordan nor were they ready to urge Kuwait to join
the AFU.

Upon his return, Uzri reported to Nuri that the two ambassadors
were not expecting quick replies to assist the AFU. Nuri, according to

Uzri, was quite upset, especially with Wright's dubious explanation for not receiving an answer to the memorandum about Kuwait. "What wrong have I done," said Nuri, "that I should be the object of all these humiliations and indignities?" He then said in despair: "I have decided to resign and let those who wanted to establish the AFU in the first place, to grapple with its problems." And he picked up the telephone and talked with 'Abd-Allah Bakr, chief of the royal court, and ordered him to inform King Faysal that he decided to resign. Nuri also instructed Uzri to let the British ambassador know that he had resigned. Uzri again paid a visit to Michael Wright later in the afternoon and apprised him of Nuri's disappointment and anxiety because his proposals about Kuwait's adherence to AFU and the grant to Jordan had received little or no attention by Britain and the United States.

Michael Wright was quite disturbed, according to Uzri, when he learned that Nuri had decided to resign and wanted to see him at once. He picked up the telephone and requested to see Nuri. But Nuri replied that he preferred to see Wright on the following day. It was agreed that they would meet at Nuri's house at 9:00 A.M. Turning to Uzri, Wright said:

> I want to assure you that I am in favor of your proposal that Kuwait should join the AFU on the basis of equality. I hope that such an arrangement would eventually be realized. . . . You have, however, to be patient and not to press the matter too hard. As to the economic assistance, there is no question about it. Unfortunately, MacMillan's visit to Washington is the reason for the delayed reply to your request.[8]

On the following day (June 10, 1958), Wright arrived at 9:00 A.M. and the meeting (attended by Uzri) lasted till about 2:00 P.M. Nuri, according to Uzri, began calmly to speak, although it was clear that his irritation (infi'al) was subdued. But very soon, Nuri's qualm came to the open and he suddenly said (as Uzri states in his Memoirs):

> I, who is well known for my friendship with the British, consider your policy in the Arab world to have completely failed. You are now at enmity with almost all Arab countries. . . . Why should not Iraq too be on the list of your enemies? You have been responsible for this sad situation because of your assistance in the creation of Israel which has become a threat to all Arab countries. Yet, when the Arabs asked for weapons to defend themselves, you have always hesitated and made all kinds of excuses for not giving them the weapons. If your policy were to continue, you are likely to lose all your friends in the Middle East. . . . When we (your friends) sought to strengthen our position in Iraq and Jordan, and requested your assistance, as the power responsible for Kuwait's foreign affairs, to urge Kuwait to join the AFU, you told us to talk first with the Shaykh of Kuwait, although we know that the matter is ultimately up to you. We have invited the Shaykh to visit Baghdad, but during his visit he avoided to talk about the subject. . . . When we tried to strengthen our position by the establishment of the AFU, we found ourselves in a very

difficult financial position. . . . I am now over seventy years old. I have in all my life sought to pursue a consistent policy of friendship with your government, because I believed that such a policy with a great power as Britain was in the interest of my country, but I have found to my regret that you treat your enemies much better than your friends. I want to assure you, Mr. Ambassador, that I am able to be a great national hero, if I were to follow the policy Arab public opinion demands—regardless whether such policy will succeed or not (probably it will not)—to take Kuwait by force. But it is not easy for me to follow such a policy. For this reason, I prefer to withdraw from public life and retire to a small isolated town in Austria, so that nobody will reproach me for instigating anybody against you. . . . [9]

The British ambassador, according to Uzri, was quite taken aback by Nuri's sharply critical remarks about British policy. He tried to calm Nuri and often interrupted him to explain the aims of British policy. Even before Nuri stopped his tirade, Wright assured him that his views would be reported to the British government. He also promised Nuri to send a cable urging the Foreign Office to take immediate action on his request for financial assistance hoping that a reply might be forthcoming within the next twenty-four to forty-eight hours. Moreover, he promised to talk with the American ambassador to send a cable to remind his government about the American assistance to Jordan. With regard to Kuwait, he assured Nuri that he had already sent a note to the Foreign Office suggesting to persuade the Shaykh of Kuwait to join the AFU. But, he added, that this question was in his opinion a matter of time, and he advised patience. The ambassador's reassurances, according to Uzri, seem to have gone a long way to clear the atmosphere from Nuri's anxiety and apprehension.

Nuri and Uzri, uncertain as to what might be the outcome of Wright's dispatches to London, went to the royal court where they had an audience with the King and the Crown Prince. Nuri, after he had reported what went on between him and the British ambassador, submitted his formal resignation. The King made it clear that he was not ready to accept it; he felt that Nuri's continuation as premier was absolutely necessary. Needless to say, he added, he had to wait until an answer about the economic assistance from the British and American governments had arrived.

Two days later (June 11, 1958) a reply to the AFU request for financial assistance arrived to the effect that an advance of twenty-eight million dollars had been approved by President Eisenhower and Premier MacMillan to be paid directly to the AFU, and the balance of the economic assistance previously paid to Jordan would be considered later, subject to the approval of Congress and the British Parliament. Upon learning the news, Nuri withdrew his resignation and asked Uzri immediately to prepare the budget for presentation to the AFU Parliament.

No sooner had the question of financial assistance been settled than Nuri left for London (June 23, 1958) to pursue the negotiations about Kuwait's membership in the AFU. At the Foreign Office, he explained his views, as stated in the memorandum about Kuwait, and assured the British that Iraq had no intention to interfere in Kuwait's domestic affairs nor to encroach on the privileges of the Shaykh and the Sabah family.

It is appropriate at this stage to give a brief account of the aims and content of the memorandum that Suwaydi, the AFU foreign minister, had submitted to the British government.[10] The memorandum made it quite clear that Kuwait's membership in the AFU was in Britain's own interest, as its inclusion might strengthen Britain's position in the Arab world and protect Kuwait from the threat of Nasir. As far as Kuwait's status was concerned, its independence and the privileges of the ruling family, as provided under the AFU constitution, were to be guaranteed. Kuwait's oil concessions to British and American companies were also to be honored. Above all, the position of the ruling families of the three countries—Jordan, Iraq, and Kuwait—well known for their friendship with Britain and the West, would be guaranteed.

In his memorandum, the foreign minister of AFU sought to provide a rationale for Kuwait's adherence to the AFU, based on Iraq's historical and legal claims. As author of an earlier note on the subject, which he had submitted to the Foreign Office twenty years previously (noted before), Suwaydi had drawn on that document without reference to it. The memorandum dwelt on the advantages of cooperation among the AFU members which would enhance their posture as a whole in the Arab world. With regard to Western interests, the memorandum states that the AFU "recognizes all oil concessions and their present provisions, as they concern the area exploited by the oil companies in this area, and the resulting financial arrangements between the various parties and those will remain as they were at present, except as required by the Arab Union to meet its financial needs." If Kuwait were to decline the invitation, states the memorandum, then the AFU will declare that all the islands adjacent to Kuwait would be considered within its own boundaries. These boundaries are "the line of the land frontier between the AFU and Kuwait, beginning from the junction of Wadi al-Awdja and Wadi al-Batin, [will] run in a straight line to Jahra and the Gulf of Kuwait."

The memorandum ends with an appeal to the British government, in which it suggests:

> to advise the Shaykh of Kuwait to choose with all speed, what is best for him, between the two solutions mentioned above. If the Shaykh of Kuwait chooses the first solution, that is, the accession of Kuwait to the Arab Union, there remains no need to discuss the frontier question. But if he chooses the second solution which concerns the frontiers, then the Arab Union is prepared to conclude a treaty of friendship and *bon voisinage* with him.

The initial British reaction was not to answer the memorandum. It was hoped, by an indirect persuasion of the United States and Jordan, the memorandum might be withdrawn by Iraq. Nuri, however, insisted that since the memorandum had already been approved by the AFU government, it could not possibly be withdrawn. But the British government made it clear that if the Shaykh of Kuwait were not ready to join the AFU, it had no intention of going back on its obligations to Kuwait nor of treating it as a "pawn in the game." The Iraqi government held that the Shaykh's position was dependent on British support; if Britain were to grant Kuwait independence, the Shaykh might be prepared to come to terms with Iraq. As it became clear that if Nuri were let down he would resign, the British realized that there was no hope of inducing the AFU to withdraw its memorandum. "One of our difficulties," the British Foreign Office held, "is that Nuri feels that his prestige is involved in Kuwait."[11] Nuri, however, an old friend of Britain, considered British support a personal obligation to him.

On June 23, 1958, Nuri made what turned out to be his last visit to England. He held several meetings with Selwyn Lloyd and other officials at the Foreign Office to discuss what was then uppermost on his mind—Lebanon. Owing to a widespread pan-Arab agitation, there was a threat to all pro-Western regimes. If Lebanon fell under Nasir's domination, Nuri pointed out, Iraq and Jordan would be next in danger. He urged Western support of Lebanon, but it was agreed that Lebanon should ask for help either from the United Nations or the United States (with British support) to intervene in order to assist the regime, provided Jordan would be consulted. Nuri offered to dispatch a force to Jordan, presumably intended to support Lebanon.

With regard to Kuwait, Nuri continued to press hard for its adherence to the AFU. "I had a talk with Nuri before his return to Baghdad," states Selwyn Lloyd in a circular to colleagues, "and found him intransigent."[12] Lloyd hoped to talk again with Nuri and other Iraqi leaders during their forthcoming visit to London on the occasion of the Baghdad Pact Council meeting on July 24. Nuri, however, was left with the impression that some kind of an arrangement would be worked out to the satisfaction of both Britain and the AFU. Two notes were dispatched to Baghdad and Kuwait, one advising Iraq to compromise and the other warning Kuwait about the danger from Nasir. "The idea of a first-stage agreement," as stated in a Foreign Office note to the British ambassador in Baghdad, was the last word Nuri had received from Selwyn Lloyd. In the note to the political agent in Kuwait, the Shaykh of Kuwait was warned that:

> The spread of radical republican nationalism will engulf hereditary regimes one after the other. Whether the ruler likes it or not, the fact is that if Nasir triumphs it will be the end of the ruling family of Kuwait.[13]

Upon his return to Baghdad (July 3) Nuri seems to have been optimistic about both Lebanon and Kuwait's adhesion to the AFU.[14]

On his way to Baghdad, Nuri stopped in Turkey. It was arranged that a meeting of the heads of state of the Muslim members of the Baghdad Pact would be held in Istanbul. King Faysal, accompanied by Nuri and the Crown Prince, was expected to arrive on July 14th. During his visit to Istanbul, King Faysal was expected to get married to a Turkish princess before the Iraqi delegation left for London to attend the meeting of the Baghdad Pact Council on July 24th.

On July 13th, a day before the King and the Iraqi delegation were to leave Baghdad, two brigades of the Iraqi armed forces, stationed to the north of Baghdad, one under the command of Brigadier ʿAbd al-Karim Qasim and the other under Colonel ʿAbd al-Salam ʿArif, were to pass through Baghdad in order to cross the river on their way to Jordan. The two commanders had received orders to proceed to Jordan, presumably for defence of that country and for possible support of Lebanon. The brigade under ʿArif, instead of proceeding to Jordan, was secretly diverted by Qasim and ʿArif to capture Baghdad. This military coup d'etat, later called the July Revolution of 1958, presumably intended to relieve the country of an unpopular regime, had virtually deprived Iraq of perhaps the most prospective attempt to settle peacefully the longstanding disputes between Iraq and Kuwait under the AFU plan.

Hardly a week after the delegation's return to Baghdad, the whole political regime of Iraq and its policy were swept away. Not only did the July Revolution dismantle the AFU structure, but it also put an end to the monarchial system to which Nuri had devoted his whole life. The King and the Crown Prince were arrested and executed on the morning of the day the army seized power. Nuri, however, had left his house early before a band of officers had arrived to arrest him. When the news of Nuri's disappearance reached the military leaders, it aroused anxiety that he may have escaped to Jordan and could organize an invasion as the premier of the AFU. A reward of £10,000 was put on his head, whether dead or alive.

But Nuri had not left the country. He could easily have escaped either via the river in disguise or by car from northwest Baghdad, since the area was open to the desert. Nuri seems to have preferred to remain, perhaps anticipating either the collapse of the regime from within or an attack from Jordan, (since after the death of King Faysal, King Husayn had become the official head of the AFU). After he left his house, Nuri passed the following day at the house of a friend at Kazimayn situated in northwest Baghdad; but he left the house disguised as a woman hoping to hide in a more friendly area. On the way he was spotted by a young man who cried out: "That is Nuri al-Saʿid!"[15] It is generally held that he was shot by one of the policemen, but we maintain that Nuri, realizing he could no longer conceal his identity, at once drew his revolver (he always carried one) and shot himself. Nuri was buried secretly at a cemetery in Baghdad North. On the following day (July 17) a mob, incited by his enemies, uncovered the tomb and began to drag his body, as they had done with the body of the Crown Prince (but not the King), down the streets and finally burned it.

The reaction to the destruction of the royal family and Nuri's death, as briefly described in *Republican Iraq*: "No one inside or outside the country protested at the assassination of Nuri or the royal family. Nuri had hopefully expected an intervention by Jordan, and when no signs of intervention were in sight, he is reported to have uttered words of despair to his allies. In fact no protests were ever made in the capitals of the powers with which he had allied Iraq. Only a few personal friends organized a small service in London in memory of him as well as the King and Crown Prince. It is an irony of history that the funeral prayers for Nuri, as well as the two great-grandsons of the Prophet Muhammed, killed by followers of the Prophet, should be given not in a mosque in Islamic lands but in a church in infidel lands."[16]

BRIGADIER QASIM'S ABORTED ANNEXATION OF KUWAIT

Brigadier Qasim, who became premier following the July Revolution, might have been able to tackle the Iraq-Kuwait relationship peacefully where Nuri had left it rather than to take, as he did later, a confrontational stand since he, not unlike Nuri, had also challenged Nasir's pan-Arab leadership. But neither Qasim nor his foreign minister, Hashim Jawad, had been informed about the trends in the Iraq-Kuwait relationship prior to the seizure of power by the Iraqi army. Only a couple of years later did Hashim Jawad learn about Nuri's negotiations with Britain concerning Kuwait as related to him by Kamil Muruwa, editor of *al-Hayat*, a daily Bayrut paper. Upon his return to Baghdad, Jawad may have called Qasim's attention to Nuri's negotiations with Britain, but Qasim, too preoccupied with domestic affairs, paid little or no attention to other matters.[17]

The Shaykh of Kuwait, relieved of Nuri's pressure to bring his country into the AFU's orbit, began to enhance his country's international status by joining some of the international organizations such as the Universal Postal Union, the International Civil Aviation Organization, the World Health Organization and others. Encouraged by Britain, he also began to conduct his relationships with the Arab countries directly. By 1960, Shaykh ʿAbd-Allah, feeling more secure with his country's enhanced international status, approached both Saudi Arabia and Iraq to appoint joint commissions for frontier demarcation. The Saudi government agreed to negotiate with Kuwait, but Iraq showed no signs of willingness to cooperate.[18]

In the meantime, there was concern in Britain about Kuwait's security and the future relationship between the two countries. It was suggested at an interdepartmental meeting that perhaps Kuwait's security might be better protected were it to become a member of the British Commonwealth as a sovereign state. Nasir, who himself had an eye on Kuwait, looked with disfavor at the prospect of seeing Kuwait brought into the British orbit. His idea that Kuwait had nothing to gain and everything to lose by such an association was reported to Shaykh Jabir by a representative of the UAR. Further unfavorable remarks in other Arab countries varied from concern that a rich Arab country like Kuwait should distance itself from the Arab world and join a foreign union to a warning that it "should not fail in its responsibility towards other Arab lands."[19]

The most violent denunciation of Kuwait's possible action to join the Commonwealth came from Qasim who denounced it in a speech on April 30, 1961, as an "imperialist scheme" to perpetuate British domination on an Arab land. He urged the Shaykh of Kuwait to oppose such a scheme and promised to support the Kuwaiti people as "Arab brothers" against foreign threats, as he maintained that there were no "frontiers between us and the Kuwaiti people." Qasim's idea of annexing Kuwait probably began at that time, as evidenced by his hinting that there were "no frontiers" between the two countries; he was beginning to learn about Kuwait's historical connections with Iraq.[20] Qasim's speech and the unfavorable reactions in other Arab countries to the Commonwealth rumor produced anxiety both in Kuwait and in Britain. While the Kuwaiti government issued a statement denying the rumor, Humphrey Trevelyan, British ambassador to Iraq, was instructed by his government to inquire about Iraq's intentions. Hashim Jawad, Qasim's foreign minister, replied that Qasim's statement was "purely historical" and of no great significance.[21]

But when Kuwait became independent as stated in an exchange of letters (June 19, 1961) between Shaykh ʿAbd-Allah and Sir William Luce, British political resident in the Gulf, Qasim sent a telegram (June 20, 1961) stating how glad he was that Britain had ended the agreement of 1899 without any word of congratulation in that message unlike the messages of congratulations that Shaykh ʿAbd-Allah had received from other Arab rulers. The absence of any word of congratulations in Qasim's message aroused the suspicion of the Shaykh, and he consulted William Luce. "The Shaykh made it clear to me then," Luce is reported to have remarked, "that if he saw anything developing out of these threats he would invoke Paragraph D." The text of the exchange of letters about Kuwait's independence consists of the following provisions:

A. The Agreement of the 23rd of January 1899 shall be terminated as being inconsistent with the sovereignty and independence of Kuwait

B. The relations between the two countries shall continue to be governed by a spirit of close friendship

C. When appropriate the two governments shall consult together on matters which concern them both

D. Nothing in these conclusions shall affect the readiness of Her Majesty's government to assist the government of Kuwait if the latter request such assistance.[22]

Four days later (June 25, 1961), Qasim publicly announced in a press conference that Kuwait was an "integral part" of Iraq on the strength of their past historical link. After an elaborate statement, Qasim declared:

> The Republic of Iraq has decided to protect the Iraqi people in Kuwait and to demand the land, arbitrarily held by imperialism, which belongs to [Iraq as part of] the province of Basra. . . . We shall accordingly issue a decree appointing the Shaykh of Kuwait as a *qa'imaqam* [district governor] of Kuwait, who will come under the authority of the Basra province. . . . [23]

Qasim's claim to Kuwait was reiterated in several other public statements, and he made it abundantly clear that he was not planning to use force, although he maintained that he was capable of achieving his aim by force. "On the contrary," said Trevelyan, "the assumption was that, since Kuwait was part of Iraq, Iraqi troops could move in as a normal measure of internal security within their jurisdiction." Trevelyan learned that the first tank regiment had gone to Basra to make accommodation for the regiment. "Iraqis told us," he added, "of hearing from friends that members of their families in the regiment in question were in Basra."[24]

Qasim talked loud but he made no move to act, although rumors abounded that forces were concentrating. It was based on these unconfirmed reports (all subsequently proved to be false) that the Shaykh of Kuwait asked for British military assistance (June 30, 1961) and informed the Arab governments that his country was under threat. On July 1st, a British force of some 7,000 troops landed in Kuwait, after being sent earlier on a British carrier to the Gulf.[25] Saudi Arabia dispatched 1200 troops to defend both the Saudi and Kuwaiti borders with Iraq at the junction of the Hafr al-Batin with Wadi al-Awja.

Meanwhile, on July 2nd, Britain requested a special meeting of the United Nations Security Council to which Kuwait was invited and complained that Iraq had threatened the "territorial independence of Kuwait." Iraq also requested a meeting, complaining of the British threat to the "independence and security of Iraq." The discussion ended without formal proposals, as the Soviet Union, in support of Iraq's contention with the Anglo-Kuwaiti exchange of letters (June 19, 1961) deprived Kuwait of independence and affirmed the continuation of British political and military domination of the country.[26] It is doubtful whether Britain had expected a settlement at the United Nations; it probably sought to explain the reasons for its action before world public opinion, as it became clear that Qasim had claimed Kuwait on historical and legal grounds short of resort to force.

From the United Nations the dispute passed to the Arab League. At the request of Kuwait to join the Arab League, a decision was taken in mid-July on how to deal with the Kuwaiti issue, and discussion was narrowed to two major points: 1) Qasim's withdrawal of his demand to annex Kuwait; 2) the formation of an Arab force by the Arab League to replace the British force. As there was no sign that Qasim was prepared to withdraw his demand, focus naturally shifted to the second point. On July 20, 1961, the Council of the Arab League, at a meeting from which Iraq's representative left in anger, passed a resolution, put forth by the Political Committee, as follows:

> I. a) The Kuwait government undertakes to request the withdrawal of British forces from its territory as soon as possible;
> b) The Iraq government pledges not to use force in anyway to annex Kuwait to Iraq;
> c) [The League] supports any wish Kuwait may have for unity or federal union with any other League member in accordance with the League Pact;
> II. a) [The League] welcomes the State of Kuwait as a member of the Arab League;
> b) [The Arab states] support Kuwait's application for membership in the United Nations;
> III. a) The Arab states undertake to render effective assistance to safeguard the independence of Kuwait at its request. The Council empowers the secretary general to take the necessary measures for carrying out this resolution at the earliest possible moment.[27]

Kuwait was admitted to membership of the Arab League, and its representative, 'Abd al-'Aziz Husayn, Kuwait's ambassador to Egypt (who attended the meeting on July 20), declared his country's readiness to fulfill all obligations under the League Pact. 'Abd al-Khaliq Hassuna, secretary general of the Arab League, undertook to implement the League's resolution. As Kuwait had already dispatched a memorandum to the League (July 18) indicating its desire to replace the British by an Arab force, an agreement between the Shaykh of Kuwait and Hassuna was reached on August 12 dealing with the technical aspect of the force. On the same day, the Shaykh of Kuwait asked Britain to evacuate its forces in preparation for the arrival of the Arab force. The total force, consisting of 3,300 soldiers, came mainly from Saudi Arabia (1,200), and the UAR (Egypt and Syria) (1,200), and the rest was provided by Sudan (400), Jordan (300), and Tunisia (200).

On October 10, Kuwait announced the evacuation of the British forces. Two days later, Egypt, owing to a disagreement with Syria (after the breakup of the UAR) decided to withdraw its force from Kuwait. But the other Arab forces remained for another year, mainly to provide moral support, as there was no real threat to Kuwait. Qasim, who had made no move to resort to force in the first place, continued to reiterate his claim, and he severed diplomatic relations with countries that had recognized Kuwait's independence. With this diplomatic action, he isolated himself rather than the countries he sought to hurt.

As to Kuwait's application to membership in the United Nations, the Soviet Union, an ally of Iraq, vetoed the proposal at the Security Council to admit it to the General Assembly on the grounds that it was and still remained a British colony. It was not until 1963, after Qasim had been removed from power and executed, that the Soviet Union stopped its efforts to block Kuwait's admission, and it became the one hundred and eleventh member of the U.N. on April 20, 1963. Meanwhile, diplomatic relations with the Soviet Union and several other Eastern bloc countries were established.

Qasim's Kuwait venture may well be considered another aborted Iraqi attempt at settling longstanding territorial and frontier issues, but Qasim failed to justify his action save on historical and legal grounds. His immediate motivation was perhaps mainly to divert attention from internal to foreign affairs, as he found the country was divided into conflicting ideological camps: Pan-Arabs and leftist groups. He sought to raise such issues as Iraq's relationships with Kuwait and Palestine to which public opinion had always responded favorably. However, the claim to Kuwait, which excited public opinion, resulted not only in aggravating internal dissension but also in isolating the country by breaking off diplomatic relations with countries that had recognized Kuwait's independence. The fall of Qasim's regime came sooner than it was expected. A counter-military-faction in an alliance with Arab nationalist groups brought down his regime on February 8, 1963.

IRAQ'S RECOGNITION OF KUWAIT'S SOVEREIGNTY IN 1963

No sooner had Qasim fallen from power than a new military regime, headed by Colonel 'Abd al-Salam 'Arif—Qasim's rival and former collaborator—was established, supported by a coalition of the Ba'th Socialist Party and a faction of pan-Arab army officers. As both 'Arif and his supporters were opposed to Qasim's dealings with Kuwait, Shaykh 'Abd-Allah, ruler of Kuwait, sent a cable to 'Arif in which he congratulated him on the fall of Qasim. 'Arif replied by cable in the same vein.

Even before they entered into negotiations, the exchange of congratulatory cables between the two heads of state implied recognition under International Law. Apart from the fact that such an exchange of letters was politically motivated, Iraq's recognition of Kuwait can be considered constitutive and not declaratory, since Kuwait had not yet acquired all the qualities of a state.[28] In order to be eligible for recognition, the state must possess an independent government, effective authority, and defined territory. But even if some sections of the frontier were in a de facto status pending final resolution, the state could still function to fulfill its obligations as a member of the community of nations if it possesses independence, effective authority, and fairly defined territory. True, when Iraq had applied for admission to membership of the League of Nations, one of the requirements for the termination of the mandate to become eligible for League membership was that it must have settled frontiers. But Iraq's admission to membership of the League of Nations was not blocked on the question of its de facto frontier with Kuwait, as noted earlier, nor did Britain raise the issue when the case of Iraq's admission came before the League Council. A case in point of a state recognized without settlement of its frontiers is Israel. It was admitted to membership of the United Nations even before a state of belligerency was terminated with its neighbors. The question of settled frontiers must therefore be differentiated from the requirement of defined territory over which the state is established.[29]

Shortly after the establishment of the new Iraqi regime, a Kuwaiti delegation, headed by Shaykh Sabah al-Ahmad, foreign minister, arrived in Baghdad to discuss the ensuing new relationships between the two countries. In response to Shaykh Sabah's request, the Iraqi government appointed a delegation, headed by Brigadier Ahmad Hasan al-Bakr, prime minister, but no specific instructions had yet been laid down for negotiations. It was, however, informally understood among the members of the delegation that Iraq had recognized the independence of Kuwait and wished to establish a peaceful relationship between the two countries.

At a meeting of the Iraqi and Kuwaiti delegations, which was held early in the evening and lasted till midnight, the principal spokesman for Iraq was not Premier Bakr but Talib Shibib, foreign minister, who was more versed with Iraq's foreign affairs than his prime minister. Shibib, with no specific instructions, began to assert in general terms that Iraq, having been able to get rid of the Qasim regime, repudiated all the hostile acts that had been taken against Kuwait. He also talked about Iraq's intention to withdraw its objection to Kuwait's application for membership in the Arab League and in the United Nations. He raised only one condition—that Kuwait should put an end to British protection. Nothing specific in Shibib's statement was implied save that Iraq was indeed ready to deal with Kuwait as an independent state and maintain a friendly relationship between the two countries.

Shaykh Sabah, on behalf of his delegation, thanked Shibib for Iraq's good intentions to establish peaceful and friendly relationships with Kuwait. He promised that upon his return, he would advise his government to propose the termination of the treaty with Britain to which Shibib had referred. He added, however, that the termination of the treaty could not possibly take place at once. It would be terminated, he said, a year after Kuwait's notification to Britain. Before the meeting came to an end, it was decided to hold another meeting on the following day in which, he suggested, the economic relations between the two countries would be discussed. Shibib, on behalf of his government, invited the Kuwaiti delegation for lunch on the following day. Thus everything seemed on the surface to have been going smoothly to the satisfaction of both sides.

When, however, Shibib was expected to be present on the following day at the Mansur Club to receive his guests, he failed to arrive. Shukri Salih Zaki, minister of economics and a member of the Iraqi delegation, volunteered to act as a host on Shibib's behalf. Shibib called Zaki to inform him that the National Revolutionary Command Council (NRCC), the highest authority in the new regime, held a meeting that lasted beyond midnight in which it categorically repudiated the statements he had made before the joint meeting of the two delegations. Shibib, accordingly, suggested calling another meeting at which he would report the action taken by the NRCC.

Early in the evening the two delegations met. Shibib, who chaired the meeting, declared with apologies that he must withdraw the statements he had made the day before, as the relationship between Iraq and Kuwait must be defined within the framework of a "union" between the two countries. Faysal Habib al-Khayzaran (a member of the NRCC) confirming Shibib's statement, said: "It is true that we have made a coup d'etat against Qasim, but we maintain that his call for the annexation of Kuwait was right." For a moment silence prevailed, but it was broken by Shukri Salih Zaki, minister of economics, who made a statement to the effect that he did not agree with the statements made by both Shibib and Khayzaran. He considered, in his own words:

> Our relationships with Kuwait have historical, geographical, economic, and demographic dimensions which no other two Arab neighbors possess. . . . The threats that may face Kuwait are the same as those that face Iraq. Suffice it to say that the ambition of the Shah of Iran to play in the [Gulf] region demonstrates that Kuwait cannot alone defend itself without support by Iraq. . . . There must, therefore, exist deeper and more intimate cooperation in all our cultural, economic, and political relationships . . . provided that these relations should never be described by such words as union, annexation, and the like.[30]

Shaykh Sabah, head of the Kuwait delegation, said that he and his delegation came primarily to congratulate the leaders of the new government on their coming to power and did not intend to discuss the matters stated in the last meeting. He had, however, suggested discussion of the economic relationship in the second meeting. But, he added, he had nothing further to say than that he would report all that he and other members of his delegation had just learned in the last two days.

A couple of months later, three Iraqi Cabinet members, headed by Salih Mahdi 'Ammash, minister of defence, went for an informal visit to Kuwait. Their purpose was primarily to negotiate for a loan, as there was a deficit in the budget owing to the continuing dwindling income from oil following Qasim's nationalization of the oil industry in 1961.

Nevertheless, they seem to have discussed pending political disputes between the two countries.

On October 4, 1963, a Kuwaiti delegation, headed by Shaykh Salim al-Sabah (Crown Prince) and composed of Shaykh Sabah al-Ahmad, foreign minister, and several other members, arrived in Baghdad to resume the negotiations about frontiers. An Iraqi delegation, composed of Ahmad Hasan al-Bakr, prime minister, Talib Shibib, foreign minister, Salih Mahdi ʿAmmash, minister of defence, and an Iraqi Foreign Office representative, but no specific instructions on the disputed frontier were given to Bakr.[31]

Bakr, who presided over the meeting, welcomed the Kuwaiti delegation and assured its members that Iraq was ready to discuss any Kuwaiti proposals concerning its relations with Iraq. Shaykh Sabah, in reply, said that a draft agreement in which Iraq might recognize Kuwait's existing frontiers had already been prepared for discussion (he was at that moment holding the draft in his hand), and he hoped that it would be agreeable to Iraq. Bakr, taken aback, quickly inquired, "Which agreement do you mean?"

"It is," Shaykh Sabah replied, "the agreement that the Iraqi delegation had negotiated before with the Kuwaiti government. . . . It has been approved by our Parliament and we hope it would be accepted without alteration, as any change would require taking it back to Kuwait's Parliament for approval." When a member of the Iraqi delegation (the official representing the Foreign Office) pointed out that prior approval by the Iraqi government was necessary before the Iraqi delegation could possibly accept it, ʿAmmash whispered to him, "Don't worry about such an agreement." "We had already come," he went on to explain, "to an understanding with several Kuwaiti army officers that, within a year or two, they would stage an uprising as a signal to the Iraqi army to occupy Kuwait!"[32]

Seemingly, it was on the strength of ʿAmmash's statement that Bakr and other members of the Iraqi delegation accepted the draft agreement Shaykh Sabah had brought in his pocket from Kuwait. The text of the agreement, embodied in the "Agreed Minutes of the Meeting between the State of Kuwait and the Republic of Iraq, October 4, 1963," states:

1. The Republic of Iraq recognized the independence and complete sovereignty of the State of Kuwait with its boundaries as specified in the letter of the prime minister of Iraq dated July 21, 1932 and which was accepted by the ruler of Kuwait in his letter dated August 10, 1932.

2. The two governments shall work towards reinforcing the fraternal relations subsisting between the two sister countries, inspired by their national duty, common interest, and aspiration to a complete Arab unity.

3. The two governments shall work towards establishing cultural, commercial, and economic cooperation between the two countries and the exchange of technical information.

In order to realize all the foregoing objectives, they shall immediately establish diplomatic relations between them at the level of ambassadors.[33]

In November 1963, hardly a month after Bakr and ʿAmmash had signed the agreement, the Baʿth Party, including Bakr and ʿAmmash, were dropped from power by President ʿArif. The Kuwaiti regime, which ʿAmmash had envisioned to overthrow within a year or two, proved more stable than the short-lived regime presided over by Bakr and his party, which hardly lasted a year. ʿArif seems to have ignored the "Agreed Minutes," consisting of Iraq's recognition of Kuwait's sovereignty and frontiers with Iraq, and never ratified it. He ruled the country with an iron hand for almost three years until 1966, when he was killed (April 13, 1966) in a helicopter accident on a visit to Basra. He was succeeded by his older brother, ʿAbd al-Rahman ʿArif, who remained in power for the ensuing two years.

On June, 1966, Shaykh Sabah al-Salim (who succeeded Shaykh ʿAbd-Allah as ruler of Kuwait in 1965) arrived in Baghdad to discuss the demarcation of the frontier that had been agreed upon in principle earlier. At a meeting headed by Premier ʿAbd al-Rahman al-Bazzaz, ʿAdnan Pachachi, foreign minister, Shukri Salih Zaki (who had joined the Cabinet as minister of finance and petroleum), it was agreed to establish a joint Frontier Commission, composed of Iraqi and Kuwaiti members, entrusted with the task of examining all relevant documents and maps on the basis of which demarcation of the frontier might be undertaken. As a quid pro quo, the Iraqi delegation demanded a loan as the Iraqi budget was running a deficit. When Shaykh Sabah asked Zaki, minister of finance, about the amount of the loan, Zaki replied that Iraq was in need of 30 million dinars (pounds). Shaykh Sabah made it clear that there was no fund in the Kuwaiti budget earmarked for a loan; but, he quickly added, there was a reserve (the amount of which he did not specify) that might be used as a loan for Iraq. The loan, intended to smooth the relationship between the two countries, proved to be a source for further suspicion and misunderstanding.

Kuwait claimed that in 1963, Iraq recognized both its independence and existing frontiers as defined under the agreements of 1923 and 1932. Neither of these agreements, as noted earlier, were ratified by Iraq. Even if the de facto frontier of 1923 and 1932 were accepted by Iraq in 1963, as Kuwait claimed, no reference was ever made in either one to demarcation. Nor was the agreement of 1963 ratified by Iraq in accordance with its constitutional procedure. True, no new constitution had yet been issued in 1963 to replace the Constitution of the July Revolution that was abolished, but under the powers entrusted to the National Council for the Revolutionary Command (NCRC) no agreements were considered binding without approval by the NCRC.[34] Thus when the text of the minutes (the agreement of October 4, 1963) came for discussion before the NCRC, it was rejected out of hand and declared unacceptable to Iraq.

In 1966, when a joint commission, composed of Iraqi and Kuwaiti delegates, met several times from 1966 to 1967 to discuss ways and means for the implementation of the agreement of 1963, there were differences of opinion between the two delegations on the nature and purposes of that agreement. The Kuwaiti delegation took it for granted that the minutes of October 4, 1963, was valid and binding on the two countries, and the purpose of the joint committee was merely to negotiate the demarcation of the existing frontier referred to in the agreement of 1963. The Iraqi delegation maintained that the 1963 agreement referred merely to indications (*mu'ashirat*), not to specifications and these were based on the agreements of 1923 and 1932, which were not only unratified but were also concluded at a time when Iraq was still under foreign control. Therefore, they argued, those agreements were not binding and should be modified in favor of Iraq if ever to be accepted. The Kuwaiti delegation rejected the Iraqi demands on the grounds that they exceeded the powers of the joint commission which met to discuss the implementation and not the legality of the agreements. In 1967, when no agreement had been reached, the meetings of the commission were prorogued sine die. The deadlock did not last too long, as the new regime that came into existence a year later showed readiness to resume negotiations.

NEGOTIATIONS FOR FRONTIER SETTLEMENT UNDER THE BA'TH REGIME

The coming of the Ba'th Party to power in 1968 opened a new chapter in the protracted frontier negotiations with Kuwait.[35] But, what both sides had hoped to be an auspicious time for understanding and cooperation turned out to be a period abounding with complications and misunderstanding. There were several factors which affected adversely Iraq's relationships with Kuwait. Some of those were ideological, but most were the consequences of changes in British policy toward the Middle East.

In 1969, Britain for largely economic reasons, announced withdrawal of its military presence in the Gulf. This situation led, in a tacit agreement between Britain and the United States, to the assumption of the role of "policeman" in the Gulf by the Shah of Iran. As the Shah considered Iraq a rival power to his role in Gulf affairs, he began to watch domestic changes in Iraq with keen interest. The overthrow of the Iraqi monarchy by the army in 1958 had alarmed the Shah who became concerned about the possibility that Iraq might become a source of danger not only for his own regime but also for other countries in the Gulf region.

In 1968 when the Ba'th Party, which advocated pan-Arab ideology, achieved power, the Shah viewed the new regime with suspicion and disfavor because it marked a significant change in Iraqi policy from cooperation with the West to dependence on the Soviet Union. The purchase of weapons was the first step taken in 1969 by the Ba'th government, and more ambitious agreements with the Soviet Union were concluded on March 3, 1970, and April 9, 1972. Under the latter, it was suspected that Iraq had granted the Soviet Union privileges to use Umm Qasr as an outlet to the Gulf, a step considered detrimental to Iranian and Western interests in the region. For this reason, the Shah began in 1969 to instigate rival military factions to overthrow the Ba'th regime. But the delivery of weapons to rival factions was uncovered, and the leaders were brought to trial and executed. The Shah's failure to overthrow the Ba'th regime did not discourage him from resorting to other means—in 1969 he denounced the Shatt al-Arab agreement of 1937 (establishing the *thalweg* in the section in front of the Khurrum Shah port as the borderline between the two countries) and demanded the *thalweg* be recognized as the frontier for all the River Shatt al-Arab from Basra to the Gulf.

Early in 1969, Iraqi-Iranian relations had so deteriorated that war between the two countries seemed imminent. For this reason, Iraq requested Kuwait to permit a small Iraqi force to be stationed on Kuwaiti territory (as part of a large military force on the Iraqi side) to protect Umm Qasr from an impending Iranian attack. Kuwait was hesitant to allow the entry of Iraqi troops across the border, but Salih Mahdi 'Ammash, minister of interior, and Hardan al-Takriti, minister of defence, proceeded to Kuwait to request permission for the Iraqi force to be stationed on its territory. Shaykh Sa'd al-'Abd-Allah, Kuwait's Minister of interior and defence, seems to have tacitly acquiesced under pressure, as the two Iraqi ministers warned that an outbreak of hostilities with Iran was impending. If it wanted, they argued, Kuwait would be welcomed to dispatch a force to be stationed near Basra or elsewhere in Iraq. On the strength of this conversation, an Iraqi force was stationed on both sides of the frontier in an area roughly about two square kilometers in size—the Kuwaiti side forming two-thirds of the area of operation. In an interview, Shaykh Sa'd, minister of defence and interior, hinted that the Iraqi force began to cross the Kuwaiti border even before the conversation started and that his tacit approval was considered an "unwritten agreement" by the Iraqi ministers. Though Shaykh Sa'd would not call the conversation an "agreement," the green light seems to have been given and the permission to station the Iraqi force was a form of modus operandi.

The impending conflict between Iraq and Iran, however, never really reached the breaking point. Nevertheless, Iraq kept its force on Kuwaiti territory on the grounds that Umm Qasr was still in need of defence as long as the Iran-Iraqi dispute over Shall al-Arab remained unresolved. Indeed, Iraq even sought to reinforce its garrison on the Kuwaiti side. In 1973, Iraq erected a defence outpost at al-Samita, a point at the end of the area of operation under the eyes of Kuwaiti soldiers who were stationed close to the Iraqi force. Despite Kuwaiti protest, the Iraqi commander demanded withdrawal of the Kuwaiti garrison when it made an attempt to stop the setting up of the post. Upon refusal, the Iraqi commander ordered his troops to open fire on the Kuwaiti garrison and forced it to withdraw. Though war between the two countries was avoided, the exchange of fire (March 20, 1973) resulted in the death of two Kuwaiti soldiers and one Iraqi.

The incident signalled the occasion for the resumption of negotiations over the frontier dispute. On March 22, 1973, two days following the attack on al-Samita, Kuwait sent a note of protest to the Iraqi government demanding the withdrawal of the Iraqi force beyond the Kuwaiti border. The Iraqi government reminded the Kuwaiti government that the borders between the two countries had never been formally agreed upon. This prompted Kuwait to dispatch another note in which it invited Iraq to discuss the dispute and warned that if Iraq were not prepared to do so, the matter would be put to other Arab states for an inter-Arab discussion. Mahmud Riyad, secretary general of the Arab League, joined by Saudi and Syrian representatives, went to Baghdad and Kuwait in April, 1973 and offered their good offices to resolve the conflict peacefully. While the Iraqi government agreed to withdraw its troops from al-Samita, it stated that the frontier dispute was a matter of direct negotiation between the two countries and none of the concern of other states.

On April 29, 1973, the Iraqi government sent a note to Kuwait, in which it proposed to discuss the frontier dispute on the basis of the previous exchange of notes, referring to them as indications (*mu'ashirat*) rather than as specific "agreements." Settlement of the dispute, the note added, should serve not only Iraqi and Kuwaiti interests, but also the interests of the Arab world as a whole to which the Ba'th Party and the Iraq government have committed themselves. In its reply (May 5, 1973), the Kuwait government ignored the ideological goals to which the Iraqi note referred and agreed to negotiate a settlement on the basis of the previous exchange of notes which it regarded as binding international agreements and not merely as "indications."

Iraq rejected the validity of the agreements (in a note dated May 17, 1973) on the grounds that they have never been ratified in accordance with Iraqi constitutional procedure. Iraq called Kuwait's attention to the radical change of circumstances and Iraq's increasing economic needs and strategic requirements which Kuwait seems to have overlooked. As Kuwait showed no signs of conceding to Iraqi requirements and insisted that the frontier agreements was still binding, Iraq proposed to postpone negotiations to a more auspicious time.

Kuwait, insisting on the need for settlement, made still another attempt to resume the negotiations. Shaykh Jabir al-Ahmad al-Sabah, heir apparent and prime minister, in an official visit to Iraq (August 20–22, 1973), tried to persuade the Iraqi leaders by hinting that settlement of the dispute would promote political and economic cooperation between the two countries. The Iraqi leaders made it crystal clear that acceptance of the de facto frontiers should be based on the inclusion of the islands of Warba and Bubiyan within Iraqi territory—at least as a lease. Shaykh Jabir made it equally clear, would not consider any change in the status quo.

Owing to Iraq's preoccupation with the Kurdish war (1974–75) in which Iran was indirectly involved, the Iraq-Kuwait frontier dispute was bound to be put aside. True, the Algiers Accord (June 6, 1975) put an end to the Kurdish war, by virtue of which Iran succeeded in obtaining Iraq's acceptance of the thalweg, the midstream line of the Shatt al-Arab frontier; the tension between the two countries evolved into a detente, but by no means did the Accord put an end to their conflicting interests in the Gulf. While Iraq's claim to the islands of Warba and Bubiyan and the stationing of forces on Kuwaiti territory began to lose weight in Kuwaiti quarters, Iraq insisted that the islands were necessary for security and demanded the two countries enter into an agreement on the matter. "Such an agreement," said Saʿdun Hamadi, Iraq's foreign minister, "is a reasonable demand in view of Iraq's security needs and is not unprecedented in the relationship between two neighbors."[36]

Kuwait continued to reject the Iraqi offer, though it implied recognition of Kuwait's sovereignty over other areas which had been contested in earlier conversations. Kuwait began to set up certain outposts and buildings as symbols of Kuwait's authority over the islands. These islands, many a Kuwaiti argue, are not a small part of Kuwait; they form nearly a quarter of its territory, and they lie so close to the coast that their control by a foreign country would not only compromise Kuwaiti sovereignty, but also might involve Kuwait in unwanted conflict with its neighbors. Kuwait's relations with Iraq became the subject of discussion in the Kuwaiti Parliament and a resolution was adopted on July 12, 1975, in which Kuwait's sovereignty over the islands within its borders was reasserted.

The question of the withdrawal of the Iraqi forces from Kuwaiti territory and the Iraq claim to the islands of Warba and Bubiyan continued to cloud the atmosphere between the two neighbors. In formal and informal talks, the Iraq government admitted that following the Algiers Accord the threat of war had receded (and Iraq withdrew its force in 1977), but it held that Umm Qasr was still in need of defence against possible future attacks. Kuwait, however, insisted on maintaining the *status que*, fearful that Iraq's appetite might be whetted even if the concession made to Iraq were very small. This was the stage where negotiations between the two countries stood when the Iraq-Iran war broke out in 1980.

Part II

IMMEDIATE CAUSES OF THE GULF WAR

Part two, consisting of two chapters, deals with the drives and events that precipitated the Gulf War. War, as the experts in strategy often warn, may be started by one country, but it can spread to many others. In the case of the Gulf War, while not intended to involve countries other than Kuwait, it ultimately drew in more than two dozen countries who responded to defend its victim.

In the first chapter of part two, we analyze the new conditions in Iraq following the eight-year war with Iran, which tempted Iraq to take a high-handed stand toward Kuwait. In the second chapter, we investigate the attempts made by Iraq and other Arab brothers to resolve the pending issues between Iraq and Kuwait to explain why the efforts made by the Arab brothers proved inadequate to avoid foreign intervention and the resort to force.

Chapter 6

Impact of the Iraq-Iran War on Iraq's Relationship with Arab Gulf Countries

I n the foregoing pages we have dealt with the unresolved disputes between Iraq and Kuwait up to the outbreak of the Iraq-Iran war in 1980. Following the eight-year war with Iran, it was hoped that the lingering differences between Iraq and Kuwait might be resolved, as Iraq had received generous financial and political support from the Arab Gulf countries, in particular from Saudi Arabia and Kuwait. This was not only the expectation of Arab Gulf countries but also the countries beyond the Gulf region.

Small wonder that when Iraq suddenly and unexpectedly invaded Kuwait, the news of Iraq's breach of the peace and its resort to occupy Kuwait by force seemed outrageous and unforgivable as reflected in almost all the Western media. But Iraq's own economic and strategic requirements, although not entirely unknown to leading policymakers in Western countries, seem to have been paid little or no attention in the decisions made to intervene in the Gulf crisis. In this chapter, we propose to discuss Iraq's views and grievances. In the following chapter, the drives and events leading up to the invasion of Kuwait will be dealt with.

IMPACT OF THE WAR ON IRAQ

In its war with Iran, Iraq emerged militarily victorious from an eight-year intermittent confrontation. But in reality, Iraq was no less exhausted than Iran and gained but little in territory and frontier modifications at an enormous cost in human and material resources.

Not only did Iraq find itself burdened with a heavy debt to foreign countries estimated then at seventy to eighty billion dollars, but it was also obliged to postpone or abandon several development projects because the war lasted much longer than expected.[1] By contrast, Iran was able to purchase most of its military requirements by cash, as only some, not all of its oilfields, were destroyed, while at the outset almost all the Iraqi oil industry was interrupted because Iran had destroyed its southern oil fields and blocked its export trade through the Gulf. Even the territory Iran had lost was recovered when Iraq, during the Kuwait crisis (1990), agreed to surrender it in an effort to persuade Iran to enter into an alliance against Western intervention in Gulf affairs.

Nor was Iraq's leadership unaware that in population, territory, and resources, Iran possesses greater military potentials than Iraq had at its disposal. Perhaps no less important is Iran's control over the entire eastern Gulf coast, including several islands, while Iraq's Gulf coast is hardly forty miles long, and almost all of it is made up of alluvial mud, unsuitable for the construction of maritime port facilities. Thus while Iraq is geographically speaking, a Gulf country, its access to Gulf waters has primarily been through the Shatt al-Arab which it shares with Iran and which has become inadequate for the country's commercial requirements.[2] Small wonder that Iraq has been concerned about the security of its maritime trade which could be exposed at any moment to Iranian threats. Nor did Kuwait respond to Iraq's request to develop a maritime port in a suitable area for navigation. Iraqi claims to Umm Qasr and the two adjacent islands (Warba and Bubiyan), which might have met its commercial and security requirements, had always been contested by Kuwait.

Iraq's concern about possible Iranian threats to its limited maritime access to the Gulf was not unfounded. Before the Islamic Revolution (1979), the Shah of Iran, in pursuit of a hegemonic policy, declared himself the policeman of the Gulf on the grounds that the region was exposed to Soviet penetration. He claimed sovereignty over the islands of Abu Musa and the two Tunbs (belonging to the United Arab Amirate), which are located near the Straits of Hormuz, the gate between the Gulf and the Indian Ocean, aiming ultimately at bringing the Gulf waters under Iranian control.[3] The fall of the Shah, however, did not put an end to Iranian claims, as Ruh-Allah Khumayni, spiritual leader of the Islamic Revolution, advocated the corollary doctrine of "the export of the Revolution," which aimed not only at controlling the Gulf region but also at extending Iranian influence beyond the Gulf in the name of Islam. There are indications that the present Iranian leadership, which honors Khumayni's essential teachings, is still entertaining the idea of achieving hegemony in the Gulf.[4] For this and other reasons, economic and geopolitical, the Iraqi leadership pursued a policy of rearmament which it started during the Iraq-Iran War. But Iraq's rearmament program aroused the concerns of Gulf neighbors as well as others in the region and beyond, including Western powers.[5]

Iraq's concerns, however, were not confined only to foreign affairs. There were groups inside and outside the regime that called for domestic reforms. For instance, following the Iraq-Iran War, the Iraqi leadership felt obliged to remove restrictions on travel abroad and on import of luxury commodities which were considered unnecessary during the war. Moreover, seeking public support, the government felt obliged to grant free expression of opinion through the press and a multiple-party system. It was rumored that Saddam Husayn, whose reputation as leader had been enhanced after winning the war with Iran, aspired to be acknowledged as a national leader and sought to solicit support by direct appeal to the public through popular elections, rather than by dependence largely on his own party. Before taking such a step, he consulted some of his close friends and followers in the high echelons of the Ba'th Party. As they seem to have shared his ideas about the need for overhauling the political regime, it was agreed that the matter should be presented before the Revolutionary Command Council (RCC), the highest authority in the regime, before any change would be undertaken.

When, however, Saddam Husayn submitted his proposals for reform to the RCC, which were discussed in two meetings (December 22, 1988 and January 16, 1989), there were reservations about some of them. The leading members of the RCC were divided into two schools of thought. One school, consisting of high-ranking members of the Ba'th Party, who had endured hardships (including years of torture in prison) before they achieved power, objected to both the principle of the multiple-party system and the removal of press censorship. They maintained that ever since the Ba'th Party had achieved power, it enjoyed a widespread popular support. There was, they argued, no urgency to allow a multiple-party system that might include some, such as the Communists, who betrayed the country in treacherous political activities abroad. As to freedom of the press, they were prepared to grant freedom in principle, but some control over the press was considered necessary. The other school, composed of a few liberal members, including Sa'dun Hamadi and Tariq 'Aziz (former Foreign Ministers and keen observers of Western political institutions) argued that full freedom of the press and a multiple-party system were absolutely necessary for the democratic form of government which the Ba'th had long been advocating.

Saddam Husayn, keen on maintaining solidarity among the members of his party, proposed to entrust the preparation of a draft constitution to a Constitutional Committee chaired by 'Izzat Ibrahim al-Duri, deputy chairman of the RCC, composed of members representing the two schools of thought. The Constitutional Committee took a long while before a draft constitution was ready for enactment as a law of the land by the National Assembly.[6]

The reasons for the delay were partly due to the steps taken to solicit public participation in the constitutional reform and partly to Saddam Husayn's preoccupation with foreign affairs. When he was confronted with an attack by Western press and with heavy foreign debt, Saddam seems to have preferred to deal with his foreign problems leaving the constitutional reform to be handled by 'Izzat al-Duri, his deputy for the Revolutionary Command Council. Nor were the leaders of the old political parties prepared to participate in political activities, as they were not quite sure that they could have full freedom to express their own ideas.[7] By the time the draft Constitution was ready for the National Assembly, the Iraq-Kuwait disputes had come to the open and the steps to be undertaken for the proclamation of the Constitution were postponed. Saddam might have even contemplated that the annexation of Kuwait would insure his election to the presidency against any rival after the Constitution had been proclaimed.

IMPACT OF THE IRAQ-IRAN WAR ON KUWAIT AND SAUDI ARABIA

The kind of support that Iraq had received from each of its Arab Gulf neighbors during the eight-year war was by no means the same, owing partly to the geographical location of each country but also to differences in the traditional foreign policy of each one. Because Kuwait might be next in line—had Iraq been overrun by Iran—it stood on Iraq's side. As it was subject to Iranian bombing, Kuwait was bound to extend financial and political support to its nearer Arab neighbor for its own survival. Thus, no sooner had the war when started Kuwait began to discuss bilateral security measures with Iraq, and its Parliament passed a general mobilization law as a measure for emergency. Even though Iran, seeking to influence Kuwait to distance itself from Iraq, warned its government by diplomatic as well as by violent means on more than one occasion, no significant change in Kuwait's attitude toward Iraq was seen until the end of the war.[8] No sooner was the danger of an immediate Iranian threat no longer looming in the horizon, than Kuwait resumed its traditional Gulf policy of the balance of power by playing the northern and eastern neighbors against one another in order to protect its own national interests. It began to contact Iran to reestablish friendly relationships with it. But this sudden reversal of policy aroused Iraq's suspicion and complicated the negotiations to resolve Kuwait's territorial disputes with Iraq.[9]

The Saudi traditional foreign policy toward its Gulf neighbors though largely determined by its national interests, has also been qualified by certain ideological sensibilities. These are the product of religious and cultural ideals—Islam and Arabism—that the Saudi leadership has taken pride to assert. Islam has flourished in its lands, and the Saudi family has played the role of the custodian of the sacred sanctuaries of Islam. As to the protection of its national interests, a tradition has been laid down by the founders of the state to the effect that Saudi Arabia should take no side in a dispute between one Arab country and another, and to offer its good offices to reconcile their differences.

As an Arab country, then, Saudi Arabia has played the role of a big brother in the family. It had already repaired ruptured relations among Arab leaders on more than one occasion. In the Iraq-Iran War, a conflict between two Muslim countries, one Arab and the other non-Arab, the Saudi leaders felt that they would be in an embarrassing position were a brother in the Arab family crushed. An Arab tradition which might throw light on this matter has it as follows: "My brother and I are against a cousin, and my cousin and I are against a foreigner." The Saudis were thus morally bound to take an ambivalent position in such situations.

In the Arab Gulf crisis of 1990, where the differences had arisen among members of the Arab family, the Saudi leaders were expected to take a more effective position to mend differences than in the Iraq-Iran War. But they did not immediately offer their good offices; they preferred first to encourage each side to meet with the other and reach an agreement by direct negotiation in the spirit of Arab cooperation and solidarity. Personal contacts between the Saudi King and the Iraqi president (as well as between the Saudi Crown Prince and the Iraqi deputy chairman of the Iraqi Revolutionary Command Council) were maintained to set an example for other Arab leaders to overcome differences and promote cooperation and solidarity. But when differences between Iraq and Kuwait were heightened, the Saudi government invited both Iraqi and Kuwaiti leaders to meet in Jidda to discuss their differences under Saudi patronage.[10]

AMIR JABIR'S VISIT TO BAGHDAD

The Amir Jabir's visit to Baghdad was intended to smooth the strained relationship between Baghdad and Kuwait. The occasion was that several Arab rulers—President Mubarak of Egypt, King Husayn of Jordan, Shaykh Zayid of the United Arab Republic, and others—began to visit Iraq and to offer their congratulations for its victory in the war with Iran. But the Amir of Kuwait, Shaykh Jabir al-Ahmad, showed no sign that he was ready to visit Iraq, arousing concerns as to the reason for his hesitation. A rumor circulating in Kuwait had reached Iraq that the Amir was expecting Iraq to send a delegation to thank Kuwait for its support against Iran which raised eyebrows in Baghdad. True, the rumor may have been intended as a reply to Iraq's claim that it won the eight-year war single-handed in defence not only of itself but also Kuwait and other Arab Gulf countries. But the rumor, it seems, took a life of its own and induced the Amir of Kuwait to have second thoughts about the wisdom of visiting Baghdad.

Owing to continuing accusations and counter-accusations, the Amir finally decided to send Shaykh Sa'd al 'Abd-Allah, Crown Prince and prime minister, on a mission to Iraq to prepare the way for Amir Jabir's state visit and to conduct preliminary negotiations on the frontier dispute—a few incidents were then recurring in the area of the frontier dispute which, according to the Kuwait press, Iraq had refused to settle. Upon his arrival, Shaykh Sa'd was so appalled to find that the Iraqi press, in reply to Kuwait's press campaign, had leveled a scathing criticism of the Kuwaiti authorities that he almost decided to cut short his visit and return home. Upon his call on the minister of defence, 'Adnan Khayr-Allah, with whom Shaykh Sa'd seems to have gotten along rather well, the question of the press campaign was raised in the presence of Foreign Minister Tariq 'Aziz. In the course of their conversation, 'Aziz suggested bringing the matter to the attention of President Saddam Husayn. Following his meeting with Saddam, it was made clear to Shaykh Sa'd that the central issue was not essentially territorial, as the press claimed, but Iraq's desperate need for a maritime port on the Gulf. Saddam pointed out that the fleets of foreign powers could find available shelters in the Gulf without difficulty while no maritime port existed for the Iraqi fleet. Shaykh Sa'd, in a friendly gesture, remarked that Kuwait might consider the possibility of providing the use of a Kuwaiti maritime port in the islands of Warba or Bubiyan without surrendering Kuwait's sovereignty over either one. Both seemed to have agreed that the matter should be carefully scrutinized by a committee consisting of members representing both sides.

When Amir Jabir finally decided to pay a state visit to Iraq (September 23, 1989), he was received in the most cordial atmosphere, as the Iraqi leadership sought to impress the Kuwaiti delegation with Iraq's earnest intention to settle long-standing disputes and establish permanent good-neighborly relationships.[11] Saddam Husayn, in a formal reception, presented to the Amir the highest Iraqi decoration, in appreciation of the support Iraq had received from Kuwait in its war with Iran. In the course of one of the conversations, it was suggested by a member of the Kuwaiti delegation that a nonaggression pact along the lines of the Iraq-Saudi Accord, might be concluded as a gesture of goodwill between the two countries. Sa'dun Hamadi, to whom the frontier question had been entrusted, remarked that it would certainly be appropriate to conclude such an accord after an agreement on the frontier dispute had been reached. Needless to say, neither a nonaggression accord was concluded nor was an agreement on settlement of the frontier dispute reached.

Amir Jabir's visit seems to have given the impression in Baghdad that the frontier dispute was expected soon to be resolved in the forthcoming negotiations. When Sa'dun Hamadi, however, paid a visit to Kuwait, three months after the Amir's visit to Baghdad, the frontier dispute was not the only question on his mind. He met with Shaykh Sabah al-Ahmad, Kuwait's foreign minister, and proposed three subjects for discussion: 1) the frontier dispute; 2) fluctuation of the world oil prices; 3) request for a loan of ten billion dollars for reconstruction and economic development. While Shaykh Sabah had expected to discuss only the frontier dispute, he was now faced with other complicated issues. Hamadi pointed out that the proposals about oil and the loan were very urgent. Shaykh Ahmad maintained that these two proposals Hamadi had raised would have first to be submitted to the Kuwait Cabinet for approval before he could enter into such negotiations.

A month later, Shaykh Sabah paid a visit to Baghdad to resume his talks with Hamadi. With regard to the frontier, they seem to have agreed to appoint a mixed commission of experts which would prepare proposals on the basis of which negotiations might lead to a settlement. Neither Hamadi nor Shaykh Sabah seem to have stated what specifically might be the purpose of the mixed commission. Hamadi held that the purpose of the commission would be to look into the whole unresolved frontier dispute. Shaykh Sabah took it for granted that the commission's function was to "demarcate" the frontier on the land, as "delimitation" had already been dealt with in earlier agreements.

The purpose of the commission was not spelled out until Shaykh Sabah, in a letter to Hamadi, indicated that the commission's purpose was to "demarcate" the frontier, contrary to Hamadi's understanding that the commission was to look into the whole questions of delimitation and demarcation. As to Iraq's request for a loan of ten billion dollars, Shaykh Sabah pointed out that since Iraq had already been given a loan (alluding to the loan extended to Iraq during its war with Iran), only another half a billion dollars might be added to it. Shaykh Sabah's dispatch to Hamadi was considered by the Iraqi government entirely unsatisfactory as it could neither meet the country's financial need nor its security requirements. With regard to the frontier dispute, Sa'dun Hamadi made it quite clear that no binding agreement on delimitation had ever been accepted by Iraq, and the reference to the commission's task to be only for demarcation was entirely unacceptable. Indeed, a mixed commission consisting of experts representing both sides, which met earlier in 1967, had already rejected Kuwait's claims to demarcation. Consequently, the frontier and territorial questions were postponed for an unspecified period. The Iraqi and Kuwaiti media, perhaps inspired by higher authorities, resumed a campaign of accusations and counter-accusations as to who was responsible for the failure to reach an agreement on the frontiers which clouded the atmosphere with suspicion and distrust.[12]

NEGOTIATIONS FOR QUOTAS AND OIL PRICES

Unable to persuade Kuwait and other Arab Gulf countries to contribute substantial funds for reconstruction, Iraq was bound to fall back on its own income from oil. But the income from oil was dwindling, because some of the Arab Gulf countries, including Kuwait, had indulged in overproduction that caused a fall in world oil prices. To resolve this problem, Iraq sought to persuade the Arab Gulf oil-producing countries to agree on a higher level of price by reducing overproduction. But how did the overproduction problem arise in the first place?

During the Iraq-Iran War, the oil production of both Iraq and Iran suddenly dropped, owing to the destruction of almost all the oil fields (at the beginning of the war, the Iraqi oil industry had almost completely been demolished) which gave an opportunity to the other Arab Gulf countries to increase their oil production considerably. After the war, when Iraq resumed oil production, most other Arab Gulf countries, including Kuwait, were exceedingly reluctant to lower their high quotas of oil production. Because of this situation, the price of oil necessarily dropped to a level as low as eight dollars per barrel, a sharp contrast to the price before the Iraq-Iran war which had reached the high level of twenty-five dollars per barrel. In addition to Iraq, other Gulf countries, like Saudi Arabia and Iran, were in favor of a higher level of prices. They proposed eighteen dollars per barrel. Iraq, desperate for cash, proposed twenty-five dollars per barrel. Kuwait, however, insisted on maintaining its war quota of oil production and was not even ready to promise that it would not produce beyond the quota assigned to it by OPEC (the Organization of the Petroleum Exporting Countries) on the grounds that it would follow instead market pressure.

At a meeting of OPEC in June, 1989, when a serious step was taken to limit Kuwait's quota of oil production to 1,037,000 barrels a day, the Kuwaiti oil minister demanded that his country should have a quota of 1,350,000 barrels per day in order to meet its budget requirements. As a matter of fact, Kuwait, as reported in the press, was then exporting no less than 1,700,000 barrels per day. True, Kuwait had its own domestic problems, such as the cost of building up its air force, payments to meet the sudden collapse of al-Manakh stock exchange (for which the wealthy Kuwaiti speculators, including members of the Sabah family, were responsible), and other economic requirements. Yet Kuwait's financial standing in the world market remained unaffected by its domestic burdens owing to its high financial reserve estimated at a hundred billion dollars in 1990. By contrast, Iraq's own reserve, which usually was equal to less than one-third of Kuwait's reserve, had already been expended. Further, a debt of over seventy billion dollars had been accumulating during and after the war with Iran. For this reason, Iraq was prepared to propose a reasonable increase, acceptable to other members of OPEC.

In November, 1989, OPEC held a meeting in which Iraq proposed to raise the price of oil up to the level of twenty-one dollars per barrel, and to resolve to not let it get lower than eighteen dollars per barrel. Saudi Arabia and the United Arab Amirate seem to have been ready to support the Iraqi proposal. As Kuwait made no promise that it would accept such a high price, Saddam Husayn sent a personal letter to Amir Jabir urging him to commit his country to an OPEC quota that would put an end to the fluctuation of oil prices. Kuwait, reluctantly accepted the OPEC quota, but its acceptance did not last long.[13]

THE ARAB SUMMIT (MAY 28, 1990)

Unable to persuade Kuwait to commit itself steadfastly to an oil quota, Iraq sought to bring pressure to bear on its leaders with an appeal to Arab heads of state either personally or in Arab summit meetings. In the meantime, Iraq was subjected to an American and British media campaign which prompted Saddam Husayn to make several public statements critical of American foreign policy in the Middle East. For example, in a speech before the third session of the Arab Cooperation Council in ʿAmman (February 25, 1990), Saddam Husayn expressed his concerns about American policy in the Arab world which he described as inimical to Iraq and called for the American fleet in the Gulf to withdraw now that the war with Iran had come to an end. Iraq's concerns were communicated to other Arab Gulf states and the Iraq media echoed them to the Arab world.

Under the circumstances, it was felt in high Arab circles that Iraq's concerns might be better brought for discussion in an Arab summit rather than to be rehearsed in the media. It was thus decided to hold a summit meeting in Baghdad (May 28, 1990) to demonstrate that the Arab states were concerned about Iraq and perhaps to persuade its leadership to pursue a policy of moderation.[14] In the opening session, attended by almost all Arab heads of state, including the Amir of Kuwait, Shaykh Jabir al-Ahmad, Saddam Husayn made no reference to his differences with Kuwait. But in a special closed meeting, to which we shall refer in the following chapter, he sharply criticized Kuwait on oil prices and overproduction.

Following the summit, the top Iraqi leaders met intermittently to review the deteriorating Iraq-Kuwait relationship. They discussed both the nature and purposes of the Kuwaiti challenge and how Iraq should respond to it. They seem to have come to the conclusion that Kuwait was determined never to give up its policy of overproduction irrespective of Iraq's financial difficulties. They suspected that Kuwait, a small country, with no significant military defence capability at its disposal, would not have taken such a firm and persistent stand unless it were counting on the support of powerful allies. There was evidence that came to the knowledge of the Iraqi leadership that Britain had encouraged Kuwait to stand firm against Iraqi demands and had promised support against any threat. Similar exchanges of views between American and Kuwaiti high government officials also seem to have encouraged Kuwait to stand firm against Iraq.[15]

Kuwait's dependence on the support of a great power is not unprecedented. As noted earlier, it has been the traditional policy of Kuwait's ruling family to seek the support of Great Britain, as British interests in the Gulf coincided with the interests of the ruling Sabah family to maintain the independence and security of the country. In the early 1970s, when Britain decided to withdraw its military presence in the Gulf, the mantle of British policing responsibility in the Gulf had fallen on American shoulders, although Britain did not completely stop its support of Kuwait. What prompted the United States, it may be asked, to take over Britain's burden in the Gulf? A little background as to how British responsibility started in the Gulf might throw light on an understanding of the American role in the Gulf.

BRITISH RESPONSIBILITY IN THE GULF

Long before the discovery of oil in the Gulf region, Admiral Alfred T. Mahan, an American authority on "the influence of sea power on history," called attention to the strategic significance of the Gulf in the Anglo-Russian contest in Central Asia. He foresaw the need for Britain to maintain a strong naval position in the Gulf long before Germany sought to include Kuwait in its plan for the Baghdad Railway, which would threaten the British position in the Indian Ocean. Mahan's anticipation of Britain's opposition to Germany's entry into the Gulf was almost prophetic.[16]

Early in the nineteenth century, British interests in the Gulf were essentially commercial. Britain sought to justify its intervention on the grounds that it was fighting disorder and prevalence of piracy that obstructed free trade in the region, although the underlying motive of piracy was local resentment of foreign intrusion.[17] Apart from trade, intervention in the Gulf became necessary to protect the British Raj in India after Napoleon set foot in Egypt in 1798 and issued dispatches to Arab rulers in ʿAdan and Masqat warning them about British colonial intentions.

For over a century and a half following French departure from Egypt, Great Britain was able to play the predominant role in the maintenance of peace and order in the Gulf at a relatively small cost. At the outset, it invited the Gulf rulers (tribal Shaykhs and dynasts) to stop making wars with one another and to enter into a series of bilateral agreements that would prohibit privateering and warfare. Gradually, almost all the Arab principalities passed under one form of British control or another, before they finally regained their full independence. At the outset, Britain was not enthusiastic about extending control over Kuwait, but Russian and German designs to construct railroads from Kuwait to the Mediterranean prompted the British Raj to extend "protection" to Kuwait in 1899, and thereby Kuwait became an important link in British imperial strategy in the region.

Britain's decision to withdraw its military presence in the Gulf by the end of 1971 raised the question as to who would then maintain peace and security. In principle, from the regional vantage point, the responsibility should fall collectively on all the Gulf countries. But in reality, there were only two that could possibly undertake the burden that Britain had undertaken in the past—Iran and Saudi Arabia. Iraq, though it aspired to play a role in the maintenance of Gulf security, was not considered a suitable candidate, because of internal instability, and its assertion of revolutionary and radical ideologies which aroused fear among its conservative neighbors.

As Saudi Arabia had shown no great interest in inheriting Britain's burden, at least on the grounds that it had not yet become militarily equipped for such a role, the obvious candidate was Iran. The Shah of Iran, Muhammad Riza, who had long impressed on the United States the need for security, seized the opportunity of British withdrawal to assert his claim to Gulf leadership as a means of checking Soviet penetration into the region. However, some of the Arab Gulf countries suspected that the Shah's ambition to play the role of policeman was linked to his territorial ambition for some of the Gulf islands in which they had vital interests like Abu Musa and the two Tunbs (which the Shah later occupied). The Shah's dependence on American endorsement of his rearmament program, although enhancing his country's position, aggravated opposition to his regime internally, since it implied American approval of his methods of governance. After the Shah's fall and the almost complete disarray of the military, the Iranian Islamic regime could hardly be considered suitable to undertake security responsibilities. Nor was it trusted by its neighbors because of its outspoken Islamic revolutionary doctrines and its declared intention to export the revolution to other Islamic countries.

Under these circumstances, had Saddam Husayn, upon his assumption of leadership in 1978, chosen a Western power as an ally of Iraq (as Iraq's rulers under the monarchy, 1921–58, had done), he probably would have been in a stronger position to claim Gulf leadership after the fall of the Shah in 1979. Iraq's role at the Arab Summit held in Baghdad (1978), aiming at solidarity and cooperation among

Arab countries, enhanced its position in inter-Arab affairs. More reassuring was the Arab Declaration of 1980, in which it was stated that
"all disputes among Arab countries shall be settled by peaceful means"
and "the prohibition of the use of force by an Arab country against
another" (Article 2). Accordingly, Iraq promised its commitment to
pursue peace and cooperation among Arab Gulf countries. Iraq thus
would have been the most prospective candidate to be the policeman
of the Gulf, had it seized the opportunity to offer its leadership for the
maintenance of peace and security. Nonetheless, Saddam Husayn,
whose regime was threatened by the Iranian clerics because it was considered secular and antireligious, chose first to settle Iraq's account with
its Iranian opponent before indulging in Gulf affairs.[18]

There were, however, further considerations which militated
against Iraq's leadership in maintaining order and security in the Gulf.
Iraq's alliance with the Soviet Union, concluded in 1972 (though
mainly to obtain weaponry), was not an asset for Iraq to assume leadership in the Gulf. Nor did Iraq's involvement in the nonaligned movement, which advocated neutrality in the East-West conflict, make it
welcome as a potential leader of countries friendly to the West. Only
when Iraq became involved in war with Iran did it begin to realize that
its national interests would be better served by cooperation with the
West than with radical groups such as the Communists or extremist
Islamic groups. American and Iraqi interests were not basically in conflict, but occasional disruptions often militated against a smooth and
continued cooperation between the two countries. Before we discuss
the tensions and conflict in the American-Iraqi relationship, perhaps a
brief account of Iraq's fluctuating relationship with the United States
might be useful.

IRAQ'S RELATIONS WITH THE UNITED STATES

From the time it achieved independence in 1932 to the Revolution of
1958, Iraq entered into an alliance with Great Britain and pursued in
no uncertain terms a pro-Western policy. It took an active part in the
implementation of Western defence plans, designed to protect the region from Soviet penetration. But when Britain was no longer capable
of undertaking full defence responsibility, the United States began
gradually to extend its support to fill the vacuum created by Britain's
withdrawal. Because it was traditionally tied up with Iraq, Britain tried
to maintain at least a limited role in a Middle East defence plan known
as the Baghdad Pact (1955), which virtually superseded the Anglo-Iraqi
Treaty of 1930. The real architect of this defence plan called the
Northern Tier, was the United States—and General Nuri al-Sa'id, prime
minister of Iraq, also played an important role both in its formation

and implementation. But General Nuri's policy ran contrary to that desired by opposition leaders who advocated a neutralist rather than a pro-Western policy. Nevertheless, so long as the monarchy presided over the destiny of the country, Iraq pursued a pro-Western policy and played an important role in regional security.[19]

The Revolution of 1958 considerably altered General Nuri's pro-Western policy, although it did not completely disrupt Iraq's traditional relationship with the West. Almost a year later, a policy of neutrality was proclaimed which adversely affected its relations with Western powers. In 1959, an agreement to initiate Iraqi-Soviet economic cooperation was concluded, but politically Iraq remained uncommitted to the Soviet Union. Public opinion, however, was divided on what attitude Iraq should take concerning the East-West relationship, because of the sharp conflict between Nationalists and Communists who advocated divergent views about foreign policy until Qasim's fall from power in 1963.

For over five years, from February, 1963 to July, 1968, Iraq took serious steps to reenter the Western fold by disregarding its agreements with the Soviet Union and resuming economic and commercial relations with Western countries. Under the 'Arif brothers' regime (1963–68) the pro-Western elements became so influential that Iraq could no longer be considered in the neutralist camp. Several actions, such as the agreement to end the Kurdish War in 1966 and Premier 'Abd al-Rahman al-Bazzaz's visit to England and the United States in 1966 and 1967, contributed in no small measure to promoting economic and technical cooperation between Iraq and the West. These steps may have alarmed left-wing parties (Communists, Ba'thists, and other elements) to whom the "revolutionary process" that was set in motion by the July Revolution of 1958 seemed to be receding and prompted them to criticize the regime. It was, however, the Six-Day War (1967) and American support of Israel that triggered the revolutionary trend and gave the army officers an excuse to overthrow, in cooperation with the Ba'th Party, the 'Arif regime.[20]

Ever since it came to power in 1968, the Ba'th Party was committed ideologically to pan-Arabism and followed a nonaligned military policy. But this policy was not intended to isolate the country from dealing with other countries in other fields, especially in economic and cultural matters. At the outset, the beneficiaries of this policy were the countries of the Soviet bloc; but the Iraqi experts began to urge resumption of relations with the United States and other Western countries, on the grounds that the Soviet Union, in accordance with the detente policy, itself was engaged in trade with the United States.[21] For this reason, trade with Western countries, which had been interrupted by the treaty of alliance with the Soviet Union, began shortly afterward to rise continuously. Only in arms and armaments did Iraq continue to depend

on Soviet supplies. Very soon, however, especially after it went to war
with Iran in 1980, Iraq began to diversify its weaponry and entered into
trade agreements with Western European countries.

At this stage not only Iraq, but also the Arab Gulf countries that
had long been pursuing friendly relationships with Great Britain,
turned to the United States. At the outset oil was the cause of the
attraction. Following World War II, American oil firms became increasingly involved in the Gulf oil industry and the American government
began subsequently to assume greater responsibility for the stability of
Arab Gulf regimes following Britain's withdrawal of its military presence
in the Gulf. But it was not only the stability of the Gulf region that
prompted the United States to provide support for Arab Gulf governments. Peace and security of the region as a whole became of concern
to the West, in order to prevent Soviet penetration into that part of
the world. It was the Shah of Iran, as noted earlier, who seized the
opportunity to emerge as the Gulf policeman, as he styled himself. His
imperial role in the Gulf, however, hardly lasted four years, as it depended in the last analysis on American backing and not on genuine
national support. Indeed, the very fact that the Shah had depended on
American military assistance for his Gulf policy turned his people
against him and became instrumental for his fall from power.[22]

The Islamic Revolution in Iran (1979) and the subsequent Soviet
invasion of Afghanistan shortly afterward prompted the American government to take the initiative in the maintenance of peace and security
in the Gulf, as dependence on one Gulf country proved inadequate.
On January 23, 1980, before a Joint Session of Congress, President Carter declared:

> Any attempt by any outside force to gain control of the Persian Gulf
> region will be regarded as an assault on the vital interests of the United
> States of America and such an assault will be repelled by any means nec-
> essary, including military force.

This declaration came to be known as the Carter Doctrine. "The
Carter Doctrine," said Brzezinski (Carter's national security adviser),
"was modeled on the Truman Doctrine, enunciated in response to the
Soviet threat to Greece and Turkey. . . ."[23] Under the Truman Doctrine, the United States provided all the means necessary for defence
to Greece and Turkey. As the rich Arab Gulf countries were prepared
to purchase the weapons necessary for defence, none—save 'Uman—
was prepared to extend the naval and air base facilities for the implementation of the Carter Doctrine as envisioned by Carter and his national security adviser. Not only in the Gulf region, but in the Arab
world as a whole, no sovereign state had normally permitted the stationing of foreign forces on its territory unless it felt there was an imminent threat of foreign aggression.

The outbreak of the Iraq-Iran War provided the occasion for the

United States and the Soviet Union to monitor one another to determine what their own attitude toward the Gulf region should be. As Iraq
and Iran were engaged in a land warfare, both the United States and
the Soviet Union declared their neutrality in the war, and the United
Nations Security Council, considering the armed conflict merely as
"the situation between Iran and Iraq," took no serious step to stop the
military conflict save to call upon "Iran and Iraq to refrain" from the
"use of force" and to settle their dispute by peaceful means. In June,
1982, Iraq withdrew its forces from Iran and was ready to settle the
conflict by peaceful means, but Iran insisted on penalizing Iraq for its
aggression and the war began to spill into the Gulf and to intensify
with fighting in the air and on the sea. Iranian aircraft began to bomb
certain coastal areas in Kuwait and Saudi Arabia.

At this stage, the Iraq-Iran War was no longer confined to two countries—it did, indeed become a Gulf war—and the United States could
not possibly remain indifferent to the expansion of the area of military
operations. Even before the bombing of the Saudi eastern coast by Iran,
the Carter administration dispatched four American AWACS aircrafts
to Saudi Arabia as necessary military precaution to deter possible foreign intervention. This was followed by the sale of planes and arms
which Saudi Arabia had requested under the Reagan Administration
for defence against Iranian attacks. Despite initial opposition by Congress on the grounds of instability of the Saudi regime, the Senate
finally approved the sale in October 1981. In reply to critics, Reagan
declared: "We will not permit [Saudi Arabia] to become another Iran."
This step has established the precedent that no friendly Arab Gulf regime would be allowed to fall, although no formal promise seems to
have been committed to writing.[24]

The American thrust into the Gulf region may be regarded as an
extension of American influence into areas such as the Arabian Sea
and the Indian Ocean, where NATO naval power had already prevailed.
In an effort to restore its prestige and influence, the Soviet Union
sought to support Iran with weaponry at a time when it stopped assisting Iraq—its ally under the Treaty of 1972—because it was not consulted before Iraq went to war with Iran. Because of Soviet coolness
(relations between Iraq and the Soviet Union remained outwardly
friendly as the treaty between them was still in force), Iraq sought to
improve its relationship with the United States. In November 1984, Iraq
resumed diplomatic relations with the United States which had been
severed in 1967. The resumption of diplomatic relations with Iraq was
described in the American press as a "tilt" toward Iraq.

But the tilt was merely a symbolic gesture for the resumption of
diplomatic relations without altering the formal neutrality that the Carter administration had declared earlier. Despite efforts to enhance
American cooperation with Iraq, pressure groups friendly to Iran (and
thus opposed to the tilt) argued that Iran was geopolitically more im-

portant than Iraq which rendered policymakers hesitant to alter American neutrality. Public concern about American hostages in Lebanon, however, and Iran's support of terrorist activities in Lebanon and other countries did not encourage the United States to restore normal relations with Iran. It was suggested to President Reagan that a friendly gesture to Iran—the delivery of weapons and spare parts—might induce "moderates" to resume Iran's friendship with the United States. But this contact with Iran, carried out through covert channels, failed to achieve the purpose of pro-Iranian policymakers, since the Iranian "moderates" who accepted the delivery of arms—their sole interest in the deal—ordered the release of only three hostages, and their attitude toward the United States did not seem to differ from that of the "extremists." The ill-advised Iran venture, ironically called Irangate, had been opposed by several members of Reagan's Cabinet, but whether the pro-Iranian elements carried out the deal with Reagan's knowledge and approval is still a matter for future research workers to determine.

Exposure of the Irangate to the public was Iraq's occasion to persuade the Reagan administration to make the "tilt" toward Iraq more meaningful. Intensified Iranian activities in the Gulf—Iran's surprise capture of Iraq's southern town of Faw in 1986 and its increasing attacks on Kuwait's tankers—induced both the Soviet Union and the United States to intervene and offer assistance to protect oil tankers. Britain and France were also concerned about the dangers to free navigation in the Gulf. It was Iran's renewal of attacks on oil tankers in the Gulf and resumption of land attacks on Iraq's territory that prompted the Security Council to adopt a mandatory resolution on July 20, 1987, by virtue of which a cease-fire was imposed on both countries to bring the war to an end. American assistance to Iraq was not in the delivery of weaponry (Iraq had already been able to persuade the Soviet Union to honor its commitments under the treaty of alliance to deliver weapons), but in other matters such as the purchase of nonmilitary technology and the sharing of secret military information about the movements of Iranian forces picked up by American AWACS. Needless to say, without Western support Iraq could not have won the war.

Following the war with Iran, Iraq sought to enhance its cooperation with the United States. Indeed, it aspired to join countries like Egypt and Saudi Arabia, regarded as American friends, in relationships with the United States. However, the events and pressures—foreign and domestic—that followed the war with Iran have created a set of forces beyond the ken and wit of the authorities on both sides to reconcile their differences. In the pages to follow, we shall deal with those events and forces that culminated in the invasion of Kuwait.

Chapter 7

Drives and Events Leading to the Invasion of Kuwait

Three underlying factors may be said to have prompted the Iraqi leadership to invade Kuwait in August 1990.

First, the eight-year war with Iran, which Iraq hoped would be followed by a period of peace and reconstruction, produced instead conditions of insecurity and suspicion among all members of the Gulf family. Since no prospect of a peace treaty establishing normal relations with Iran was in sight (only a U.N. cease-fire), Iraq began to suspect that Iran might, at any moment, resume the war in order to impose its own terms in a peace treaty. For this reason, when Iraq began to reduce its standing army, it decided at the same time to reinforce its rearmament program not only for defence against Iran, but also for security in the Gulf region. As a consequence, the rearmament program, as well as the servicing for the huge foreign debt, became a heavy burden on the budget while the country's income from oil export was diminishing owing to overproduction by several members of the Gulf countries beyond the quotas set by OPEC. As noted earlier, Kuwait, the principal opponent to fixed oil quotas (on the grounds that OPEC members should pursue oil production in accordance with the pressure of the world market) brought down the price of oil and affected adversely Iraq's income from oil.

Second, Iraq's rearmament program aroused Israel's concern which encouraged its supporters in the Congress and the press to influence the American government to take steps that might restrain Iraq from becoming a threat to its neighbors. What particularly disturbed Israel was Iraq's program for the acquisition of weapons of mass destruction (such as chemical, biological, and nuclear weapons) which would undermine its qualitative military superiority over the Arab world. Israel entertained the idea of destroying Iraq's nuclear plant before it reached the stage of producing nuclear bombs. In 1981, in a surprise air attack, Israel virtually destroyed the Tammuz (Osiris) nuclear plant situated to the south of Baghdad. Owing to its preoccupation with the war with Iran, Iraq did not retaliate. After the war, when Iraq resumed its rearmament program, Israel seems to have been ready for another raid on Iraq's plants. In a speech which he made on April 1, 1990, Saddam Husayn warned that Iraq would retaliate if Israel attacked again. Saddam's warning that he would use the binary chemical weapon if Israel attacked reverberated in Western political circles, and the press reported Saddam's statement as an unprovoked threat to Israel.

Third, because Iraq had entered into a treaty of alliance with the Soviet Union, Iraq was looked upon with suspicion and disfavor throughout the Western world. The treaty, however, was primarily for the purchase of weaponry and not a military alliance against the West, as Iraq was a member of the nonaligned movement and pursued a neutralist foreign policy. After it went to war with Iran, the United States extended credit to Iraq with which it purchased nonmilitary technology and foodstuffs. It also received military intelligence about the movement of Iranian forces that contributed in no small measure to bringing the war to an end in 1988.

American indirect support of Iraq, however, was not intended to treat Iraq as an ally, least of all to win a war over Iran. It was rather intended to end the war without a winner or loser. American policymakers, hoping that Iran might soon resume its friendly relationship with the United States, certainly did not want Iran to be a loser. But Iraq, taking advantage of American support, won the war. No sooner had the war been over than Iraq, hoping its relations with the United States would be enhanced, was disappointed to learn that the United States was not ready to take it into its confidence. There were still lingering suspicion and distrust from the Reagan administration that militated against the development of a friendly relationship between the two countries. A brief review of American-Iraq relationships following the Reagan administration might be illuminating.

AMERICAN RELATIONS WITH IRAQ UNDER THE BUSH ADMINISTRATION

American policymakers under the Bush administration sought to pursue a policy of the balance of power in the Gulf region so that neither Iraq nor Iran would be able to single-handedly control the Gulf. Iraq, however, claiming victory over Iran, aroused suspicion among Arab neighbors, particularly Kuwait, as it might be a danger to their security. For this reason, American policymakers, concerned about the security of the Gulf, were neither satisfied with Iraq's military victory over Iran nor comfortable with its rearmament program. In their eyes, Iraq seemed to have become potentially an aggressive and not a moderating regional factor.[1]

There were, however, two schools of thought as to what American policy should be in the Middle East. One school, advocating cooperation with Iraq, made an attempt to persuade U.S. leadership to pursue a policy of peace and moderation in line with American policies toward other Arab countries that have long maintained cooperation and friendship with the United States. This school prevailed over the White House after 1986 (following the failure of Reagan to persuade Iran to deliver American hostages, often called the Irangate scandal) and the State Department during the Bush administration until early 1990. The other school, advocated by the Defence Department and supported by the Congress and the press, maintained that the Iranian Revolutionary regime would sooner or later be replaced by another moderate regime which might pursue the traditional Iranian foreign policy of cooperation and friendship with the United States. Even if the present Islamic regime in Iran were to survive, they maintained, it would gradually become more moderate—there were already some moderate elements in the regime, like Rafsanjani, president of Iran—as it is in Iran's own national interest to cooperate with the United States after the Cold War had come to an end.

Neither school seems to have adequately assessed how Iraq and Iran would conduct their foreign policy, because they assumed that the foreign policy of each country would be essentially based on national interests. The Iranian regime, based on Islamic classical doctrines, advocated ideological principles which considered Western standards adverse to Islam. Nor were the moderate elements, on whom the American experts had high hopes, able to influence significantly Iran's new foreign policy in order to come to an understanding with the United States.

In Iraq the situation was more complex. There were always two factions within the Ba'th Party, one ideological advocating cooperation with the Soviet Union, and another secular in favor of cooperation with the West. After Saddam became president in 1979, the faction advocating secularism became more influential, in particular when the Islamic Revolutionary regime in Iran was instrumental in instigating Iraqi religious elements (essentially Shi'is) against the Ba'thist regime. For this reason, Iraq was gradually moving in favor of cooperation with the West, particularly in view of the support it had received from Western countries during the war with Iran.

In the United States, however, while the Bush administration was in favor of cooperation with Iraq (hoping that its government would become a force for moderation and peace in the Middle East), there were strong elements in Defence and Intelligence, and even stronger groups in the Congress and the press, opposed to cooperation with

Iraq. As a result, while the American government was sending statements through official channels in favor of cooperation with Iraq,
groups in Congress (particularly in the Senate) and the media were
denouncing Iraq, often using harsh statements, citing its rearmament
program and its record in human rights. Small wonder the Iraqi leaders
were often puzzled and bewildered as to what precisely the American
objectives toward Iraq were. Several Iraqi men in high offices paid visits
to Washington and met with a number of American policymakers to
understand where Iraq stood in their eyes. For example, on October
6, 1989, during his visit to the United States, Tariq ʿAziz, Iraq's foreign
minister, met with President Bush and Secretary Baker and complained
about a hostile campaign against Iraq. Baker, surprised about ʿAziz's
accusations, denied that there was any American hostility toward Iraq.
Both seem to have come to an understanding that the two countries
should cooperate to maintain peace and stability in the Middle East
and enhance trade relationships between them. But the attacks in the
press and Congress continued to concentrate on Iraq and particularly
on Saddam Husayn's style of leadership. Such attacks were considered
unfair and a pretext for interference in domestic affairs. Iraq complained in vain through its Embassy in Washington, but the attacks did
not stop.[2]

It was felt on both sides that perhaps clarification of the misunderstanding was necessary. On February 11, 1990, John Kelly, assistant
secretary of state for Middle Eastern affairs, visited Baghdad and met
with Saddam Husayn. For almost two hours, Saddam expressed his
views about the international situation following the declining position
of the Soviet Union and its impact on American relations with Iraq. He
said that the Soviet Union as a world power was finished, and the
United States could have a "free hand" in the Middle East for a period
of five years. Saddam was obviously sending a message that he was ready
to cooperate with the United States in the maintenance of peace and
security in the Middle East. Aware of Israel's influence on American
policymakers through the media, he was uncertain as to whether the
United States was ready to pursue "constructive purposes" or follow
Israel's own goals, owing to its profound pressure on American policymakers through the media.

Kelly tried to explain the nature of the American political system
which permits such political activism. He also called Saddam's attention
to the forthcoming annual report on human rights in which there were
some critical statements about Iraq's record. Saddam made it clear that
he would not object to criticism provided it were not destructive. But
when the report was published a month later, it was broadcast on the
Arabic program of the Voice of America from Washington, including
highly critical remarks expressing the views of the State Department.
As the broadcast contradicted the spirit of Kelly's assertion of American
goodwill towards Iraq, the American Embassy in Baghdad was in-

structed to apologize about the tone of the broadcast, claiming that it was a mistake to broadcast the report on the Arabic program. When the State Department's apology was reported to Saddam Husayn, he remarked that the only thing he understood from the apology is that "in this matter [American] policy has two phases."[3]

A few days later, it was announced in Washington that an Iraqi citizen was arrested in California and accused of an attempt to kill an Iraqi fugitive, presumably a member of the Iraqi U.N. Mission in New York. As a protest, the State Department decided to expel a member of the Iraqi mission in New York. On the same day, Iraq reciprocated by expelling a member of the American Embassy in Baghdad.

These incidents can happen among countries with close working relationships on higher governmental levels. But in the case of Iraq, such incidents touched sensitivities on higher levels which often affected adversely Iraq's endeavors to cultivate friendly relationships with the United States. Nor were the incidents arousing Israel's sensitivities very helpful. For instance, on February 20, 1990, when American planes reported that six Iraqi scud missile launchers were stationed at an Iraqi base near the Jordanian border, Israel declared that the existence of an Iraqi force near Jordan was a threat to its security and that it would not close its eyes. Regardless whether such an Iraqi force was in Jordan or near its frontiers, Iraq had on more than one occasion dispatched, at the request of Jordan, a force deemed necessary for its security requirements. No sooner had the news about the Iraqi missiles reached the United States than the Congress threatened to pass a resolution to stop the export of farm products to Iraq which confirmed the suspicion of Iraqi leaders that the American government was in fact acting contrary to its own stated intentions that it sought to pursue a good relationship with Iraq. While Iraq was wondering why the United States was so antagonistic to it, Bush sought to indicate his disapproval of the Senate action by declaring that he would veto the resolution which dissuaded Congress from action.[4]

Not only did the threats in Congress and the American press create ill-feelings between the two countries, but also a number of incidents that were occurring in Iraq aggravated the situation. For example, on March 9, 1990, Farzad Bazoft, an Iranian press reporter for the *Observer*, holding a British passport, was arrested by the Iraqi authorities because he had entered a prohibited military area (presumably it included a missile factory) and was accused of being a spy taking pictures of the area. He was taken to court where he made a confession about the purpose of his visit. No sooner had the news of his arrest and confession been broadcast through the media than it aroused a campaign in the British press against Iraq on the grounds that the accusation was false and unfounded. The *Observer*, retaliating for the arrest of Bazoft, described Saddam Husayn as the "Butcher of Baghdad." Attempts at pressuring Iraq to release Bazoft seem to have annoyed the Iraqi authorities, particularly the intercession by Premier Thatcher over the media rather than through normal diplomatic channels. Bazoft was condemned to death by the court, and was executed on March 15.[5]

A week later (March 22) Gerald Bull, the Canadian expert in the production of the so-called "super-cannons", who was accused of entering into an agreement with Iraq to provide the cannons—parts of which were on order from England—was assassinated in Brussels. Some members of Bull's family were reported to have said that Bull had already been warned that the Mosad (Israel's Intelligence Service) was after him. A few days later, the British authorities announced that a number of high technological instruments, including parts of Bull's super-cannon were confiscated before they were shipped to Iraq. Indeed, strict instructions were issued for a thorough search of travelers' baggage to Iraq to stop shipment of technological instruments to Iraq, although the government had officially permitted it.[6]

The war of words reached a climax on April 1, 1990, when Saddam Husayn made a speech, which was widely publicized, in which he threatened to burn with the binary chemical weapons half of Israel, were it to attack Iraq. "By God," he added, "we will make the fire eat up half of Israel, if it ever tries to do anything against Iraq."[7] This speech prompted General Ehud Barak, Israel's chief of staff, to make a statement to the effect that Israel would always be ready to strike at any time if it felt Iraq's forces had become a danger to Israel.[8]

For his speech, Saddam was highly complimented by the Arabs because he stood up to Israel, but he was denounced in Western countries and, in a State Department statement, Saddam's words about Israel were described as "inflammable, deplorable, and irresponsible."[9] Saddam complained that his statement about the use of the binary chemical weapon against Israel was quoted out of context, as he said he made it only as a warning to Israel "if it ever tries to do anything against Iraq," which was omitted in the press reports.

THE AMIR BANDAR MISSION

Owing to the heightening tension with Israel that might involve the whole Gulf region, Saddam Husayn called King Fahd, and, in a telephone conversation, it was agreed that the American president and the British prime minister should be alerted about the impending Israeli threat. King Fahd decided to send Amir Bandar, the Saudi Ambassador to the United States, to meet with Saddam Husayn and carry messages from him to President Bush and Prime Minister Thatcher. In the meantime, Husni Mubarak, president of Egypt, contacted Bush to assure him that Saddam had no intention of attacking Israel. He also dispatched a letter to Israel in which he warned that the situation had become critical.

Amir Bandar arrived in Baghdad on April 5 and met with Saddam Husayn at Sarsank, a resort in northern Iraq.[10] Saddam told him that he had suggested the meeting to explain his position toward Israel, as he was wrongly depicted to have taken an offensive position against Israel. In his speech, he said, he would attack only if Israel had attacked. Israel had already struck the nuclear research plant in 1981, and another surprise strike was expected at any moment. "I want to assure President Bush and His Majesty King Fahd that I will not attack Israel." He also said that he expected the United States to obtain a commitment from Israel that it would not attack Iraq. Bandar inquired whether Saddam wanted to "mention" that matter to Bush or to carry a "message" to him. "It is a message from me to the president," replied Saddam.

Leaving Baghdad for Saudi Arabia on the same day, Bandar reported his conversation with Saddam to King Fahd who told him to relate Saddam's message to Bush. Four days later, Amir Bandar went to see President Bush at the White House and told him that King Fahd asked him to relay the message he had received from President Saddam that "he [Saddam] had no intention of attacking Israel." Bush wondered why "Saddam has to say he would not attack Israel, if he did not intend it." Saddam, Bandar replied, suspected that there was a conspiracy against him. Bandar also told Bush that Bazoft, as Saddam told him, had the telephone number of an Israeli official in his pocket when he was arrested, evidence that he had links with Israel.

Following Bander's meeting with Bush, Saddam was waiting for an answer about Israel's assurances not to attack Iraq. King Fahd, at Saddam's insistence, called Bandar to inquire about Israel's assurance. Bush told Bandar that he did not want "anybody to attack anybody," and promised to talk to the Israelis. Upon contacting Israel, Bush was told that "if Iraq did not launch anything against them, Israel would not launch anything against Iraq." This assurance was passed directly to Saddam and the danger of a crisis seems to have passed.

THE UNITED STATES SENATE'S MISSION TO IRAQ

Hardly a week after Bandar had met with Saddam Husayn, a bipartisan delegation of the United States Senate headed by Senator Robert J. Dole and composed of four other senators—James A. McClure, Alan K. Simpson, Howard M. Metzenbaum, and Frank H. Murkowski—visited the Middle East to talk with Egyptian, Israeli, and Palestinian leaders about the peace process that was then under discussion which was encouraged by the United States. While the delegation was visiting Egypt, Mubarak suggested that it should talk with Saddam Husayn, as he would be an important Arab leader for any discussion about peace in the Middle East. Saddam was described in the American media as a man who threatened to attack Israel, but Mubarak told the delegation that he was a man for peace and it was important to talk with him. Dole and other members of the delegation welcomed the suggestion. As they told Bush that they were planning to visit only Egyptian, Israeli, and Palestinian leaders, Dole talked with Bush (April 11, 1990) on the telephone and each member of the delegation spoke with him.

Mubarak contacted Saddam about the senators' intention to visit Iraq, and Saddam welcomed the visit. On the following day the delegation met with Saddam in Mawsil (Mosul) in northern Iraq. Dole handed him a letter in which the purpose of their visit was stated. "Iraq plays a key role in the Middle East," states the letter, and the purpose of the delegation was "to see improved bilateral relations between our nations." Dole showed two press reports (given to Iraq's foreign minister) which reported that Iraq was engaged in producing biological weapons. On the basis of this report some members of the U.S. Congress had called for imposing sanctions against Iraq. But Senator Spector, who had met Saddam and had a "positive impression" of him, wanted the Senate to know more about Saddam and had urged Dole to visit Iraq. For this reason, Dole told Saddam, "we want to know what we can do to strengthen our relations.[11]

In an elaborate statement, Saddam welcomed the delegation and stated his ideas and concerns about Iraq's relations with the United States. In particular, Saddam raised the question of the American provocative position toward Iraq. "It has ben claimed," said Saddam, "that Iraq threatened Israel, although my words clearly state my conviction, that this campaign has been intended to provide psychological propaganda and political cover for Israel to attack us, as it did in 1981." Dole replied that the American government was not the cause of the campaign and that it condemned the Israeli attack in 1981; but Saddam pointed out that the United States had known about it, according to some reports that had surfaced.

Saddam then turned to explain his position toward Israel and the use of biological and nuclear weapons. He said, as he publicly stated before, "if Israel strikes, we will strike against it." He went on to explain:

> I believe that this is a fair position, and that such a known, previously stated position is what help peace, and not the opposite. For, perhaps Israel would avoid striking when it knows that it will be struck. At the same time, if the West really wants peace, a course such as this is in the interest of peace. They should only be disturbed by it if they want Israel to strike Iraq without Iraq retaliating. I said that if Israel uses atomic bombs, we will strike it with binary chemical weapons. . . .

> Are chemical weapons more dangerous to mankind than nuclear bombs? . . .

I know that there is a difference between possessing weapons and using them. I consider it the right of the Arabs to possess any weapon that their enemy possesses. Iraq does not possess atomic bombs. If we did, we would announce that, to preserve peace and to prevent Israel from using their atomic bombs.

We are definitely not warmongers or warlords. We want peace. We do not want atomic, chemical or biological weapons to proliferate. If the West really does want the same thing, then it should promote the declaration that the entire region be free of such weapons. . . .

As Saddam had just learned that the American Congress was considering applying sanctions against Iraq on the grounds of its possessing chemical and biological weapons, he wondered why the Congress and the press were so hostile against Iraq. Senator Dole assured Saddam that neither the press nor Congress represent Bush or the government. "Bush will oppose sanctions," Dole said, "and he might veto them. . . . We in the Congress are striving to do what we can in this direction." Dole also maintained that biological, chemical, and nuclear arms should be abolished, and "we hope this will be part of a total disarmament to make this region free of these types of weapons."

But Dole had another important matter to raise with Saddam. "We would like to ask how is it possible for us to improve our relations when we read that U.S. television reported yesterday that in the Salman Bak area south of Baghdad you are developing a virus for use in warfare that could wipe out entire cities. . . . Are you developing this virus, these biological weapons?"

This question led to a debate on whether the United States and Israel possess biological weapons. Dole said that biological weapons have been banned in the United States since the Nixon administration. But when Saddam asked whether there was any research on them, Dole replied: "We are conducting research but not production of this type." Saddam assured Dole that Iraq had no biological weapons; but, he admitted, it had "chemical weapons." "However," he added, "can President Bush tell me or the members of the Iraqi National Congress, as I told you about Iraq, that Israel does not have biological weapons?" He reiterated his proposal that all such weapons—chemical, biological, and nuclear—should be prohibited and that the Middle East should be declared free of such weapons.

Dole seems to have agreed with Saddam on this matter, as he said that "I highly welcome what you have just said and that this policy is the exact policy that our government follows. "But," he added, "how will we carry out what you have said?" "This is another issue." "But I [Dole] believe we will try to do this."

Senator Murkowski made a short statement urging Saddam to "compromise." He said that he knew the history of the Middle East and that the United States views the Middle East as "a powder keg."

"We have come to you, Mr. President, with good intentions." With regards to Israel, he pointed out, there was discussion about peace among its leaders, and there seems to be an opportunity to reach a compromise. He also stated that in the letter they brought from President Bush, he "urges you . . . to join other leaders in this region" to cooperate and not to let this opportune moment pass.

Senator Metzenbaum, after he stated that he was encouraged by Bush to visit Iraq, said "with regards to the things raised in the United States about Iraq, the same things had been said about the Soviet Union. ""But now," he added, "Secretary Baker and Foreign Minister Scheverdnadze have become friends and go fishing together in the river." Foreign Minister ʿAziz remarked that "there is no Gorbachev in Israel." Senator Alan Simpson pointed out "someone might come along." Saddam said that a wise person in Israel, striving to achieve the impossible, should make peace now, not ten years later. Metzenbaum insisted that there was no "conspiracy" in the United States, in England or in Israel, to do anything against Iraq.

Senator Simpson, addressing himself to Saddam's complaints about the American government, picked out the press as the spoiler in American-Iraqi relations. "I believe," said Simpson, "your problems lie with the Western media, and not with the U.S. government." "As long as you are isolated from the media," he went on to explain, "the press— and it is a haughty and pampered press—they all consider themselves political geniuses. . . . They are very cynical." "What I advise is that you invite them to come here and see for themselves." Saddam replied: "They are welcome. . . . We hope they will come to see Iraq. . . ."

Senator Dole, reiterating his call for peace, said that he lost his right arm forty years ago because of the war. "That reminds me daily," he pleaded, "that we all must work for peace. . . . We all have differences. . . . This leads me to the other final point I would like to make. We must work at our bilateral relations and if there is anything at all that we can do to improve our relations, it will be to both our countries' benefit."

"Finally," said Senator Dole, "if there is any message you would like us to relay on your behalf to President Bush. . . ."

Saddam replied: "Relay to him my regards, and tell him what I have said. Tell him that Iraq also wishes to establish relations based on mutual respect, and to serve the interests of the two countries and to serve the cause of peace and security in the world as well as in our region."

The exchange of views went very well. Saddam spoke his mind openly and the senators, speaking sympathetically, told him what the United States expected from him—peace and compromise with Israel. The senators also reciprocated Saddam's openness and promised to cooperate in reporting his interest in peace to President Bush and Congress. They also warned him about the Western media and advised him how to deal with it. They promised to talk with Israeli leaders while visiting Israel and to express his keen interest in pursuing a peaceful process and expressed their hope that relations between Iraq and the United States might steadily improve.

What did the Dole delegation accomplish upon its return home? Its members did talk with Bush, who seems to have been pleased with their exchange of views with Saddam, and they also talked with other members of the Senate. Proposals to impose sanctions against Iraq were abandoned, and Bush issued orders to provide trade credit for Iraq to purchase farm products, although high technological commodities were still denied to Iraq. Saddam hoped that that commodity, which was still prohibited, would soon be made available to Iraq.[12]

CONFRONTATION WITH KUWAIT

From his conversation with several emissaries—particularly with the Bandar and the Dole missions—Saddam Husayn must have realized that the president of the United States was opposed to a confrontation between Iraq and Israel. In the meantime, the campaign in the Congress and the press began to subside. As a consequence, Saddam seems to have felt, since all was quiet on the Western front, he could therefore safely turn his attention to the Gulf to deal with such urgent issues as oil prices, overproduction, and Kuwait's de facto frontier with which his mind had already been preoccupied.

In the last chapter, it will be recalled, an Arab Summit meeting (May 28–30, 1990) was held in Baghdad, called at the instance of several Arab leaders to demonstrate that Iraq was not standing alone in the Arab family against foreign threats. During that Summit, two closed meetings were devoted to sensitive issues. In one of them (May 30), it will be recalled, Saddam Husayn brought to the attention of Arab leaders Iraq's differences with Kuwait. He spoke his mind openly about the difficult financial position of his country, resulting from the lowering of oil prices due to overproduction by some of the Arab Gulf countries. "Iraq," he asserted, "is in a state of economic warfare." "It was created," he added, "by some Arab countries whose heads of state are present at this meeting."

> They [Saddam went on to explain] have pursued a policy of oil overproduction leading to the lowering of oil prices to its lowest level. . . . To Iraq, every lowering of one dollar in the prices of oil has resulted in a loss of one billion dollars a year. . . . We request our [Arab] brothers who do not intend to wage [economic] warfare against Iraq to realize that there are limits to what one can endure; but we have reached the point where we cannot sustain more pressure. . . . [13]

No reaction from Shaykh Jabir, Amir of Kuwait, was noted, who seemed either to have paid no attention to Saddam's appeal or assumed that the remark of the Iraqi president was not specifically directed to Kuwait. Following that meeting, King Fahd of Saudi Arabia, in agreement with Iraq's viewpoint on oil prices, met privately with Saddam Husayn and told him that he was worried to see him in "a mood of anger." "I am in more than a mood of anger," replied Saddam, "I felt that flames of fire were about to come out of my nose, but I tried to control myself." Fahd inquired whether an agreement had ever been reached with Kuwait? Nothing had been reached, replied Saddam. King Fahd, realizing that the central issue was financial, suggested that a mini-summit of oil-producing countries might be convened to resolve the problems of oil prices and overprodction. Shaykh Jabir, the Amir of Kuwait, also talked with Saddam before he left Baghdad, intimating that "there is a solution for every problem." This was taken by Saddam as a hint that further negotiations might lead to a resolution of the differences between them.[14]

Saddam's conversation with King Fahd and Shaykh Jabir prompted him to dispatch Saʿdun Hamadi (June 23, 1990) on a mission to the Arab Gulf countries to follow up his appeal to resolve the issues raised over oil prices and overproduction. The four Arab Gulf countries—Saudi Arabia, Kuwait, United Arab Amirate, and Qatar—seem to have been agreeable to holding a smaller Arab summit provided it was preceded by a preparatory meeting of the Arab oil ministers. During his visits to Arab capitals, Saʿdun Hamadi met with several heads of state and their oil ministers, the majority of whom seemed to have been sympathetic with Iraq's position. In his meeting with the Amir of Kuwait in the presence of the foreign minister, although Hamadi was assured that the OPEC oil quota for Kuwait was agreeable to them, the foreign minister remarked that Kuwait should have the freedom of raising its quota. Hamadi, rightly or wrongly, seems to have gotten the impression that the Foreign Minister's remark meant that Kuwait would not be bound by the OPEC quota.[15]

During the month of June, Saddam Husayn held several joint meetings of the Revolutionary Command Council (RCC) in which, among other things, Iraq's differences with Kuwait were discussed. As Kuwait had shown no sign that it was ready to settle those differences, it was decided to bring them before the Arab League Council for consideration in its forthcoming meeting in July. On July 16, 1990, Saddam Husayn publicly raised Iraq's differences with Kuwait in his speech on the occasion of the twenty-second anniversary of the Baʿth Revolution. In that speech, he accused the Arab Gulf rulers of consciously lowering the price of oil which reduced Iraq's income from oil and affected adversely its program for economic development.[16]

Meanwhile, Tariq ʿAziz, foreign minister, submitted a memorandum to the Arab League (dated July 15, 1990) a day after Saddam had delivered his speech.[17] The Iraqi memorandum opens with a few rhetorical statements such as that "the Arabs are one nation" and that "the Arab lands, despite its division into several states, form but one home for the Arabs." The security of any section of that home, the memorandum states, should be looked upon not from the narrow security of that section, but from the overall security of the Arab home. "It is on the basis of these national and brotherly principles," the memorandum asserts, "Iraq has dealt in its relationship with Kuwait." "But unfortunately," the memorandum adds, "Iraq has been treated contrary to those principles. . . . Kuwait has deliberately pursued a policy that hurt Iraq . . . at a time when it was facing an imperialist Zionist campaign for its stand in defence of Arab rights."

With regard to Iraq's relations with Kuwait, the memorandum states, there were three sets of differences. First, there was the frontier differences, the legacy of foreign control over Arab lands, which Iraq sought in vain to resolve in the sixties and seventies. No sooner had the war with Iran started than Kuwait discretely began to encroach on Iraqi lands beyond the de facto borders and to establish military and security centers. Following the war with Iran, Iraq proposed to settle the frontier differences, but Kuwait unexpectedly showed no readiness to reach an agreement, which aggravated the tension between the two countries. Second, Kuwait and the United Arab Amirate began to increase their oil production beyond the quotas assigned by OPEC which resulted in the lowering of oil prices and affected adversely Iraq's income from oil. Moreover, Kuwait began to drill oil from the South Rumayla oilfield, which Iraq considered within its borders. Third, Iraq proposed the establishment of an Arab Fund for Development to be provided by Arab oil countries, each to contribute a dollar from the extra annual income from oil provided the price of a barrel exceeded twenty-five dollars. The memorandum ends by an appeal to Kuwait to cancel its debt to it on the grounds that the war with Iran had cost Iraq over 106 billion dollars for the defence of Kuwait as well as other Arab countries against the threats of the Islamic Revolution in Iran. Iraq's debt to Kuwait, estimated at ten billion dollars, was in Iraqi eyes a small amount compared with Iraq's expenditure in money and blood in defence of Arab lands. The memorandum reminds Kuwait of the Marshall Plan with which the United States volunteered to contribute for the reconstruction of the European countries that fought against the Nazi aggression. Iraq requested the Arab League secretary to circulate the memorandum to all the Arab states. Only two—Kuwait and the United Arab Amirate—accused of tampering with oil prices and of overproduction, replied to Iraq's memorandum.

The Kuwaiti reply (dated July 19, 1990) states that the Iraqi memorandum was received with surprise and resentment owing to its presumptions and accusations without any basis in reality. Nor were its contents consistent with the spirit of the brotherly relationship that existed between Kuwait and Iraq during and after the bloody war with Iran. Kuwait, the reply memorandum states, has always dealt in its relations with Arab brothers in accordance with the principles and values embodied in the Arab League Pact, particularly the principles of good neighborly relationships, recognition of the independence and sovereignty of the state, and noninterference in domestic affairs. "Iraq claims," states the memorandum, that "Kuwait sought to undermine Iraq's position while the whole world knows the support Kuwait had extended to Iraq at a time when its lands and oil-carriers were exposed to foreign attacks." Kuwait's memorandum, however, did not answer Iraq's questions concerning oil prices and territorial claims, save its offer to discuss the demarcation of the frontier which Iraq had rejected, because the frontier treaty (1963) was not ratified by Iraq. Nor did it reply to Iraq's complaints about its debt to Kuwait and its losses in the lowering of oil prices.[18]

The reply of the United Arab Amirate (July 19, 1990) was polite and very brief. It simply rejected Iraq's accusations and insisted that as far as the oil prices were concerned, it was prepared to accept the quota assigned by OPEC. Moreover, it had always been ready to cooperate with other Arab countries to protect their common interests. Disagreement among Arabs, it pointed out, could hurt Arab interests and benefit none other than their enemies.[19]

In another memorandum to the Arab League, (July 21, 1990), Tariq 'Aziz rejected Kuwait's claim that it pursued Arab principles and values and pointed out that the Kuwaiti authorities were displeased simply because he had exposed their negligence and mistreatment of Iraq before the Arab nation. He stressed Iraq's complaints that Kuwait had never consented, contrary to its claim, to reach an agreement on frontiers with Iraq, as it had always sought to procrastinate and postpone any attempt to reach an agreement with Iraq. Iraq rejected all of Kuwait's counter-accusations, particularly its claim that Iraq had encroached on Kuwaiti territory during the war with Iran. Moreover, Iraq reproached Kuwait for its letter to the United Nations Security Council about their dispute; Iraq considered it inappropriate to turn an Arab family dispute into an international issue.[20]

The Iraqi memorandum to the Arab League, submitted first to a meeting of the Arab Foreign Ministers before it came before the League Council, aroused an unexpected uproar, and confusion resulted from accusations and counter-accusations between the Iraqi foreign minister and his opposite numbers in the Gulf countries. It was reported that the Iraqi foreign minister, in reply to one of his critics, said that Kuwait's action was equivalent to a "declaration of war." In the meantime, the news that Iraq had deployed military units near the Kuwaiti frontier had become known to the Arab League, and the consideration of the Iraqi memorandum by the League Council was postponed. The news of the deployment of the Iraqi forces, confirmed by

American observation planes in the region, had already been known to Saudi Arabia, Jordan, and Egypt.

Under these circumstances, because the Iraqi leadership had appeared "belligerent" in Western eyes, American policymakers in the White House and in the State Department often met to discuss what the American government should do to toughen its stand toward Iraq in order to encourage a course of moderation and peace in Iraq's relations with its neighbors. Some suggested cancelling all the credit programs, as some irregularity in the use of American credit by the Atlanta branch of the Italian Banca Nazionale del Lavoro had granted over three billion dollars in unauthorized letters of credit. But this matter had been settled. However, although the American credit was continued, it was suspended on May 29 for a time while American policy was reviewed. Baker and some of his advisers did not think "it was wise to take irrevocable actions," as some of the Arab leaders had been urged to "cool things down." True, Saddam had indulged in some rhetorical statements, but there was no sign he was contemplating action.

On July 16, 1990, it will be recalled, Iraq had submitted a memorandum (dated July 15, 1990) to the Arab countries in which Iraq accused Kuwait of aggression against Iraq, to which Saddam had referred in his speech at the celebration of the twenty-second anniversary of the Ba'th Revolution, and which brought the differences with Kuwait into the open. References to American support were made. Three days later (July 19), following discussion about American policy in embassies in the Middle East, a dispatched sketched "a new policy guidance on the Iraq- Kuwait dispute": first, "all disputes should be settled by peaceful means, not intimidation and threats of use of force; second, the United States takes no position on the substance of bilateral issues concerning Iraq and Kuwait." The dispatch also stated that the United States was committed to ensure free flow of oil and the independence and integrity of the Gulf countries.[21]

In the meantime, President Mubarak contacted the heads of state of four Arab countries—King Fahd of Saudi Arabia, the Amir of Kuwait, the King of Jordan, and the ruler of the United Arab Amirate—to exchange views as to what should be done to reduce tensions. It was decided that their foreign ministers should meet in Alexandria (July 22, 1990) a day before the anniversary of the Egyptian Revolution to discuss the situation. The upshot of the meeting was an agreement to ask President Mubarak to fly to Baghdad on July 24 and impress on Saddam Husayn the urgency of the need to settle his country's differences with Kuwait by direct negotiations before a serious crisis might be created.

Meanwhile, the Saudi foreign minister, Amir Saud al-Faysal, made a quick visit to Baghdad on July 22 to meet with Saddam Husayn. After a brief conversation, they agreed to propose a meeting between Shaykh Sa'd, Kuwait's premier, and 'Izzat Ibrahim al-Duri, deputy president of the Iraq Revolutionary Command Council—the two highest ranking figures next to the heads of state of their countries—to be held in Jidda under the auspices of King Fahd in order to settle their differences amicably. At a meeting of the Arab foreign ministers in Alexandria, to which Amir Saud reported Saddam's acceptance of the idea of an Iraq-Kuwait meeting in Jidda, Mubarak was requested to carry a message to this effect in person to Saddam Husayn.

On July 24, Mubarak met with Saddam in Baghdad and the Jidda meeting was approved. Mubarak's main concern, however, was about the danger from the concentration of an Iraqi force near Kuwait's border. Saddam did not deny the fact that military units had been moved to southern Iraq. But, it seems, a misunderstanding about the purpose of the force had developed between the two Arab leaders. Mubarak understood that Saddam had no intention of using force against Kuwait. Saddam maintained that he told Mubarak he had no intention of using force while the negotiations at Jidda were underway. As it was not customary to keep records in closed meetings among Arab heads of state, it was exceedingly difficult to determine whose statement was correct.[22]

On his way back to Alexandria, Mubarak stopped in Kuwait and Saudi Arabia to report the agreement for holding a meeting in Jidda, which he was almost certain would resolve the crisis amicably. He assured both Kuwait and Saudi Arabia that Saddam Husayn had no intention of using force. Highly optimistic about the forthcoming meeting in Jidda, Mubarak told the foreign ministers in Alexandria that he was convinced the crisis would be over by the end of July.

THE SADDAM-GLASPIE CONVERSATION

Before the Iraqi and Kuwaiti delegations met in Jidda (July 31), Saddam Husayn, aware of the fact that the Gulf is important to American strategic interests in the Middle East, wanted to know how safely he could deal with Kuwait without inviting foreign intervention.

On July 25, a day after Saddam's meeting with Mubarak, Nizar Hamdun, deputy foreign minister, called Ambassador April Glaspie to invite her to a meeting at the Foreign Office. As Glaspie had already met with Hamdun earlier on the same day to seek an answer about a question from Washington concerning Saddam's speech on July 16th (in which Saddam had referred to American pressures), she thought that perhaps her meeting would be with Tariq 'Aziz, Iraq's foreign minister, as Saddam Husayn, whom she had never met before, was not in the habit of receiving foreign diplomats. He delegated this function to 'Aziz who, holding the position of deputy prime minister in addition to foreign minister, used to receive all diplomatic representatives on behalf of the president. Upon her arrival, Nizar Hamdun, waiting in his car outside the Foreign Office building, told Glaspie that the meeting would be in another building and he escorted her in his car. Only after arrival at the presidential Palace did Glaspie realize that the meeting would be with President Saddam Husayn in the presence of his foreign minister.

In explaining the purpose of the meeting, Saddam told Glaspie that he wanted his conversation with her to be a "message to President Bush." The "message" covered several subjects. It dealt with the resumption of Iraq's diplomatic relations with the United States (severed in 1967), American foreign policy in the Gulf, and Iraq's differences with Kuwait.[23]

With regard to Iraq's resumption of diplomatic relations with the United States, Saddam said that Iraq had decided to reestablish the diplomatic relations early in 1980 (shortly after he had become president), but when Iraq became involved in the war with Iran, it was postponed till 1984. Because of the broken relationship, he said, it was obviously difficult for the United States "to have a full understanding of the events in Iraq." But after the resumption of relations, he added, "we hoped for a better understanding and closer relationship because we too did not understand the background of many American decisions." For example, he mentioned the Irangate and other events, which harmed Iraq, but, he said, "we wiped the slate clean."

In his conversation about American foreign policy, Saddam expressed his misgivings about the attitude of the press and the American government toward Iraq. Following the war with Iran, he pointed out, the "media began to meddle in our politics, and our suspicions were renewed because we began to wonder whether the United States felt uneasy about the outcome of the war by virtue of which we liberated our land." He also indicated that there were a number of people in the State Department and in the intelligence community as well as "in certain quarters" who did not like the idea that Iraq was able to liberate its lands (he added quickly, however, that he did not mean by "certain quarters" the president or the secretary of state). But he also stated his unhappiness with the American-Iraq relationship:

> We do not accept [he went on to explain] threats from anyone because we do not threaten anyone. We would like to say, however, that we hope the U.S. will not entertain too many illusions and will seek new friends rather than to increase the number of its enemies. . . .

And he added:

> The United States must have a better understanding of the situation and declare who it wants to have relations with and who its enemies are. But it should not make enemies simply because others have different points of view regarding some subjects like the Arab-Israeli conflict.

Saddam then began to discuss his country's expectations of the United States. He expressed his hope that a friendly relationship between the United States and Iraq would be established. "I do not be-

lieve," he said, "that anyone would lose anything by making friends
with Iraq." He hoped that such a friendship would be developed not
only with Iraq but also with other Arab countries.

Saddam then turned to discuss the American relationship with Kuwait. He complained that American support of Kuwait's attitude toward
Iraq had undermined Iraq's economy. He learned that some Americans
who did not like Iraq's victory over Iran became very active in Arab
Gulf politics. "They began to contact Gulf states and to inspire them
with fear of Iraq and to persuade them not to give Iraq economic aid."
Saddam bitterly complained that their activities "resulted in the drop
of oil prices and in undermining Iraq's position and depriving its people of higher economic standards."

Saddam maintained that American support of Kuwait revealed
"prejudice against Iraq," because it encouraged Kuwait to disregard
"Iraq's rights." "Iraq has its own rights," said Saddam, and he complained: "We cannot understand the attempt to encourage some parties to harm Iraq's interests." To prove his point, Saddam told Glaspie:
"But go and look for yourselves. You will see the Kuwaiti border patrols,
the Kuwaiti farms, the Kuwaiti installations—all built as closely as possible to this line to establish that land as Kuwaiti territory." Saddam
hinted that he might use force. "If you use pressure," he said, "we will
deploy pressure and force." "We don't want war," he added, "but do
not push us to consider war as the only solution to live proudly and to
provide our people with good living. . . ."

Glaspie had ample time to reply to Saddam's questions and also to
address her own questions to him. First, she thanked him for his "conversation" as a "message" to President Bush. As to Saddam's inquiry
about American "friendship," she called his attention to the letters
sent to him by President Bush on the occasion of the Iraqi National
Day. Moreover, she told him that she had "direct instruction from the
president to seek better relations with Iraq." "But how?" remarked
Saddam, "We too have this desire." "But matters are running contrary
to this desire," said Saddam, and he again complained about the press
campaign against Iraq. Agreeing with him on this matter, Glaspie
pointed out that this situation in the United States happens even to
American politicians. She assured him that "President Bush wanted
better and deeper relations with Iraq, but he also wants an Iraqi contribution to peace and prosperity in the Middle East. . . . He is not going to declare an economic war against Iraq."

Turning to the question of oil prices, Glaspie pointed out that the
United States did not want higher prices for oil. Saddam replied that
he did not want "too high prices for oil." Tariq ʿAziz, confirming Saddam's point said that "our policy in OPEC opposes sudden jumps in
oil prices." Saddam maintained that Iraq's proposal of "twenty-five dollars a barrel is not a high price." Glaspie agreed and stated that "we
have many Americans who would like to see the price go above twenty-

five because they come from oil-producing states." Saddam complained
about the price of oil because it had dropped to twelve a barrel resulting in a reduction in the income from oil of some six to seven billion
dollars. Such a reduction, he said, "is a disaster" to his country.

Glaspie remarked that she "understood this," in view of the extraordinary efforts to rebuild the country. "I know," she said in expressing her sympathy with the plans for the reconstruction of his
country, "you need funds . . . and our opinion is that you should have
the opportunity to rebuild your country." "But," she added, "we have
no opinion on the Arab-Arab conflict, like your border disagreement
with Kuwait."

Glaspie then turned to the important question of the deployment
of a force in the south of Iraq. "Normally," she said, "that would not
be any of our business. But when this happens in the context of what
you said on your National Day . . . then it would be reasonable for me
to be concerned. . . . For this reason, I received an instruction to ask
you, in the spirit of friendship—not in the spirit of confrontation—
regarding your intentions."

Saddam assured Glaspie that all what he wanted was "to find a just
solution," and insisted that "we are not an aggressor but we do not
accept aggression either."

Glaspie asked him if he could give "an assessment of the efforts as
to whether anything has been achieved?"

Saddam replied that President Mubarak told him the Kuwaiti premier agreed to meet with 'Izzat Ibrahim; he just phoned to say that the
Kuwaitis had agreed to meet in Saudi Arabia.

Glaspie, satisfied with the answer, said, "Congratulations."

Saddam remarked, "A protocol meeting will be held in Saudi Arabia and then it will be transferred to Baghdad for deeper discussion
directly between Kuwait and Iraq. We hope that the long-term view and
the real interests will overcome Kuwaiti greed."

Glaspie asked, "When do you expect Shaykh Sa'd to come to Baghdad?"

Saddam said it would be on Saturday or Monday at the latest.

Glaspie replied, "This is good news."

Saddam said Mubarak told him the Kuwaitis were scared. They said
troops were only twenty kilometers north of the Arab League line (in
reference to the existing de facto border). Saddam told Mubarak to
"assure the Kuwaitis and give them our word that we are not going to
do anything until we meet with them." "When we meet, and when we
see that there is hope, then nothing will happen." Glaspie seemed
satisfied and told him she was planning to go to the U.S. (Indeed, she
actually left for London on the following day, and learned about the
Iraqi invasion of Kuwait shortly after her arrival in London.)

In his conversation with Glaspie, Saddam was very critical of the
American policy toward Iraq. He was obviously neither conciliatory in

tone nor even ready to show the moderation he displayed in his conversations with John Kelly or with the Dole mission. He considered
Kuwait's intractable attitude toward Iraq as an indirect pressure aimed
at undermining his leadership and his efforts to develop the country's
industrial potential. He hinted that he was expecting military confrontation either directly with the United States or indirectly through an
attack by Israel. He was obviously hurt by the attacks in the media and
by Congressional attempts to cut off trade with his country. Pride seems
to have prevented him from submission to pressure or threat even
though he could not match American military power.

Earlier on the same day Glaspie had seen Nizar Hamdun to discuss
a message she had received from Washington asking for clarification
about Saddam's critical speech of American policy which he had made
on July 16 on the occasion of the twenty-second anniversary of the Ba'th
Revolution in 1968. Nizar Hamdun must have told Tariq 'Aziz about
his meeting with Glaspie. When she was called later by Hamdun, her
mind was preoccupied with what she would say to him. Her instruction
from the State Department was, along the lines of Kelly's conversation
with Saddam, to reaffirm American government intention to pursue
peace and cooperation with Iraq.

Before her meeting with Saddam Husayn, Glaspie had received
only two dispatches from Washington concerning the Iraq-Kuwait dispute. The first was the letter dated July 19, 1990, from the secretary of
state, James A. Baker, to which we referred earlier. The substance of
the other letter that Glaspie had received from the State Department,
which she relayed to Nizar Hamdun before she met with Saddam, emphatically stated that the United States "can never excuse settlement
of disputes by other than peaceful means."[24]

Glaspie may have too gently expressed herself, but her instructions
were clear to stress peace and cooperation, and she did warn against
resort to force. Her statement that the United States had no position
on Arab-Arab conflict such as the border dispute, for which she was
criticized, was based on the two letters she had received shortly before
she saw Saddam on July 25. Hoping that the border dispute would be
resolved in the forthcoming Jidda meeting, she left Baghdad for London, unaware of what the three military units near Kuwait's border
would do.

THE JIDDA MEETING

On July 31, by invitation from King Fahd, Iraq and Kuwait were formally
invited to a meeting in Jidda to be held for direct negotiations between
the two countries. The purpose of the meeting, as it had been agreed
between the two sides, was to review their differences and make proposals for a settlement to be finalized at another meeting in Baghdad.

Iraq appointed ʿIzzat Ibrahim al- Duri, deputy president of the Revolutionary Command Council, as head of the Iraqi delegation, and Kuwait appointed Shaykh Saʿd, prime minister, as head of the Kuwaiti delegation. The fact that the head of each delegation held the second highest ranking position in his country gave the impression that both sides were serious about their determination to reach an agreement based on compromise.

Shortly before the Jidda meeting took place, however, when Kuwait was approached by Jordan to agree to some of Iraq's proposals—such as accepting OPEC oil quotas, concessions on the Rumayla oilfield, and a lease for the islands of Warba and Bubiyan—the Shaykh of Kuwait was adamant and refused to accept any proposal. He only agreed that his prime minister, Shaykh Saʿd, would meet with the Iraqi representative to review the situation. Before he left for Jidda, Shaykh Saʿd received his instructions from Shaykh Jabir. In a footnote on the bottom of King Fahd's letter of invitation to Jidda, Shaykh Jabir's instructions to Shaykh Saʿd read as follows:

> We attend this meeting under the same conditions we agreed on. . . .
>
> Whatever you may hear from the Saudis or the Iraqis about brotherhood and Arab solidarity, forget it. Every one of us has his own interests. The Saudis want to weaken us . . . so that they can press us in the future to give them concessions in the neutral zones. The Iraqis want to compensate for their losses in the war at our expense. Neither of these should happen. That is the view of our friends in Egypt, Washington, and London. Insist on your discussions. We are more powerful than they imagine. With all my wishes for your success, Jabir.[25]

Nor were the instructions given to ʿIzzat Ibrahim al-Duri, head of the Iraqi delegation, less stringent. In his instructions to Duri, Saddam Husayn said: "If the Kuwaitis were to reveal their well-known obstinacy, then you may tell them that we have pictures of Kuwait when it was a mud-walled town, the only border we are ready to recognize are those walls."[26]

The official records of the Jidda meeting have not yet seen the light. There are, however, three firsthand accounts by Arab leaders who attended the meeting. One is by King Fahd, who sponsored the meeting, and who made a speech at a Saudi press conference (November 26, 1990) in which he related some of his recollections about what went on in the Jidda meeting.[27] The second account is by Shaykh Saʿd, Kuwait's prime minister and head of its delegation, who made a speech in London (September 4, 1990) in which he gave a brief account of the events that preceded the invasion of Kuwait, including the meeting in Jidda.[28] The third account is by Saʿdun Hamadi, member of the Iraqi delegation, who kept personal notes about the meeting.[29] None gives us a complete record of what went on behind closed doors. While they are in agreement about fundamentals, there are differences about details.

Shaykh Sa'd, according to his account, arrived in Jidda on July 30, a day before his opposite number, 'Izzat al-Duri. It is likely that Shaykh Sa'd wanted to meet with King Fahd and arrived earlier to talk with him. On the following day (July 31st), 'Izzat Ibrahim al-Duri, head of the Iraqi delegation, accompanied by Sa'dun Hamadi, former minister of foreign affairs, arrived shortly before noontime. The delegation, met by Amir 'Abd-Allah, Saudi Crown Prince and deputy prime minister (with whom Duri had good personal rapport), was escorted to the Conference Palace in Jidda where Shaykh Sa'd and his delegation were staying.

At 4:00 P.M., the heads of the two delegations went to the Hamra Royal Palace where King Fahd was ready to receive them. In welcoming them, the King explained that the purpose of the Jidda meeting was to bring the two sides together in order for them to have the opportunity to meet alone and freely discuss their differences. He wished them success in their endeavors. To achieve their purpose, Amir 'Abd-Allah said, he would open the first meeting and provide all facilities for the two delegations, but would leave them alone hoping that agreement might be reached. He also extended an invitation to a dinner in their honor at 9:30 P.M. The protocol meeting at the Hamra Palace hardly lasted forty minutes, according to Sa'dun Hamadi's record.

At about 6:00 p.m., after their return to the Conference Palace, the two delegations held two meetings, preceded by a short tête-à-tête meeting between the heads of the two delegations (opened by Amir 'Abd-Allah). According to Shaykh Sa'd's account, which confirms Hamadi's record, there were indeed two meetings preceded by a closed one between Shaykh Sa'd and Duri. No sooner had Shaykh Sa'd began to submit in detail Kuwait's views about the Iraqi claims, than Duri, who had made no significant remarks, suggested that the two delegations should hold a joint meeting. The closed meeting between Shaykh Sa'd and Duri seems to have been too short, it hardly lasted twenty minutes, according to Sa'dun Hamadi's record.

Before the two delegations started, Duri went to a corner of the Conference hall to perform the sunset prayer, as he was keen not to miss the prayer. It is not clear which delegation began to present its proposals first, as Shaykh Sa'd's account gives the impression that he started first to present Kuwait's views about Iraq's claims. But Hamadi's record clearly indicates that Duri presented Iraq's proposals and indicated Kuwait's transgressions in addition to the ones related to the de facto frontier such as drilling oil in the South Rumayla oilfield, lowering oil prices through overproduction, and denying a request to allow Iraq's commercial airflights through Kuwait's airspace. These proposals, he stated, were based on the memorandum which Iraq had submitted to the Arab League in mid-July.

In reply, Shaykh Saʿd pointed out that the Iraqi memorandum to the Arab League could not possibly be considered the basis of negotiations as it was rejected by Kuwait. He also stated that Iraq's claim to the South Rumayla oilfield had no basis in law, as the oilfield is within Kuwait's territory, separated from the Iraqi Rumayla oilfield by some seven kilometers. He also rejected the proposal for a fixed oil price. Nor did he accept Iraq's request for permission to allow commercial airflight through Kuwait's airspace, although such a privilege had already been accepted under an agreement reached by the five Arab oil ministers. No specific counter-proposals seem to have been offered by the Kuwaiti delegation and the meeting ended without reaching an agreement as it was expected, according to Hamadi.

When they met at dinner, King Fahd, simply asked: "How is it going?" As they both smiled, he thought it went very well and began to talk in general terms about the need to discuss Arab differences amicably as the best way to protect their national interests. But the two men did not openly bring their differences before the King, and the meeting was expected to be resumed on the following day. Duri must have called Saddam Husayn to report that the Kuwaiti premier had shown no sign that he was ready to accept any of the Iraqi proposals so that Saddam ordered him to return. On the following day (August 1st), the Iraqi delegation left for Baghdad after Duri had paid a quick visit to Madina to pray at the Mosque where the Prophet was buried. Before the Iraqi delegation had departed, the Kuwaiti delegation wanted to issue a joint statement to the effect that the two delegations had reached an agreement on "positive issues," but the Iraqi delegation replied it preferred that each delegation should issue its own statement.[30]

On the following day, when King Fahd learned that the Iraqi delegation had left, he met with Shaykh Saʿd, who stayed a little longer for a meeting with him. Shaykh Saʿd told King Fahd that he had been flexible and offered a number of compromises to meet Iraqi demands. For example, he claimed that Kuwait was ready to grant Iraq military facilities on the islands of Warba and Bubiyan and had offered to forgive the Iraqi debt. As to the Rumayla oil field, he suggested that it should be settled by arbitration. In his conversations with Duri, however, Shaykh Saʿd did not really commit himself to any specific proposal, as he probably thought that final commitments should be made in Baghdad. Thus the Jidda meeting, which the Arab leaders had expected to ease tensions and settle disputes, turned out instead to be a complete failure and to aggravate suspicion and hard feelings.

Part III

STAGES OF
THE GULF WAR

This part consists of six chapters. In the first chapter, the steps taken by Iraq leading to the invasion of Kuwait are dealt with. A regional conflict such as Iraq's invasion of Kuwait was expected to be resolved by a regional organization as the Arab League. Since the Arab League did not move quickly to resolve the issue, foreign powers intervened to settle the issue by the use of force, called the Coalition War, under the leadership of the United States. These events are discussed in the first three chapters of this part. The immediate consequences of the Coalition War, such as the Shi'i and Kurdish uprisings are dealt with in the last three chapters of this part. Not all the consequences of the Coaliton War are dealt with in this work, as most of them are still pending for future settlement.

Chapter 8

The Invasion of Kuwait

The Jidda meeting, which was eagerly expected in Arab capitals to resolve the disputes between Iraq and Kuwait, proved extremely disappointing when it came to an abrupt and unexpected end. While Kuwait considered the meeting but one step leading to another in Baghdad where the two heads of state might reach a final agreement, Iraq held that if the meeting turned out to be another encounter in which Kuwait showed no sign that it was ready for compromise, then there would be no need for another meeting in Baghdad. Thus, when in the first meeting in Jidda, Kuwait seemed intransigent, 'Izzat Ibrahim al-Duri must have called Baghdad to report that the Kuwaiti delegation had rejected all Iraq's proposals, and he was at once ordered to return home.

Early in the evening of August 1st, shortly after Izzat al-Duri had returned from Jidda, Saddam called a meeting of the Revolutionary Command Council (RCC) to hear Duri's report on the Jidda meeting. After a brief discussion, Saddam proposed the use of force to annex not merely the area of South Rumayla oilfield (al-Ratqa) and the islands of Warba and Bubiyan, but also the rest of the country. This option was not on the minds of the RCC members when they met to hear Duri's report about the Jidda meeting. A fortnight earlier, the RCC had adopted the option to use force only in the event Kuwait were to persist in denying Iraq's legitimate claim to the South Rumayla oilfield and the two islands.[1]

Why did Saddam, it may be asked, change his mind and propose the option of occupying the whole of Kuwait?

Two reasons seem to have prompted him to change his mind: one was essentially geopolitical and the other ideological.

First, Kuwait, although a small country surrounded by three more powerful neighbors—Iran, Iraq, and Saudi Arabia—has always been able to protect itself by depending on the support of a great power (first England and later the United States), whose vital interests in the Gulf were served by Kuwait. As Kuwait had shown no sign that it would accept Iraq's claims to the South Rumayla oilfield and the two islands, Saddam concluded that the Kuwaiti rulers must be counting on foreign support, leading to a war of attrition, which might undermine his regime. If the whole of Kuwait were occupied and the Sabah regime were replaced by another friendly to Iraq, foreign forces, according to Saddam, could not attack Iraqi forces as traditionally Saudi Arabia would not allow the landing of foreign troops on its land. Nor could a foreign force enter from the Gulf coast, as Iraqi forces would be in control over the entire coast of Kuwait. No other Arab country outside the Arabian Peninsula, Saddam maintained, save Syria, was expected to go to war with Iraq for the sake of the Sabah family.

Second there were ideological considerations. Apart from Iraq's legal claims, a widespread opinion in Iraq asserted that Kuwait, on historical grounds, was but a part of Iraq. The relationship between the two countries was symbolized by the slogan that "Kuwait is a branch of the (Iraq) trunk." For this reason, when British protection over Kuwait was terminated in 1961, Brigadier Qasim at once declared that Kuwait was part of Iraq, but he was faulted because he took no immediate action to annex the country by force before the British had landed troops to defend its territory. Saddam, in order to avoid such possible public critique, opted to occupy the whole of Kuwait. He also hoped that by the annexation of Kuwait, his own reputation as a pan-Arab leader would be enhanced. Saddam's military advisers seem to have been quite enthusiastic about Saddam's option for the occupation of Kuwait.

What was the opinion of other RCC advisers, particularly Sa'dun Hamadi and Tariq 'Aziz, former foreign ministers, who were well-acquainted with Gulf affairs? As both had often been frustrated in dealing with Kuwait, they seem to have also come to the conclusion that some form of pressure was necessary against the Kuwaiti regime. Nor were the experts on Western affairs very helpful, as they told Saddam that the American public was not ready to go to war with a foreign country. Thus Saddam's military option was adopted.[2]

RESPONSE TO IRAQ'S INVASION OF KUWAIT

The United States and Britain were the first Western countries to protest without hesitation against the invasion of Kuwait, because the invasion had threatened Western vital interests in the region. As British imperial interests in the Gulf and the Indian Ocean had declined since World War II, the mantle of protecting the independence and security of the Arab Gulf countries had fallen on American shoulders. Consequently, the United States was bound to react quickly and took the lead, politically and militarily, to reverse the invasion and reestablish the status quo ante in the Gulf.

When, however, Iraq invaded Kuwait in the wee hours on the morning of August 2 (it was the early evening of August 1 in Washington, D.C.), the views of the various American governmental departments about the political events in the Gulf region were not quite the same, because each department was watching developments in the region from different perspectives. Before the invasion of Kuwait, policymakers in the White House and the State Department, primarily concerned about the maintenance of peace and security in the region, sought to persuade countries like Iraq and Iran to cooperate with the United States by pursuing a policy of moderation. Only after the invasion, when they viewed Iraq's action as a threat to American interests in the Gulf and the Middle East region as a whole, did they begin to discuss ways and means to reverse the invasion. The Defence and Navy Departments, concerned about the security of the Gulf even before Iraq's invasion of Kuwait, began to prepare plans for defence. The intelligence agencies have always been active in watching events and gathering information for policymakers in the various departments of government.[3]

When an Iraqi force was first deployed near Kuwait's border in the latter part of July 1990, and later expanded from three to five divisions, it was immediately spotted by the Defence Intelligence Agency (DIA), and the information about the movement of this force was reported almost every day to high military authorities.[4] This information, however, was not reported to the White House and the State Department until the Iraqi force had reached a distance of three miles from the border, as the DIA was not sure that the aim of this force was to cross Kuwait's border. The Defence Department had a plan called CENTOM whose headquarters was at a base in Florida (because the Gulf countries were not in favor of a visible American presence on their territory) and another plan to protect the ruler of Kuwait who represented the legitimate government of Kuwait (this plan had already been prepared during the Iraq-Iran war to save his life in the event his country was overrun by Iran or Iraq).[5]

The White House and the State Department, however, did not at first pay enough attention to the evidence that Iraq was ready to invade Kuwait. Thus when the news about the movement of the Iraqi force toward Kuwait was reported to the President shortly before the invasion had taken place, it was not taken seriously, as it was construed on the strength of the advice of Arab leaders friendly to the West as a form of pressure to induce the Kuwait authorities to concede to Iraqi demands concerning borders and oil production.

Owing to repeated warnings from the Defense Department and the CIA, a meeting at the State Department was finally held on July 27 to review the situation in the Gulf. It was decided that a direct message was required from the secretary of state, James Baker, to Saddam Husayn, in which he was assured that "the United States was trying to get along with Iraq and attempting to establish a way to work with him, and that Iraq must reciprocate." The Defence Department had urged a stronger message, but the general opinion was in favor of the "restrained message," as "Saddam was not going to cross fellow Arab, Mubarak."[6] As a result, the dispatch that Baker sent to Saddam (July 29, 1990) was not strong enough to deter him from resorting to force.

Since Saddam showed no willingness to cooperate with the United States, the White House and the State Department suddenly began to change their attitude toward Saddam, and several proposals were suggested not only to reverse the invasion but also to disarm Iraq of all kinds of chemical and nuclear weapons. One high official in the White House even suggested that "Saddam had to be toppled."[7] All the steps that were undertaken to achieve these objectives under the aegis of the United Nations were decided in several subsequent meetings at the White House.

AMERICAN DIPLOMACY TO RESOLVE THE GULF CRISIS

Following meetings with his political and military advisers at the White House and Camp David, President Bush made it crystal clear to the American public that he was determined in the first place to reverse the invasion and restore the legitimate government to Kuwait. In order to carry out his plan through the United Nation, Bush had to seek the cooperation of Western as well as the leading Arab countries, in particular Saudi Arabia and Egypt, whose participation was deemed absolutely necessary for any political and military action to be taken against Iraq.

The first and most important ally of the United States was England. Bush had already discussed with the British prime minister, Margaret Thatcher, the situation in the Gulf, who held even stronger views about Iraq's aggression and offered to cooperate with the United States to restore the legitimate government of Kuwait. Bush's contacts with the leading Arab leaders were at the outset not very encouraging, as they sought first to deal with the crisis as an Arab problem, but they were in agreement with Bush in principle that Iraq should withdraw from Kuwait and its legitimate government should be restored.[8]

Turkey and Iran, two non-Arab neighbors of Iraq, were important, as any sanction, economic or otherwise, imposed on Iraq would be of little or no effect were those northern and eastern neighbors to open their countries for Iraq's oil. Since Iraq and Iran had been at war for eight years and no peace treaty (only a cease-fire) had yet been concluded, no official cooperation was expected between the two countries. But Turkey, where an important Iraqi pipeline for the export of oil to Europe was in operation, proved to be an absolutely necessary ally, if an embargo on oil, and therefore the most important Iraqi income from foreign trade, were to have any significant effect on Iraq to withdraw from Kuwait. After he returned from a meeting with his military advisers at Camp David (August 4), Bush was ready to contact President Ozal of Turkey. By coincidence, Ozal had himself called, and Bush, after a brief talk with journalists, had a conversation with Ozal who indicated that he was opposed to Iraq's invasion of Kuwait, but explained the political and economic events that were likely to ensue, were Turkey to join in an embargo against Iraq. Three days after the U.N. economic sanctions were imposed, Baker went to Turkey and promised Ozal that Turkey's losses would be taken into consideration. Not only did Baker promise one billion dollars from the United States, but also another one billion to be provided by the World Bank. Had it stood neutral during the Gulf crisis or failed to cooperate with Western countries, Turkey's membership in NATO would be compromised. Moreover, Baker told Ozal that the United States had formally endorsed Turkey's application to join the European Community.[9]

Bush had no great difficulty in persuading Gorbachev to cooperate with the Western democracies, as he needed American support to deal with his domestic problems. The Gulf crisis was a test case. Had the Soviet Union (the only power that could have saved it by casting a veto against mandatory sanctions) sided with Iraq, then Gorbachev would appear as wholly uncommitted to full cooperation with the United States. Since Iraq had not consulted the Soviet Union before it invaded Kuwait, as required under the Soviet-Iraq treaty of alliance, Gorbachev must have felt free to relieve himself from the obligation to help Iraq in order to cement his relationship with the United States.[10]

But when Bush sought to enlist the Soviet Union in the Coalition army that would be sent to Saudi Arabia, Gorbachev was not prepared to join such a military expedition. Baker telephoned Shevardnadze to urge Soviet participation. After consulting with Gorbachev, Shevardnadze replied that the Soviets would not join the military coalition. The Soviet military who supplied Soviet weapons to Iraq and served as advisers to the Iraq military were putting enormous pressure on Gorbachev to dissuade him from joining the Coalition in which the Soviet army might find itself facing the Iraq army fighting with Soviet weapons. The Soviet "Arabists," said Baker, were furious about the "joint statement" in which Shevardnadze had joined with Baker to denounce Iraq's aggression.

Since the Soviet leaders had shown reservations as to what extent they would cooperate with the United States, Bush decided to send his secretary of state, who had won the confidence of Shevardnadze, to Moscow in order to seek Soviet commitment for further pressure on Saddam to withdraw from Kuwait. The Soviets had agreed on economic sanctions. But these appeared to the American government inadequate

to influence Saddam to withdraw in the foreseeable future. It appeared
to the American government that differences among the Coalition powers might come to the surface, on which the Iraqi leaders were counting, and the U.S. decided to escalate sanctions, including the use of
force. For cooperation among the five permanent members of the Security Council, the agreement of the Soviet Union and China to use
force was necessary as even France and possibly England were not sure
that economic sanctions will work in the long run. Bush and Baker had
met with Gorbachev and Shevardnadze in Helsinki (September 9,
1990) and discussed, among other things, the Gulf crisis. While they
were in agreement on forcing Iraq to withdraw through the use of
economic sanctions, there was no agreement to go beyond that level.
For this reason, further attempts to discuss the matter were made.

On November 3, Baker left Washington for visits with most of the
countries represented at the Security Council. In particular, he wanted
to talk with the Soviet and Chinese foreign ministers. By coincidence,
Qian Qichen, the Chinese foreign minister, was on a visit to Egypt, and
on his way to Baghdad. It was arranged that Baker would see him in
Cairo. The talk between them was not only about Iraq, it included
American-Chinese relationships. Baker explained to Qian the use-of-
force resolution that the United States had in mind to introduce to the
Security Council. Qian told Baker that China was committed to full
implementation of the U.N. resolutions. But when Baker asked him to
tell Saddam that China would support that resolution, he was noncommittal. Baker, however, understood that China would abstain from ob-
jecting to the U.S. resolution.

On November 7, Baker arrived in Moscow. He had extended talks
with Shevardnadze. The Soviet position at the outset was that economic
sanctions would work. It was a matter of time, according to Shevardnadze, who thought at first it would take a couple of months. As the
Soviet leaders were in contact with the Iraqi leaders, they were still
hoping that Iraq would withdraw from Kuwait without the use of force.
Aware of the fragility of the Coalition, Shevardnadze warned that if the
war were necessary, then, "You have to know that you will succeed."
Baker, who trusted Shevardnadze, invited Howard Graves to explain
the American military strategy. Graves, said Baker, "delivered a highly
detailed classified briefing on our war plan." Highly impressed, it
seems, with the American military preparation and Baker's persuasive
argument, Shevardnadze agreed to support the American position on
the resolution to be introduced at the Security Council. He arranged
a meeting with Gorbachev and both went to see him on the following
day.

The discussion with Gorbachev was mainly about the wording of
the Security Council resolution, and he agreed to go beyond economic
sanctions. "He is reluctant to use force," Baker felt, "but prepared to
do so." The outcome of Baker's visit to Moscow was that the Soviet

Union promised to vote in favor of a resolution implying ultimately the use of force, but felt that further nonmilitary efforts to persuade Saddam to withdraw must be attempted. Baker's visit to Moscow as well as to other Western capitals, including Arab countries, proved highly successful.

The only members of the Security Council that voted against most of the mandatory sanctions were Yaman and Cuba. Since neither one was a permanent member of the Security Council, their negative votes were considered merely protest gestures, as there was always a majority of nine in favor including the five permanent members designated under the Charter (Article 27).

Bush was able to rally not only the support of members of the Security Council, but also other members of the United Nations, particularly the leading Arab countries and Turkey. The only Arab countries that stood on the side of Iraq were Jordan, Algeria, Tunisia, Libya, Sudan, and Mauritania. On the domestic level, however, Bush had a much harder task persuading the Congress of the United States to vote in favor of the use of force as provided under the Security Council Resolution 678. Nor was the American public at first in favor of war, despite the intensive media campaign against Iraq's rearmament program and its threats to Israel, as opinion was that the economic sanctions had not been given long enough time to work as an alternative to war.[11]

THE ARAB SEARCH FOR PEACEFUL SETTLEMENT

No sooner had the Iraqi forces crossed Kuwait's border in the wee hours on the morning of August 2, 1990, than King Fahd, shaken by the invasion, called King Husayn on the telephone and told him that "President Saddam should be urged to limit his invasion to the extent of the disputed boundaries between Iraq and Kuwait until the whole dispute could be resolved peacefully," according to King Husayn's report.[12] King Husayn keenly felt he should meet with Saddam; but before he went to Baghdad, he first had to meet with President Mubarak to coordinate the efforts of three Arab rulers—King Fahd, President Mubarak, and himself. Mubarak was upset that Iraq had resorted to force, as Saddam had promised him not to use force (Saddam said later he had told Mubarak that he would not use force before Iraq and Kuwait had met at the Jidda Conference).[13] On his way to Alexandria, King Husayn called President Bush on the telephone (he had learned that Bush had called to talk with him and with President Mubarak). From their talks with Bush, King Husayn and Mubarak found the American president was quite upset by Saddam's resort to force. He considered the invasion of Kuwait "an aggression," and he had already made a public statement to that effect. "Saddam had challenged the United

States" Bush told the King Husayn, and he was ready to "accept the challenge."[14]

Bush was surprised, according to King Husayn, that the Arab countries had not condemned the Iraqi invasion and wondered why the Arab foreign ministers in Cairo were still talking and could not reach a decision. Nor did King Fahd, said Bush, ask for American assistance; only Kuwait had requested assistance soon after the invasion started. "The United States will act independently," Bush added, "regardless whether other countries will cooperate or not." King Husayn replied that he wanted the Arab leaders to be given time to deal with the situation. Finding Bush convinced that the Arabs were not ready to act, King Husayn pleaded with him: "Give us forty-eight hours . . . no more!"[15]

The three Arab rulers—King Husayn, King Fahd, and President Mubarak—sought to find a way to convince Saddam that withdrawal from Kuwait was absolutely necessary before the Western powers had intervened to make their own decision as to how the crisis should be resolved. Although Mubarak was upset by Saddam for his resort to force (believing that Saddam had given him unqualified promise not to use force), he suggested to call an Arab mini-summit meeting in Jidda to cope with the situation. Highly optimistic about the prospect of holding such a summit, King Husayn proceeded with enthusiasm to Baghdad to inform Saddam about it. Before he left, Mubarak had told King Husayn that Iraq should withdraw from Kuwait and its legitimate government should be restored. These, according to King Husayn, were proposals for discussion, but not conditions laid down before the summit had met in Jidda. In his visit to Baghdad (August 3rd), King Husayn was able to persuade Saddam Husayn to attend the Jidda summit and discuss the crisis, including Iraq's withdrawal from Kuwait and the restoration of the legitimate Government. Saddam promised to bring these proposals before the Iraqi Revolutionary Command Council (RCC), provided the Arab foreign ministers, then meeting in Cairo, would not condemn Iraq nor make withdrawal and return of the legitimate government conditional. These were merely considered proposals to be brought before the mini-summit in Jidda for its consideration. Meanwhile, Saddam presented King Husayn's proposals to the Iraqi RCC and its approval was reported to King Husayn on the same day. Before King Husayn had returned to 'Amman, however, the Egyptian government issued a statement in which the Iraqi invasion of Kuwait was condemned and the Arab foreign ministers, in line with Egypt's action, also proposed condemnation of Iraq.

Why did the Egyptian government issue the condemnation before the Arab leaders had an opportunity to meet at an Arab mini-summit? In the Jordanian *White Paper*, an account of what had taken place, after King Husayn's visit to Baghdad, states:

At the same time that his Majesty [King Husayn] was discussing the proposals jointly agreed upon between himself and President Mubarak, the Egyptian government issued a statement condemning the Iraqi invasion of Kuwait. Upon his return, His Majesty called President Mubarak to inform him of the agreement he had reached with President Saddam Hussein, and to express his regret at the Egyptian statement. President Mubarak's explanation to His Majesty was that he was under great pressure, and that he had spoken with His Majesty King Fahd who was very angry at the situation. President Mubarak was now unwilling to accept the agreement reached by His Majesty with President Saddam Hussein, and insisted on Iraq's unconditional withdrawal from Kuwait and the immediate restoration of the Kuwait ruling family. . . . [16]

Several attempts by a number of Arab leaders to resolve the ensuing crisis were made from August 3 to 10, including visits to Baghdad and Riyad, but suspicion began to cloud the atmosphere leading to division of the Arab rank into two camps: King Fahd and Mubarak, on the one hand, were not sure that Saddam was ready to withdraw from Kuwait, while King Husayn and Yasir ʿArafat (who also visited Baghdad), on the other, had been assured by Saddam that he was prepared to withdraw if an Arab summit were to meet and discuss the crisis. Meanwhile, the Cheney mission to Jidda and the landing of an American force in Saudi Arabia seem to have aroused Saddam's suspicion as to the purpose of the mission and prompted him to declare the annexation of Kuwait as an answer that he was not prepared to withdraw from Kuwait under the threat of foreign intervention. He felt particularly insulted when, at a meeting of the Arab League called by Mubarak on August 10, a resolution in which Iraq was condemned and called upon for immediate withdrawal from Kuwait, including the restoration of its legitimate government (in conformity with the Security Council Resolution 660) was adopted. The differences that suddenly came to the surface among Arab leaders seem to have put an end to collective Arab mediation, and the prospect of an Arab solution for the Gulf crisis became almost nil. But King Husayn, firmly believing that the crisis could have been resolved by peaceful means, never ceased offering his personal mediation on several subsequent occasions, to no avail.

From August to September, 1990, King Husayn visited seven Arab countries—Yaman, Sudan, Libya, Tunisia, Algeria, Mauritania, Morocco—and five European capitals—Spain, Britain, Germany, France, and Italy—hoping to enlist the cooperation of their governments to support his mission of mediation. On September 19, following a meeting with King Hasan of Morocco, attended by Chadli Bin Jadid, president of Algeria, King Husayn addressed a letter, dated September 22, 1990 to Saddam Husayn, in which, as stated in the Jordanian *White Paper*, he expressed:

the fear felt . . . that beneath the immediate problem between Iraq and Kuwait lay designs on the resources and lands of the Arab, and that the crisis was a trap set for Iraq into which it was in danger of falling. . . . It was made clear to President Saddam that Jordan and other Arab governments could not accept the acquisition of territory by war, not only as a matter of principle, but also because failure to maintain this principle could constitute a dangerous precedent of which Israel would take advantage. Iraq's invasion and annexation of Kuwait could not be tolerated, its reversal would not be a defeat for Iraq, but on the contrary, a source of gain for Iraq, and the Arab world as a whole: The real achievements of the Iraqi nation over two decades would be preserved, attention would be drawn to the need to address the problem of the growing gap between the rich and the poor Arab states . . . [and] show that the Iraq occupation was an act of self-defence against an inflexible position and not just expansionism or a wish for hegemony; it would rectify the wrong, contain the crisis, and pave the way for its resolution.[17]

Saddam's reply to King Husayn's appeal was not very encouraging (September 29, 1990). He agreed with King Husayn's analysis of the background to the crisis, but did not agree with the choices before Iraq. The questions put by the King, said Saddam, should have been addressed to the other party—what did it want from Iraq? Saddam indicated that he would accept an Arab solution as suggested by King Husayn during his visit to Baghdad on August 3. The alternative would be an international conference to consider not only the Gulf crisis, but also other problems. As to the rejection of the acquisition of territory by force, Saddam said, it should be respected as a matter of principle and applied to all cases, not only to Kuwait. In this respect, Saddam argued that he would put the Palestine question before the international community. But he complained that similarities between his case and the Palestinian problem were rejected by the United States and Britain.[18]

King Husayn, however, was not discouraged from his firm belief that a peaceful settlement of the crisis was absolutely necessary in order to avoid destructive consequences to the Arab world. As all attempts to arrange an Arab solution failed, he tried other means—seeking the help of European members of the Coalition, and of the Soviet Union. He tried to plead for the release of foreign nationals held in Iraq since August 1990. Following his visit to Baghdad on December 4, it was announced by the Iraq government that foreign nationals were released. But it was not only King Husayn who appealed to Iraq—Willy Brandt, former chancellor of Germany; Edward Heath, former British prime minister; and Ramsey Clark and Jesse Jackson, two prominent American public figures—also used their influence to plead with Saddam Husayn.

The last important occasion for King Husayn's peaceful efforts was when, following the urging of several countries to give peace a chance before the use of force, he visited London, Bonn, Rome, and several other capitals, and urged for a final effort to avert war. He also warned

Iraq about the consequences of the war. Even after the Coalition War started, he appealed for an end to the destruction caused by air raids not only on Iraqi people but also on Jordanian citizens. Although peaceful efforts had no chance to succeed, King Husayn never accepted the idea that the Gulf war was inevitable.

FORMATION OF THE COALITION UNDER AMERICAN LEADERSHIP

In order to liberate Kuwait from occupation, President Bush sought not only to enlist the cooperation of Western countries, but also the Arab countries, particularly Saudi Arabia and Egypt, in order to demonstrate that the aim of the Coalition was not just another Western imperial intervention in Arab affairs, but an attempt to assist the Arab family against the actions of one of its own members that threatened peace and security.

Following his talks with Thatcher at Aspen, Bush had already started to arrange the formation of an international coalition composed essentially of Western powers. Through his initial contacts with King Fahd of Saudi Arabia, he learned that although King Fahd was completely outraged by Saddam's action, he showed no interest in participating in a military action, and in Bush's talks with King Husayn and President Mubarak, it appeared they also preferred to resolve the crisis through Arab mediation. After his return to Washington, Bush had several conversations with European allies who promised cooperation to resolve the crisis. They suggested enlisting the participation of leading Arab countries in order to make it clear that the liberation of Kuwait would not be construed as Western intervention in Arab affairs but a "collective measure" by a "coalition," in which the Arab countries would play an important role in carrying it out.

It was also suggested that a mission to Saudi Arabia should be sent to offer support against possible attack by Iraq. Prince Bander, Saudi Arabian ambassador in Washington, was invited to the White House to discuss the subject as to how King Fahd might be persuaded to cooperate in the event of an attack by Iraq. Upon talking with Bandar, Bush assured him that he was serious about his plan and gave his "word of honor" that he was determined to act. Prince Bander left Washington for Riyad on August 4, two days ahead of the Cheney mission, to acquaint King Fahd with the realities of the American position—particularly Bush's own ideas and plans—to assist the King in deciding the role Saudi Arabia might take in the unfolding drama of the liberation of Kuwait.[19]

It is a Saudi tradition that whenever an important matter of policy is facing the country, the top Saudi members of the family meet in camera to express their views from both the perspective of the security of the country as a whole and the family's own perspective with regard to the stability of the regime. It seems that some of the senior members of the family stressed the traditional policy that no foreign power should be allowed to entertain military presence in the country while most of the younger members pointed out that Saddam Husayn's invasion of Kuwait, if it were not reversed, would be a danger to the security of the country as a whole. No formal act is ordinarily taken, but the King is vested with the privilege to make decisions on the basis of consensus. If Saudi Arabia were to take a constructive step to maintain security and stability, a force composed of Arab and foreign brigades was deemed necessary, provided it was invited at the pleasure of Saudi Government and agreed to leave after it had fulfilled the mission. When Cheney arrived in Jidda and presented a plan for the deployment of a defensive force, the King had already been mentally prepared to accept the offer, but he wanted to have at his disposal all the details about the plan before a formal invitation had been issued.

After the meeting, Cheney called Bush to inform him that King Fahd had formally invited the United States to dispatch a defensive force to his country. On his way back, Bush asked Cheney to stop in Egypt and Morocco to acquaint President Mubarak and King Hasan with his mission to Saudi Arabia and to seek their participation in the defence of that country after an invitation had been issued to them from King Fahd. Syria was also invited to participate, but King Husayn, who insisted that the crisis might be resolved by peaceful means, took no part in the forthcoming military operations in the Gulf.

Toward the end of November, when Saddam Husayn had shown no sign that Iraq would withdraw from Kuwait, the Security Council adopted Resolution 678 which allowed the use of force to compel Iraq to withdraw from Kuwait. From the time Resolution 678 (November 29, 1990) was adopted to the middle of January 1991, Iraq was given "a pause," as stated in the Resolution, to consider that unless it decided to voluntarily withdraw from Kuwait the Coalition would drive it out by force. As war was imminent, it was contemplated that in early 1991 the weather would be more suitable than any other time to conduct military operations in the region. It was hoped that the Coalition War might accomplish its task before the Muslim holy month of Ramadan, in which Muslims are prohibited from fighting. Meanwhile, the Coalition had already begun to pursue aims beyond the defence of Arabia. In retrospect, those aims may be summed up as follows: 1) concentration of the Coalition forces in Saudi Arabia; 2) the liberation of Kuwait; 3) destruction of Iraq's chemical, biological, nuclear, and other weaponry beyond domestic needs; 4) release of all prisoners of war; 5) reparations for damages done by Iraq's invasion of Kuwait; and 6) replacement of Saddam's regime by another friendly to the West.

The United States and Britain were the two principal powers that provided the military forces necessary to achieve the objectives of the

Gulf war. They were joined by France with a considerably small military force, as it did not want to be the only Western democracy that did not join the Coalition. Most of the Arab countries dispatched only symbolic forces, but the Saudi Army took an active part in the military operations. Moreover, Saudi Arabia, as the host country, extended all the facilities necessary for the Coalition force to perform its task from the moment it set feet in the country until its departure.[20]

Chapter 9

The Role of the United Nations

The role of the United Nations in the Gulf crisis is unique. Its resolutions and the celerity with which they were adopted had never been witnessed before. For no sooner had Iraq started to invade Kuwait on August 2, 1990, than the Security Council met on the same day and adopted its first mandatory resolution against Iraq demanding withdrawal from Kuwait "immediately and unconditionally" on the basis of an appeal by the ruler of Kuwait, Shaykh Jabir, and his prime minister, Shaykh Sa'd, who had fled the country to Saudi Arabia. In the meantime, President Bush, on the strength of the request of the Kuwaiti ambassador to the United States, instructed the State Department to bring the crisis before the Security Council.

The American delegation to the United Nations at once became very active. Upon its initiative, several members of the Security Council met informally, and a draft resolution, prepared in consultation with Kuwait's representative to the United Nations, was sponsored by the United States, the United Kingdom, France, and several other members, and formally submitted to the president of the Security Council. The representatives of Kuwait and Iraq to the United Nations, although not members of the security council, were invited to participate in the discussion when the Council met on the evening of August 2, 1990.

Muhammad Abu al-Hasan, representative of Kuwait, was the first to address the Council. After a passionate speech in Arabic, he presented his country's case as follows:

> We ask the Security Council to put an immediate halt to the invasion and to exercise its duty to ensure, by every means available, that Iraq withdraw immediately and unconditionally to the international boundaries that existed before the invasion. Kuwait appeals to and urges the Council in the

name of justice and the sovereignty of the United Nations to adopt a
resolution in conformity with the Charter and with international laws and
norms.[1]

The representative of Iraq, Sabah Qudrat, a member of the Iraqi
Mission to the United Nations ('Abd al-Amir al-Anbari, chief of the
mission, was then on leave), presented his government's case. After a
few words in Arabic, he read a statement which he had just received
from Iraq:

> First, the events taking place in Kuwait are internal matters which have
> no relation to Iraq.
>
> Secondly, the Free Provisional Government of Kuwait requested my gov-
> ernment to assist it to establish security and order so that Kuwaitis would
> not have to suffer. My Government decided to provide the assistance
> solely on that basis.
>
> Thirdly, the Iraqi government energetically states that Iraq is pursuing
> no goal or objective in Kuwait and desires cordial and good-neighborly
> relations with Kuwait.
>
> Fourthly, it is the Kuwaitis themselves who in the final analysis will deter-
> mine their future. The Iraqi forces will withdraw as soon as order has
> been restored. This was the request made by the First Free Provisional
> Government of Kuwait. We hope that it will take no more than a few
> days, or at least a few weeks.
>
> Fifthly, there are reports that the previous Kuwaiti government has been
> overthrown and that there is now a new Government. Hence, the person
> in the seat of Kuwait here represents no one, and his statement lacks
> credence.
>
> Sixthly, my Government rejects the flagrant intervention by the United
> States of America in these events. This intervention is further evidence
> of the coordination and collusion between the United States Government
> and the previous Government of Kuwait.
>
> My country's Government hopes that order will be swiftly restored in
> Kuwait and that the Kuwaitis themselves will decide upon their future,
> free from any outside intervention.[2]

Qudrat's statement was not taken at its face value. His reference to
the "Free Provisional Government of Kuwait," which seems to have
been announced after the invasion of Kuwait, elicited some sarcastic
remarks from Pickering, the American representative, and Tickell, the
British representative. Had 'Abd al-Amir al-Anbari, an experienced law-
yer-diplomat, not been on leave, he would probably have made a more
specious statement on behalf of his country.

At the outset, however, the attitude of the Council was not on the
whole hostile toward Iraq. Indeed, several members expressed friendly
feelings toward both Iraq and Kuwait, but they deplored the "use of
force." Pickering, the American representative, declared that his gov-

ernment "will stand shoulder to shoulder with Kuwait."[3] Other representatives—the French, the British, and the Soviet—in line with the American position, condemned Iraq's resort to force in principle, but they stressed the need for peaceful means of settlement and welcomed the mediation which the Arab states had offered. No statement by any representative seemed to imply that there was any intention to call for sanctions, economic or otherwise, as the dispute was essentially regional, and the Arab League was expected to resolve it.

Invoking Articles 39 and 40 of the U.N. Charter, the Security Council passed Resolution 660 (1990) by virtue of which it: 1) condemned Iraq's invasion of Kuwait; 2) demanded that Iraq withdraw "immediately and unconditionally" all its forces to the positions in which they were located on August 1, 1990; and 3) called upon Iraq and Kuwait to "begin immediately intensive negotiations" to settle their differences. This resolution passed with no dissent save Yaman's abstention, as its representative had received no instructions from his government; he decided that he was not prepared to participate in the voting. Thus the votes in favor were fourteen out of fifteen.

With regard to the longstanding Iraq-Kuwait differences—frontier and oil-price disputes and others—the Security Council considered them regional disputes which could be resolved either by direct negotiations or through the Arab League. In its first meeting, the Security Council had on the whole handled the matter fairly well, and there were reasonable expectations that the dispute might soon be resolved by peaceful means.

THE SECURITY COUNCIL RESOLUTION 661: THE ECONOMIC SANCTIONS

Hardly four days later, before even giving Iraq and other Arab countries long enough time to consider ways and means for settling the crisis peacefully, the Security Council met again (August 6, 1990) to impose economic sanctions on Iraq under Chapter VII of the U.N. Charter. Despite the attempts of several Arab leaders, King Husayn of Jordan and others, who urged settling the crisis as an Arab question, the leading permanent members of the Security Council demanded settlement of the crisis through the United Nations on the grounds that it was not merely an Arab but also an international issue. To deal with the Gulf crisis as an international case before first giving the Arab League an opportunity to resolve it seemed inconsistent with the U.N. Charter which empowered regional organizations to deal with all "such matters as are appropriate for regional actions" (Article 52).[4]

The draft Resolution 661 (1990), imposing economic sanctions on Iraq, was sharply criticized by several members of the Security Council, in contrast to the response to Resolution 660, which had been endorsed by all save one, the Yaman representative for lack of instructions from his government. Moreover, while the Council's attitude was on the whole friendly to Iraq in its consideration of Resolution 660, its attitude in the adoption of Resolution 661 had completely changed four days later. The Council's hostile attitude was shown by the celerity with which it had adopted Resolution 661, due to the pressure which the American delegation exercised on other delegations. In the drafting of the Resolution, the American delegation had consulted only the five permanent members of the Council and few other members, including the Kuwaiti but not the Iraqi delegation (neither were permanent members, but they were invited to attend the Council's meetings to participate in its consideration of resolutions affecting their countries), and the draft Resolution 661 was distributed among other delegations on the same day it was submitted to the Council shortly before it held its meeting. Objections to these procedures and other critical remarks were voiced by the Iraqi representative as well as by others who voted against Resolution 661. Quotations from the principal speakers, for and against Resolution 661, may perhaps demonstrate the depth of the controversy as to how the Security Council was dealing with the Gulf crisis.

Muhammad Abu al-Hasan, the Kuwaiti representative, and ʿAbd al-Amir al-Anbari, the representative of Iraq, were the first to present the views of their countries about Resolution 661. Abu al-Hasan requested approval of the draft Resolution on the grounds that "no one [in Kuwait] has agreed to cooperate with the usurper and aggressor," and that Iraq had refused to withdraw its troops, as required under the U.N. Resolution 660. He went on to explain:

> We reached the conclusion that Iraq was not committed to Resolution 660 (1990), either in form or content. Thus it is your turn, your role, your historic responsibility to prove to the whole world that the security of nations, whether large or small, is not a commodity that can be bought or sold or used for terrorism or threats. By taking a position vis-a-vis this draft resolution which is before us now, you are reaching a historic shift in the work of the Security Council and demonstrating its influence in ensuring that the will of the international community is exerted through the imposition of sweeping sanctions—an overall embargo against a country that has refused the will of the international community.[5]

In reply, ʿAbd al-Amir al-Anbari, the Iraqi representative, sought in vain to point out that the new draft resolution contradicted Resolution 660. He said:

> On August 3 my government announced that it intended to start the withdrawal of its forces on August 5. My Government in fact started to withdraw its troops at 8 o'clock local time . . . [T]he draft resolution that has been submitted does not help at all to resolve the crisis, nor does it help . . . to withdraw.

> With all due respect for the Council . . . I cannot fail to stress one fact that is known to everyone: This draft resolution was prepared by a single state. Pressure was exerted on all the other states to go along with it. That makes the draft resolution null and void, because anything imposed by force and threat is not legitimate under the principles of the Charter.[6]

Most members, however, were not prepared to listen to Anbari's appeal, perhaps mainly because no sufficient material evidence was provided by Iraq to persuade the leading members of the Security Council that Iraq had indeed the intention to withdraw. Anbari insisted that the manner in which the draft resolution was drawn could not be conducive to quick withdrawal of the Iraqi forces.

The American position, as stated by Pickering, is as follows:

> Iraq, through its actions has rejected United Nations Security Council's Resolution 660 (1990). . . . Its response to the world community has been scorn. The United Nations Security Council states unequivocally today that we will use the means available to us provided in Chapter VII of the United Nations Charter to give effect to United Nations Security Council resolution 660 (1990), which we adopted on August 2. Iraq must learn that its disregard for international law will have crippling political and economic costs, including, but not limited to, arms cut-offs. Our concerted resolution will demonstrate that the international community does not—and will not—accept Baghdad's preference for the use of force, coercion, and intimidation.[7]

Other permanent members of the Security Council—the United Kingdom, the Soviet Union, France, and China—declared that they would vote in favor of the draft Resolution, each giving its own rationale. While the French and the Chinese representatives in line with the American representative, supported the draft resolution in principle, they did not indicate that the draft Resolution should apply only to economic sanctions, contrary to the American representative's claim that it included all the means provided under Chapter VII of the U.N. Charter. It thus devolved on the British representative to clarify the matter. He stated that two points were important to bear in mind about the draft Resolution:

> The first is that the draft resolution will remain in effect only so long as Resolution 660 (1990) is not complied with. Secondly, economic sanctions should not be regarded as a prelude to anything else. Here I obviously refer to military action. Rather, economic sanctions are designed to avoid the circumstances in which military action might otherwise arise.[8]

The Soviet representative, Lozinsky, instructed by his government to vote for the draft Resolution despite the fact that the Soviet Union was an ally of Iraq, must have had a difficult task to justify his government's decision. In his own words, Lozinski said:

> The decision to vote in the Security Council today to support this draft Resolution on sanction was a very complicated matter for the Soviet Union. It was a difficult decision, because the draft Resolution directly affect a whole set of relationships between us and Iraq that have been developing over many years now. We value the relations of cooperation with Iraq. . . . We could not, however, fail to make a principled evaluation of what had occurred. Neither our principles nor the new political thinking allow us to use double standards here. . . . [W]e therefore have supported the coordinated action which the international community has been forced to take by the situation that has developed. . . . [9]

While critical remarks about "hardships" imposed by the draft resolution were made by several members, it was denounced by only two representatives—'Abd-Allah al-Ashtal, representative of Yaman, and Alacon de Quesada, representative of Cuba. Al-Ashtal warned that "the draft resolution . . . will not be a pretext for intervention in the area," and insisted that his country would like to continue its efforts for peaceful settlement. "Therefore," al-Ashtal concluded, "we will not adopt any attitude at this meeting that would negatively affect the efforts undertaken by the Republic of Yaman to find a solution to the conflict."[10]

A more devastating statement against the draft Resolution came from de Quesada, the Cuban representative. In agreement with Yaman's representative, he noted that the draft Resolution might "complicate the situation even more at a time when Iraq has begun withdrawing its troops. . . . [T]he draft would also impede the current actions and efforts of the Arab states to arrive at a solution." As de Quesada had found that the text of the draft Resolution was originally received by all of the Security Council in a version almost identical to the one that was delivered to them by the American delegation on Friday, August 3, he made a harsh attack against the United States on the grounds that:

> The plan to impose sanctions on Iraq actually existed before we entered this new phase of Security Council deliberations, at a time when no one even knew about the statement made by the Iraqi government, also on August 3, to the effect that it was going to commence the withdrawal of its troops from Kuwait.[11]

Most members of the Security Council, however, had already made up their minds to vote in favor of the draft Resolution. Thus the possibility of Iraq's withdrawal, to which the Iraqi and Cuban representatives referred, was not taken seriously. Nor was the appeal by Yaman to give the Arabs an opportunity peacefully to settle the dispute listened to. A majority of thirteen members voted in favor of Resolution 661 (1990) which called, on "all states," to impose economic sanctions on Iraq. Yaman and Cuba abstained.

THE ANNEXATION OF KUWAIT

On August 9, 1990, hardly a week after the occupation of Kuwait, Iraq suddenly declared that it had annexed Kuwait to become the nineteenth province of the country. No sooner had the news reached the Security Council than it met on the same day and adopted Resolution 662 by virtue of which it was declared that the "annexation of Kuwait by Iraq . . . has no legal validity, and is considered null and void." Iraq was also ordered to "rescind its actions purporting to annex Kuwait."

Three reasons may have prompted Iraq to take such a drastic step: 1) as the Provisional Kuwaiti regime which had been established to replace the Sabah family rule could not muster national support, its head, ʿAla Husayn al-Khafaji, resigned because he was unable to recruit a sufficient number of compatriots to cooperate with him in the governance of the country; 2) The Arab League had failed to provide a face-saving formula which Iraq had requested in order to justify its withdrawal from Kuwait; and 3) As an impending foreign intervention was expected, the Iraq invoked the notion of "Arab unity", to which Arab leaders often resort to enlist Arab cooperation against foreign threats. In his statement, at the Security Council, al-Anbari pointed out that while Iraq had just started to withdraw on August 5, the United States and Britain did not want the "withdrawal to proceed peacefully" and sought by intervention in Arab lands (a reference to the dispatch of American troops to Saudi Arabia) to resolve the crisis by force rather than by peaceful means. He rejected the allegations that Iraq had any hostile intentions against Saudi Arabia, as Britain and the United States claimed.[12]

Upon Iraq's invasion of Kuwait (August 2, 1990), Qudrat, the Iraqi representative, had already stated before the Security Council that the Provisional Government of Kuwait would determine its own future. But before Kuwait had been made a province of Iraq, neither the people nor the Provisional Government of Kuwait were called upon to express their wish about whether they wanted to become a province of Iraq or remain as a separate country. Furthermore, the Kuwaiti representative did not raise the question at the Security Council as to whether the wishes of the Kuwaiti people were expressed on Kuwait's becoming the nineteenth province of Iraq; he only denounced the annexation on the grounds of legitimacy and sovereignty. His reference to the existence of "a genuine struggle . . . waged by the people of Kuwait under occupation" may have been vaguely construed to mean that the people were opposed to annexation. By its annexation of Kuwait, however, Iraq did not seek the support of Kuwait's public opinion, but the support of Iraqi public opinion. As noted earlier, there has always been a widespread Iraqi opinion that Kuwait was part of Iraq. The annexation of Kuwait was thus construed as merely an act to remove the boundary between the two countries which had been imposed by foreign intervention.

IMPLEMENTATION OF THE ECONOMIC SANCTIONS

No sooner had the Security Council passed the resolution to impose mandatory economic sanctions on Iraq than it began to call on all members of the United Nations as well as nonmembers to cooperate in their implementation. The Security Council established a committee to examine the process of implementation and to report periodically on its progress to the Security Council.[13]

The United States was the first U.N. member to take steps to implement the economic sanctions. President Bush issued two executive orders blocking all Iraqi and Kuwaiti government property in the United States and prohibiting all transactions with Iraq. Further Executive Orders prohibited other forms of transactions such as exports to and imports from Iraq as well as prohibiting travel by American citizens to Iraq or by Iraqi citizens to the United States save for official business or journalistic purposes. The United Kingdom and several other members of the European Community followed the lead of the United States.[14]

Several U.N. members, however, especially Jordan and Bulgaria, finding themselves faced with great difficulties in enforcing the sanctions, notified the Security Council that they would like to be allowed certain exceptions in their economic and financial relationships with Iraq. In a letter (August 20, 1990) to the Security Council, Jordan stated that both the geographical location and the economic interdependence between the two countries made it exceedingly difficult to apply most of the economic and financial sanctions. In a memorandum, Jordan indicated that the loss in income from foreign trade (quoting the figure for 1989) were sixty-five million dollars. The loss of export income to Iraq in 1990 was expected to be $200 million. The income from the ʿAqaba Port charges, transportation, and packing activities was estimated to exceed $250 million annually. As all of Jordan's import of oil was from Iraq and Kuwait, Jordan could not afford to shift to new sources without loss of concessionary supplies. Grants to the budget and loss of remittances from Jordanians working in Kuwait who were forced to return home entailed serious losses. Jordan's expected losses from all these sources were estimated to exceed two and a half billion dollars. For these reasons, Jordan felt that its economy would collapse unless arrangements were made to obtain grants, oil with concessionary conditions, and long-term soft loans in order to enable the country to overcome its economic predicament.[15]

In the case of Bulgaria, its economy was based almost exclusively on oil. In a memorandum, it outlined the losses that the country might face as a result of the suspension of its trade with Iraq and Kuwait. On the basis of these estimations, it invoked Article 49 and 50 of the U.N. Charter to discuss with the Security Council possible solutions to the problems arising from the imposition of mandatory sanctions. The Security Council decided to refer the case of Jordan to a committee which would prepare a special report on the subject. This report would then function as a guide in allowing other countries hurt by the embargo to be treated like Jordan.

The committee presented its report on Jordan to the Security Council on August 27, 1990. The Council, having approved the committee's report, referred its recommendations to the Secretary General to "develop methods for the purpose of receiving information from States about the contribution which they have or are preparing to make to alleviate the longer-term hardships confronting Jordan as a result of its application of economic sanctions against Iraq."[16] In the case of Jordan, it took the U.N. Secretary General quite a while before he was able to persuade countries such as Saudi Arabia and the United States to help reduce its dependence on trade with Iraq. Nevertheless, Jordan could not completely stop its trade with Iraq owing to geographical and other considerations—long frontiers, location of desert areas on both sides of the frontiers, and public pressures in favor of assisting Iraq— although some measures were taken to restrict trade and business transactions with Iraq.

NAVAL AND AERIAL INTERDICTION

Under the economic sanction Resolution, the Security Council called upon the whole community of nations to stop all transactions and trade with Iraq. As some of the countries could not enforce the embargo, Iraq continued to trade with them by sea. The United States and Britain warned Iraq that they would search its boats in the Gulf to prevent them from carrying on trade with third party countries by both naval and aerial interdiction. At the NATO meetings in Brussels (August 10 and 13; December 17 and 18, 1990), when the subject of a maritime blockade was discussed and subsequently the use of force under Resolution 678 was adopted, the United States and Britain announced that they had the right to resort to the use of force to prevent trade between Iraq and third-party countries under Article 51 of the U.N. Charter which allows the right of individual and collective self-defence.[17] Indeed, the Kuwaiti government, through its U.N. representative, informed the Security Council in a letter that it had "requested some nations to take military or other steps necessary to ensure the effective and prompt implementation of Security Council resolution 661 (1990)." On the basis of that request, the United States and Britain declared that they had been given the right to defence by the government of Kuwait.

The American and British decisions aroused the protest of both Iraq and other countries. On August 15, 1990, the Libyan representative to the U.N. transmitted a letter from Colonel Muʿammar al-Qadhafi, to the U.N. Secretary General in which it was stated that "an act of aggression under international law" and "a flagrant violation of the Charter of the United Nations" had been committed in the Gulf by some members of the United Nations. For this reason, Qadhafi requested that the Security Council consider the acts of the forces that existed in the Gulf "as a matter of urgency." He also questioned the legality of the existence of American forces in Saudi Arabia. "We believe," he maintained, "that it threatens security in the region and that the only possible action is the replacement of American forces with Arab League forces to defend the Kingdom of Saudi Arabia." Qadhafi, in reference to a statement made by the U.N. Secretary General, said that a blockade in the implementation of Article 51 of the Charter should be under the name of the United Nations. With regard to Article 51, Qadhafi said:

> We wish to reaffirm clearly that there is absolutely no justification for invoking Article 51 of the Charter in the current situation, given that that Article is aimed only at repulsing an act of aggression against the territory of the state calling for the implementation of that Article. The state in the Gulf, however, is not being attacked by Iraq or by any other state.[18]

In the meantime, the Iraqi representative to the United Nations transmitted two letters from his government (August 19 and 20, 1990) in which Iraq complained that two tankers *Baba Kurkur* and *al-Karama* were subjected to harassment by British and American military aircrafts on their way to the Gulf. In the Gulf, off the port of Fujayra, *al-Karama* tanker was "requested information on its port of departure, port of registration, and port of destination." Later, the tanker was asked the same questions by an American warship which continued to trace the tanker. "The Iraqi government," the letter added, "objects strongly to the autocratic and unlawful acts of piracy and aggression carried out by the United States and British forces against Iraq." Iraq called on the United Nations to adopt appropriate measures to prevent such acts.

Because of the dubious legal grounds on which the interdiction was applied, the British foreign secretary, Douglas Hurd, announced (August 24, 1990), that the British government was "working very hard to get a fresh [U.N.] resolution" in order to provide the "legality of enforcing the blockade." Hurd stated that he had received information that an Iraqi tanker, *ʿAin-zala*, discharged oil at the refinery in ʿAdan, a port in south Yaman, on August 21.[19] In addition to Iraq's denouncing the harassment of the tanker, Colonel Qadhafi dispatched to the U.N. secretary general a letter (August 17, 1990) in which he protested

against the American orders to inspect shipping in the Gulf and neighboring areas. "The orders," he insisted, "should be issued by the Security Council, not by the United States."[20] On the strength of the
information provided by the British Foreign Secretary and the complaints of Iraq and Libya, it was deemed necessary to call a meeting of
the Security Council to consider the matter. Before such a meeting was
held, the secretary general of the United Nations, Perez de Cuellar,
paid a visit to the Middle East.

DE CUELLAR'S MISSION TO THE MIDDLE EAST

The mission of the U.N. secretary general to the Middle East was
prompted not only by a need to report on the implementation of the
embargo, but also by criticism of Iraq's refusal to allow foreign nationals to leave the country in violation of human rights and privileges. His
mission was also intended to include discussion of the Gulf crisis with
Arab leaders in order to resolve the crisis by peaceful means.

It was arranged that de Cuellar would meet Tariq 'Aziz, deputy
prime minister of Iraq, in 'Amman, Jordan. He met with 'Aziz twice. In
the first meeting (August 31, 1990), he discussed all questions relating
to Iraq's occupation of Kuwait—the U.N. resolutions demanding Iraq's
withdrawal, the release of foreign nationals, and several other matters—
but no conclusive agreements were reached. On the question of withdrawal, 'Aziz seems to have explained in detail Iraq's territorial claims
and its security requirements, and insisted that Iraq was not prepared
to withdraw before some of those problems were resolved. De Cuellar
was thus left with the impression that Iraq, at least at that stage, would
not withdraw from Kuwait. At a press conference, when 'Aziz was asked
by a press reporter about withdrawal, he replied: "You cannot resolve
such a situation by a magical solution. . . . We need patience, we need
some degree of quiet diplomacy." As to foreign nationals, 'Aziz told de
Cuellar that Iraq was ready to release them provided the United
Nations would guarantee that Iraq would not be attacked by Western
military forces. In his press conference, de Cuellar told reporters that
he "considered Iraq's gesture to allow women and children to leave
. . . an important step forward," but he hoped it would "be followed
by other decisions which will allow all foreigners to leave the area."[21]

In their second meeting (September 1, 1990), 'Aziz and de Cuellar
resumed their conversation about the Gulf crisis and Iraq's withdrawal.
To his great disappointment, de Cuellar received no positive reply
about Iraq's compliance with the Security Council resolutions. In his
answer to reporters, 'Aziz said that his talk with de Cuellar was "useful"
and he was "open-minded." "I am always at his disposal," he added,
"and we would like to continue our contacts in the future, in order to

seek and to explore the ways and means to bring about peace, justice, and stability to the region as a whole."

Before he left, de Cuellar did not disguise his disappointment that Iraq had given no hint about withdrawing from Kuwait. When he first met with ʿAziz, de Cuellar told press reporters his purpose was to persuade Iraq to accept the Security Council resolutions that demanded withdrawal from Kuwait. "As I leave ʿAmman," he added "I must acknowledge a certain disappointment . . . that real progress had [not] been made." De Cuellar, however, admitted, as ʿAziz had told him, that there has been a "double standard" in American willingness to deploy military forces to drive Iraq out of Kuwait while failing to use its power to force Israel into acceptance of United Nations resolutions calling for withdrawal from occupied Arab lands. "I totally agree, as I had said before," de Cuellar said in a reply to one reporter's question, "that all resolutions of the Security Council should be implemented." He also said that the Kuwait crisis was in part an "outgrowth of Arab frustrations over Israel." In his report to the Security Council, de Cuellar said that he relayed all that he had learned from his trip, but still the members of the Council insisted that before negotiations were to proceed to resolve the crisis, Iraq must first withdraw from Kuwait.[22]

PROPOSALS FOR PEACEFUL SETTLEMENT BY MEMBERS OF THE SECURITY COUNCIL

While the secretary general of the United Nations was in the Middle East, other attempts by European leaders to resolve the Gulf crisis were made by at least two permanent members of the Security Council: France and the Soviet Union. The French and Soviet initiatives were made with prior consultations with Arab leaders, in particular with King Husayn of Jordan and King Hasan of Morocco.

On the occasion of the forty-fifth United Nations General Assembly session, President François Mitterand delivered a speech on September 24, 1990, in which he sought to resolve the Gulf crisis in a package with the Lebanese and the Arab-Israeli problems, as suggested by Saddam Husayn in his declaration of August 12, 1990, and to establish a broader "dialogue" to enable peace and security in the Middle East. In the absence of an Arab solution, he said, it would be his hope that Western diplomacy might prevail over confrontation.[23]

Mitterand proposed several steps to be taken to resolve the crisis: 1) Iraq's withdrawal from Kuwait and the release of hostages; 2) the international community guaranteeing the withdrawal of its military forces from the region, the restoration of Kuwait's sovereignty, and "exercise of the democratic will of the Kuwaiti people"; and 3) "We must replace confrontation in the Middle East with the dynamics of good-neighborliness and security and peace for each and every country." In this respect, he said, he had in mind: a) to resolve the Lebanese problem by its regaining full sovereignty over its territory which was still occupied by foreign troops and divided by opposing forces; b) to allow the Palestinians to have their homeland and to create a state of their own choice; c) to allow Israel, living in constant insecurity, to have peace and security in its relationship with neighbors provided that every agreement reached between Israel and its neighbors would be approved by the United Nations; and d) to achieve the reduction of armaments in the region, cooperation among all countries from Iran to Morocco, and the stability and prosperity in the region.

The response to Mitterand's proposals varied from complete rejection to silence, especially his reference to the exercise of the "democratic will of the Kuwaiti people," which was considered cynically intended to undermine the legitimate ruling Sabah family. It was rejected in particular by Bush who insisted on "complete, unconditional, and immediate withdrawal" from Kuwait. Mitterand left New York on the day after his speech and embarked on a trip to the Gulf region to talk with Arab leaders about his proposals for a settlement of the Gulf crisis by peaceful means. Two days after Mitterand made his speech, Shaykh Jabir, the deposed Amir of Kuwait, made a speech before the General Assembly in which he tearfully appealed to the community of nations to put an end to the occupation of his country by Iraq.[24]

With regard to the Soviet Union, an ally of Iraq, its leadership had not yet definitely decided to let Iraq down. There were, it seemed, differences of opinion between the civil and military leaders. The military maintained that Iraq, an ally, had been supplied with the best Soviet weaponry and with Soviet military advisers who supported Iraq during its war with Iran, and had continued to do so after Iraq had invaded Kuwait. For this reason, they urged, Iraq should be saved from a military confrontation with the West. The civilian leaders held that Iraq had created a dilemma for them. As Gorbachev was counting on Western support for his political and economic reform plans, Iraq's confrontation with the West seemed quite embarrassing to him. True, in its treaty with the Soviet Union, Iraq was entitled to purchase Soviet military equipment and to seek the advice of military experts. But Iraq, which was expected under the treaty of alliance to consult with the Soviets on all matters of foreign policy, did not even inform the Soviet leadership about its plan to invade Kuwait. For this reason, the Soviet representative was instructed to vote with other permanent members of the Security Council in favor of all the sanctions against Iraq save the one permitting the use of force, concerning which the Soviet representative abstained from voting.[25]

When, however, Mitterand proposed negotiations to resolve the Gulf crisis including the Arab-Israeli conflict (concerning which the Soviets had always sought to participate in favor of the Arabs), Gorbachev contemplated that the time had come to offer Soviet good offices to Iraq in response to the Soviet military demand. Early in October, 1990, Yevgeny Primakov (a specialist in Arab affairs and a member of Gorbachev's Presidential Council) was sent on a mission to persuade the Iraqi leadership to withdraw from Kuwait as a step to be followed by negotiations to resolve the Gulf crisis. The mission, though broad in its objectives, was in fact most specifically intended to urge Iraq to withdraw from Kuwait and to arrange for the evacuation of Soviet citizens from Iraq.

Upon his arrival at ʿAmman, Jordan (October 3, 1990), Primakov met with King Husayn and handed him a letter from Gorbachev which stated, as he told Jordanians over television, that the Soviet leadership was seeking possibilities for "a peaceful and political settlement." Coinciding with Primakov's visit to ʿAmman, Taha Ramadan, deputy premier, who represented hardliners in the Iraqi leadership, denied that Iraq would withdraw from Kuwait.

From ʿAmman, Primakov went to Baghdad (October 4, 1990). He told reporters that his purpose was to achieve a "very serious exchange of views." He talked with Tariq ʿAziz and delivered a letter from Gorbachev to Saddam Husayn. The content of the letter was not disclosed, but the purpose, Primakov said, was "to find a political solution to prevent slipping into a military course" in the Gulf. As Saddam Husayn was not prepared to withdraw without a face-saving promise that he would realize some gain, the Primakov mission was not expected to succeed. Nevertheless, Gorbachev continued to talk about peaceful means of settlement with several Arab leaders who visited Moscow. He told Qays al-Zuwawi, vice premier of ʿUman, that he had no plans to send troops to the Gulf as "there [were] already more than enough troops there." As Primakov returned empty-handed, the Security Council was bound to adopt further resolutions to tighten the sanctions against Iraq.[26]

SECURITY COUNCIL RESOLUTIONS ON HUMAN RIGHTS AND OTHER RELATED ISSUES

Long before de Cuellar had visited the Middle East in August, 1990 to deal with the condition of hostages, complaints about the condition of foreign missions and the situation of foreign nationals (hostages) in Iraq and Kuwait had been brought to the attention of the Security Council. On September 14, 1990, a draft Resolution on human rights, specifically dealing with foreign nationals, was adopted as Resolution 666 (1990) by a majority of thirteen members. The purpose of this Resolution was to assist the foreign nationals (hostages) in Iraq in receiving food and medicine which the Iraqi government had not made available to them.

The Yaman representative, al-Ashtal, objected to Resolution 666, because it provided means to insure distribution of food and medicine to foreign nationals without regard to the Iraqi people who were deprived of adequate food, mainly because of the harsh economic sanctions that had so tightly been applied. The Cuban representative, de Quesada, called the Council's attention to the complaints which he and other members had received about thousands of people reaching virtually the starvation level in Iraq and Kuwait.[27]

In reply, Pickering, the American representative, attributed the complaints of 100,000 starving Indians, Sri Lankans, and Filipinos to the "deliberate policy of Iraq . . . to feed first its military, . . . [which created] conditions of famine for foreign nationals trapped in Kuwait."[28] The problem, however, as other Security Council members realized, was more complicated, owing to internal and external conditions—rising prices, inefficiency in the distribution of food and medicine, and restrictions on imports from abroad—which created confusion that hit foreign workers in Iraq and Kuwait hard.

Toward the end of September, 1990, the Security Council held several meetings to consider a number of other pending issues. One of the Resolutions dealt with de Cuellar's report on his trip to the Middle East in which he pointed out that Iraq was not prepared to withdraw under the conditions stated in the Security Council Resolutions. The representative of Yaman, al-Dali, warned that if war broke out, it would spread to other regions and would not be confined to the Gulf. He proposed to the Council: "to take positive measures in order to contribute positively to a peaceful resolution of this crisis that would lead to the withdrawal of Iraq from Kuwait so that the Resolutions adopted by the Council would not be used as a justification and pretext for war." He proposed the submission of a draft Resolution calling on all parties to intensify efforts in exploring peaceful means to resolve the Gulf crisis. But the Yaman and Cuban efforts did not materialize, as no significant support from other members of the Security Council was forthcoming.

On October 29, 1990, the Security Council held a meeting to consider further possibilities for resolving the Gulf crisis, as neither de Cuellar nor the Primakov missions had succeeded in persuading Iraq to withdraw from Kuwait. The Iraqi representative, 'Abd al-Amir al-Anbari, sought in a solemn critique to underscore the causes for the failure of the Security Council to resolve the Gulf crisis.

First, al-Anbari argued that while the Security Council, under Article 24 of the Charter, bears the responsibility for the maintenance of international peace and security, its members were in the meantime expected to act "in consonance with the purposes and principles of the United Nations." The primary purposes of the United Nations, he said, are not only to maintain peace and security, but also to bring about peace with justice. Yet the Security Council, al-Anbari pointed out, had not hesitated to adopt Resolutions to use force under Chapter

VII of the Charter that threatened peace and security. Moreover, he added, the Council had not deemed it appropriate to consult with Iraq on any Resolution it adopted since August 2, 1990, despite the fact that the resolutions concerned Iraq and affected its independence, sovereignty, and national security. "In so doing," he said, "the Council has ignored its obligations under the Charter to observe the principles of justice and International Law." The Security Council Resolutions, in his words, "were adopted in a form that was akin to an ultimatum calling for capitulations, rather than a form that urged peace."

Second, al-Anbari said, the Security Council Resolutions were adopted under pressure. For example, Resolution 661 (1990), which imposed economic sanctions, was adopted only three days after the adoption of Resolution 660 (1990), in order to "allow the United States to ensure cover for its acts of aggression against Iraq." "It does not," he held, "allow a blockade of Iraq." The Iraq government considered the Resolution unjust and declared that it was contrary to the U.N. Charter. "The naval blockade has led to a situation of anarchy and piracy." For example, he said, one Iraqi vessel, the *Tadmur*, was searched three times; even the foodstuffs on board for the sustenance of the vessel's crew were seized.

Third, the use of force is prohibited under the Charter save in self-defence. This right, however, whether to use force in individual or collective self-defence, is subject to a time limit specified by Article 51. Under this article, the right of self-defence is authorized until such time as the Security Council has seized control of the situation. Until the conflict is resolved, said Anbari, no state—whether the United States or any other—has the right to use force. Nevertheless, the United States dispatched forces to the region while the Security Council was still seized of the situation.[29]

Several jurists have disagreed about the right to use force beyond reasons of self-defence under Article 51 of the U.N. Charter. For example, J.N. Moore, in support of the force under Article 51, argues that there were "two sufficient and independent legal bases for coalition nations to have assisted Kuwait in resisting and ending the illegal Iraqi aggression against Kuwait and in restoring the international rule of law." First, he cites the Security Council authorization under Resolution 678 (1990), pursuant to Chapter VII, for the use of "all necessary means" by U.N. members to implement Resolution 660 (1990) and to reestablish peace and security in the area. Second, he argued that the United States and other members of the United Nations were requested (August 12, 1990) by the government of Kuwait to assist it to exercise the right of individual and collective defence under Article 51. Abram Chayes, however, maintains that once the Security Council passes Resolutions on any crisis, it automatically "has taken measures necessary to maintain international peace and security." Anbari's and Chayes's interpretation of the clause "until the Security Council has taken the measures necessary to maintain peace and security'' seems to correspond correctly to the meaning implied under Article 51. Because of the differing views expressed about the interpretation of Article 51, an advisory opinion of the International Court of Justice should have been sought on the matter.[30]

In the meantime, several members of the Security Council had been arguing that peaceful means were ineffective and urging the use of force. The American and the British governments were concerned that time was in favor of Iraq, presumably because if differences were to develop among the permanent members of the Security Council, it would be exceedingly difficult to adopt further mandatory Resolutions. On September 24, 1990, when Mitterand offered his proposals for peaceful settlement of the Gulf crisis and Gorbachev sent Primakov to Baghdad, the American and British governments became restive about the steps taken by the French and Soviet governments lest they persuade other Coalition powers to accept settlement of the Gulf crisis on terms agreeable to Saddam Husayn. Thus when Bush met with Gorbachev in Helsinki (September 29, 1990) he raised the question of the need for cooperation to force Saddam to withdraw from Kuwait. Gorbachev assured Bush that the Soviet Union was committed to all the U.N. Resolutions concerning the Gulf crisis. Early in November 1990, it will be recalled, Baker visited most of the Coalition countries to impress them with the need to use force as economic sanctions were inadequate to compel Saddam to withdraw.

SECURITY COUNCIL RESOLUTION 678 (1990): THE USE OF FORCE

Before the end of November, consensus seemed to have been reached among the permanent members of the Security Council that the time had come to use force, as Iraq had shown no sign that it would comply with the Security Council Resolutions to withdraw from Kuwait. During that month, it was the turn of the American representative to chair the meetings of the Security Council, as the rule requires the rotation of the chair (in alphabetical order) on a monthly basis. A draft Resolution 678 (1990) sponsored by the United States, United Kingdom, the Soviet Union, and Canada, was ready before the Security Council for its meeting on November 29, 1990. The American secretary of state, James A. Baker, decided to lead the American delegation and chair the meeting. The U.N. secretary general issued an invitation to the Foreign Ministers of the countries represented in the Security Council to attend that historic meeting. The foreign ministers who attended were (in alphabetical order): Canada, China, Colombia, Cuba, Ethiopia, Finland, France, Malaysia, Romania, the Soviet Union, the United Kingdom, the United States, and Zaire. Two countries that were members—Côte d'Ivoire and Yaman—were represented by their chiefs of mission. The foreign ministers of Iraq and Kuwait were also invited, while the latter was represented by Shaykh Sabah al-Ahmad, Kuwait foreign minister; the former was represented by al-Anbari, chief of the Iraqi mission, as the Iraqi foreign minister, Tariq 'Aziz could not attend. (He had requested permission to travel by an official plane for security reasons, but permission for his plane was denied, and he was informed that he could travel only on a commercial plane.)

In his opening speech, welcoming the foreign ministers of 12 countries, Baker prefaced his speech with a quotation from the address of a former head of state delivered in Geneva fifty-five years earlier, as follows: "There is no precedent for people being the victim of such injustice and of being at present threatened by abandonment to an aggressor . . . [and] barbarous means—[were] used against innocent human beings. . . ."

> Those words, [said Baker], I think, could well have come from the Emir of Kuwait, but they do not. They were spoken in 1936, not in 1990. They come from Haile Selassie, the leader of Ethiopia, a man who saw his country conquered and occupied, much like Kuwait has been brutalized since 2 August. Sadly, that appeal to the League of Nations fell ultimately on deaf ears. . . .
>
> History has now given us another chance. . . . We must not let the United Nations go the way of the League of Nations. . . .
>
> Our aim today must be to convince Saddam Hussein that the just and humane demands of this Council and of the international community cannot be ignored. If Iraq does not reverse its course peacefully, then other necessary measures, including the use of force, should be authorized. We must put the choice to Saddam Hussein in unmistakable terms.[31]

The eloquent words of the American secretary of state were addressed to more than one audience. In welcoming the foreign minsters, he reminded them of the seriousness of the Gulf crisis, and raised the question as to whether it should be resolved by violence or by peaceful means. Baker's words were also addressed to another audience—to Iraq—and he warned its president that if he did not heed "the just and humane demands" of the Security Council to resolve the crisis "peacefully" then other measures, including the use of force "should be authorized." Baker's words were also addressed to still another audience—the members of the Security Council—to remind them that their aim should be to achieve "peace and for justice across the globe."

Both Shaykh Sabah and al-Anbari also made statements stressing peace and justice in principle. Shaykh Sabah complained that Kuwait was "the victim of aggression and atrocities"; for this reason it was in favor of the draft Resolution which was "the only avenue to ensure the restoration of our rights."[32] Al-Anbari, however, addressed himself to two subjects. One was legal, to which he had already referred earlier concerning Article 51 which allows the use of force only in self-defence. The other, he said, was political. He referred to the claim against his country that it did not want peace. "This is a tendentious stance," he strongly objected, as his government had already declared that it wanted peace provided it were a "comprehensive, durable, and just process." He ended his statement on this note: "If the United States imposes war on us, then that will be our destiny," but he insisted that "our people will not kneel down," as they will be defending "the right against injustice and tyranny."[33]

Following the representatives of Kuwait and Iraq, several other members of the Security Council made statements indicating the position they would take on the draft Resolution. All of them paid lip service to the need for peaceful settlement and hoped that Iraq will voluntarily withdraw from Kuwait, but the opinion of each varied concerning the vote for the draft Resolution. Two, the representatives of Yaman and Cuba, declared that they would vote against the draft Resolution. The representative of China, while he did not want to cast a veto which would vitiate the Resolution, also did not want to vote in favor of it. In other words, he simply decided to abstain.

Al-Ashtal, representative of Yaman, stated that his government had supported the Security Council Resolutions calling for the withdrawal of Iraq from Kuwait, but insisted that the search for an Arab solution to the problem would have been more agreeable to his country. Since Yaman had already declared that it would seek an Arab peaceful solution, it could not support a draft Resolution that would authorize the use of force. For this reason, Yaman decided to vote against the draft Resolution.[34] Like the representative of Yaman, the Cuban representative stated that his government had condemned the invasion of Kuwait. It had, however, called for peaceful means to achieve the withdrawal of Iraqi forces. For this reason, "Cuba believes that it would not be advisable to adopt a Resolution which is a virtual declaration of war." Like Yaman, Cuba voted against the Resolution.

The British and French representatives stood for peace in principle. "We are gathered here," said Hurd, British foreign secretary, to make a strong bid for peace." But, as Dumas, the French foreign minister, stated: "Although my country is deeply committed to the search for a political settlement, in the final analysis law must prevail." "It is in this spirit," he added, "my country voted in favor of this Resolution."[35] Other non-permanent members of the Security Council followed the lead of Britain, France, and the United States.

The abstention of China in the voting on Resolution 678 raises a query as to whether this Resolution is valid under the U.N. Charter. A close examination of Article 27(3) indicates that the abstention of one permanent member of the Security Council may not fulfill the requirement as stated in the text of the Charter. Article 27(3) reads:

> Decisions of the Security Council on all other matters [other than pro-
> cedural] shall be made by an affirmative vote of nine members including
> concurring votes of the permanent members. . . .

Taken literally, the meaning of the clause "concurring votes of the permanent members" without qualifications means all the five permanent members of China, France, the Soviet Union, the United Kingdom, and the United States as specifically stated under Article 23(1) of the Charter. Nevertheless, the concept of the "veto" to explain that the meaning of "abstention" is not negative in the voting process has been used by the Security Council. But the concept of the veto does not exist under Article 27 to define the meaning of abstention. Unless an amendment of the Charter is made to allow the use of a "veto," the abstention of one or more members means that the concurring votes of all the five permanent members are still necessary for a Resolution to be binding.

THE GENEVA MEETING

Before the adoption of Resolution 678 by the Security Council, a number of suggestions were made inside as well as outside the United Nations that before the use of force was implemented further initiatives to resolve the Gulf crisis by peaceful means should be attempted. True, the U.N. secretary general, President Mitterand, and other personages —Willy Brandt, Edward Heath, and Ramsey Clark—were able to achieve the release of hostages, but no direct attempt was ever made by the Security Council or by the United States to discuss possibilities with the Iraqi government for peaceful means of settlement. Even the visits of King Husayn to Baghdad and his talks with President Saddam Husayn were personal missions and could not be considered a mandate from other Arab countries or the Arab League to induce the Iraqi leadership to withdraw from Kuwait. For this reason, a gesture of goodwill, called "a pause of peace," was inserted in Resolution 678 to give Iraq a last opportunity to make up its mind to withdraw without military confrontation.

As the French and the Soviet governments had in vain tried to persuade Saddam to withdraw, it devolved on the United States to try its hand on behalf of the U.N. to induce Iraq to withdraw. Since the "pause of peace" was roughly for six weeks (from November 29, 1990 to January 15, 1991), it was envisioned that there was still time enough for the foreign minister of Iraq, Tariq 'Aziz, to visit Washington and meet with President Bush, and the American secretary of state, James Baker, to visit Baghdad and meet with Saddam Husayn. As Baker requested his visit to take place before 'Aziz had visited Washington, the

Iraqi leadership became worried that changing the order of the two visits might perhaps mean that the purpose of Baker's mission would be merely confined to delivering an ultimatum to Iraq to withdraw from Kuwait. After an exchange of views between the two countries, Iraq decided to invite Baker to visit Baghdad any time after January 13, two days before the end of the "pause." This arrangement was completely unacceptable to Washington. To resolve the issue, it was decided to cancel the visits to Baghdad and Washington; instead, it was agreed that Baker and 'Aziz will meet in Geneva on January 9. The Geneva meeting, replacing the direct communications between the two presidents through confiders, was taken to fulfill merely a procedural function, to communicate the U.N. Resolution, but not considered a serious attempt to resolve the Gulf crisis by peaceful means.

The two delegations, headed by Baker and 'Aziz, arrived in Geneva on January 9, and the meeting started on the following day at the Intercontinental Hotel. The diplomatic procedures were keenly observed as evident in the calmness and polite exchange of views during the conversation between the heads of the two delegations. Before the meeting started, they accepted an invitation by photographers to shake hands giving the impression that they would talk not as enemies but as gentlemen who had already met before and knew each other quite well.

The meeting took the form of a prolonged dialogue and seemed to proceed smoothly, with each man deferring to the other whenever either one wished to interrupt and reply to a specific point. We are using the Arabic text as our source of information, as it seems fairly accurate (and unofficially it has been confirmed as fairly accurate in high official circles). Instead of giving a brief summary of the dialogue, the principal matters presented by each side will be summed up as follows: 1) the questions raised by Baker, including his reply to 'Aziz's queries; 2) the questions raised by 'Aziz, including his reply to Baker.[36]

Before the conversation started, Baker handed 'Aziz a letter from Bush addressed to Saddam Husayn. 'Aziz opened the letter, at Baker's request, as it was relevant to the subject of discussion. After reading it, 'Aziz returned the letter to Baker; he told him that he could not carry a letter full of threats and written in a language not usually used between heads of state. Baker did not pick up the letter where 'Aziz had left it. Neither the American nor the Iraqi delegation had picked it up after the meeting was over.[37]

Baker asked 'Aziz whether he wanted to speak first. 'Aziz replied that he wished to know what Baker had to say first. In his presentation, Baker reiterated emphatically some of the matters dealt with in Bush's letter, and also made critical remarks, referring to Iraq's "miscalculations."

In the first place, Baker stated that the purpose of the meeting in

Geneva was not to negotiate but to communicate the U.N. Resolutions which demanded that Iraq must comply with the will of the international community that it withdraw, otherwise it would be compelled to withdraw by force. The purpose of this meeting, Baker added, was to explain American responsibilities and that there was no intention to exercise pressure or threats against Iraq. Baker also warned that in the event force was used and Iraq might use chemical and biological weapons, the American purpose will not be only to liberate Kuwait but also to overthrow the existing regime, and those responsible for it would be liable for punishment. Moreover, Iraq would face destruction and would become a weak state.

Second, Baker pointed out that Iraq committed too many miscalculations. It miscalculated, he said, the international response to the invasion of Kuwait, its pillaging of that country, its holding of foreign nationals as hostages, and its attempts to divide "the international community and gain something thereby from its aggression." Iraq, he added, should not miscalculate again.

Had there been an opportunity to meet earlier, ʿAziz replied, a lot of misunderstanding might have been removed. Since Baker had spoken at length about Iraq's misunderstandings, said ʿAziz, he wanted to make it clear that "we have not made miscalculations." Iraq, ʿAziz pointed out, was very well aware of the situation and denied that his country's leadership was ignorant of what the American intentions were. "It had known everything," he said.

ʿAziz then turned to explain the general situation in the Arab world. There were, he said, wars, instabilities, hardships which existed for several decades, and the Gulf crisis was necessarily the consequence of those events and problems. If the United States were ready and seriously thinking about bringing peace in the Arab world, ʿAziz said, Iraq was ready to cooperate. But, ʿAziz went on to explain, such peace, in order to be lasting, must be based on justice. As to the new world order, ʿAziz assured Baker, Iraq was ready to participate in it.

Talks about justice and the new world order necessarily led to a discussion about the relationships between Israel and the Arab countries. As Baker maintained that Iraq's invasion of Kuwait had nothing to do with the Palestinian question or with helping the Palestinians, ʿAziz tried to make it clear that "the Palestinian question is a matter of security to Iraq." "If the Palestinian question is not resolved," ʿAziz pointed out, "we do not feel secure in our country." In its attitude toward Israel and the Arabs, ʿAziz remarked, the United States had pursued a double standard.

In the polite dialogue between Baker and ʿAziz, there were several exchanges of recriminations on specific matters. For example, ʿAziz criticized the United States for pressuring other members of the Security Council to vote in favor of most of the mandatory Resolutions against Iraq. Baker denied that the United States pressured other countries and called his attention to the fact that the whole community of nations was against Iraq's invasion of Kuwait. He also accused Saddam Husayn of lying to Husni Mubarak, president of Egypt, when he told him that Iraq was not going to use force against Kuwait. ʿAziz denied the accusation and went on to explain that Mubarak misunderstood Saddam. One of the questions often raised during the discussion was about the U.N. demand that Iraq should withdraw from Kuwait, and Baker frequently warned about the disaster that might befall Iraq were it to refuse to heed the calls to withdraw. ʿAziz maintained that the United States had ignored Iraq's legitimate rights in its disputes with Kuwait. For this reason, he said, the Iraqi people felt they had been wronged and ill-treated by the United States. "When the people have such a feeling," said ʿAziz, "and were threatened by resort to force, they were bound to fight in order to defend themselves rather than submit to oppression."

Baker seemed on the defensive when ʿAziz complained that the United States, claiming to pursue a new world order based on peace and justice, had applied a "double standard" in its relationship with Israel and the Arab countries. ʿAziz remonstrated that Iraq was not treated in the same way as Israel, although Israel too had failed to comply with all the U.N. resolutions, yet the United States had "covered the Israeli position [and] protected it politically at the Security Council." "So if the matter is respect of international law," ʿAziz pleaded in protest, "we would like you to show the same attention to all Security Council Resolutions. . . . [I]f you do that, a lot of differences between us will be removed."

The Geneva meeting lasted over six hours. As it went on much longer than expected, it gave the impression that both sides were perhaps trying to achieve a solution to the crisis. There were three breaks during the meeting, including one hour for lunch. At lunch, ʿAziz met with the Algerian foreign minister, Ahmad Ghazali, and the PLO foreign policy chief, Faruq Qaddumi. It is reported that ʿAziz told them: "We are not going to make any progress in these talks. . . . They will not discuss the 15th of January. . . . We can't negotiate with them unless they do."[38] After lunch, the talks were hardly more than a continued articulation of the differing views, without any evident intention of reaching a compromise.

Like the Jidda meeting, there was no common ground on which Baker and ʿAziz could reach an agreement. Baker was given instructions not to negotiate an agreement; his task was to make it clear to ʿAziz that he had no choice but to accept withdrawal without reward. ʿAziz also was instructed not to talk about withdrawal unless there was a possibility of addressing some of Iraq's grievances. Like the aftermath of the Jidda meeting, there were talks about the need for further mediation, but only one—de Cuellar's last visit to Iraq—was undertaken.

DE CUELLAR'S FINAL MISSION

The de Cuellar mission was initiated by Bush, as the United States was criticized for its unwillingness to take advantage of the "pause" to resolve the crisis by peaceful means. Bush seems to have asked de Cuellar to visit Baghdad in order to persuade Saddam to withdraw from Kuwait. After he arrived in Baghdad on January 11, de Cuellar could not meet with Saddam, as Daniel Ortega, former president of Nicaragua, was then meeting with him. De Cuellar's standing in Iraqi eyes, however, was not so high as to have any effect, as he had played no effective role in the Iraq-Iran War. Thus, when de Cuellar met with Saddam, two days after his arrival on January 13, Saddam had already been told by Ortega that de Cuellar was visiting Baghdad at the insistence of Bush and not in his capacity as the U.N. secretary general. Saddam thus was not very enthusiastic about his meeting with de Cuellar and let him know that he had known quite well how he had acted during the Iraq-Iran War.

Following Saddam's half-hearted words in welcoming him, de Cuellar also made it clear that he was not charged with any "mandate." He complimented Saddam for his decision to release the foreign hostages which helped to diffuse tensions. Recalling Saddam's initiative of August 12, in which it was declared that Iraq would withdraw from Kuwait as part of an overall solution of the Palestine question, de Cuellar pointed out that Saddam had called world attention to the need for resolving that problem. He also complimented him for the initiative he had taken to end the war with Iran. He appealed to him in the same spirit to find a way of adhering to the U.N. Resolutions, including Resolutions 660 and 678, which called for withdrawal from Kuwait. If this step were undertaken, de Cuellar said that he had put down "something said by Mr. Bush on a small piece of paper," which might be of interest to Saddam. Bush said:

> The United States will not attack Iraq or its armed forces if withdrawal from Kuwait has been achieved and the situation has returned to what it was prior to August 2. The United States will not attack Iraq or its armed forces in the region; it will support negotiations between the parties concerned, and I shall accept any decision by those parties.[39]

Saddam showed an interest in some of de Cuellar's points about the relationship between the Gulf crisis and the Palestine problem, but he said virtually nothing about withdrawing from Kuwait. Saddam also told de Cuellar that what rendered the crisis more difficult to resolve was the threat that Iraq felt, because Kuwait had become a base from which the United States could attack Iraq. He went on to explain that Iraq had already agreed to attend a summit meeting in Saudi Arabia to settle the crisis, but Egypt and Saudi Arabia preferred to invite American forces to Saudi Arabia before such a summit had met. Nevertheless, Saddam said, Iraq announced that it would withdraw some of its forces. But when American forces continued to arrive in increasing numbers, Iraq stopped the pull-out and the crisis was aggravated. Saddam indicated that he was convinced that if withdrawal occurred without any prospect of discussing Iraq's legitimate complaints, peace would not be achieved in the region, since Kuwait had become a base of threats against Iraq. For this reason, Saddam told de Cuellar, Iraq could not possibly withdraw from Kuwait. But when de Cuellar inquired whether he understood correctly that Saddam's position on Kuwait was "irreversible," Saddam at once replied that he did not say that. What he meant, in his own words, is as follows:

> If you find out that the Americans are in the position of one seeking an outlet from a predicament and that they are searching for a way in which they will not lose but will not necessarily achieve all they want, it is possible to formulate guidelines for this purpose, and the Arabs could search for a solution in accordance with these guidelines.[40]

Saddam's position was clear. Unless some of Iraq's legitimate territorial claims, including settlement of the Palestine problem, were conceded, he was not prepared to talk about withdrawal. This position was also made clear by 'Aziz to Baker in Geneva. Thus when de Cuellar left Baghdad for New York, stopping in Paris to see Mitterand, he looked despondent after he arrived on January 14. In France, he learned that several attempts to offer mediation were made, but since they were conditional on Iraq's prior acceptance of withdrawal, they were rejected by Iraq. Even when Gorbachev made a last attempt, at Iraq's request, in response to which Iraq agreed to withdrawal, it was rejected by Washington.[41]

CRITIQUE OF THE UNITED NATIONS ROLE

The actions taken by the Security Council to resolve the Gulf crisis have been criticized by Iraq on both procedural and substantive levels. In the Iraq-Iran Gulf war, which lasted over eight years, the Iraqi and Iranian armies were virtually at each other's throats in several pitched battles, yet the Security Council made no move to invoke the relevant Articles under Chapter VII which would empower the Security Council to take action as it had done later in compelling Iraq to withdraw from Kuwait. Nor did the Security Council give, at the outset, the impression that it was indeed prepared to stop the Iraq-Iran War. It held a meeting one day after the war broke out (September 22, 1980) only to exchange "views in informal consultation," before it issued, a week later (September 28, 1980), its first Resolution, calling upon Iran and Iraq to "refrain" from the use of force and to "settle their dispute by peaceful means." In addition, the Security Council did not take effective action when seven years later it invoked Articles 39 and 40 under Chapter VII

by virtue of which it demanded that "Iran and Iraq observe an immediate cease-fire [and] discontinue all military actions"; there were no
warnings that further actions would be taken if "an immediate cease-
fire" were not observed.

By contrast, the Security Council moved so quickly and effectively
to deal with Iraq's invasion of Kuwait that its action has aptly been
considered unprecedented in the annals of the United Nations. For
hardly had Iraq started to move its forces across Kuwait's border (August 2, 1990) than the Security Council met on the same day and issued
its first Resolution demanding an "immediate and unconditional withdrawal" of the Iraqi forces from Kuwait. Within the following four
months, the Security Council issued a dozen Resolutions demanding
not only withdrawal from Kuwait, but also the demolition of all weapons
of mass destruction. It issued further Resolutions after Iraq's withdrawal
dealing with territorial and frontier disputes, which would, in the long
run, have been more in the interest of the parties concerned were they
settled by negotiations rather than by mandatory Security Council Resolutions.

Perhaps even more serious criticism about the use of force was
leveled at Security Council Resolution 678 (1990) because its action
was considered contrary to the U.N. Charter which stresses peaceful
means for the Resolution of disputes before the use of force. The Gulf
crisis could have been resolved by peaceful means, as al-Anbari, Iraq's
representative to the United Nations, had time and again pointed out
in his speeches before the Security Council. Tariq ʿAziz, foreign minister of Iraq, had also told James Baker, the U.S. secretary of state, at
the Geneva meeting, that Iraq was ready to resolve the Gulf crisis in
the context of other Middle Eastern problems at an international conference.

In the course of their conversations at Geneva, ʿAziz complained
to Baker that in its relationship with Iraq, the United States had used
a double standard—it sought to apply force against Iraq under U.N.
Resolution 678 (1990) while it had pursued peaceful means with Syria
and Israel about their actions in Lebanon and the West Bank. ʿAziz's
exchange of recriminations with Baker led to a discourse on peace and
justice as aims of the United Nations. In its dealings with the Gulf crisis,
ʿAziz accused the United States of ignoring justice in seeking the Resolution of the crisis by resort to force. Baker replied that since Iraq
had refused to comply with the United Nations demand to withdraw,
the use of force was deemed necessary to compel Iraq to withdraw
before the crisis could be resolved. In their discourse, ʿAziz seems to
have implied in his complaint to Baker that justice should first be
achieved before peace could be established. But, one may ask, which
of the two, peace or justice, should first be achieved in order to avoid
resort to force.

Achieving peace and justice in the relationships among nations is the primary purpose of the United Nations. The U.N. Charter, under the Preamble and Article 1, states that the purpose of the United Nations is to achieve both peace and justice in order to "save succeeding generations from the scourge of war." Peace and justice, according to the Charter, could be achieved in the world by establishing "conditions under which justice and respect for the obligations arising from treaties and other sources of International Law" (Charter's preamble).

Peace and justice, idealists and realists are agreed, must be observed under any world order if it were ever to endure. But they disagree about the interrelationship between them, as to which of the two is superior and takes precedence. The idealists maintain that peace will never endure if it is not based on justice. For a world order devoid of justice tends to breed tensions and conflicts and ultimately will destroy the foundation on which peace is established. It is thus tempting to argue that justice is the key to a lasting peace, as peace and justice cannot be completely separated. Yet in human experience justice has proved so compelling a goal that its pursuit often prompts men to break the peace. In their interrelationship, however, peace proves to be the proximate, but justice is the ultimate objective, if public order is ever to endure.

Finally, a query might be raised, against whom were the U.N. sanctions issued: the governors or the governed? In theory, the purpose of the sanctions is to compel the governors who represent the "state" to meet its obligations under the U.N. Charter and the norms of International Law. In Western democracies, the principle of "government by the consent of the governed" is the basis on which most of the governors are elevated to power. It follows that the "governed" must ultimately be considered responsible for any action taken by the "governors." For if the "governed" were in disagreement with the "governors", the latter would be replaced, directly or indirectly, by public expression of opinion exercised by one form or another.

In the Middle East, however, the relationships between governors and governed vary considerably from one country to another. In the traditional countries of the Arabian Peninsula, there are certain institutions such as the formal or informal consultative councils by virtue of which the governors keep in touch with the governed and the views of both sides are often presented and debated. These organizations give an expression to the Islamic principle of "consultation" (*shura*) which is legally binding on both governors and governed under both Islamic law and Arab tribal (customary) law. The "governor" would lose the confidence of his followers and consequently his right to rule would be questioned were he to disregard completely the views of the governed.

But in countries where the governors have been elevated to power through the military, the consent of the governed has in most cases been disregarded. Ever since the overthrow of the monarchy in 1958,

Iraq has been ruled by a military under which the governed have had almost always no voice in the rise or fall of the military regimes. In the Gulf crisis, in the decision to settle the Iraq-Kuwait dispute by resort to force, the governed had not been consulted, although one may argue that the Iraqi public was in favor of unity with Kuwait, but not necessarily by resort to force. It would therefore seem unjust and counterproductive that the incidence of the U.N. sanctions should be borne to a large extent not by the governors but by the governed. True, the sanctions, have in theory, allowed food and medicine to be imported for the benefit of children, the elderly and the sick, but such commodities were not, in fact, made available, and the incidence of sanctions has, as a result, hit in most cases the innocent for whom the Resolutions had not, at least in principle, been intended.

ROLE OF ARAB REGIONAL ORGANIZATIONS

Well before the United Nations took action to consider Iraq's invasion of Kuwait, Arab leaders had already been grappling with the Gulf crisis hoping that it might soon be resolved before becoming a pretext for foreign intervention. There were four regional organizations which, either individually or collectively, might have dealt with the crisis, each in accordance with its own standards and procedures. Yet only the Arab League and the Islamic Conference Organization took the Gulf crisis seriously and might have resolved the issue—had the Western powers not intervened and had they allowed the Arab leaders long enough time to resolve it in accordance with their own standards and time-consuming processes. The other two Arab regional organizations—the Arab Gulf Council (composed of Saudi Arabia, Kuwait, Bahrain, Qatar, United Arab Amirate, and 'Uman) and the Arab Cooperation Council (composed of Iraq, Jordan, Egypt, and Yaman)—did not deal with the Gulf crisis directly because the crisis was on the agenda of the Arab League in which all the members of the Arab Gulf Council and the Arab Cooperation Council were represented.

THE ARAB LEAGUE

The League of Arab States is the oldest organization in the Arab world designed to deal with Arab regional affairs as defined under Article 52 of the United Nations Charter. It was established during the closing days of World War II, almost simultaneously with the convocation of the San Francisco Conference which laid down the Charter of the United Nations in 1945, although the idea of some form of an Arab union had been on the minds of many Arab leaders for a long while.[42]

Before the establishment of the two Arab subregional organizations, the Arab League had already dealt with several Arab disputes such as the Franco-Syrian dispute in 1945 and the Arab-Israeli conflict ever since it was ensued in 1948. In 1961, we have already noted how Brigadier Qasim threatened to annex Kuwait after it achieved independence, which prompted the Arab League to dispatch Arab military forces that replaced the British force to defend Kuwait. Most of those forces remained until Iraq finally recognized Kuwait's sovereignty in 1963 following the fall of Qasim's regime. The League's success in resolving the Kuwait crisis in 1961 was partly due to the ample "cooling off" time given to the parties concerned in order to discuss the situation, but mainly to the Arab League's ability to coordinate Arab activities and to deploy the military forces required for the maintenance of order and peace in the Gulf.[43]

In 1990, when the second Kuwait crisis suddenly and unexpectedly rose, the Arab League had neither a full grasp of the Iraq-Kuwait conflict nor had it been given the time to deal with the differences among Arab leaders in discussing how to resolve the crisis. Western intervention, first through diplomatic pressures and later by resort to force, was so quick and overwhelming that it virtually gave Arab leaders no chance to resolve the crisis by peaceful means.

Before the U.N. mandatory sanctions were imposed on Iraq (August 2), Arab leaders quickly but ineptly started to talk about ways and means to persuade Saddam Husayn to withdraw as a step in resolving the crisis as an Arab issue. As noted earlier, there was a great deal of confusion and misunderstanding about procedural matters before the Arab leaders finally agreed to discuss the crisis at a meeting of the Arab League on August 10. Even before the Arab League Council convened, there were haggling and emotional controversies among the Arab leaders as to whether a preliminary meeting of foreign ministers was necessary to formulate proposals for consideration by the League Council. Because of the extraordinary circumstances, a decision was made by the Arab League secretary (presumably after consultation with some of the Arab heads of state) who announced that there was no need for a foreign ministers meeting.[44]

The long awaited meeting started at 7:15 P.M., chaired by President Husni Mubarak, head of the host country. A Saudi proposal was submitted, Mubarak announced, prepared at an informal meeting by the foreign ministers of Egypt, Syria, Lebanon and the Gulf countries. Several speeches were made by the president of Algeria, Amir Jabir of Kuwait and his premier, Sa'dun Hamadi, Iraq's deputy premier, and Yasir 'Arafat, chairman of the PLO. The Algerian president warned that if an agreement for settlement were not reached, foreign intervention would be inevitable. The Kuwaiti premier and Iraqi deputy premier exchanged sharp words and wondered whose country had stabbed the other in the back.[45]

Yasir 'Arafat, realizing that accusations and counter-accusations were useless and waste of time, quickly took the floor and said: "I have a practical suggestion, which we have already discussed before the meeting." He proposed to appoint a delegation of three—one representing the Arab Cooperation Council, another from the Gulf Cooperation Council, and a third from the Maghrib—to carry a message to Baghdad and ask Saddam Husayn to withdraw from Kuwait. As he had already talked with Saddam about withdrawal, ʿArafat maintained that a "dignified appeal" from the Arab League would surely be acceptable to him. ʿArafat's proposal was not favorably received, as some doubted that Saddam was ready for such an appeal. What complicated the situation and undermined ʿArafat's proposal was a broadcast over the Baghdad Radio in which Iraq made an appeal to the peoples of Egypt and Saudi Arabia inciting them to rise up against their rulers just as President Nasir of Egypt used to appeal to Arabs over the heads of their own rulers to overthrow them. This was unexpected news which discouraged anyone from visiting Baghdad during such a time of emotion and confusion. It prompted the president of Sudan to reiterate the admonition of Jadid, the Algerian president, about the dangers of foreign intervention and warned that "we should not give any excuse for foreign presence in our land." This prompted Hafiz al-Asad, president of Syria, to remind him that those who occupied Kuwait were responsible for the foreign presence. As the news that foreign forces were already on their way to Saudi Arabia, King Fahd stood to explain the situation in his country:

> Our brother from the Sudan is mixing issues. I was not going to comment on what he said, but I feel obliged to do so. The forces present now in Saudi Arabia will never be used in an offensive act unless it is provoked to defend itself.

In a statement on Saudi television, King Fahd had already announced the presence of foreign troops in which he said:

> These forces from brotherly [Muslim] and friendly [American] powers are here temporarily. They are to help defend the kingdom, participate in joint exercises, and will leave as soon as the kingdom so demands.[46]

As Mubarak felt that the meeting might go on indefinitely, he put the Resolution to the vote. ʿArafat protested: "President Mubarak, please wait, please delay the voting," but to no avail. There were complaints that Mubarak had become impatient and wanted to end the meeting. For this reason, the Iraqi delegation walked out and proceeded directly to the airport.

The voting was considered to be in favor of the Resolution. Some of the delegates argued that it was unbinding because it belonged to the category of collective action on national security and therefore the vote must be unanimous. According to the Arab League Pact, Resolutions are binding only if they are voted unanimously. Owing to the difficulty of obtaining unanimity, the rule was modified to the effect that in the case of a majority, the Resolution would be binding only on those who voted in its favor. But the majority rule did not apply to Resolutions concerning collective measures about national security. For such Resolutions the unanimity rule must apply. After careful scrutiny of the votes, it was announced that ten were in favor of the Resolution, and nine varied between rejection,, abstention and reservation.

The Resolution may be summed up as follows:

1. It condemned the aggression against Kuwait and called upon Iraq to withdraw its forces immediately to its position prior to August 1st.
2. It reaffirmed the sovereignty, independence, and territorial integrity of Kuwait as a member of the Arab League and the United Nations as well as calling for the restoration of the legitimate government of Kuwait. It also supported all measures that Kuwait might adopt for the recovery of its territory and independence.
3. It condemned Iraq's threats against other Arab Gulf countries and the deployment of forces along Saudi Arabia's border. It also supported the rights of Saudi Arabia and other Arab Gulf countries to self-defence under the treaty of Joint Defence and Economic Cooperation (Article 2), the United Nations Charter (Article 51), and the U.N. Security Council Resolution 660 (August 2, 1990).
4. It decided to "comply with the request of Saudi Arabia and other Arab Gulf states that the Arab forces should be deployed to assist its armed forces in defending its soil and territorial integrity against external aggression."[47]

The Arab League Resolution, while it reaffirmed the U.N. Resolution 660, stopped short of the economic sanctions imposed under Resolution 662, and tacitly allowed further negotiations to persuade Iraq to withdraw its forces and enter into negotiations with Kuwait to resolve differences on debts, oil, and the frontier. No serious efforts, however, were made by the League to implement its Resolution as the Arab countries were split into two camps and the differences between them were aggravated. The door for individual endeavors to find a face-saving formula remained wide open, to which we have referred, but none could have claimed to have had any prospect of success.

THE ISLAMIC CONGRESS ORGANIZATION

Perhaps a little background on Islamic movements and organizations might be useful before discussing the role of the Islamic Congress in the Gulf crisis. The Islamic Congress, composed of representatives of the Islamic states, is perhaps the most comprehensive organization which formally addressed itself to Islamic affairs throughout the Islamic world. It grew out of the Islamic organizations that developed after World War I following the abolition of the Ottoman Caliphate.

The Ottoman Empire, the last ecunemical Islamic state in the annals of Islam, was governed by the Sultan-Caliph who combined, as head of state, both religious and political authorities. The new state system that replaced the old Ottoman system was modeled after a Western pattern based on national and secular concepts. For this reason, the Caliphate was abolished, and the religious authority in each Islamic country became subordinate to political authority. The modern Islamic state accordingly became implicitly secular, although no formal step was taken to declare it secular save in Turkey, and the religious organizations in most Islamic countries came under the control or guidance of the civil authorities.

Because of the subsequent separation between the religious and political authorities, two sets of ideas and ideologies began to spread throughout Islamic countries and to influence political development in various degrees of intensity. The new ideologies opposed to Islam were nationalisms and secularism. Turkey, which had been exposed to such ideas before the ecumenical Ottoman system had collapsed, formally pursued secularization (often called Westernization) after the end of World War I when it declared itself a secular and national state. In other countries, especially in northern Arab lands, nationalism was stressed in order to maintain internal unity, and concessions were made to religious groups opposed to secular ideas by including Islamic elements in the legal and administrative systems.[48]

But there was opposition to the secular and pan-Arab ideologies in the traditional Islamic regimes of the Arabian Peninsula, where Islam was born and spread to other countries. In the Middle Ages, Islam became the religion and symbol of a spiritual unity of an empire extending from the Atlantic to the Indian Ocean. Saudi Arabia, where the holy places of Islam exist today, is formally considered the custodian of the holy sanctuaries of Islam and the protagonist of the principle that political and religious authorities are combined. King ʿAbd al-ʿAziz (often called Ibn Saʿud), founder of the modern Saudi state, pursued the traditional unity between the political and religious authorities, although he also allowed the importation of Western technological advancement which he considered necessary for the development of the country, particularly since oil was discovered during World War II.

King Faysal, second son of Ibn Saʿud, who ascended the throne in 1984, pursued his father's emphasis on Islam as the basis of the political system. He also was determined that his country should take the lead in establishing an Islamic organization, representing all Islamic countries, which would promote cooperation among them to enhance their position in regional and international affairs. With the enhancement of its position as the third greatest oil-producing country in the world, Saudi Arabia began to contribute in no small measures to Islamic countries that have limited resources for their cultural and economic development.

In line with the policy to cooperate with Arab and Islamic countries, Faysal sought to coordinate the activities of Islamic societies and associations by holding Islamic conferences in which all issues that might threaten or undermine Islamic lands could be thoroughly discussed and dealt with. Faysal was motivated by Islam as a more powerful bond of unity than nationalism which often led to rivalry among Arab countries and weakened their stand against foreign pressures and interventions.

The Islamic Congress Organization, which came into existence in 1972, was the first permanent institution representing Islamic governments to which Saudi Arabia offered not only resources to assist other Islamic countries in their domestic affairs but also its leadership to enhance their standing in world affairs. Although Faysal had no intention of interfering in the domestic affairs of other countries, he was, however, ready to offer his country's good offices to reduce tensions and conflicts among Islamic countries. He was motivated by a sense of Islamic patriotism to help Arab and Islamic countries as well as to enhance the standing of his own country by asserting its leadership. Faysal's policy of assisting Arab countries, whether through the Islamic Congress and the Islamic Bank in Jidda or by offering Saudi mediation, was continued after him by King Khalid (d. 1982) and later by King Fahd as demonstrated in their endeavors to contain the Islamic Revolution in Iran and the assistance extended to Iraq during the eight-year war, to which we have referred earlier.[49]

As to the Kuwait crisis, the Islamic Congress, then meeting in Cairo on August 2, 1990, on the same day the Iraqi army had invaded Kuwait, considered the conflict between the two Islamic countries as part of its responsibility, but preferred to move slowly step by step. At first, it instructed the secretary general of the Islamic Congress, Hamid al-'Abid, to make a statement on its behalf in which it called on Iraq to withdraw its forces from Kuwait and to seek peaceful means to resolve the crisis. On the following day (August 3) before it adjourned, it passed a Resolution along the line of the Arab League's Resolution, in which it condemned Iraq's invasion and called for immediate withdrawal of the Iraqi forces and settlement of the crisis by peaceful means. All members voted in favor of the Resolution, except five— Jordan, Sudan, Mauritania, Yaman, and the Palestine Liberation Organization. (Libya and Jibuti's foreign ministers did not attend the meeting). In its meeting on September 14, 1990, the Congress passed a Resolution condemning the Iraqi aggression toward Kuwait and demanded the withdrawal of Iraq's forces from Kuwait. It also called for the restoration of the legitimate authorities to Kuwait and payment for all the damages resulting from the invasion. Finally it called for the formation of an Islamic force to be made available for the settlement of conflicts among Islamic countries under the guidance of the Islamic Congress Organization.

On January 14, 1991, a day before the U.N. Security Council Resolution 678 was to take effect by the use of force against Iraq, the secretary general of the Islamic Congress Organization appealed to Saddam Husayn "to issue his orders to the Iraqi forces in Kuwait to withdraw quickly and without conditions in order to avoid unforeseen consequences." This act, the secretary general said, would be "an Islamic obligation" on behalf of Islam toward the Muslim peoples today and of the future generations. the secretary general also offered his services at the disposal of Iraq to establish "a bridge" between Iraq and Kuwait which might resolve the differences between the two countries and restore an atmosphere of confidence and good will.[50]

The Islamic Congress Resolutions, representing the official standing of the Islamic states, may be regarded as a vote of confidence on behalf of the Islamic world for the policy pursued by the Saudi leadership to resolve the Gulf crisis. They can also be taken as ratification of King Fahd's decision to accept the United Nations resolution to use force, composed of Arab and foreign armies, to defend Saudi Arabia from possible attack and to compel the Iraqi forces to withdraw from Kuwait.

RETROSPECT

The Arab regional organizations, composed of Arab countries, sought to protect Arab regional interest. In contrast, the Islamic Conference, composed of Muslim countries from all over the world (membership is open to all Islamic countries irrespective of ethnic-cultural differences), pursues Islamic interests on ecumenical matters irrespective of national differences. Its discussions and decisions must be made in accordance with Islamic principles and standards as prescribed under Islamic law and religion. For this reason, when the Iraqi forces invaded Kuwait, the Islamic Congress sought to discuss the situation from the perspective of what Islam prescribes when an Islamic country resorts to force against another Islamic country. In the case of Iraq's invasion of Kuwait, four Gulf countries—Bahrain, the United Arab Amirate, Qatar, and 'Uman—decided not to take part in the military operations on the grounds that their military forces were relatively small and confined to defensive purposes only. But Saudi Arabia, the leading Gulf Power, joined by Egypt, Syria, and Morocco, condemned Iraq and participated with other countries in using force in order to compel Iraq to withdraw from Kuwait. As Islam prefers peaceful means for settlement, the Islamic Conference decided that before resort to force, an appeal to Iraq to withdraw was necessary and the secretary of the Islamic Conference offered his good office to Iraq before the military operations had started.

The other Islamic organizations—the Arab League, the Arab Gulf Council, and the Arab Cooperation Council—are regional organizations, whose main purposes were to cooperate with other countries to maintain peace and security only as far as the Arab world was concerned. True, the members of these organizations are Islamic countries, but almost all have adopted in various degrees secular measures, and their decisions, particularly on matters relating to foreign affairs, are not only based on Islamic principles, but also on secular standards that serve national interests and the norms and practices acknowledged by other nations in international affairs. Thus when the Iraq invasion of Kuwait was first discussed at a meeting of the Arab foreign ministers and then at the Arab League Council, there was, it will be recalled, a sharp division among the members between those who voted to condemn Iraq's action and those who wanted to appeal to Iraq for withdrawal from Kuwait in a spirit of reconciliation without condemnation. While the members who advocated both proposals called for settlement of the crisis by peaceful means as required under Islamic standards, none was solely guided by a single standard, as each sought to protect Arab national interests from the perspective of its own subregional interests. As noted earlier, neither proposal was carried by unanimity, as required under the League's voting rules, and the failure of the Arab League to resolve the crisis necessarily invited foreign intervention.

Chapter 10

The Coalition War

The failure of the Geneva meeting to persuade Iraq to withdraw from Kuwait before January 15, 1991 meant that Iraq must be driven out of Kuwait by resort to force. In other words, there would be "war" between the Coalition powers and Iraq. As such a "war" is prohibited under the U.N. Charter, save in "self-defence" under Article 51 of the U.N. Charter, the "war" that the Coalition had launched was not carried out by a "declaration of war" against Iraq, as defined under International Law, but as a "police action," ordered by the higher authority of the United Nations which represent the will of the community of nations. As a "police action," the Coalition War implicitly meant that Iraq was liable to punishment for its aggression against another state. Indeed, the manner the Coalition War was prosecuted seemed not only to drive Iraq's forces out of Kuwait, as it was announced, but also to punish a nation by the destruction of its industrial and infrastructure centers contrary to the norms governing war as defined under International Law.

The Coalition War was carried out in three stages. The first, called Operation Desert Shield, was a defensive arrangement carried out after Iraq's invasion of Kuwait to defend Saudi Arabia and other Gulf countries, in the event Iraq were to attack one of them. In the previous chapter, we have already dealt with the steps taken to dispatch an American force to be stationed in Saudi Arabia for defensive purposes. The dispatch of the American forces was also intended to be a form of pressure to induce Iraq to withdraw from Kuwait.

The second stage of the Coalition War, called Operation Desert Storm, may be said to have begun after the Security Council had adopted Resolution 678 (November 29, 1990). The strength of the American force in Saudi Arabia was doubled from about a quarter of a million to half a million. As a Coalition expedition, the American force in Saudi Arabia was joined by British, French, and, in much smaller numbers, by other expeditionary forces. In the second stage, the use of force was in the form of air warfare. The whole operation was planned to destroy strategic targets. It was decided that these targets were to consist of the following: 1. Iraq's command, control, and communications in order to render its regime incapable of directing its military forces; 2. areas where the weapons of mass destruction were located; and 3. the Republican Guard, the most efficient Iraqi force, in order to reduce Iraq's ability for effective defence and threaten one of the pillars of its regime.

The first stage, called "Operation Desert Shield," was started five days after Iraq had invaded Kuwait. Under the command of General H. Norman Schwarzkopf, it consisted of an American military build-up on the Saudi and Kuwaiti borders. Its declared purpose was to deter any possible Iraqi aggression against Saudi Arabia. As such, it was a defensive measure, and it was not initially considered "a prelude to an attack on Iraqi forces." As far as Saudi Arabia was concerned, the American and Saudi forces were under the joint command of General Schwarzkopf and General Khalid Bin Sultan. When the political and economic sanctions were not able to persuade Iraq to withdraw from Kuwait, the use of force was authorized under Resolution 678 (1990), and carried out under the second and third stages of the Coalition War. The purpose of these two stages was to protect the Coalition forces and to reduce the Iraqi defence forces and weaken one of the pillars of its regime.

The second stage began on January 16, 1991 (EST) and lasted thirty-eight days. In this stage, the Coalition operation aiming at crippling Iraqi's ability to wage war was carried out in three separate steps. The first was to conduct a strategic air campaign in which the air raids would focus on the main strategic targets: to cripple the Iraqi Air Force which would reduce the Republican Guard's military capability and to demolish the supply lines to Kuwait. The second step was to focus on obtaining air supremacy by a complete elimination of the air force and enemy supply line. The third and final steps were to concentrate on battlefield targets, such as supply lines, Republican Guards, and centers where nuclear, biological, and chemical weapons might have existed. The third and final stages of the Coalition War were the land invasion of Kuwait and southern Iraq by the multinational forces. This offensive began on January 16, 1991 and lasted till Iraq asked for a ceasefire.

The military operations started exactly at 12:01 A.M. (EST) on January 16, 1991, the deadline set by the U.N. Security Council under Resolution 678 which stated that if Iraq did not agree to withdraw unconditionally from Kuwait then the Coalition powers were authorized to liberate Kuwait by the use of force. Seventeen hours later, at 7:00 P.M. (EST), Marlin Fitzwater, the White House spokesman, announced that the "liberation of Kuwait had begun." Two hours later President Bush announced in a televised address that:

... the allied countries have exhausted all reasonable efforts to reach a peaceful resolution, and have no choice but to drive Saddam from Kuwait by force. . . . this will not be another Vietnam, our troops will have the best possible support in the entire world, and will not be asked to fight with one hand tied behind their back.[1]

While Bush was making his address, hundreds of air attacks were taking place against strategic Iraqi targets. Colonel McCausland gave a report of the first hours of the air raids which states:

At approximately 0100 on 17 January, eight American Apache helicopters from the 101st Airmobile Division escorted by four Air Force MH-53 Pave Low special operations helicopters crossed the Iraqi border flying low, without lights and at high speed. Using laser-guided missiles and gunfire they destroyed two early-warning radar installations. The attack lasted only a few moments and sustained no casualties. This assault created a 'rader black' corridor in the Iraqi air-defense network, and eight F-15 fighter bombers immediately crossed into Iraq. They were the leasing element of 700 allied aircraft that had assembled beyond Iraqi radar detection. An hour later 30 F-117A Stealth aircraft began bombing government installations in Baghdad and southern Iraq. Once their attack was finished, the Iraqi capital was struck by cruise missiles launched from US Navy ships and B-52 bombers that had departed 11 hours earlier from bases in the U.S. During the first 24 hours, allied air forces flew more than 1000 combat sorties, and the U.S. fired 151 cruise missiles.[2]

These sorties, performed with the help of British and Saudi combat aircraft, were intended to hit many strategic targets in Iraq and Kuwait. These initial missions seem to have been able to knock out many strategic targets in Iraq with precision. Sophisticated weapons such as the Tomahawk cruise missile, laser-guided missiles, and stealth aircraft proved to function well under their first combat trials, not to mention providing a total and complete technological edge throughout the entire war.

On the Iraqi side, the only real effective part of the Iraqi defence was in the use of the modified Scud missiles. The Scud missiles were used against Israel, aimed at cities such as Tel Aviv and Haifa, as well as against Saudi Arabia. The first of the Scud attacks took place on January 17–18; seven were shot at Israel, and one landed at Dhahran in eastern Saudi Arabia. These missiles, however, did not carry the anticipated chemical or biological weapons, but were all conventional weapons. The Scud missiles, however, are known for being highly inaccurate, and quite an ineffective weapon. The reason is that their Soviet guidance systems are very primitive. Nor do they contain very powerful warheads. Reports have shown that those missiles have carried very low explosive warheads; indeed, in one case it was found that an Iraqi warhead was made of cement.

Iraq's Scud missile attack on Israel was intended to draw it into the war. Israel was not a member of the Coalition, as its participation in the war would have resulted in Arab refusal to join the multinational force. For this reason, Iraq attacked Israel with Scud missiles in order to draw Israel into the war which might break up the Coalition and turn the war into another Arab-Israeli conflict. Israel was persuaded not to retaliate, despite a few casualties suffered by its civilian population. Israel would have liked to retaliate, but were dissuaded by the American offer of the deployment of military hardware to Israel, particularly the Patriot anti-ballistic missiles which were intended to inspire high morale among Israeli citizens in danger of being hit by Iraqi Scud missiles. This system was originally designed as a Surface to Air Missile (SAM) system, but was modified during the war to act as an anti-missile system. By the third day of the war, the United States had supplied the Israeli military with many of these systems, as well as the qualified personnel to man the two batteries of this complex defence system.[3]

The parties did not offer full protection to the civilian population. Of the eighty-eight launched Scud missiles on Israel and Saudi Arabia, thirty-two people were killed and over 250 were injured.[4] One of the downfalls of the Patriot system became apparent on February 25, when the U.S. Army reserve barracks in Dhahran was struck by a downed Iraqi Scud missile.[5] The problem that became evident was that the Patriot system was not very effective, and even if it hit the Scud, the warhead was in many cases still intact, and could still cause damage wherever it fell, as in the case of the army barracks. The Patriots themselves also caused some damage. True, the Patriot could divert the Scud from hitting its original tactical target, but it still posed a threat to anything in its path. For the civilian damage done by the Scud missiles, Israel was compensated by financial assistance. The European Union contributed $100 million, Germany gave $3.2 million, and the United States gave $1 billion. These generous gifts seem to have aroused Iraq's leadership to protest Western double standards in dealing with the region. Meanwhile, anti-war protests which took place in Washington, D.C. and some European capitals, were supported by larger street demonstrations in several Arab and Muslim countries including Jordan, Sudan, Morocco, and Algeria.

By January 23, the Coalition had flown over 12,000 sorties.[6] It was estimated that by this time the Coalition air raids had achieved most of their objectives in the first two stages of "Operation Desert Storm," although later the number of targets hit was reassessed to a much lower figure. It appeared that out of the sixty-six airfields in Iraq, only five were operational, and that ninety-five percent of the Iraqi defence radar system had been destroyed. General Colin Powell claimed that the Coalition had gained "general air superiority."[7] At this point the next step of the operation was to immobilize the Iraqi army itself. "Our strategy," Powell added, "for dealing with this army is very simple: First we're going to cut it off, then we're going to kill it."[8]

By the second week it was believed that the Coalition had exhausted the highly strategic targets, mainly: airfields, weapon depots, early warning rader, the air force, and so on. The increase in Scud attacks, however, prompted the Coalition to shift the fixed and mobile missile launchers to the top of the priority bombings. This in turn slowed the effectiveness of the air campaign, because it was difficult to find the location of the mobile launchers in desert areas. This necessarily shifted focus away from the attacks on the targets that would feed the Iraqi military.

The Coalition forces were effective in the destruction of key military targets. The Stealth Fighters and Tomahawk missiles destroyed or rendered useless the nuclear reactors at Samarra and at Abu Ghurayb. The British force was able to destroy a munitions depot in Basra, and the French managed to destroy an ammunitions dump at Quwayla in southern Kuwait. The intention of this bombing was to separate and isolate the Iraqi troops in southern Kuwait from their resources. This lead to a relentless aerial bombardment by the Coalition troops in southern Iraq. Another attempt was made to sever centralized communications for the coordination of Iraqi troop efforts by the so-called attack on "dual-use targets," such as public highways, railroads, bridges, and public communications systems.[9] In this operation, however, there was the danger that the focus on "dual-use targets" might increase the chances of killing civilians. This issue was raised in a press conference held by President Bush, in which he stated that "We are doing everything possible to minimize collateral damage . . . ," but he added, "Saddam is now relocating some military functions, such as command and control headquarters, in civilian areas around schools. . . ."[10]

The Coalition decision to target these installations was made on the grounds that their location relative to the civilian neighborhoods was quite misperceived. True the Coalition possessed high surveillance technology that could identify military targets. But the reality was something else. For example, the attack on the civilian bomb shelter in the Baghdad suburb of 'Umariya, occurred because the shelter was inaccurately identified as a command-and-control center for the Iraqi military operations.[11] The official Iraqi report is that the civilian toll was over 400 deaths, ninety-one of which were children, although the final figures actually were over one thousand.[12]

By the end of the second week, the United States made claims that were reevaluated soon after. It claimed that the Coalition destroyed eleven out of twelve chemical and biological weapon production plants, and three refineries which reduced the Iraqi production of oil by fifty percent. The continuing bombardment induced the Iraqi government to give up attempts to keep centralized control of the air force.[13] There were some exaggerated claims made by the Pentagon. It was estimated that two-thirds of the airfields in Iraq had been destroyed, while actually two-thirds were still operational. Iraq also regained one-fifth of its radar abilities. Most of the Iraqi Air Force was safe in Iran, only fifty combat aircraft had been destroyed. Despite constant aerial bombardment, Iraq managed to save a majority of its high-grade anti-aircraft artillery systems. As for the tanks, it is estimated that 4700 of the 5500 still remained safe, and twenty-two of thirty Scud batteries were still operational. Moreover, the Iraqi mobile communications systems remained intact.

On January 30, the Iraqi military made a final attempt to demonstrate its military capabilities. This attempt was made against the allied positions in Saudi Arabia. The operation consisted of an estimated fifty tanks and 1,500 Iraqi soldiers.[14] The attack killed twelve American Marines and thirteen Iraqis. This was a surprise attack to the Coalition.[15] The operation took place along the seventy kilometers of coastal area from Khafji to Umm Hajjul with the eventual capturing of the port city of Khafji. The capture of Khafji showed a breakdown of the Coalition reconnaissance information and a lack of coordination among the multinational forces. The Saudi Arabian and Qatari troops immediately engaged the invading Iraqi troops in the city, and, with back-up from United States Marines, the Saudi Arabian troops eventually recaptured the city.[16]

The Coalition War clearly demonstrated the benefits of having air superiority in a land battle. No less important was the role of the centralized command-and-control. In an attempt to end the war with a negotiated settlement, the Soviet foreign minister Bessmertnykh, although he expressed support for the U.N. resolutions, voiced concern about the direction that the conflict was taking. He felt that the destruction of Iraq was not consistent with the spirit of the U.N. resolutions. Soviet leaders began to express concern that the war might deviate into a conflict leading to a complete destruction of Iraq's infrastructure. They also held that with the end of the Gulf War the Arab-Israeli conflict should come to an end. The Soviets considered these to be the two most pressing issues in the Middle East. The Bush administration tacitly agreed with the Soviet viewpoint, but the idea that there was a link between the two situations was denounced by Israel.

On January 25, 1991, Saddam Husayn decided that it would be beneficial for him to let Western journalists return to Baghdad to view the massive bombardment by the Coalition air strikes. It is considered one of the most intensive bombardment in history as the sorties reached 3,000 a day.[17] The Western journalists came to the conclusion that the laser-guided "smart bombs" were fairly inaccurate. The decision to let the journalists back into Iraq was an attempt to arouse world sympathy about the damage that had been done to the civilian population as a result of the Coalition bombings.

A prime example of the inaccuracy of these weapons came on a raid on the 150-foot telecommunications towers in the city of Diwaniya. In four raids the Coalition had managed to blow the tops off of two hotels and to destroy about sixty shops in the nearby market, but left the towers completely untouched.[18] The journalists also visited children's schools and clinic in Hilla that had been hit by Coalition bombings on January 18 and 26—the second bombing of the school had killed five and injured twenty-five. In an attempt to hit a nearby road on January 23, the Coalition air raids hit instead a house in al-Haswa three times.

The second week of the war witnessed an increase in Iraq's use of Scud missiles against Saudi Arabia and Israel, causing extensive damage and tension despite the use of the Patriot missiles. The Coalition continued their air attacks against Iraq. The Iraqis were able to shoot down a number of planes. This week witnessed a huge leak of oil, caused by war damage, in the waters of the Gulf. The Coalition accused Iraq of ecological terrorism. Thousands of tons of oil covered an area fifty kilometers long and fifteen kilometers wide.

By this time the Coalition air strategy had become known. It consisted of four stages. The first was the destruction of Iraq's strategic targets, command and communication, control centers, and factories of mass destruction weapons. The second was the bombing of Iraq's strategic reserves and the disruption of communications between the leadership and its forces in Kuwait. The third was pressuring Iraqi forces on the tactical level and preparing the ground for land invasion. The fourth was the use of land and naval forces to drive Iraq out of Kuwait and to enter into Iraq. The Iraqi resistance, however, led to a change in the initial plans leading to a prolongation of the bombing campaign. At this time, two Coalition military leaders criticized the conduct of the war and questioned its objectives. The Pakistani chief of staff General Mirza Aslam Beg, whose forces were in Saudi Arabia, accused the West of a conspiracy to weaken the Muslim world by encouraging Iraq to invade Kuwait in order to provide it with a justification to invade and destroy Iraq. The French defence minister, Chevenement, who resigned, also accused the Coalition of wanting to overthrow the Iraqi regime and decimate the country. President Gorbachev warned that the conflict might become a broader war and called for a new peace initiative.

As it had become clear that the war to liberate Kuwait was likely to spread to Iraq, President Mubarak and King Fahd met in Riyadh and declared that their forces would not fight inside Iraq. Pope John Paul II also issued his denunciation of the war. U.N. Secretary General de Cuellar protested the killing of eight Jordanian truck drivers along the Baghdad-Amman road. Bush accused Jordan of "moving way over to Saddam Husayn's camp."

India, a leading member of the nonaligned movement, called the attention of the Security Council (February 9, 1991) to the necessity that the Coalition should not go beyond the terms of Resolution 678. On the same day Turkish and Russian high officials, meeting in Anakara, called for an end to the destruction of Iraq. The Iraqi government also launched its own diplomatic campaign when Sa'dun Hamadi, member of the Revolutionary Command Council, arrived in Tehran and said that the peace proposal submitted by Iraq was being seriously considered in his country. One day later in 'Amman, Hamadi announced that Iraq was ready to negotiate an end to the war if the United States would be excluded from the talks. As he was speaking, the Coalition was launching the most intensive ground and air operation of the war.

On February 12, President Gorbachev sent his special envoy, Yevgeny Primakov, to Baghdad to persuade the Iraqi government to accept a diplomatic solution that would meet the requirements established by the U.N. in order to avert a land war which might be costly to both sides. After his meeting with Saddam Husayn, Primakov announced that Baghdad was ready to cooperate to find a peaceful way to end the war.

On February 15, Iraq declared that it was willing to deal with Security Council Resolution 660 provided the subsequent resolutions were abrogated. It also said that the American forces must leave the region and that Kuwaiti nationalist and Islamic forces would be allowed to participate in the decision as to what the future of the country would be. In addition, it said that Israel must withdraw from the occupied Arab territories, and the countries that took part in the war against Iraq should help in rebuilding what had been destroyed. President Bush responded by describing the plan as a "cruel hoax," designed to drive a wedge between the United States and its allies, and called on the Iraqi people and Army to force Saddam to move aside and comply with U.N. resolutions. The Soviet foreign minister said that Iraq's offer opened a new stage and must be pursued.

On February 18, Iraq's foreign minister, Tariq 'Aziz, went to Moscow in an effort to end the war and stop its spreading into his country which seemed imminent. He submitted a peace plan to Gorbachev to be communicated to Bush who rejected it and proposed his own conditions for an avoidance of a land campaign and the war. These included "immediate and unconditional" Iraqi withdrawal before a ceasefire could be put in place; the evacuation to be completed in four days from Kuwait (by February 23rd); restoration and recognition of the Kuwait government, and payment of reparations to Kuwait by Iraq; and continuation of the sanctions on Iraq.[19] Britain and France supported the Bush position while Italy supported Gorbachev's plan. Baghdad called the conditions "shameful."[20]

On February 19, Sa'dun Hamadi, while returning to Baghdad via Tehran from a nonaligned conference on the war in Yugoslavia, gave the first figures on casualties to an Iranian newspaper. He said the bombing campaign had killed 20,000 people, wounded 60,000 and caused damages estimated at 200 billion dollars. Following a meeting with Tariq ʿAziz, Iran's foreign minister said that ʿAziz had already told him that Iraq's conditions for withdrawal were "matters that could be addressed."[21]

On February 21, the Iraqi government responded to Gorbachev's eight-point peace plan including a declaration of its intent to withdraw from Kuwait, a cease-fire, and actual withdrawal. It added, however, that U.N. sanctions must be lifted once two-thirds of its forces had withdrawn and the abrogation of all resolutions once withdrawal was completed. Iraq called for the monitoring of the cease-fire by a U.N. force.[22]

Bush rejected the Gorbachev plan on February 22 and gave Iraq less than twenty-four hours to accept the White House's conditions. A few hours later the White House spokesman, Marlin Fitzwater, listed twelve conditions: Complete withdrawal within a week; facilitating the arrival of the Kuwaiti government to Kuwait City; the release of all prisoners within two days; removal of all explosives from oilfield installations and giving the Allies information on all mines; giving up control over Kuwaiti airspace to the allies. For their part, the Coalition would promise not to attack retreating Iraqi soldiers.[23]

A few hours later, the Russians and the Iraqis submitted a six-point plan agreed to by Gorbachev and ʿAziz which included unconditional and immediate Iraqi withdrawal; an Iraqi evacuation within a day of the ceasefire agreement; the withdrawal to be completed in three weeks, and the abrogation of all Security Council resolutions once the withdrawal occurs. Less than five hours later Iraq officially accepted the Gorbachev plan. On February 23, ʿAziz declared that Iraq, following the acceptance of the Soviet plan, had decided to withdraw from Kuwait immediately and unconditionally.

The Bush administration at once dismissed the latest Soviet plan and reiterated the ultimatum to Baghdad to begin pulling out on February 23 by 17:00 GMT. Half an hour later in a conversation with Bush, Gorbachev sought—without much success—to convince him to delay the land offensive by twenty-four hours since an acceptable compromise was only one day away. Similar phone conversations with the leaders of Germany, Britain, France, Syria, Egypt, and Jordan ended in failure. At the Security Council, Western countries opposed any talk of postponing the land invasion. At 18:00 GMT Bush ordered U.S. to proceed with the military operation: The land operation in Iraq.

On February 24, 1991, "Operation Desert Sabre" began, with the firing of the sixteen-inch guns of the U.S.S. Wisconsin and U.S.S. Missouri anchored off the coast of Kuwait. Then followed an amphibious landing on the beaches to link up with the ground Coalition troops waiting to fight the battle at the border. The American Airborne Corps, moving toward southwest Iraq, was shelling southern Iraq, while the Iraqis were unaware of enemy positions. Since the middle of January, the British, French, and American forces had been discreetly moving from Saudi Arabia across the undefended southwestern Iraqi border.

On February 24, these forces, which deceived the Iraqi Military Command (it had already lost its air force and was unable to discover the movement of the Coalition forces) launched its offensive on two fronts: on one the forces that proceeded across the Kuwait-Iraq border; and on the other across the Saudi-Kuwait border. This operation was entirely not what the Iraqi military command had expected, as it had been deceived into believing that the Coalition forces were going to attack from Kuwait.

Iraq's miscalculation led to a series of lost battles. Its forces were confronting an overwhelmingly superior force. The Iraqi position was hopeless and the retreat from Kuwait across the Iraqi border was to save as many troops and tanks (and other war *matériel*) as possible. Southern Iraq was exposed to Coalition forces and the question who had won or lost the war was not in doubt. It is outside the scope of this study to discuss the military operations that took place in Kuwait and southern Iraq, as there are several works by military men who took part in the operations as well as scholars who dealt with the subject, to which readers may be referred.[24]

At 18:00 GMT on February 26, 1991, the U.N. secretary general received a letter from Tariq 'Aziz, accepting most of the U.N. resolutions, excluding 661, 665, and 670. These three resolutions dealt with the continued embargo of Iraq. The five permanent members of the Security Council reviewed the letter and decided to reject it. At that time, President Bush was briefed by a letter from General Colin Powell and Dick Cheney that "all military objectives had been achieved."[25] Although the operation had completed all of its intended tasks, General Schwarzkopf ordered the heaviest bombing on Baghdad. This mission brought the total number of allied sorties against Iraq to a massive 106,000 in forty-two days. The attacks continued against Iraqi forces which had begun their evacuation from Kuwait. On February 26, the Kuwait resistance group had reported that Iraqi troops had abandoned Kuwait City and its suburbs using all available transport including stolen cars and buses as well as military vehicles.

The fleeing Iraqi troops were stopped in their tracks just twenty miles west of Kuwait City at Mitla Ridge and at Highway 80 which came to be known as the "highway to hell" in what Colin Smith of the *London Observer* called "one of the most terrible harassments of a retreating army from the air in the history of warfare."[26] Allied assault aircrafts using a range of sophisticated and lethal bombs and missiles relentlessly bombarded the front and the tail end of the retreating columns leaving the retreating Iraqi soldiers hopelessly trapped. The attacks were described as "Turkey shoots," killing untold thousands of half-starving and totally defeated soldiers who were trying to flee Kuwait.[27]

The Coalition leaders apparently did not want to see an Iraqi withdrawal. From their perspective "this [retreat] represented an unexpected problem: how to publicly counter Iraq's announcement that the troops trying to flee north to Iraq were part of an orderly withdrawal from the Amirate designed to comply with U.N. resolutions.''[28]

The reports and grizzly pictures from the scene shocked not only the correspondents but even American military commanders and White House officials and threatened to undermine the carefully orchestrated image of a "clean" and unblemished victory. They put tremendous pressures on President Bush and his close aides to end the war.[29] President Bush halted the combat and demanded that Iraq must comply with all of the U.N. Security Council resolutions. The liberation of Kuwait was complete, but a terrible price had been paid.[30]

Estimates of total casualties in the war paint a grim picture of the effectiveness of modern weapons and tactics. The total number of Iraqi deaths related to the war continues to be surrounded by controversy and mystery. Neither the Iraqis nor the Americans have given official numbers. The figures range from a high of 200,000 to General Schwartzkopf's figure of 150,000 and to Hiro's figure of 82,500.[31] Total U.S. losses in the entire seven-month period of the crisis were 376 dead in both combat and accidents related to the build-up and execution of the war.[32]

Having been satisfied with the accomplishment of all of the goals of the war, President Bush declared, on February 27, 1991, an end to the war. "Seven months ago," Bush said, "America and the world drew a line in the sand, we declared that the aggression against Kuwait would not stand, and tonight America and the world have kept their word.''[33] Iraq declared that it would accept the cease-fire announced by President Bush. On March 2, 1991, discussion between the Iraq and Coalition delegations began. On the following day, March 3, 1991, it led to the formal acceptance of the cease-fire and complete cessation of hostilities as well as the immediate release of prisoners of war from both sides and the disclosure of Iraqi minefield information. Meanwhile, the Security Council adopted Resolution 686 (1991) in which it demanded that Iraq "implement its acceptance of all twelve resolutions" that had been adopted by the Security Council. The secretary general of the United Nations was requested to report on the implementation of this resolution and appoint committees to assist not only in the implementation of this resolution but also other decisions adopted by the Security Council.

Chapter 11

Iraq under the Aegis
of the United Nations

The purpose of the dozen Resolutions that the Security Council had adopted before the resort to force under Resolution 678 was to put pressure on Iraq to withdraw from Kuwait by using economic sanctions. But no sooner had the Coalition powers driven the Iraqi forces from Kuwait than almost another dozen Resolutions were issued by the Security Council under which Iraq was subjected to further demands concerning the demolition of weapons of mass destruction, payment for foreign debt to countries that supplied weapons to Iraq, and reparations to all the parties concerned that suffered injury before as well as during the Coalition War. Since the Iraq regime was weakened by the defeat of its forces, the opposition leaders, mainly among dissatisfied Shi'i elements in the southern and Kurdish elements in the northern areas revolted against the regime leading to civil war which prompted the central authorities in Baghdad to crush the uprisings. While the Shi'i uprising, receiving half-hearted support from Iran, was suppressed, the Kurds in the northern area sought refuge in Iran and Turkey. The Kurdish exodus called for foreign intervention which prompted the Security Council to issue further Resolutions which restricted the central government's control in the northern area.

Because the uprisings and the problems that have arisen in the country brought foreign intervention, Iraq seemed to have become no longer free to deal with its own problems, as the limitations set under the U.N. Resolutions, including the economic sanctions, rendered its national government no longer free to exercise its powers under the control of the higher authorities of the United Nations. Restrictions of the attributes of sovereignty and independence have become the theme of complaints by the Iraqi leaders and sympathizers with Iraq's predicament, which have often been voiced in public statements made at the

United Nations and in the country's media. In this work, it is not our purpose to deal with all the events and problems that have arisen in Iraq following the Coalition War, as to do justice to such a task would need a separate volume to cover not only one of the momentous periods of Iraq's history but also its impact on the Arab world as a whole. In this work we intend to deal with three fundamental subjects that have directly resulted from the Coalition War: 1) The Security Council's Resolutions that have been adopted following the Coalition War, their content and impact on Iraq, will be summarized; 2) Another chapter will be devoted to the Shi'i and Kurdish uprisings; 3) The demarcation of the Iraq-Kuwait boundary, a perrenial issue that has bedevilled the relationships between the two countries, will be discussed.

THE SAFWAN ACCORD AND THE UNITED NATIONS RESOLUTIONS

Following the exchange of several notes, a cease-fire was formally accepted by Iraq in a meeting at Safwan, an Iraqi town near the de facto frontier, under which a formal cease-fire was signed on March 3, 1991. The Safwan Accord called on Iraq to comply with all of the United Nations Security Council Resolutions pertaining to the Iraqi occupation of Kuwait as well as a number of ancillary agreements designed to help the Coalition forces to undertake the steps necessary to fulfill both the terms and spirit of the U.N. Resolutions and to allow the Security Council to monitor Iraqi compliance of the Resolutions. The Safwan Accord forbade Iraq to fly any fixed-wing aircraft in the country, and also to abstain from taking any action that might endanger the Coalition forces in southern Iraq. This ban was relaxed after the withdrawal of these forces, but Iraq was not officially informed. The Coalition, however, claimed that Iraq violated the Accord in its movement of surface-to-surface missiles and Iraqi flights into the no-fly zone. Coalition attacks were launched against Iraqi targets in retaliation.

On April 3, 1991, the Security Council considered Resolution 687, under which the terms of the Safwan Accord were included. It was adopted by twelve votes. Cuba opposed while Yaman and Ecuador abstained. Under this Resolution Iraq was required not only to recognize its de facto frontiers with Kuwait as defined under the 1963 Agreement, but also to accept the demarcation of borders and the establishment of a demilitarized area, unequally penetrating six miles into Iraq and three miles into Kuwait. Moreover, it demanded that Iraq should release all detainees and return to Kuwait all property taken during the occupation. Finally the Resolution demanded the dismantling of Iraq's weapons of mass destruction—nuclear, chemical, and biological—and banned the development of such weapons in the future. The Resolution, however, lifted, under the economic sanctions, the prohibition on foodstuffs and medicines, but it retained the air embargo.

A United Nations Special Commission (UNSCOM) was given authority to undertake over 100 missions to Iraq and largely completed the process of identifying and destroying Iraqi weapons of mass destruction, particularly chemical and nuclear weapons as well as ballistic missiles. As the Resolution also required the destruction of all ballistic missiles with a range of more than 150 kilometers, all key technical and industrial installations which might have been used in the nuclear program were also destroyed in 1992. All nuclear-fuel reactors, both fresh and irradiated, were removed in February 1994. On May 11, 1994, the group given the task of destroying chemical weapons declared that all chemical weapons, agents, precursors and wasted chemical would be destroyed by June 14, 1994. UNSCOM also declared Iraq's accounting of its ballistic weapons program was completed, but there were still, and are up to the present day, questions about Iraq's biological weapons program.

On April 5, 1991, the Security Council adopted Resolution 788 by a ten-to-three vote with two abstentions. The Resolution demanded an end to the repression of Iraq's Kurdish and Shi'i communities and for allowing international humanitarian organizations into the country. On May 24, 1991, Iraq, not without initial opposition, signed an agreement permitting the presence of U.N. Security guards as replacements for allied forces in northern Iraq. Two days earlier, Iraq was pressured to withdraw its police from the northern city of Dahuk and to have them replaced by Western noncombat military and foreign relief workers.

The United States, Britain, and France unilaterally acted to establish two exclusion zones, one in the north and the other in the south. They claimed that these no-fly zones were established pursuant to Resolution 788. Iraq rejected these no-fly zones and in vain challenged them in December 1992 and January 1993. On January 13, 1993, American planes attacked Iraqi missile sites and other facilities in southern Iraq on the grounds of security. Similar attacks were launched against ground radar stations in northern Iraq, and American planes downed an Iraqi Mig flying in the area on January 18 and 19, 1993. On January 19, Iraq offered a cease-fire in its confrontations with the United States on the eve of President Clinton's inauguration and offered to allow an American plane to fly into Baghdad without conditions. Two days later, American planes fired a missile and dropped cluster bombs on an Iraqi ground radar in the northern no-fly zone, when its beam was directed at coalition aircraft, but the Iraqi authorities said there were no defence batteries at that location. Other attacks occurred at radar sites on January 23.

On August 15, 1991, the Security Council adopted Resolutions 705 and 706 under which Iraq could sell up to $1.6 billion worth of oil over six months provided that thirty percent of the proceeds would be taken as war reparations. Furthermore, five percent would be assigned to pay for the UNSCOM expenses and an additional portion would pay for other U.N. expenses in Iraq, including paying half of the cost of the Iraq-Kuwait boundary demarcation commission. The remainder was to go into an escrow account for the distribution of food and medicine to the Iraqi people. Iraq rejected the plan on the grounds that it infringed its sovereignty.

Iraqi attempts to deny access or to prevent UNSCOM inspectors from using their aircraft for security or political reasons had led earlier to the adoption of Resolution 707 on August 15, 1991, calling for the granting of full access to inspectors and for disclosure of weapons programs and names of suppliers. Iraq's complaints (September, 1991) about the flying of U.N. inspectors into "limited areas" and their taking of aerial photographs, and calling for Iraqi "specialists" to accompany them were rejected and the United States threatened to send additional aircraft to escort U.N. inspectors. One week later, a confrontation developed with U.N. inspectors who sought to remove documents from a facility in central Baghdad. Iraq claimed the documentary contained information on its scientists and the information might be turned over to Israeli and Western intelligence and jeopardize the lives of Iraqi scientists. Iraq's deputy prime minister accused David Kay, the U.N. team leader of being an American spy. The confrontation ended on September 27 when the inspectors were allowed to leave with the documents. It was also revealed (September 30th) that Kay had sent the information he had gained about Iraq's nuclear program to American officials in Washington before reporting to his U.N. superiors. This kind of confrontation seems to have recurred several times. The latest, following the defection of Husayn Kamil, must have been based on information from Kamil.

On February 8, 1992, Iraq accused the U.N. of violating diplomatic immunity by entering the Baghdad offices of the Arab Scientific Research Council without permission. The United States, Britain, and France declared a no-fly zone in southern Iraq purportedly to protect the Shi'i community and barred Iraqi planes and helicopters south of 32nd parallel. Iraq claimed that this was a violation of International Law.

On October 2, 1992, the Security Council adopted Resolution 778 which provided for the seizure of frozen Iraqi accounts by U.N. member states, and releasing them to the U.N. to pay for U.N.-related expenses in Iraq. On October 6, Saddam Husayn accused the U.N. inspectors of trying to strip Iraq of industrial and technological capability. On February 5, 1993, the Security Council adopted Resolution 806 which called for a phased deployment of additional U.N. troops to the demilitarized zone between Iraq and Kuwait. Iraq also asked the Security Council on March 8 to stop all surveillance flights claiming that information was being passed to Israel. The Bush administration launched massive raids on January 17, 1993, aimed at forty-five cruise missiles at the Za'faraniya manufacturing complex outside Baghdad, which had been made inoperable by inspectors. One missile hit the al-Rashid Hotel and killed three civilians. This was followed by other raids on the January 18 and 19, particularly on defence installations.

On May 7, 1993, Kuwait informed the United States that it had discovered what it claimed to be an Iraqi-sponsored attempt to assassinate former President George Bush while on his trip to Kuwait (April 4–16, 1993). Following American investigations of the evidence, the Clinton administration, responding to calls for retaliation in Congress, decided that Iraq was responsible for orchestrating the event. On June 26, 1993, the United States launched twenty-three Tomahawk cruise missiles carrying 1000-pound warheads at the Baghdad headquarters of the Iraqi intelligence organization. The United States invoked Article 51 of the U.N. Charter—allowing states to use force in case of legitimate self-defence—as justification for its action. Skeptics, however, cited a classified CIA report which said that the evidence might have been manufactured to make an infiltration appear as an attempt to assassinate Bush. The plotters were said to be too inept to be closely tied to Iraqi intelligence. This action was unilateral and therefore not within the jurisdiction of the U.N. Security Council Resolutions pertaining to Iraq. Some of the missiles hit civilian targets killing thirty-eight people including one of Iraq's leading female painters at her home, and wounding several others. The United States launched attacks on Iraqi air-defences in the southern air exclusion zone on August 25 and again on August 29, 1993.

On March 26, 1994, Iraq informed UNSCOM officially that it was accepting the long-term monitoring of its weapons of mass destruction under Resolutions 618 and 715. Iraq's compliance and the deteriorating health and food conditions in the country gave an impetus for other states to call for the lifting of the embargo, as it was done by Turkish President Demerel on January 17, 1994 and Jordan's prime minister on January 18. On May 17, 1994, the U.N. Food and Agriculture Organization and the World Food Program sounded the alarm about commonly recognized 'pre-famine indicators' in the country.

In September, 1994, Iraq massed troops on its border with Kuwait. It was speculated at the time that Iraq was attempting to focus international attention on its efforts to have the sanctions lifted. Iraq's action prompted the United States to deploy emergency military forces to deal with a possible renewed invasion of Kuwait. Most American allies reacted against Iraq's moves although France's defence minister accused the American government of hyping the incident for election-year purposes. The Iraqi government tried to persuade the international community to lift the sanctions because they were creating a human crisis. Since the invasion of Kuwait, Iraq has been under an international economic-sanctions regime that has halted its export of oil (except for a small amount that is smuggled across the border into Turkey and Iran or sold to Jordan). Therefore Iraq has had no source of foreign exchange to finance its purchases of imported goods such as foodstuffs and medicines. The cumulative effect of the sanctions has been exceedingly hard on Iraqi citizens.

In March, 1995, more than 35,000 Turkish troops, claiming "hot pursuit" of separatist Turkish Kurds who had attacked Turkish troops as well as engaged in terrorist attacks, launched an invasion of northern Iraq in hot pursuit to destroy the Kurdish Workers Party (PKK) training camps and capture stores of arms and ammunition. While the United States, claiming that it "understood" Turkey's position, did not object to the invasion, France and other European countries objected strongly to the Turkish invasion.

IMPACT OF THE UNITED NATIONS SANCTIONS ON IRAQ

While the Coalition powers sought to achieve political and military goals through the application of economic sanctions, the impact of the sanctions on civilian citizens proved highly disastrous, contrary to the United Nations reservations that the sanctions should not apply to food and medicine. Despite reports by U.N. officials as well as by humanitarian organizations that health conditions were deteriorating, the economic embargo continues to the present. A report by the United Nations Undersecretary General Marti Ahtissari published on March 22, 1991, states that the U.N. sanctions "seriously affected" Iraq's ability to feed its people. This was noted by the drafters of the Security Council's Resolution 687, a long and comprehensive document of thirty- four paragraphs. It was adopted on April 3, by twelve votes to one (Cuba), with two abstentions (Yaman and Ecuador). It removed the embargo on foodstuffs, eased restrictions on essential civilian needs, and unfroze Iraq's foreign assets. However, the lifting of the remaining restrictions was tied to the elimination of Iraq's non-conventional weapons and other provisions, concerned with the demarcation of borders between Iraq and Kuwait, peacekeeping, international terrorism, and other matters.

The list of demands—military, political, economic, and geographic—that Iraq must meet if the sanctions were to be lifted, was outlined in several Security Council Resolutions as noted earlier. Judging by the international politics of sanctions as they have been practiced since they were imposed in 1990, their removal will obviously have to result from a political act. This means that either the American government will change its policy toward Iraq, or Iraq will have to change its policy and comply to all the terms of the U.N. Resolutions. Neither of these changes seemed to be imminent. Indeed, at the Geneva meeting, James Baker warned Tariq 'Aziz that the United States would bomb Iraq back to the pre-industrial age, presumably to let 'Aziz know that the Bush administration was determined to bring Iraq to its knees if it did not withdraw from Kuwait. 'Aziz, however, was not forthcoming, as he knew that higher authorities in Baghdad were in no mood to acquiesce to American pressure. As a result, the economy has no chance but to continue its downward slide.[1]

Due to this catastrophe, Iraq appeared to be in an appalling condition. For example, the paralysis of electric-power plants deprived the people of drinking water, interrupted agricultural irrigation through pumping stations, and clogged the sewage system. Hospitals without generators were unable to perform surgery. A Harvard University health study team undertook the first systematic and comprehensive on-site examination of public health in Iraq.[2] After the Coalition War, the team visited all the major cities and a number of smaller towns all over the country from April 28 to May 6, 1991. The study found the existence of "a public health catastrophe." It estimated that at least 170,000 children under five would die in the coming year from the "delayed effects of the war." This figure represented a doubling of infant and child mortality. The study found prevalence of severe malnutrition which indicated the real possibility of famine, cholera, and typhoid.[3]

While the focus of the Coalition's strategic bombing was on military targets, it is clear that many of the targets were also vital parts of the civilian infrastructure, since they had dual-use purpose. More importantly, the definition of strategic targets by the Coalition forces was expanded to include targets such as telephone and communications facilities, power and industrial plants, and key headquarters, many of which were outside the area of military operation and some deep inside Iraq.[4] Moreover, while telephone lines and electricity as well as roads and bridges may be used for military purposes, the bulk of their use is in fact civilian in nature. The United Nations approved some sanctions that left a severe impact on the country's food stock as well as on its industries which were dependent on the outside world for spare parts, raw materials, and machinery. About 16,000 private ventures had either shut down or were close to halting their activities by the fall of 1990.[5] The massive destruction of the civilian infrastructure and the high number of casualties was considered one of the highest rates of killing in "organized warfare" in recent history.[6]

One of the most serious features of the economic sanctions was to require Iraq to apply to the Security Council for permission and procedures to engage in trade (i.e., how much oil can it sell, which exporting terminals may the oil go through, how much to import, what to import and other questions). Furthermore, Resolution 687 (1991) stipulated that a special U.N.-administered compensation fund be created for which thirty percent of Iraq's oil revenue is to be earmarked to pay reparations for claims against Iraq for any direct-loss damage (including environmental damage and depletion of natural resources) and injury to foreign governments, nationals and corporations, as a result of the invasion of Kuwait. Moreover, about 130 million must be assigned to replenish the Kurdish area and to pay for all expenses of U.N. commissions that visited Iraq for inspections and demolition of weapons for mass destruction. By accepting such a Resolution, Iraq in effect must agree to mortgage its oil revenues for a long time to come. Although the sanctions continue to be in effect, Iraq is able to generate small amounts of foreign currency from several sources such as the sale of small quantities of oil to Jordan, Iran, and Turkey, the sale of gold by the government, the smuggling of public-sector machinery and equipment to Iraq, the sale of privately owned gold, liquidation of privately owned, foreign-held balances to finance trade, and the release of small amounts of frozen assets by certain foreign governments. Such foreign exchange earnings are used by the government and the private sector to import small amounts of food, medicines, and other commodities. For this reason, the Iraqi people are frustrated with the sanctions' unreasonable rules.

According to a report written by independent Iraqi experts, Iraq's oil revenue once U.N. sanctions are lifted will not be enough to meet its minimum requirements for feeding its people and rebuilding its shattered economy. The experts calculated that Iraq would earn around $11.4 billion a year in the first five years after the sanctions disappear. But it estimated that annual expenditure for that period would total no less than twelve billion dollars—three billion to service Iraq's debt, four billion for Gulf War reparations, three billion for food and medicine imports, and two billion for reconstruction. These calculations were based on an Iraqi oil output of 2.5 million barrels a day with crude selling at an average of fifteen dollars a barrel throughout the five-year period.[7]

Part of Baghdad's strategy aimed at getting the sanctions lifted has been to lure foreign oil companies with lucrative post-sanction contracts, thus securing the support of the governments of their home countries for an end to the U.N. embargo. Some of the negotiations, particularly with the Russians and French, are at an advanced stage and contracts could be signed within weeks of the U.N. Security Council lifting the sanctions in part or as a whole.

Attempts by France and Russia to persuade the Security Council to consider a partial lifting of the economic sanctions was based partly on the grounds that Iraq had already cooperated with the United Nations Commission for the destruction of Iraq's weapons of mass destruction and partly because of the deterioration in the health conditions which caused an increasing rate of death among the children. But the United States and Britain, opposed to Saddam Husayn's regime and expecting its replacement by another friendly to the West, rejected the proposal of partial lifting of the sanctions and held that it might even strengthen Saddam's regime and prolong its existence in power.

Owing to the deterioration in health conditions, especially the increasing rate of death among children, the United States and Britain proposed Resolution 986, which was adopted by the Security Council on April 14, 1995, by virtue of which Iraq would be allowed to sell oil in the amount of two billion dollars during a six month period (with possible renewal for another six months period to sell oil for two more billions of dollars) for the purchase of food and medicine. As Resolution 986 stipulated that the distribution of food and medicine among the people should be carried out under a United Nations Special Commission, the Iraq Government refused to accept the Resolution on the grounds that the United Nations supervision is an interference in domestic affairs which would infringe Iraq's sovereignty and independence. Iraq also objected to the distribution of food and medicine in the Kurdish area, which has already been considered a secluded province under United Nations supervision, because it might also compromise Iraq's sovereignty, as the Kurdish area is still part of Iraq.

In 1996, owing to further worsening health conditions, the Iraq Government agreed to cooperate with the United Nations on the implementation of food distribution partly under domestic pressure which called for the acceptance of Resolution 986 and partly under the urging of friendly Arab and European governments. Iraq also sought that by further cooperation with the United Nations, it hoped that the economic sanctions as a whole might be lifted in the near future. Whether these expectations will ever be realized would depend on the degree of cooperation between the Iraqi authorities and the United Nations Commission.

Chapter 12

Shi'i and Kurdish Uprisings

The Iraqi Army's defeat by the Coalition powers and the massive destruction of military and civilian areas released pent-up anti-regime feelings among the opposition groups inside and outside the country. Above all, it reinvigorated opponents to the regime among the Shi'is in southern Iraq and the Kurds in northern areas who had long been awaiting favorable opportunities for uprisings against the central government.

The Shi'i and Kurdish uprisings erupted spontaneously when the cease-fire brought the Coalition's military operations to an end. They were given impetus by the coordinated efforts of several opposition groups, and were encouraged by the Coalition powers. It was almost taken for granted that the end of the regime was near at hand after President Bush's announcement (February 27, 1991) that he was bringing a halt to Operation Desert Storm. The truce was formalized at Safwan on March 3rd when the military leaders from the two sides agreed to the terms of a cease-fire that left about one-sixth of Iraq's territory under the control of the Coalition's forces.

The Iraqi opposition to the regime represents a wide range of individuals, organizations, political and religious parties, and movements with varying degrees of support inside Iraq. The overall number of opposition organizations that have suffered, and continue to suffer, splintering and rivalry range between sixty-five and seventy. These consist of a variety of religious and ethnic groups such as Shi'is, Kurds, Turkomans, and Assyrians, as well as Communist, Islamist, secularist, pan-Arabist parties, and other independent figures.[1] Their opposition to the Ba'th regime is perhaps their only unifying factor. Deep personal, ideological, and political differences continue to exist between them. Their ability to form a viable opposition and to overthrow the regime is generally viewed with skepticism even by many of their regional and Western supporters. Most of their leaders have lived in exile for many years and are unknown to most Iraqi citizens. They generally lack strong organizations or a solid base for support inside the country.

The group with the largest base of support are the Kurdish parties: the Kurdistan Democratic Party (KDP) and the Patriotic Union of Kurdistan (PUK). The KDP is led by Mas'ud Barzani, the son of Mullah Mustafa Barzani who founded the party and led the Iraqi Kurds from the 1940's until his death in 1979. The PUK is lead by Jalal Talabani who emerged in the 1960's as a rival and critic of Mullah Mustafa Barzani. Other than the two large parties on the Kurdish scene, there are small, but growing, Islamist groups such as the Islamic Movement of Kurdistan led by Shaykh 'Umar and 'Uthman 'Abd al-'Aziz and the Kurdish Hizb Allah led by Adham Barzani which are also active along with influential tribal feudal groups who will be discussed below. The Kurdish Workers Party (PKK) that has used northern Iraq as one of its bases in its fight against the Turkish government has also made some gains among the Iraqi Kurds. The Iraqi invasion of Kuwait and the international response to it gave renewed life to a very weak opposition. In 1990, opposition groups, which for the first time included Shi'i representatives, met in Damascus where they launched the National Joint Action Committee to formulate a strategy designed to coordinate their activities to overthrow the regime. The Kurdish and Shi'i groups played a major role in the unsuccessful uprisings launched at the end of Desert Storm.

During the uprisings of March, 1991, the opposition groups met in Bayrut and agreed to work for the replacement of the Ba'th regime by a federal and democratic system in which the Kurds would enjoy a broad level of autonomy. These groups, however, were unable to work together despite attempts to establish a more effective opposition umbrella organization. In June, 1992, two hundred delegates representing secular Kurdish and Shi'i opposition groups met in Vienna where they formed the Iraqi National Congress (INC). In October 1991, INC representatives met in the Kurdish area that was protected by the Western allies to elect a three-man leadership and a twenty-six-member executive council. The executive council was headed by Ahmad Chalabi, a secular Shi'i banker. The council consisted of Hasan al-Naqib, a pan-Arab and former Iraqi Chief of Staff who broke with the regime in 1978 while he was ambassador to Syria, Kurdish leader Mas'ud Al-Barzani, and Muhammad Bahr al-'Ulum, a moderate Shi'i cleric who did not favor the establishment of an Islamic state. Despite foreign support, most of the opposition groups continue to suffer from factionalism and the absence of deep-seated support inside Iraq.

Within a few days following the Coalition War, the uprising in the southern part of the country quickly spread to the Kurdish area in the north. The "popular uprising," as it was described, began on March 2nd when a group of armed men from Suq al-Shuyukh, a town under the control of U.S. troops, arrived at Nasiriya and organized hundreds of deserters to attack government headquarters in the area. Nasiriya lies on the edge of the marshes where Iraqi deserters from the war had taken refuge along with Shi'i opponents of the regime.

Similar events occurred in Basra. Angry and disgruntled infantry soldiers who had returned to the city, bringing with them tales of their devastating defeat and humiliation, launched attacks against Ba'th Party offices, its Popular Army, and security headquarters. The rebels seem to have solicited the Coalition forces to help them in overthrowing the regime. Hardly had the uprising begun in Nasiriya and Basra than it spread to a number of other southern towns including the Shi'i holy cities of Karbala and Najaf. It was in these cities that the insurgents were joined by thousands of armed followers of the Supreme Assembly of the Islamic Revolution in Iraq (SAIRI) and launched attacks against Ba'th members and military and security officials and their families. These events were a spontaneous anti-regime reaction that exploited the weakness of the Iraqi Army caused by its haphazard and bloody withdrawal from Kuwait. Basra, Iraq's second largest city, became an important bellwether for what was to take place in other areas.[2]

A number of observations might be made about the nature of the uprising and its leadership. First, the uprising seems to have occurred in areas where the people and the civil infrastructure were not equipped to handle the large numbers of troops and equipment that were retreating from Kuwait. Second, the uprising began as an expression of the state of anarchy in a Basra that was crowded with huge numbers of heavily armed soldiers who were still reeling with bitterness from the military defeat and the sheer weight of the Coalition's attacks by planes, ships, missiles, and laser-guided bombs as well as from hunger resulting from the economic sanctions. Third, it is clear that the uprisings did not come about as a result of a well-planned action nor was it able to offer a political program or alternative vision for the future. It also became clear that the uprising lacked the political leadership from inside the country who could offer a plan for a new and viable regime. What emerged instead was a disorganized popular movement in areas which had a Shi'i majority and which armed itself in the early stages with weapons taken mostly from the army or from the weapons distributed by the regime to defend against Coalition attacks. No less important is the rumor that the insurgents believed, as a result of the American call for the overthrow of the regime, that Saddam was finished. It is true that President Bush made an explicit call on February 15 for the Iraqi people and military to overthrow Saddam's regime. He stated that if they wanted to end the bloodshed they should take "matters into their own hands to force Saddam Husayn the dictator to step aside."[3] However, the insurgents in the North and South believed that "Saddam was finished."[4] But no serious American assistance was offered.

Several top Iraqi military leaders, were said, according to an unconfirmed report, to have held a secret meeting at a military base outside the city of Nasiriya. The meeting was attended by such important military leaders as Mahir ʿAbd al-Rashid, the former commander of the Republican Guard and a hero of the Iraq-Iran war who was dismissed at its conclusion. It was reported that the military leaders expressed their views as follows:

> Defeat is inevitable and the political leadership must pay the price. Instead of letting the others make the choice, it is better for us to choose an alternative leadership in order to safeguard Iraq's territorial integrity . . .

As to how the power would be transferred, the report stated:

> At the end of the meeting and the acceptance of the conditions of a cease-fire, provided that the cease-fire is followed by Saddam Husayn's announcement within two weeks that he would step down from power and transfer his leadership to a military leadership comprising three officers. These were named from among the participants [in the meeting]. This was on condition that the military council could guarantee the safety of Saddam Husayn and his family.[5]

Even if such a decision had been carried out, it is clear that no credible organized leadership could replace Saddam Husayn as the threats to Iraq's survival as an independent and united country doomed any chance that the army and the upper echelons of the Baʿth Party would turn against the regime that could maintain the unity of the country. For example, on February 24, 1991, Salah ʿUmar al-ʿAli, a former member of the Iraqi opposition, called in vain on the Iraqi people to overthrow Saddam's regime over the clandestine Voice of Free Iraq:

> The tyrant of Iraq, like all other tyrants before him, totally disregarded the innocent blood, did not think of your national interests. . . . he thinks of himself alone. . . . You have no option but to put an end to the dictator and his criminal gang in an effort to survive and defend the homeland. Rise and save the homeland from the clutches of the dictatorship. . . . prove to your people and nation that you are faithful and honorable sons of this generous country and this honorable nation.[6]

Nor did the opposition groups united under one leadership appeal to the people as a way to preserve the country's unity. The uprisings which broke out in different parts of the country were based mainly on sectarian and ethnic lines rather than on party-based political lines, while the Sunni Arabs played little or no part in it. The Sunni leadership in Iraq had always called for unity on national grounds, but they were opposed to Shiʿi dissident groups, as Shiʿi political ascendancy might invite Iranian intervention in Iraq's domestic affairs.[7]

While the Kurdish uprising received the most attention in the Western media, the uprising in southern Iraq was largely dependent on local support and appeared as the bloodiest and most threatening to the regime. For example, the rebels in Basra voiced the slogans "*Maku wali illa 'Ali*" and "*La hakim illa Ja'fari*" which mean: "There is no authority except 'Ali" and "No ruler other than a Ja'fari (Shi'i)".[8] Other slogans declared that the government must neither be Eastern nor Western, but Islamic.[9] These slogans were reminiscent of the Iranian Revolution and unacceptable to secular opposition leaders who had called for a secular regime friendly to the West.

The extremism and violence of the uprising in the South aroused concern not only in northern Iraq, but also among Shi'i moderate groups. Bloody massacres occurred in places such as Kut, 'Amara, Najaf, and Karbala, which witnessed the worst incidents where some officials and their families were cut to pieces, beheaded, and dragged through the streets, and sometimes burned. The Iran-based Iranian Revolutionary Guards and the al-Badr and al-Tawwabin brigades, under the leadership of the Supreme Assembly of the Islamic Revolution in Iraq (SAIRI) which had infiltrated southern Iraq became involved in these incidents and provided direction and leadership to the uprising during the first few days in March. These forces also included small numbers of Iranian Revolutionary Guards. The Tawwabin was comprised of Iraqi POWs who refused to return to Iraq after the war with Iran. Muhammad Baqir al-Hakim, the head of SAIRI, claimed that Iran did not play an important role in the uprisings in Iraq.[10]

By March 5th, the uprising spread to Najaf where Ayat-Allah Abu al-Qasim al-Khu'i, the leading Shi'i religious authority had resided. Al-Khu'i, an Iranian by origin, had criticized Khumaini's concept of Islamic government on theological grounds, but during his residence in Iraq had avoided involvement in political affairs. Al-Khu'i, as well as other religious leaders, was overcome by the extremism of the events. He was greatly concerned about the killings and destruction of public and private property. He issued two *fatwas*, or religious edicts, dealing with the uprising. In the first, he called on the insurgents to protect the property of private and public citizens and institutions and to conduct themselves in accordance with Islamic law which prohibits harming people and the destruction of property and requires that corpses lying in the streets should be buried. On March 8th he issued another *fatwa* establishing a higher committee to protect "public good" to be composed of nine high-ranking religious leaders who would act on his behalf. It is not clear whether this committee could be viewed as an alternative government, as some have held, or merely as a temporary arrangement until public order was restored. Regardless of intent, the committee helped to calm down matters somewhat—prisoners at shrines were released, soldiers were provided food by the clergy, and citizens were urged to return to work.[11]

The central government in Baghdad, which at first appeared to have been overwhelmed by the Coalition War and by the joint uprisings in the North and South, quickly realized that it had to fight not only for its survival as the loss of the Shi'i Arab South, unlike the loss of the Kurdish North, would not only undermine its own authority but also might threaten the country's territorial integrity and independence. For this reason, the government at once became very active. It mobilized its forces from the North and center, especially the Republican Guard, to suppress the Shi'i uprising in the South. In less than three weeks, Baghdad was able to bring under its control every major rebel-held city and town. The holy cities of Karbala and Najaf were reportedly ravaged.

At Karbala, the number of rebels had swelled by army defectors, deserters, and SAIRI forces to almost 50,000.[12] They were largely dependent on weapons and ammunition either abandoned by Iraqi soldiers who fled the battlefield or brought along by those soldiers that defected. Some of the insurgents fled Karbala after the arrival of government troops, but most of them put up fierce resistance. As they were pushed back, some 3,000 along with a small number of civilian supporters barricaded themselves inside the holy shrine where they thought government soldiers might refrain from attack. After a short attempt to force their surrender by siege, the army was ordered to attack. Heavy tank and artillery fire quickly brought an end to the resistance. Six-hundred people, mostly civilians, were killed in the confrontation, and the rest were taken prisoner, including sixty Iranians according to an Iraqi official. These figures, however, probably are less than the actual number of casualties.

The Shi'i dissident movement, without substantial help from foreign sources, had no real chance of standing against loyal military and Ba'th Party elements which had been built over the years. As Iraqi troops appeared to be gaining control over the insurgents, Iran's spiritual leader, Ayat-Allah Khamene'i on March 13, urged the Iraqi army not to fire on Muslims as this was forbidden by Islam and called for the establishment of an Islamic state in Iraq. Basra, however, had been retaken by March 12 and Karbala by March 13.

The Iraqi army met stiff resistance at Najaf, where the insurgents, like those at Karbala, retreated to the holy shrines. The army attempted to keep them under siege, but as resistance continued, the heavy guns and surface-to-surface missiles were turned on them and their resistance quickly ended. In both Karbala and Najaf, an unknown number of civilians and combatants were killed, estimates ranged from 600 to 6,000. There were reports that between 3,000 and 6,000 were taken prisoner, including members of the Iranian Revolutionary Guards.[13]

Meanwhile, *al-Iraq*, a pro-government newspaper warned that, "hostile forces seeking to annihilate Iraq by disintegrating its national unity in accordance with their inherited colonialist principle of 'divide and rule'."[14] It added that "Iraq belongs to all its citizens and sons," and urged them to confront the colonialists by strengthening the national unity. It described the current stage as a "challenge." The army's paper confidently predicted, on March 8th, that "the coming days will prove that the calculations of Iraq's enemies are mere illusions."[15]

On March 16, 1991, Saddam Husayn delivered his first speech since the end of the Coalition War. Focusing on recent events, he blamed:

> The herds of rancorous traitors falsely carrying Iraqi identity infiltrated from inside and outside the country to spread terror, devastation, sabotage, and looting in a number of southern cities those renegades and traitors began to attack some of the army units and barracks to capture weapons and began to burn people's property, loot Government offices, schools, hospitals, houses, and dishonor women. . . .[16]

He also blamed Iran for trying to harm Iraq and warned that "any attempt to change the system of government during war with the assistance of foreign forces cannot be considered a nationalist event." Saddam declared that Iraq has never been and will not belong to a certain sect or faction, thus making possible sectarian rivalry. He warned that the transformation of Iraq's diversity into divisions leads to the "fragmentation of the country and would be like entering the dark maze that Lebanon has experienced for over fifteen years."

The Shi'i uprisings in the South, where the majority of people are Shi'is, demonstrated that there was a deep-seated resentment against the regime.[17] But, despite the speed with which it spread, the opposition seemed unable to gather sufficient Shi'i and other support even at a time when the regime was at its weakest. During the recent decades of its history and particularly during the Iran-Iraq war, it appeared that the idea of Iraq as an Arab country had made significant inroads, especially among the generations that grew up after World War I, over a traditional, religious, or sectarian identity. This is also true among other non-Muslim communities in Iraq.[18]

In the South the situation remained generally calm after the harsh suppression of the uprisings. The opposition leaders remarked that the government had begun at that time to drain the marshes, where Shi'i followers had resided for centuries, and to divert water to rivers and canals. In response, the government pointed out that the project was intended for long-planned agricultural projects that go back to the early 1950s and were recommended by American companies. There is no doubt that some of the diversions were also aimed at forcing residents to relocate in order to deny the opposition viable bases of resistance. On August 26, 1992, the United States, Britain, and France inaugurated a limited no-fly zone south of the 32nd parallel similar to the Kurdish area. Since 1991 the Iraqi army has been able, with tribal and party support, to maintain a firm grip on the security situation in the South. Low-level anti-regime activities by Iranian-based opposition groups continue, but appear to have had little impact on the regime's overall control of the South.

After the collapse of the uprising, the United States and its allies sponsored the adoption of Security Council Resolution 688. This resolution demanded that the Iraqi government end the repression of its citizens in the North and South of the country and that efforts by international humanitarian organizations be allowed to reach all persons in need. Ironically, this was done at a time when the Iraqi people as a whole continued to suffer the impact of the crippling sanctions. A memorandum of understanding between U.N. and Iraqi government representatives allowed for the presence of 600 U.N. relief workers and 500 guards for the humanitarian efforts. After a lapse of the agreement, a new memorandum was signed in October, 1992 which allowed for 300 guards, an unspecified number of relief workers, and a $180–200 million relief program for the country to provide some food supplies and to help restore sanitation and health-care facilities.

These efforts were briefly suspended following a series of bombing and other terrorist incidents aimed at U.N. supply trucks. A new agreement was signed in 1993. Despite this help, however, a U.N. report released in July, 1993 warned that the Iraqis were facing pre-famine conditions and urged that the U.N. sanctions be lifted.

The Shi'i uprising in southern Iraq gave an impetus to a more serious uprising in the Kurdish area to achieve autonomy. In order not to alienate foreign support or to scare neighbors such as Iran and Turkey upon whose good will they depended to wage their struggle against Baghdad, Kurdish leaders appealed for autonomy, rather than independence. The Kurdish leader, Jalal Talabani, expressing the aspirations of many Kurds, said:

> I have the right to dream of an independent Kurdistan and the Kurdish people has the right to self-determination, but for political reasons we cannot change the existing boundaries. . . . What we favor is the establishment of democracy within the framework of Iraq.[19]

The Kurds have long aspired to have an autonomous or semi-independent status in Iraq. They inhabit the mountainous region including large areas in Iran, Iraq, and Turkey. There are Kurds who also live in Syria and Armenia. The population of Kurdistan is indeterminate but is generally believed to number around three-to-four million in Iraq, seven-to-eight million in Iran and thirteen to fifteen million in Turkey. In Iraq, the Kurds live in the northern area, also known as southern Kurdistan. They inhabit the northeast sector of the old Mawsil (Mosul) province, three-quarters of the Irbil province, almost all of Sulaimaniya province, and half of Kirkuk province, as well as a small part of Diyala (Ba'quba) province. The Kurds, like other inhabitants of the area, are a racial mixture that owes it composition to the migrations and invasion by various groups that have ruled the area at different times. From ancient records we get a picture of a proud and tough people, unresponsive to foreign powers. To this day, the Kurds remain a distinct and separate people. This may be attributed to their mountainous territory that forms a geographic barrier between them and their neighbors, to their ferocity in defending their territory, and to their self-sufficient economy that reduces their need for contact with outsiders. The Kurds indeed have never possessed an independent status; they have been ruled and oppressed by many foreign rulers. This situation has led to the growth of a strong tribal and feudal system. The tribal and religious leaders have played a leading role in the recent history of the Kurds.[20]

Yet many of the factors which helped to protect the Kurdish identity have also helped to divide them. The fact that Kurdistan was remote and inaccessible combined with the lack of a modern transportation system made communication difficult. The development of a strong tribal system increased intra-Kurdish rivalries and suspicions. Since World War I, the Kurds have been divided among four countries— Turkey, Syria, Iraq, and Iran. The variety of spoken dialects further impeded communication; even in Iraqi Kurdistan, the Kurds speak dialects that vary from region to region. The majority of Kurds are Sunni Muslims. But there is a small minority of Shi'i Kurds who live mostly in southern Kurdistan, Kirmanshah, and Luristan, where other small minorities including Yazidis, Christians, and Ahl al-Haq (who deify the Imam 'Ali) live.

The Kurds were latecomers to the concept of nationalism which had spread among the various Middle Eastern peoples under the Ottoman Empire. Kurdish opportunity for the creation of a state offered itself after World War I when independence would have been recognized under the Treaty of Sèvres (Articles 62, 63, and 64). Kurdish and Armenian hopes were however dashed by the emergence of the Turkish nationalist movement under the leadership of Mustafa Kamal that denied independence to the Kurds.[21]

Kurdish nationalist aspirations have been expressed in a variety of forms. The Kurds have made attempts at dialogue with national regimes of the countries in which they inhabit, with international bodies, and within the Kurdish community itself. They have also traveled the road of violent struggle. For their part, the Kurds have not, however, established a unified community with an organized program for action. Instead, they have always been torn apart by feudal, tribal, religious, and political forces and differences. The countries in which the Kurds have resided were preoccupied with their own national or international objectives and were often led, at best, to the Kurds or give them little more than verbal and often transitory support. Small wonder that the Kurdish uprisings before World War II were considered little more than tribal insurgencies and were manipulated by Britain and France.

The history of the Iraqi Kurds in the postwar years offers an excellent example of the impact of new ideologies and foreign intervention. The Iraqi Kurds at one point were edged by foreign powers into positions near autonomy, only to find that such a policy was remanded.

Tribal uprisings were often encouraged or discouraged, depending upon the extent to which they served the political interests of foreign powers or neighboring countries, such as the rival claims to Mawsil between Turkey and Iraq.

Following World War I, several tribal uprisings which began to take nationalist overtones were suppressed by the Iraqi government. In the 1940s cooperation between Mulla Mustafa Barzani, a charismatic tribal leader, and a group of several Kurdish nationalists led to an uprising with clear nationalist demands.[22] The suppression of this uprising drove Barzani to support the Soviet-backed autonomous Kurdish Republic of Mahabad in Iran. After the collapse of the Mahabad regime, he fled to the USSR where he remained until the overthrow of the Iraqi monarchy in 1958.[23] The new government, under Brigadier ʿAbd al-Karim Qasim, invited Barzani to return and provided him with arms and money. Qasim, however, was noncommittal on Kurdish autonomy, although the Constitution recognized the Kurds as partners with equal rights in the country. An uneasy alliance between Qasim and Barzani lasted until 1961 when competing interests and demands led to a confrontation.[24]

Overthrown by the Baʿth Party and pan-Arab officers, the Qasim regime came to an end in 1963. Under the Baʿth regime, the initial efforts at negotiations with Kurdish leaders quickly deteriorated into an armed conflict.[25] The Kurds were suspicious of the Baʿth emphasis on Arab nationalism. In 1966, Premier ʿAbd al-Rahman al-Bazzaz offered amnesty to Kurdish rebels and a twelve-point program to resolve the Kurdish dispute. It was a compromise between Arab and Kurdish nationalism. The military, however, opposed to Kurdish autonomy, caused the collapse of the regime.

Following their return to power in 1968, the Baʿthist leaders realized that to resolve the Kurdish problem, they must come to terms with Kurdish nationalists. In 1969, the Baʿth government adopted several measures, partly based on the Bazzaz program, aimed at the reconciliation with the Kurds. A Manifesto, composed of fifteen articles was issued on March 11, 1970. This manifesto tacitly recognized a Kurdish identity with the admission that the Iraqi people consist of two main nationalities, Kurdish and Arab. Autonomy was promised to the Kurds within four years in those areas where they form a majority of the population. The Kurdish language was given official status, and Kurds were to be taken into the government on the basis of their numerical proportion of the population. A Kurdish vice-president and Kurdish ministers were to be appointed to the government, and an amnesty was granted to Kurdish rebels and Kurdish detainees were to be released. The Government promised also to help in the reconstruction of the Kurdish area. In return, the Kurds promised to disband their army (*peshmerga*) and to hand over their heavy weapons and radio transmitters to the government. The Manifesto offered the Kurds an opportunity to run their own local affairs through an autonomous regime. The Manifesto and the autonomy law of 1974 granted limited control to the Kurds over natural resources, but reserved internal security, defence, and foreign affairs for the central government. The law made it clear that the Iraq government considered the "Kurdistan area" and its people to be an indivisible part of Iraq.[26]

The March Manifesto was intended to provide security for the Kurds and end the persistent conflict that had plagued Iraq since 1958. It literally transformed Iraq into a formal federal state composed of Kurdish and Arab areas. Cultural pluralism was a recognized fact and the political system would be adapted to meet these requirements. A solution, however, was not to be so easily found. While the first year witnessed implementation of a number of projects, disagreements soon arose and distrust replaced cooperation. Mulla Mustafa, who was encouraged by promises of assistance from the United States, Iran, and Israel, became suspicious of Ba'thist goals following two attempts on his life and escalated his demands.[27] Among other things, he insisted that oil-rich Kirkuk should be included in the Kurdish area and that the Kurds be given the authority to maintain their own forces and to establish contacts with foreign powers. In 1974, when negotiations failed, the government announced that it was ready to implement the March Manifesto in the areas under its control, and it appointed the members of a legislative assembly and an executive council to administer it. These actions, however, did not dissuade the Kurdish leadership from going into an armed struggle.

Heavy fighting ensued in the Spring and continued until the Autumn. The Iraqi armed forces, better trained and equipped than the Kurdish irregulars, were able to make costly but steady advances against Barzani's force. Mulla Mustafa's appeal to foreign powers for help prompted the Shah of Iran to increase his aid to the Kurdish army. But when the Shah's assistance proved insufficient, it was increased with possible Iranian entry into a war with Iraq. The gravity of the situation led to mediation efforts by Algeria and the two sides reached a compromise on March 6, 1975. The Algiers Accord resulted in gains for both sides. For Iran it meant that Iraq accepted Iranian demands that the Shatt al-Arab boundary between the two countries run along the thalweg line and that Iraq put an end to its support of all opponents to the Shah's regime. For Iraq, it signified an end to the costly Kurdish rebellion and recognized the status quo concerning land frontiers.[28]

The Iraqi government followed a policy that combined severity with leniency in dealing with the Kurds. It began to implement major development programs in the area intended to improve the living standards of the people by establishing hospitals, schools, anti-literacy centers, factories for light industry, and tourist centers. It also began to implement land-reform programs by virtue of which it sought to weaken the tribal and feudal structure of society. Meanwhile, the Iraqi government began to implement tough security measures on the basis of which thousands of Kurds were relocated in other Kurdish or Arab areas of Iraq, leading to the creation of a strategic border zone stretching from six to twelve miles along the border of Turkey and Iran. The government also resettled some of its returning refugees from Iran in areas other than their own homes. But as a result of growing opposition to this policy and because some Kurdish groups began to take up arms against the regime, the Government modified its policy. Kurdish guerrilla activities became isolated and ineffective until the outbreak of the Iraq-Iran war.[29]

Since Mulla Mustafa's death, a struggle for leadership has ensued among the younger urban generation who have sought to pursue Mulla Mustafa's assertion on larger concessions for Kurdish autonomy. Jalal Talabani, the leader of the PUK, challenged Barzani's leadership and has show readiness to cooperate with the regime. But Mas'ud Barzani, who inherited his father's leadership of the Kurdish Democratic Party, asserted large concessions for Kurdish autonomy and a struggle for power between the two leaders has ensued. A faction from each of the two parties began to cooperate with the government in the implementation of the March Manifesto as they maintained that the Kurdish people would obtain greater concessions by cooperation rather than by resorting to force. At any rate, they argued, the Kurds could not possibly win by confrontation, as the Iraqi government had at its disposal greater military force than the Kurds.

When the Iraq-Iran war broke out in 1980, both Mas'ud Barzani and Talabani sought to cooperate with Iran, hoping that if Iran would win, Iraq might come to term with the Kurds and either seek their support or by pressure from Iran. Neither expectation proved in their best interests. Chemical weapons were also used against them. A case in point is the attack on Halabja, a town in Iraq's Kurdish area near the Iranian border, where a large number of Kurds died. On March 16, 1988, Iraq was accused by Iran and the Western press of launching a chemical attack.

While there is no doubt that Halabja was the target of chemical weapons and Iraq was held responsible for using them, it is not yet completely clear who fired them. An American Defence Department study, reported in the *Washington Post* states that both Iran and Iraq used gas, but a "conclusive intelligence" has shown that Iran may have been the first to fire artillery shells filled with cyanide gas into Halabja, and medical teams visiting the sight said most of the victims died of cyanide gas.[30] According to American officials, "Iraq does not use cyanide gas. . . . We are sure that Iran uses cyanide." Another study (commissioned by the U.S. Army War College Strategic Studies Institute) held that perhaps both sides fired chemical weapons at Halabja: "Iraq was blamed for the Halabja attack, although it was subsequently brought out that Iran too had used chemicals in its operation, and it seemed likely that it was the Iranian operation that killed the Kurds.[31]

During the last months following the war with Iran, the Iraqi government pursued a harsh policy, known as the al-Anfal campaign, against the Kurdish insurgents accused of collaborating with Iran. The government pursued a policy of destroying Kurdish villages and towns and relocated hundreds of thousands of Kurds in areas far away from their homes in the mountainous borders. A Congressional staff report, given credence by Secretary of State George Schultz, made new accusations, denied by Iraqi officials, that Iraq also used chemical weapons.[32] The repression brought an unprecedented degree of unity among Kurdish groups. The Kurdish leaders became very active and formed a Kurdish Front ready to cooperate with other opposition groups. It was, however, the Gulf War that gave the Kurdish leaders an opportunity to achieve full autonomous status over which the Iraqi government had no control, owing to the support the Kurds received from the Coalition powers.

Jalal Talabani, who was responsible for foreign affairs in the Iraqi Kurdistan Front, visited the United States soon after Iraq invaded Kuwait. In talks with American officials, he offered to provide military intelligence and cooperation in the war against the central government, on the condition that the United States give the Kurds financial, military, and political support.[33] He was told the United States was reported to have agreed to offer money and guns, but not direct formal recognition of the Kurds.[34] This offer was rejected by the Kurds, although the United States may have given the Kurds weapons when the Coalition War had started.[35] The Kurds in any case were ready to go into confrontation with the Iraqi government at any opportune moment.

No sooner had the Shi'i uprising in the South started than the Kurdish uprising followed it a few days later. It began at the town of Raniya on March 4th near the Iranian borders and quickly spread to other towns and cities including Sulaymaniya, Dahuk, Irbil, 'Aqra, and Zakho. The uprising was emboldened by the defection of the Kurdish auxiliary forces, officially known as the National Defence Brigades, which took place in mid-March. Some of these have been encouraged to defect by Barzani and Talabani, and by the broadcasts of the clandestine *Radio Free Iraq*.[36]

The Kurdish auxiliaries numbered as many as 100,000, and, according to some sources, it numbered over 200,000.[37] These Kurdish forces had earlier played a crucial role in the central government's efforts to suppress Kurdish-nationalist activities throughout the 1970s and 1980s. They helped the government to maintain its control over the Kurdish area during the war with Iran when government forces were badly needed elsewhere. Most of these forces were recruited from anti-Barzani and anti-Talabani Kurdish tribes whose leaders were being

paid and given positions by the government. These Kurdish tribal leaders may have been motivated by the same general view, widely shared
after the end of the Coalition War, that the Baʿthist regime could not
survive. The Shiʿi uprising in the South had encouraged many Kurdish
towns to join hands with those who had already rebelled. Moreover,
when the Kurds learned that the Coalition forces had occupied a large
area of the country and there were rumors that their forces were poised
to move into northern Iraq from Turkey, they came to the conclusion
that the time had come for the North to be freed from the control of
the central government.[38] Their expectations were heightened by mid-
March when the American forces effectively grounded the Iraqi air
force's fixed-wing planes—although not the helicopters—by its threat,
"If you fly, you die." The Kurds enthusiastically began to call President
Bush "*Hajji Bush*" (Pilgrim Bush), a term of respect reserved for men
who have made the pilgrimage to Makka, because of his war against
the Iraq.

The Kurds were encouraged to learn that Turgot Ozal, the president of Turkey, had talked about a federal solution for Iraq's problems
and hinted about Turkish territorial claims in northern Iraq.[39] Meanwhile, when the under-secretary of the Turkish Foreign Ministry met
with Talabani and Muhsin Dizai, advisor to Masʿud Barzani, in Ankara
on March 22, 1991, he told the Kurdish leaders that Turkey had no
intention of establishing an independent state in northern Iraq, but
would favor a federal or confederal arrangement.[40]

The Kurdish Front leaders were also encouraged by Iran and Syria
to move against the regime and to coordinate their activities with the
insurgents in the South. There were also contacts between Kurdish and
Shiʿi opposition groups to coordinate their activities and launch attacks
once the regime was defeated by the Coalition powers. Detailed plans
were made on how to accomplish their objectives and to coordinate
their activities. The timing and the events of the uprising in the South
and in the North may have taken these leaders by surprise. They, however, moved quickly to take control of the uprising and were encouraged by opposition leaders who met in Bayrut (March 11–13) to
coordinate their activities against the government.

The uprisings in northern Iraq started on March 4, 1991, at the
city of Raniya. They quickly spread to the Kurdish cities of ʿAqra and
Zakho, and then moved to Mawsil, which is predominantly an Arab
city. The uprising then moved to the oil-rich city of Kirkuk and its
environs. Kirkuk has been a hotly contested city between the Kurds and
the central government.[41] In 1970, the Kurdish leaders wanted to include Kirkuk in the Kurdish autonomous area, but their demand was
opposed by the Turkoman and Arab leaders. The issue was raised again
in 1991 to no avail during the negotiations between the central government and the Kurds.

Kirkuk had never been controlled by the Kurdish leaders even at the height of Mulla Mustafa's Kurdish wars in the 1960s and 1970s. In March, 1991 when most of the Kurdish area had come under Kurdish military control, Kirkuk fell into Kurdish hands. At Sulaymaniya fierce clashes occurred between Kurdish insurgents and Government security forces, including Ba'th party members, leading to the killing of over 900 pro-Government officials. Jalal Talabani said that the Kurds took about 100,000 Iraqi soldiers and officers prisoner and released them without killing one officer but that "not one single individual of the intelligence and security officials survived.... The governor of Sulaymaniya was among those killed."[42] The Kurds, however, generally avoided killing army and Fursan (auxiliary) members. According to Hushiyar Zibari, "Only agents and security officials were killed but not military or government officials."[43]

Kurdish leaders were surprised by their rapid successes and were overtaken by the events.[44] Barzani said that, "the result of seventy years of Kurdish struggle is at hand now.... It is what I had wanted to see all my life."[45] Some of the leaders were initially hesitant about launching an uprising because they were still not sure that their allies among the opposition would be able to deliver. They also became concerned about their ability to control the chaotic situation created by the collapse of the central authorities, the defection of the Fursan, the quick turnover of major cities, and of feeding the population remaining in a region devastated by many years of war, internal rebellions, and repression.

During the last two weeks of March, the Kurdish insurgents were in full control of most of northern Iraq. The insurgents had captured huge arsenals of weapons, including tanks, armored cars, trucks, and cannons, as well as an airfield with several Iraqi planes from army units which had surrendered to the Kurds. Likewise, at Sulaymaniya, Dahuk, 'Aqra and 'Imadiya attacks were launched against security and party headquarters, and hundreds of government and party officials were killed. The Kurdish uprising sought to eliminate government control over the Kurdish area. The Ba'th party and security headquarters were burned, and its offices and army barracks were looted. Most of the police, security officials, and Ba'th party members were killed. Soldiers were imprisoned and a few were taken as hostages to the mountains. During this time a clash took place between Kurdish forces moving south toward Kirkuk and units of the Mujahidin Khalq, the Iraqi-based Iranian opposition forces. The Mujahidin claimed that Iranian Revolutionary Guards infiltrated Iraq dressed as Kurds and attacked their bases near Sulaymaniya and Kirkuk, while Kurdish sources claimed that the Mujahidin refused to yield and about 100 prisoners were taken.[46] Fierce clashes took place also in the small town of Qara Hanjir where, according to the Iranian news agency (IRNA), the Mujahidin "gouged the eyes of Kurdish women and children."[47] The rumors of massacres at Qara Hanjir and that the central government might use poison gas, napalm, and missiles in retribution created panic among the Kurds. This led to the mass flight of refugees.[48]

The Kurds were unable to sustain their advances in the face of superior weaponry and disciplined forces. Mas'ud Barzani was forced to fight with only his own personal bodyguards at his side.[49] The quick collapse of the rebellion and the rumors about possible use of poison gas and massacres and the failure of the Coalition powers to intervene on their side may have been the last straw for the hapless Kurds. A Kurdish leader was quoted as saying that "All hope was in outside assistance—the Americans and the allies—otherwise, I wouldn't have asked my friends to rise up."[50] This statement is a strange echo of what the legendary Kurdish leader Mullah Mustafa said in the wake of the 1975 collapse of the Kurdish rebellion, "Were it not for American promises, we would not have become involved to such an extent."[51]

By early April, panic and fear drove over a million and a half Kurdish peasants, professionals, businessmen, tribal leaders and fighters to flee toward the Iranian and Turkish borders. The Iraqi government claimed that the Kurdish leaders encouraged the Kurdish population to flee in order to attract international attention, but Mas'ud Barzani claimed that he and other Kurdish leaders urged their followers to stay home.[52] Civil war and repression inevitably led to mass exodus. Over one and a half million people were on the move in the harsh cold weather of Iraqi Kurdistan. The horrifying pictures of the Kurdish refugees brought many Western journalists to cover the humanitarian crisis. The situation became more dangerous when Turkey, in sharp contrast to the Iranians, refused to allow the Kurds to enter. The tragic events at the border raised questions about American intentions. The Kurds accused the United States of betrayal. They said that American policy was similar to that of 1975 when the Kurds were abandoned after a deal was struck between Iran and Iraq.

During the military operation after the liberation of Kuwait, President Bush urged the people of Iraq "to take matters into their own hands . . . and force the dictator to step aside."[53] It was, accordingly, a great disillusionment for the Kurds when they learned that the United States would remain neutral in the Iraqi civil war. "We don't intend to involve ourselves in the internal affairs of Iraq," said the White House spokesman Marlin Fitzwater on March 16.[54] It is not clear what kind of private promises were made to the Kurds. It is obvious that high-level American officials did not meet with the Kurds. Indeed, Bush refused to meet with a Kurdish delegation during the last days of the war.[55]

American contacts with Kurdish opposition leaders began shortly before the end of the Iraq-Iran war when the Kurds had sent messages to Washington, but the response was negative.[56] The Kurds were interested in getting American weapons, but they also wanted autonomy. When Talabani visited Washington in 1988 he warned: "Iran might withdraw and you need a foreign backer."[57] Contacts were made with American Embassy officials in London leading to Talabani's visit to the United States. He spoke at the Wilson Forum at the State Department. Owing to Iraqi protests, an appointment with the Defense Department was cancelled. Talabani, however, met informally with some White House officials and with Senator Claiborne Pell and his aide, Peter Galbraith.[58]

The Kurds postponed their planned uprising against the government because of a lack of communication. They expected to receive support and were hoping for the arrival of American troops. Some Kurdish officials claimed that the United States promised its support, which never came, if they rose up against the Iraqi government. A number of Kurds claimed that American intelligence officials promised the Kurds that if they rose up, they would back them.[59] The Kurds believed that the Ba'th regime was about to collapse. Some Kurdish leaders were advised not to negotiate with the regime because the Americans would overthrow Saddam and any agreement with him would have undermined American credibility and strengthened the government. President Bush had on several occasions called on the people of Iraq to overthrow their leader. On February 15, he suggested that, "There's another way for the bloodshed to stop, and that the Iraqi military and the Iraqi people [should] take matters into their own hands to force Saddam Husayn, the dictator, to step aside and to comply with the U.N. resolutions and then rejoin the family of peace-loving nations."[60]

The American government, needless to say, wanted to see the fall of the Ba'th regime but it hoped that such an outcome would be achieved by a military uprising which would bring to power a new leadership that could preserve Iraq's territorial integrity and unity, provided it would not pose a problem to American allies in the region, such as Turkey, Egypt, and Saudi Arabia. As one U.S. National Security Council aide put it: "Our policy is to get rid of Saddam Husayn himself, not his regime."[61] A Kurdish victory might mean a possible partition of Iraq and instability in the region, particularly in Turkey, a close U.S. ally, where the Kurdish Workers Party (PKK) was waging a fierce campaign for Kurdish rights since 1984. Egypt, Saudi Arabia, and some Arab Gulf countries would also have been fearful of the emergence of an Iranian dominated Shi'i regime in Baghdad. The Saudi Commander of Desert Storm Prince Khalid bin Sultan was quoted as saying: "The rebellion against Hussein [is] an internal matter and the business of the Iraqi people."[62]

President Bush's popularity, which reached unprecedented heights during the war, was also founded on his concern for the lives of American troops, a theme he often repeated, but public discomfort grew over the problem of the refugees, dramaticized nightly on television by journalists who were delighted to embarrass the Bush administration after the lifting of the tight restrictions on media coverage by the military during the war. On April 13, Bush declared that "Internal conflicts have been raging in Iran for many years, and . . . we're going to continue to help these refugees. But I do not want one single soldier or airman shoved into a civil war in Iraq that's been going on for ages. And I am not going to have that."[63]

As the Iraqi army recaptured one town after another in the Kurdish area, the size of the exodus of Kurds increased, reaching about half of the Kurdish total population of the area. On April 1, Mas'ud Barzani issued an urgent appeal to the United States, Britain, and France to act through the U.N. to save his people from "genocide and torture" as Kurds risked death from exposure and disease on the mountains and valleys of Kurdistan rather than face Iraqi troops.

In the meantime, Iraq, as was reported by the U.N. Under-Secretary General Marti Ahtisari on March 22, was no longer able to feed its people due to the war and the sanctions under Resolution 687. The allies, however, were preoccupied with the drafting of the final cease-fire terms with Iraq and Resolution 687 and the events on the ground did not fit the military scenario they had envisioned. Two days later, the Security Council adopted Resolution 688 in response to the humanitarian crisis, and condemned Baghdad's repression of its civilian population, including the Kurdish-populated areas. It demanded not only that Iraq end its repression of minorities, but also that it allow immediate access to those in need of assistance by international human-rights organizations, and the Resolution directed the secretary general to pursue humanitarian efforts. It also appealed to all states and humanitarian groups to contribute to relief efforts.

On April 6, the Iraqi RCC declared that "Iraq has totally crushed all acts of sedition and sabotage in all cities of Iraq."[64] The Iraqi response to the Security Council Resolution 687 and 688 was reflected in several Baghdad radio broadcasts, such as the following, issued on April 11:

> By uprooting treason and sabotage and purging its north of strife, Iraq foiled all the hostile alliances wagers on those traitors and adventurers, who had been implementing and continue to implement the plans of their masters in Washington, London, and the capitals of the other covetous forces. It has become clear that the U.S., British, and French administrations have been driven to desperation by the failure of their agents and mercenaries. They have all of a sudden become the protectors of the Iraqi Kurds and the defenders of their national and human rights.[65]

The radio broadcast also added:

> A general amnesty has been announced, security and supremacy of the law have been established in all parts of Iraq, including the northern area, and a large number of citizens have returned to their homes. There

is nothing to prevent the remainder from returning to all towns and villages of the autonomous region.

Questions continued to surround the uprising and the reasons behind its collapse. Iraqi opposition leaders as well as critics of the American policy at the end of the War have argued that the main reason behind the collapse of the revolt lies at the door of the Bush administration and its coalition allies and their failure either to stop the Iraqi government from using its remaining helicopter gunships against the insurgents and to provide them with weapons or for not going all the way to Baghdad to overthrow the Husayn regime.[66]

Owing to continuing pressures on the Coalition powers, President Bush announced on April 16 that the American, British, and French forces would build tent cities in dry, low terrain areas and would encourage and assist the movement of refugees to those areas. This commitment was to be protected by allied "rapid-reaction" forces based in Turkey. This action, which became known as Operation Provide Comfort, aimed at providing relief aid to the refugees and intended to help them return home. Iraq, which had reached a cease-fire with the Kurds on April 16 in order to begin negotiations, denounced the American plan on April 18 as an "interference in its internal affairs."[67] The cease-fire left some areas in the north under Kurdish control and paved the way for Iraqi-Kurdish talks.

The newly formed safe area (called "safe haven") for the Kurds was to be established around the cities of Zakho, Dahuk, and ʿImadiya. Initially there were calls for the establishment of an "enclave" not to be touched by Iraqi forces. North of the 36th parallel the Iraqi troops could not use fixed-wing airplanes or helicopters, and Iraqi forces were also forbidden from interfering in relief work in that area. Meanwhile, the number of Kurdish refugees soared to new highs. In late April, there were over 468,000 refugees in southeastern Turkey and close to a million in or near Iran which, unlike Turkey, opened its doors to the refugees. International and non-governmental organizations became involved in massive relief efforts.

The United Nations began to establish a presence in Dahuk on May 13, 1991, sending eight food trucks in accordance with an agreement (March 18) to set up humanitarian, non-military centers to help displaced Iraqi people in several hard-hit parts of the country. The United Nations also took over the administration of the Zakho refugee camp from the United States.

While the United Nations secretary general's envoy on refugees, Prince Sadr al-Din Agha Khan visited Baghdad to get Iraq's consent to grant the United Nations police powers on its territory in northern Iraq, the United States increased its pressure on Iraq to reconsider its rejection. Relating to this issue, the secretary general of the U.N., Perez de Cueller, in a meeting in the White House on May 9 said,

Today I have received a very clear rejection from the Iraqi government. They do not want a U.N. police force. Therefore, since Baghdad refuses U.N. police forces, the authority must come from the Security Council in the form of a new resolution.[68]

The Iraqi government, after retaking the cities, called on the Kurds to send a joint KDP-PUK delegation. Upon its arrival, the delegation was warmly received in Baghdad.[69] The issues of democracy and a federal system was suggested by the Kurds. Talabani, after insisting on receiving Barzani's backing for his negotiating with Baghdad, demanded also that he would choose the Kurdish delegation.[70] The Iraqi government said anything was possible short of partitioning Iraq and was willing to sign an agreement provided both Mas'ud Barzani and Talabani attended.

The Kurds enjoyed greater international sympathy and support than at any previous time and were at the same time negotiating with a weakened Iraqi government which would be making concessions. In addition, some Kurdish leaders believed that care must be taken not to lose this opportunity to achieve full autonomy by direct negotiation with Baghdad and not by regional or international interventions as they had already been disappointed earlier by dependence on foreign support.[71]

During the first and following rounds of negotiations, four working papers were drafted dealing with democracy and human rights, autonomy, normalization and security, and national unity.[72] In the paper on democracy and human rights, the Kurds demanded that Ba'thist monopoly control of the political system be ended and a separation of the party from the state be declared necessary. Political and press freedoms were to be guaranteed as well as a freely elected convention held to prepare a new constitution to be voted on by the people. On Kurdish human rights, it was agreed that any relevant norm recognized under international law would be accepted by the Iraqi government. Finally, the Iraqi government demanded that the Ba'th would be the vanguard party and Saddam's leadership of the country acknowledged, but it was willing to accept a nonsectarian multiparty system.

In the paper dealing with autonomy and the borders of the autonomous area, the Kurds held that responsibility for security must be in the hands of the Kurds and that the areas of Khanaqin, Mandali, and Kirkuk, demanded previously by the Kurds in the 1972[73] negotiations, must be recognized as part of the Kurdish region. The Kurds demanded that all schools and universities would be free of government control. The government responded that all security matters are the responsibility of the presidency, educational institutions would be under the jurisdiction of the ministry of education, and the governors of all provinces must be linked to the minister of interior. It agreed that the Kurdish language would be used at all levels of the government and in all educational institutions in the autonomous area.

In the paper dealing with normalization of relations, the Kurds called for an end to policies of deportations and Arabization and the need for rebuilding destroyed villages and towns. The government maintained that Arabization would not apply to the area within the boundaries of the autonomous region, but would not be stopped outside of this area, particularly in the mixed areas such as Khanaqin and Kirkuk, where the Kurds are not in the majority.

With regard to the last paper regarding the strengthening of national unity and territorial integrity, and combatting "chauvinist and separatist tendencies," both sides were in agreement. The initial meeting was followed by negotiations led by Mas'ud Barzani. On April 25, 1991, Jalal Talabani, PUK leader, announced after the first round of talks that the Kurds would receive greater autonomy, based on the March Manifesto of 1970 agreement.[74] In addition to the subjects dealt with in the four main papers, Talabani requested further negotiations concerning Kirkuk, a major oil city of importance to both parties, as well as the need for international guarantees (i.e., by the U.N. and the United States).

In subsequent negotiations, Mas'ud Barzani the KDP leader, stressed the importance of democracy and of oil falling under the jurisdiction of the central government. He insisted that defining the border of the autonomous region was the key point, although he showed flexibility on the issue of Kirkuk saying that the city's oil would come under the jurisdiction of the central government. The upshot of Barzani's negotiations consisted of the following six major points: separation of party and government, constitutional legitimacy, political and party pluralism, separation of judicial, executive, and legislative functions, holding of elections, and freedom of the press.[75] The *peshmerga* (the Kurdish irregular army) would become part of the Iraqi forces. Barzani's statements met opposition from Sa'd Salih Jabr, chairman of the Iraqi Free Council, and an open appeal from the Iraqi opposition was made to Barzani and Talabani to cease negotiating with Saddam Husayn in a way which produced such results as praising Saddam's love for the Kurds.[76] Barzani continued his negotiations in Baghdad until June 16, when agreement was reached in principle, although not yet signed. The "Autonomy Draft Law," the agreement which Barzani brought with him, was based on the March 11, 1970 Manifesto. While Barzani was enthusiastic about it, Talabani was not. In late June when Talabani and Barzani met, Talabani stated that resolution would only occur if the proposals of a unitary Iraqi state and the joint use of the city of Kirkuk were addressed. Kurdish leaders said that what made agreement between the Kurds and the Iraqi Government more difficult to accomplish was not "The Autonomy Draft Law," but Saddam Husayn's demands for certain concessions from the Kurds.[77] The Draft Law required that the Kurdish militia (*peshmerga*) and the radio broadcasting stations be handed over to the Iraqi central authority, and the Kurds should cease independent cooperation or contact with foreign powers. In order to achieve the objectives of Iraqi national unity, Kurds should support the Ba'th Party and the Kurdish Front should accept a national program to be drawn by the Ba'th. As no agreement on fundamental issues like the formation of the autonomy area was reached, negotiations came to a standstill.

Differences ensued between Barzani and Talabani, partly on the proposals raised by the Iraqi government, but also on the attitude of each leader as to how to deal with Iraq.[78] Barzani appeared to believe that the Manifesto should be signed, despite its shortcomings, for the following reasons: 1) The Kurds have suffered greatly over the past decades and they needed to live a normal life; 2) The outside world was not serious about providing support for the Kurds and the support given them was primarily humanitarian and not political; 3) This is the best time to deal with Baghdad and the best time to negotiate with the government; and 4) the Kurds are part of the region and must coexist with its people.

Jalal Talabani, however, had a different perspective. He opposed the deal with the regime because: 1) Saddam could not be trusted and would attack the Kurds whenever he is stronger; 2) A deal with the government would strengthen radical Islamic and nationalist Kurdish groups such as the PKK and the Kurdistan Islamic Movement in Iraq; 3) International public opinion is more aware of the Kurdish plight and would not allow them to be crushed again; 4) The deal with Saddam divides the Iraqi opposition; and 5) A deal must include Kirkuk as Saddam will not be able to survive since the Western powers will bring him down and support the Kurds.

Following the failure of negotiations between Baghdad and the Kurdish leaders, Iraq withdrew its troops and officials from the Kurdish area and imposed its own economic blockade, leaving a vacuum in the Kurdish region. The Iraqi Kurdish Front led by Barzani and Talabani later organized its own election for a regional parliament. The two main parties, Barzani's KDP and Talabani's PUK, received a relatively equal number of votes with a tiny lead for the KDP. A power sharing arrangement was reached whereby each side received fifty seats in the 105-seat parliament. Five seats were given to the Assyrian Christian community. This arrangement and the failure of Barzani and Talabani to directly participate in the Kurdish authority proved to be a major stumbling block.

In addition, major differences erupted in 1993–94 between the factions loyal to Barzani and those loyal to Talabani over the collection and division of revenues and over growing concerns about the changing balance of power within the Kurdish region resulting from three small parties joined the KDP, thereby raising the PUK's concerns regarding an imbalance of power. The PUK also entered into a military confrontation with the Islamic Kurdistan Movement. Later, in May 1994, a major military confrontation occurred between the KDP and the PUK, leading the latter to occupy the regional Kurdish capital of Irbil. Thousands were killed during the fighting. In addition, a series of costly political and military confrontations between the Iraqi Kurdish organizations and the radical Kurdish Workers Party (PKK) which has fought against the Turkish government in the name of Turkey's Kurds has further undermined Kurdish unity and the image of the Kurdish leaders. Separate efforts at negotiations sponsored by the French, the Americans, the Turks, and the Iranians, led to the signing of agreements-in-principle between the antagonists that have yet to be implemented.

As a result of the Gulf War, the Kurds of Iraq had gained a new and unique status whereby they gained control over an area and established, under Western protection, an entity just short of independence. Even the Ba'th Party's paper *al-Thawra* admitted, in a series of articles in early April, 1991, that the uprisings were a sign of the failure of the regime and the Ba'th Party to end ethnic and sectarian divisions in the country.[79] Nevertheless, intra-Kurdish feuding and personal rivalries, exacerbated by interference and manipulations by some of their external supporters, have greatly undermined the credibility of the Kurdish leadership at home and abroad. This situation has led to questions about the future of this latest attempt at a Kurdish entity in Iraq. Rivalry among Kurdish leaders invited foreign intervention, presumably to support Kurdish national aspirations; but considered by Arabs to serve the self-interests of the foreign powers.

Chapter 13

Demarcation of the Frontiers

The border disputes between Iraq and Kuwait, a perennial issue between the two countries, influenced several other issues such as the claim to adjacent islands and the demarcation of boundaries that Kuwait sought to resolve in order to assert its sovereign independence. Small wonder that Kuwait found in the Coalition War, when Iraq was at the mercy of the Security Council, an opportunity not only to assert its sovereignty and territorial integrity, but also to settle once and for all the border disputes with Iraq. It was upon Kuwait's request that the settlement of the boundary dispute became one of the conditions specified under Resolution 687 (April 3, 1991) which Iraq had grudgingly accepted in order to bring the Coalition War to an end. Not only did Resolution 687 declare "the restoration to Kuwait of its sovereignty, independence, and territorial integrity;" it also reaffirmed the agreement concluded between Iraq and Kuwait, signed in Baghdad on October 4, 1963, which dealt with the boundary dispute:

> 2. ... Iraq and Kuwait respect the inviolability of the international boundary and the allocation of islands set out in the "Agreed Minutes [1963]. . . .";
> 3. Calls upon the secretary-general to lend his assistance to make arrangements with Iraq and Kuwait to demarcate the boundary between Iraq and Kuwait drawing on appropriate material, including the map transmitted by Security Council document S/22412 and to report back to the Security Council within one month;
> 4. Decides to guarantee the inviolability of the above-mentioned international boundary and to take as appropriate all necessary measures to that end in accordance with the Charter of the United Nations. . . . [1]

Under Resolution 687, the Security Council had also requested the U.N. secretary general to submit, after consultation with Iraq and Kuwait, a plan for the appointment of observers "to monitor the Khawr 'Abd-Allah and a demilitarized zone, which is hereby established, extending ten kilometers into Iraq and five kilometers into Kuwait from the boundary . . . [in order] to deter violations of the boundary [and] to observe any hostile or potentially hostile action mounted from the territory of one state to the other."

The Kuwaiti foreign minister, Shaykh Sabah al-Ahmad al-Sabah, welcomed the adoption of the Security Council Resolution 687 without hesitation, as it promised to provide his country with almost all what it had aspired to achieve in the settlement of its frontier dispute with Iraq. The Iraqi foreign minister, Ahmad Husayn, highly defiant of the Resolution, dispatched a response (April 6, 1991) in which he denounced it as an "unprecedented assault on the sovereignty" of Iraq. He also objected to the steps taken by the Security Council to determine in advance the boundary between Iraq and Kuwait before an agreement had actually been reached between them. Moreover, he also rejected almost all the terms relating to the frontier dispute with Kuwait.

With regard to the agreement of 1963, based on an exchange of letters between Iraq and Kuwait in 1932, Resolution 687 considered it binding because it was signed by the Iraqi prime minister and accepted by the ruler of Kuwait. In his letter to the Security Council, the Iraqi foreign minister objected to the decision of the Security Council to consider it binding on Iraq, because it was not ratified by the president of Iraq in accordance with the country's constitutional processes which requires all laws, including treaties and agreements, to be signed by the head of state. Thus Iraq considered the demarcation of the boundary, based on the agreement of 1963, invalid in accordance with its constitutional process. On matters of principle, the foreign minister objected to the "double standard" pursued in treating Iraq differently from other countries, such as Israel and Syria, which have not yet withdrawn from occupied Arab territories. He also objected, as a matter of principle, to Resolution 687, since it is contrary to Resolution 660 which stated that the two sides would settle their differences through bilateral negotiations.

On May 2, 1991, the secretary general, Perez de Cuellar, after consultations with Iraq and Kuwait, established the Iraq-Kuwait Boundary Demarcation Commission (IKDBC) composed of five members. Three independent members were appointed by the secretary general (one of them served as chairman). The other two, representing Iraq and Kuwait, were nominated by the two countries concerned. Iraq nominated Riyad al-Qaysi and Kuwait nominated Tariq A. Razzuqi. The three members selected by the secretary general were: Mukhtar (Mochtar) Kusuma-Atmaja, former Indonesian foreign minister as chairman, Ian Brook of Sweden, and William Robertson of New Zealand, as technical experts. From the beginning of the commission's work, it was agreed that its task was technical, not political, and its specific function was the demarcation of the boundary. The Commission requested Iraq and

Kuwait to submit all relevant documents and other materials for its consideration. Since the Security Council had received a British map of the frontier, as stated in Resolution 687, the map was submitted to the Commission.

It is to be noted that there were two separate groups assigned to work in the demarcation process: the observers, to which Resolution 687 referred, and the IKDBC, which was set up by the secretary general and approved by the Security Council. The first was to monitor the Khawr ʿAbd-Allah and the demilitarized zone; the other to demarcate the boundary and establish pillars on the line that separate the territory of one side from the other. During the fulfillment of their functions, there was a considerable number of conflicts over jurisdiction in the demilitarized zone; such incidents occurred during almost the entire period for the demarcation in which both Iraqi and Kuwaiti authorities were involved. An account of these events may be found in the secretary general's interim reports to the Security Council.

For example, one important incident may be of interest to cite about rumors and unconfirmed information. Under Resolution 687, the secretary general was requested to appoint observers to monitor the demilitarized zone (ten kilometers on the Iraqi side and five kilometers on the Kuwaiti side). While the Demarcation Commission was carrying out its work there were violations made by both Iraqi and Kuwaiti policemen presumably in dealing with smugglers, but these were considered unavoidable by the observers. On August 28, 1991, the Kuwaiti Coast Guard captured twelve small boats and detained forty-five Iraqi men in the Khawr ʿAbd-Allah. According to the Kuwaiti authorities, an armed Iraqi force, estimated at eighty men, attacked the Bubiyan Island with gunboats. The Kuwaiti press claimed that "the Iraqi force used heavy weapons and were backed by gunboat reinforcements" dispatched by Iraq from Faw. In an effort to defend Bubiyan, the Kuwaiti military were able to sink seven boats and to capture over forty Iraqi men while others escaped. The Kuwaiti representative to the U.N. informed the Security Council that Iraq committed "armed aggression," and he went on to explain that "this dangerous development demonstrates once again the aggressive intentions by Iraq against the security and peace of Kuwait and shows that Iraq has not learned its lessons." The United States congratulated Kuwait for defending itself, and the British representative to the U.N. supported the Kuwaiti complaint and the British Foreign Office condemned Iraq's action in an official note. The United Nations observers found that the whole affair was the work of private profiteers who collect weaponry for black-market sale and that there were no traces of boats "allegedly sunk by the Kuwaitis."[2]

The Iraq-Kuwait Demarcation Commission (IKDBC) held eighty-two meetings during the period from 1991 to 1993 before it could complete its work. It laid down its own rules of procedure and divided its work on delimitation into three sections: 1. the Western section, as described in official agreements, "from the intersection of the Wadi al-Awdja and the Batin and thence northwards along the Batin to a point just of the latitude of Safwan; 2. the northern section, the official agreements state, "thence eastwards passing south of Safwan Wells, Jabal Sanam and Umm Qasr leaving them to Iraq and so on to the junction of the Khawr Zubayr with the Khawr 'Abdullah;" and 3. the eastern section (often called the Khawr 'Abd-Allah section) consisted of "the islands of Warba, Bubiyan, Maskan (Mashjan), Faylaka, Awhah, Kubbar, Qaru, and Umm al-Maradin appertain to Kuwait." In its work for the demarcation of each section, the commission decided to depend on all the documents that dealt with the interpretation of the delimitation of the borders during the period from 1940 to 1950 when Britain offered its mediation to reach an agreement between Iraq and Kuwait. According to the documents relevant to borders, the British government provided its own interpretation as to delimitation, which Iraq had agreed to accept, provided either Umm Qasr port and Warba Island were given to Iraq or the whole Khawr 'Abd-Allah would become under Iraqi control. Britain almost succeeded in working out a compromise on delimitation, but in each step taken either Iraq or Kuwait raised objections and the British mediation came to nought. While dependence on the documents used for mediation during 1940–51 can be very useful, they by no means could be fully satisfactory for demarcation, as those documents aimed at reaching an agreement dealing essentially with delimitation leaving the question of demarcation for the future. This led partly to sharp differences between the Iraqi and Kuwaiti representatives and perhaps to the resignation of the representative of Indonesia, chairman of the IKDBC.

In his final report on demarcation to the Security Council, (May 20, 1993) the secretary general provided a summary of the most important documents on the basis of which the IKDBC established the demarcated border between Iraq and Kuwait. Apart from the basic agreements that defined the delimitation of the frontier, such as the unratified agreements of 1923, 1932, and 1963, the fundamental documents on the basis of which the demarcation was established by the IKDBC may be summarized as follows.[3]

First is a document by H.R.P. Dickson, British political agent in Kuwait, in which he pointed out that in 1935, "on the basis of a new map," it was always understood that "the northern boundary to run in a due east-west straight line from the Batin center line to the notice-board, and thence, also in a straight line, to the junction of the Khawr Zubayr and the Khawr 'Abd-Allah." But, Dickson added, the map published in the following year, contained several errors, including the most important about "the underestimated distance between Umm

Qasr and the junction of the Khawrs.'' This map became the basis for almost all considerations of the boundary by the British and Iraqi authorities till 1963.

Second, in 1937, C.J. Edmonds, British adviser to the Iraqi Ministry of Interior, in a memorandum to the minister of interior, proposed that "the boundary should follow the thalweg of the Batin, thence run due to a point one mile south of Safwan palms and onwards, in straight line, to the junction of the thalwegs of the Khawr Zubayr and the Khawr 'Abd-Allah. From the junction of the Khawrs, the boundary followed the thalweg of the Khawr 'Abd-Allah to the open sea." The Iraqi government adopted the Edmonds memorandum on the basis of which it claimed the Iraq-Kuwait boundary as it had existed, and the Kuwait government adopted Dickson's formulation of the boundary as understood to have existed on the basis of a map presumably prepared by experts in the service of the British Raj in India.

A noticeboard on the crossroad between the two countries, laid down on the basis of Dickson's boundary formulation, was placed. In 1939, this noticeboard was removed. In 1940, it was replaced by the British political agent assisted by Kuwaiti experts. But Iraq protested on the grounds that the noticeboard had been placed one thousand meters south of the Iraqi customs post, that is, 250 meters north of the Iraqi boundary. In 1940, in an exchange of letters between Iraq and Kuwait via the British government, the boundary between the two countries was described, under the 1932 agreement, as suggested by Edmonds and Dickson to clarify two matters: one to specify the low water (*thalweg*) line on the southern shore of the Khawr Zubayr (on which both sides were agreed), the other (on which they disagreed) on the question of the site of the noticeboard, a point one thousand meters south of the Iraqi old customs post. As Edmonds, British adviser in Iraq, was responsible to the British Foreign Office in London, and Dickson, British agent in Kuwait, was responsible to the British Raj in India, the differences between the two offices, as noted earlier, varied considerably, perhaps partly because Edmonds sought to assert Iraqi interests, while Dickson asserted Kuwaiti interests. These proposals, including documents issued in the 1950s providing further information and maps about borders, were made available to the IKDBC.

On the basis of these documents, the commission held several meetings to determine the demarcation of the three sections of the boundary. The lack of precision in the information provided in the documents about the point south of Safwan, the lines of the boundary in the Batin, Umm Qasr, and the Khawrs of Zubayr and 'Abd-Allah was not clear in the language of the delimitation formulas. "Of particular concern," stated the U.N. secretary general report, "were whether it was technically possible to demarcate the boundary without a turning point at Safwan, whether the thalweg or the median line concept should be applied in the northern part of the Batin to divide the graz-

ing areas equitably and whether there had been a shift in the junction
of the Khawrs over the past decades." For this reason, it was decided
that a new mapping was necessary to provide more precise evidence
for the decisions required on controversial issues. The fieldwork undertaken by the experts through aerial photography and mapping provided further evidence that assisted the Commission in deciding the
demarcation of the third area, the Khawr ʿAbd-Allah section, as well as
certain parts on the land-boundary sections. Resort to equity to determine the line of demarcation obviously raised the question as to
whether the commission had the power of delimitation, as its frame of
reference under the Security Council resolution was to demarcate, not
to delimitate the frontier. This and other points of differences led eventually to the resignation of the Iraqi representative, Riyad al-Qaysi, who
refused to attend meetings after July 15, 1992 as the commission appeared to him biased in favor of Kuwait, and the chairman of the commission, Kusuma Atmadja, resigned on November 20, 1992, perhaps
also on the grounds that it exceeded its powers of demarcation, although the report of the secretary general states that he resigned for
"personal reasons."[4]

Following the fieldwork of aerial mapping of border areas and
other technical information, including the Rumayla boundary areas,
the IKDBC began to discuss and make decisions on the demarcation
of the three sections of the boundary: the western, northern, and
Khawrs sections. The final decisions in brief are as follows:

First, the western section. The demarcation of this section was
based on the delimitation set forth in the 1932 agreement, and in the
Edmonds memorandum (1940) which clarified the clause about the
frontier to follow the "*thalweg*" (the line of the deepest depression)
and accepted by Iraq in 1952 provided "the cession of Warba Island
settled before proceeding with demarcation." As Kuwait rejected the
ceding of Warba Island, Iraq withdrew its acceptance of the thalweg as
the line of demarcation. The Commission decided that "the line of the
lowest points (the *thalweg*)," as proposed by Edmonds, would be the
basis of the demarcation of the boundary along the Wadi al-Batin." It
also decided that "the boundary would be marked by a series of straight
lines, approximately two kilometers in length, such that the aerial extent by which the thalweg departs from the boundary on the Kuwaiti
side was equally balanced by the departure on the Iraq side." The Commission also decided that "the northern end of the boundary in the
Batin be located at the intersection of the thalweg of the Wadi and the
latitude of the point south of Safwan."[5]

Second, the northern section. On the basis of the 1932 agreements,
this section begins "from the intersection of the thalweg of the Wadi
al-Batin with the parallel of latitude that runs through the point just
south of Safwan, eastward along that parallel south of Jabal Sanam to
the point just south of Safwan, and thereafter along the shortest (ge-

odesic) line to the port of Umm Qasr, and from there to the junction of the Khawr Zubayr with the Khawr ʿAbd-Allah.'' In the demarcation of this section, the commission divided it into three subsections: a) from the Wadi al-Batin to the point south of Safwan; b) from the Safwan to the intersection of the Khawrs; and c) Khawr ʿAbd-Allah.

With regard to the first subsection, the Commission, on the basis of the 1932 agreement, found that all the maps agree that the boundary line follows a latitude to a point south of Safwan. However, the noticeboard that indicated this point, which is fundamental to determine the line of demarcation, had been removed after sixteen years from the time the maps indicated it after the agreement of 1923 was concluded in an exchange of letters between Sir Percy Cox and the Shaykh of Kuwait. Dickson, the British political agent in Kuwait, who had known Sir Percy Cox, and was acquainted with the 1923 agreement, stated in 1935: ''We have always understood the northern boundary of the frontier to run in a due east and west line from the Batin (center line) to a point one mile south of Safwan Wells, where a large noticeboard exists on the side of the road which today marks the boundary.'' In 1940, the reestablishment of the noticeboard prompted Iraq to protest the location of the new noticeboard and insisted that its location was 250 meters north of the distance of 1,000 meters from the customs port. In these circumstances the Commission came to the conclusion that:

> The two most probable positions for the noticeboard were nearly 1,609 (1 mile) and 1,250 meters south of the south-west extremity of the customs port. In the absence of other reliable evidence, the commission gave equal weight to both measurements and decided on the mean distance of 1,430 meters from the southwest extremity of the old customs port along the old road as the most probable location of the noticeboard. The location of the point thus determined by the commission is 180 meters further south than the distance specified in the 1940 Iraqi protest note and 430 meters south of the claim made then later for Kuwait.[6]

On the basis of the mean figure, the Commission made its decision and the location was determined to be the line of demarcation between the end of the boundary in the Batin and the beginning of the northern boundary.

With regard to the second northern subsection, from Safwan to the junction of Khawr Zubayr and the Khawr ʿAbd-Allah, the Commission first sought to identify the *thalweg* of the channel in order to determine the location of the junction of the two Khawrs. After an examination of the maps, charts, and aerial photographs that were at its disposal, the Commission considered the thalweg had not changed its location and on that basis the demarcation of the junction of the Khawrs was determined. As to the straight line from the point south of Safwan to the junction of the Khawrs, ''the Commission found that such a line would have sliced into the northern shore of the Khawr Zubair, thereby closing off the mouth of the Khawr." It came to the conclusion that there were errors and distortions in the maps of 1917 and 1936 made available to it and descriptions of the Khawrs positions. For this reason, the Commission decided to make its decision on maps prepared earlier as well as more recent ones and came to the conclusion that no "significant effects or accretion around the junction of the Khawrs during the period covered by the material studied." As it had done earlier to adopt the principle of the "mean position" to determine the demarcation line south of Safwan, the Commission also applied the same principle to "the demarcation of intersection of the boundary with the shoreline at Umm Qasr should be in terms of the position of the Khawrs as shown on the 1936 map as it was considered that that was the position of the boundary as envisaged and intended from that time." On this basis, the demarcation left only the Umm Qasr port complex and Umm Qasr village to Iraq, but the area south of it was considered within Kuwaiti territory.

Third, the Khawr ʿAbd-Allah section. This section consisted of the maritime, or offshore, boundary from the junction of Khawr Zubayr and Khawr ʿAbd-Allah to the eastern end of the Khawr. From the evidence at the disposal of the Commission, it was clear that there was a general agreement between the two sides on the boundary in the Khawr, although the Iraqi side considered the islands to have been assigned to Kuwait by Britain without Iraq's consent.[7] The Commission decided to demarcate the border on the basis of the principle of the median line, but it was "understood that navigational access should be possible for both states to the various sides of their respective bordering the demarcated boundary." The Commission's decision to determine the median line was based on the documents, photographs, and charts that were made available to it. Hydrographic techniques were used to identify base points. All these were submitted to Iraq and Kuwait for approval or to provide alternative provisions. Kuwait accepted the Commission's propositions, but Iraq did not respond, as its representative did not attend the Commission's meeting, nor was his government prepared to accept the demarcation decisions taken by the Commission.[8]

Following the decision concerning the points where the pillars would be established for demarcating the land boundary, the Commission entered into a contract with the Eastern Asphalt and Mixed Concrete Company of Bahrain for the manufacture of boundary markers. Work on the emplacement of pillars in the fall of 1992 was completed within less than two years. On the land boundary 106 pillars and twenty-eight intermediate boundary markers were established. The boundary line in the Khawr Zubayr was not physically demarcated, but plaques were emplaced on the jetties where a low-water springs line continued beneath them and on some other marks indicating demarcating lines.

No sooner had the IKBDC completed its work, a report on the demarcation was sent to the U.N. secretary general, Perez de Cuellar, on April 16, 1992. It was submitted to the Security Council which approved the demarcation on May 27, 1993, and was forwarded to Kuwait and Iraq as a binding document. A summary of the demarcated boundary was simultaneously made public when it was delivered to de Cuellar. Needles to say, Iraq was not expected to accept the demarcation as set in the U.N. secretary general's report to the Security Council (May 20, 1993). Its representative had not attended the meetings of the Commission since July 15, 1992. However, since Iraq had accepted the Security Council Resolution 687 (1992) under which the IKDBC was established to demarcate the line and place the notice pillars (as de Cuellar stated in his letter to the Iraqi foreign minister, dated April 30, 1991), the demarcation of the boundary, as set in de Cuellar's report to the Security Council and approved was considered binding. But Iraq publicly rejected Cuellar's report as both Tariq ʿAziz, deputy premier and Ahmad Husayn, foreign minister, denounced the demarcation as "not based on legal documents," denoting that the border problem remained unresolved. Public opinion in Iraq has always been in favor of unity between the two countries, and the leaders of almost all shades of opinion maintain that Kuwait had encroached on Iraqi territory. Even the opposition leaders outside the country made critical statements to the effect that the U.N. demarcation report was unacceptable to them.[9]

In Kuwait, the IKDBC demarcation report was received with great satisfaction as it not only confirmed its claim that the rich South Rumayla oilfield (Ratqa) and the two islands of Warba and Bubiyan fall within its frontier, but also designated that Umm Qasr, the only maritime area that Iraq had used as an alternate to Basra, was divided between the two countries; its southern portion is now within the demarcated boundary of Kuwait. The Kuwaiti rulers seem to have hoped to share the Khawr Zubayr with Iraq, but the whole of it was confirmed to fall within Iraqi borders. No official statement has been made about this matter save a statement to this effect, reported in the *Kuwaiti Times* (May 4, 1993).[10]

Ever since the Security Council sought to impose demarcation of the boundary on the basis of the delimitation specified under the unratified agreement of 1963, Iraq has objected in principle to accept demarcation before an agreement had been reached on delimitation by negotiations, taking into consideration the validity of its claims and vital interests.

The Security Council, however, has refused to lift the economic sanctions until Iraq had accepted all its Resolutions, including the recognition of Kuwait's sovereignty, territorial integrity, and the demarcated boundary laid down by the IKDBC. As the economic sanctions have adversely affected not only the conditions of health and morale of the country but also isolated it from the rest of the world, the Iraqi government was prompted to accept the advice of its former allies and friends, particularly Russia and France with whom Iraq had had commercial dealings, to intercede on its behalf with other permanent members of the Security Council to allow the export of Iraq's oil to world markets. Since the United States and Britain have invariably insisted that Iraq must fulfill all its obligations under the Security Council Resolutions, including the demarcation of boundaries, the Iraqi government finally agreed to recognize Kuwait's sovereignty, territorial integrity, and its demarcated boundary, and a formal letter to this effect was delivered to the Security Council through the secretary general of the United Nations on November 10, 1994.

Has the frontier problem, including demarcation, been resolved by Iraq's acceptance of the IKBDC's demarcated boundary under the Saddam Husayn regime? A variety of views on the subject have been expressed ever since the U.N. secretary general's report on demarcation was made public in 1993. Three sets of views might be examined on the subjects of the sovereignty and independence of Kuwait and the delimitation-demarcation of the frontier between Iraq and Kuwait. Before discussing the subjects of the recognition of sovereignty and frontiers, it should be remembered that the procedure for recognizing the sovereignty and independence of the state is not the same as that for concluding an agreement on frontiers which define the line between two (or more) states. Under International Law, the recognition of the sovereignty and independence of one state by another is ordinarily done by an exchange of letters between the two heads of state or by the establishment of normal diplomatic relations between them.[11] But the delimitation and demarcation of frontiers are different matters which have always been settled by a treaty or agreement between the two (or more) states and ratified by the heads of state in accordance with the constitutional process of each side in order that the agreement reached between them would become a law binding on each side.[12]

In the Iraq-Kuwait frontier case, there has been considerable confusion on the questions of Kuwait's sovereignty and independence as well as on the validity of the three agreements of 1923, 1932, and 1963. Kuwait and its supporters, as mentioned earlier, have always considered the validity of the de facto borders implied under the recognition of its sovereignty and independence by Iraq. As far as Kuwait's sovereignty and independence are concerned, Iraq had recognized them by implication, specifically, it had exchanged cables of congratulations with Kuwait and established diplomatic representation between the two countries in 1963. As to the validity of the agreements of 1932 and 1963, this is an entirely different matter. True, these agreements had been ratified by the Shaykh of Kuwait, and the text of the 1963 agreement had been reported by Kuwait to the United Nations and published in the U.N. Treaty series before Iraq had taken action to ratify it. It is also true that the agreement of 1963 was signed by the prime minister of Iraq, who chaired the meeting between the Iraqi and Kuwaiti delegations, and the foreign minister of Kuwait, who headed the Kuwaiti delegation. But if this agreement were to be valid, it should have been approved by the Iraqi Cabinet and ratified by the president before it could become law for Iraq under its constitutional processes. When the agreement of 1963 came before the Iraqi Cabinet for approval on the same day it was signed by the Iraqi premier, who led the Iraqi delegation, it was rejected by the Iraqi Cabinet and never ratified by the president. On more than one occasion, Kuwait was notified about the matter.

In 1994, under the impact of the United Nations economic sanctions, Saddam Husayn notified the United Nations that Iraq was ready to recognize Kuwait's sovereignty and the demarcated boundary by the IKDBC. This step, taken under pressure, produced different reactions among the Iraqi leaders inside and outside the country. Needless to say, Iraq's recognition of Kuwait's sovereignty and independence, which actually had been done earlier, was the fulfillment of a longstanding Kuwaiti aspiration to achieve peace and security in its relationships with all neighbors. As Kuwait surely is not unaware that Iraq's recognition under Saddam Husayn's regime was undertaken under pressure and could at any time be repudiated by a future Iraqi government, it may argue that the recognition of its sovereign independence and demarcated boundary are not ultimately dependent on Iraq's recognition but on the Security Council Resolution 687 which considered not only the agreement of 1963 valid and binding, but also the IKBDC's demarcation of the boundary as defined under that agreement.[13]

As the Iraqi regime that accepted the demarcated boundary under Resolution 687 was not elected by the people to express an opinion on the matter, the Iraqi opposition leaders outside the country felt it was their duty to speak on behalf of their compatriots. When they met with the members of the IKBDC, they expressed their concerns and requested postponement of the final decision until Saddam Husayn's regime had been replaced by another elected by the people. The IKBDC replied that its function was merely technical—to demarcate the boundary on the basis of the 1963 agreement, in accordance with Security Council Resolution 687. As to the 1963 agreement, its validity is a matter on which the Security Council must decide on the basis of an advisory opinion of the International Court of Justice.

The Iraqi opposition leaders made their views public through the press. They made it clear that they were not unsympathetic with Kuwait's requirements for peace and security and insisted that Kuwait's sovereignty and independence should be acknowledged by Iraq. But, they maintained that the demarcation of the frontier ought to be postponed for the time being and should not be imposed by foreign powers, as the future peace and security between the two sister Arab countries could not possibly be guaranteed by freign powers.[14]

Kuwaiti men in high authority, as well as others in unofficial organizations, have almost all responded swiftly and indignantly against the position taken by the Iraqi opposition leaders, and a press campaign was conducted denouncing them as unfit leaders for Iraq to replace Saddam Husayn's regime. The Kuwaiti minister of state for Cabinet affairs, Dari al-Uthman, stated that the Security Council, upon Kuwait's request, decided to settle the question by the appointment of a demarcation committee, which acted on the basis of the 1963 agreement. As to the objections raised by the Iraqi opposition leaders, the minister of state replied that the frontier is a question that must be dealt with between the authority of one state with the other irrespective of domestic differences among leaders. The deputy foreign minister of Kuwait, Sulayman al-Shahin, said that the validity of Kuwait's boundaries with Iraq, based on the agreement of 1963, had become well-known to third parties as they had received the relevant official documents on the subject. As to the present conditions in Iraq, which have been raised in the press, al-Shahin said that Iraq has always been stronger than Kuwait in the past, and still is in the present. The assistant deputy minister of defense, Shaykh Sabah al-Nasir, said that Iraq had already possessed the Bakr Port and Umm Qasr on the coast of Khawr al-Zubayr which are quite adequate for its trade through the Gulf contrary to the opinion of those who claim that Iraq was deprived of maritime ports. The Iraqi authorities, however, have always complained that neither the Bakr nor the Basra ports were adequate for commercial purposes and claimed the islands of Warba and Bubiyan should be returned to Iraq for security requirements.

Perhaps the most important defense on behalf of the Iraqi opposition leaders, was by Sa'd Salih Jabr, president of the Free Iraqi Council, which may be summarized as follows:

1. The Iraqi opposition leaders, aware that Saddam Husayn has committed many unforgiven wrongs, were opposed to the invasion of Kuwait because it was contrary to Arab and Islamic traditions as well as to the norms of International Law.
2. The Iraqi opposition leaders were just as much concerned about the maintenance of peace and security in the Gulf as Kuwait. For this reason, they were anxious to settle the border question directly between Iraq and Kuwait.
3. The Iraqi opposition leaders were not opposed to the demarcation of frontier in principle. "In our conversation with IKBDC," he said, "we have already told its members that we would welcome a permanent demarcated boundary capable of survival in order to avoid falling in the same tragic situation as that of the Algiers Agreement [concerning the Iraq-Iran frontier] which Saddam had concluded and later denounced, leading to war resulting in the loss of over a million men."

4. Because the present regime in Iraq has denied the people a voice in the governance of the country, the Iraqi opposition leaders maintain that the postponement of demarcation to more auspicious circumstances would be in the interest of both countries until the people could elect their own rulers to maintain peace and security.[15]

The foregoing Iraqi and Kuwaiti views reported through the press has underscored a fundamental procedural difference between the two countries: should the agreement on the boundary between the two countries be dependent on the support of foreign powers or on an agreement reached between regimes elected by the people? While both the Kuwaiti rulers and Iraqi opposition leaders were agreed that the Iraqi regime under Saddam Husayn could not be trusted and must be replaced by another elected by the people, they disagreed as to how an agreement on the boundary between the two countries should be reached.

Kuwait, a small state, has pursued a policy which developed that its independence as a state would be dependent on the support of a foreign power that has an interest in the Gulf ever since it entered into an agreement with Great Britain in 1898. When British interest in the Gulf began to decline, the United States inherited the British legacy. Kuwait has thus conducted its foreign relations on the understanding that its sovereign independence and security are guaranteed by the United States and by its membership in the United Nations. The Iraqi opposition leaders, however, insisted that the best guarantee for Kuwait in the future would be an agreement reached with a government elected by the people of Iraq rather than by dependence on a foreign power.

The views of the Iraqi opposition leaders, however, were unacceptable to Kuwait and its Western supporters. In these circumstances, Iraq has been advised by some of its former allies, particularly Russia and France, to accept the United Nations boundary demarcation so that it could recieve assistance from them in the lifting of the economic sanctions. But since Iraq has recognized Kuwait's demarcated boundary under pressure and by a regime that was not elected by the people, any future government might be reluctant to accept it as enduring and valid. Frontiers between any two (or more) states can be the source of continuing trouble so long as they have not been settled by an agreement freely reached between them.[16]

Part IV

RESPONSIBILITIES FOR THE WAR

This part, consisting of four chapters, deals with the question of how to assess the responsibility of each principal party involved in the Gulf War. In the experiences of nations, the standard of responsibility for war has varied from age to age and from nation to nation. For this reason, an attempt in the first chapter of this part is made to scrutinize the standard of responsibility recognized by Muslim countries. Chapters two and three are devoted to the assessment of the Arab countries and their leaders on the one hand, and the Western countries and their leaders on the other, on the basis of the standards of justice recognized by each one of them.

The final chapter deals with the question, often raised by both Arab and Western leaders, as to whether the Gulf War was inevitable. The various schools of thought on the subject—the advocates of determinism, free will, and others—are discussed. In the final analysis, however, we maintain that the war was not inevitable.

In the assessment of responsibilities for the war, the Iraqi rulers pursued the wrong methods in asserting otherwise legitimate claims to territory and frontier by resorting to pressure and force. Kuwaiti rulers, however, used peaceful methods to assert their control over disputed territory and frontier by resorting to diplomacy.

Chapter 14

Standards of Responsibility

Responsibility, etymologically defined, is that for which the individual "must answer." Just as every individual, as a member of a community, is under obligation to respect the rights and privileges of other members, so also in the relationship among nations, each nation today is under obligation to respect the rights and privileges of other nations—the rights of sovereign equality, independence, territorial integrity, and others—for the breach of which it would be held responsible.

Unlike individual responsibility, however, where the standard for individuals in each state is defined under its legal system, no well-defined standard of state responsibility existed in the past. In the modern age, serious attempts to establish a standard acceptable to all nations have been made. Since World War I, the standard of state responsibility under the League of Nations Covenant was essentially confined to the maintenance of peace and security in the world. Under the United Nations Charter, the standard of responsibility has been extended to include not only peace and security but also to achieve "justice" and protect "human rights," concerning which the League of Nations Covenant was silent. With regard to human rights, the United Nations has made an earnest attempt to establish a minimum standard of "human rights," embodied under the "Declaration of Universal Human Rights." As a "declaration," however, it is not necessarily binding on all nations, but since it has been signed by most nations it is considered morally binding on all.

On the regional plane, the standards of rights and responsibilities has not always been in harmony with the standard set under the United Nations Charter, which is largely drawn on Western standards, while some of the regional standards are based on religious and other tra-

ditional values. The Middle Eastern standards are perhaps the oldest
in the world and the people take pride in their rich heritage. Islam
which is not only a religion but also a political system, is the basis on
which the Arabs established an empire that challenged the religious
and political systems of Western Christendom during almost the entire
Middle Ages. Today, the Arabs have manifestly been reasserting Islamic
values and concepts as the standard not only for regional relationships
but also for their relationships with Western countries. The declaration
of the *jihad* during the Gulf crisis was not the first time it has been
invoked in the modern age, as it had often been declared by Muslim
leaders without regard as to who was the competent authority to declare
a *jihad*.

THE ISLAMIC STANDARD OF RESPONSIBILITY

Like Western standards of responsibility, the Islamic standard is partly
based on ancient standards that preceded Islam, such as the Persian,
Greek, and Roman, although in theory the basic source is the divine
revelations. The Persians and the Greeks, who had been in almost continuous state of warfare before Islam, considered themselves superior
to each other and went to war on the basis of disparities in race and
culture. Aristotle, who laid down a standard of responsibility for the
Hellenes, considered war with the barbarians (Persians and others) a
"just war."[1]

The Roman Empire, which dominated the whole ancient Mediterranean world, was engaged in almost continuous warfare with its neighbors and sought to justify its actions on the grounds that the barbarians
were making trouble on the frontiers. Upon the suppression of disorder, the barbarian territories were annexed, and all the communities
that came under Roman rule were entitled to Roman citizenry, as peace
and order were considered Rome's standard of responsibility.[2]

In the Middle Ages, following the fall of Rome, the standard of
responsibility for war began to change. In the Christian and Muslim
doctrines, the scale on which the concepts of law and order was
weighed differed considerably from the classical scale. The laws of
Christendom and Islamdom, the two rival powers throughout the Medieval period, were in principle derived from and aimed at the assertion
of God's peace and justice on Earth. Each maintained, however, that
only its own system of religion and law was valid under God's revelations and each denounced the validity of the other's system, claiming
that it was its responsibility to extend the benefits of its own revealed
religion and law to other nations at the point of the sword. Islam's
instrument for achieving its objective was the *jihad*, a duty that might
be achieved by peaceful as well as by violent means. Christendom,
equally feeling the responsibility for the validity of its doctrines, coun-

teracted with the Crusades. To Islam the *jihad* was the litigation between the belief in the oneness of God and polytheism just as the Crusade was the litigation between Christianity and paganism.[3]

The *jihad*—often called, but not quite correctly, a "holy war"—is one of the most misunderstood concepts of Islam, as it has been used by the Western press and many writers to denote "summons to massacre." Thus Gibbon, the famous historian of the *Decline and Fall of the Roman Empire*, wrote: "Muhammad, with the sword in one hand and the Koran in the other, erected his throne on the ruins of Christianity and Rome."[4] But to scholars well versed in the religion and law of Islam, the *jihad* is essentially a duty to achieve as much spiritual salvation as necessary to protect the Islamic community. Islamdom, like Christendom, is a political community. It conceived the world to have been divided into: *dar al-Islam* (the house of Islam), where the believers lived and the *dar al-Harb* (the house of war) where the unbelievers lived.

The *dar al-Islam* was in theory neither at peace nor necessarily in permanent hostility with the *dar al-Harb*, as Islam had acknowledged the existence of Christendom (indeed, it had entered into interim peace agreements with a number of Christian communities) but it had not recognized it as a valid legal system. The relationship between the *dar al-Islam* and the *dar al-Harb* may be described as a "state of war," to use a modern legal terminology, because the ultimate aim of Islam was to establish peace and justice with communities that had acknowledged the Islamic public order. But the *dar al-Harb*, although viewed as in a "state of war," was not treated as a no-man's land without regard to justice. Islam proposed to regulate its relationship with *dar al-Harb* in accordance with a branch of its legal system (*Shari'a*) called *al-Siyar* (conduct of state), consisting of the norms governing the relationship between Islam and other communities in war and peace.

The instrument with which Islam sought to achieve its objective was the *jihad*. Islam prohibited all kinds of warfare save in the form of *jihad*. But the *jihad* did not necessarily call for sabre-rattling, even though a state of war existed in theory between the two *dars*—*dar al-Islam* and the *dar al-hard*—since Islam's ultimate goal might be achieved by peaceful as much as by the sword.

Strictly speaking, the word "*jihad*" does not mean "war" in the material sense of the word. Literally, it means "exertion," "effort," and "attempt," denoting that the individual is urged to use his utmost endeavors to fulfill a certain function or carry out a specific task. Its technical meaning is the exertion of the believer's strength to fulfill a duty prescribed by the law (*Shari'a*) in "the path of God (*Qur'an*, LXI, 10–13), the path of right and justice. The *jihad* may therefore be defined as religious and legal duty which must be fulfilled by every believer either by the heart or tongue in combatting evil and spreading the word of God by the hand and sword in the sense of participation in fighting. Such war, called in Western legal tradition "just war" (*bellum justum*), is the only valid kind of war. All other wars are prohibited. But resort to *jihad* must be declared by the Caliph, the head of state, not by irresponsible individuals.

The *jihad* was the just war of Islam. But war in the sense of resort to force is not a priority as other peaceful means should first be attempted before resort to the sword. In the Qur'an, God specified salvation of the soul as the ultimate aim of the *jihad*: "He who exerts himself (*jahada*), exerts only for his own soul" (Q. XXIX, 5).

True, the classical doctrine of the *jihad* made no distinction between defensive and offensive war, but later jurists, when fighting between Christendom and Islamdom came to a standstill and peace treaties were often concluded to establish peace (though lasting for only ten years in principle, capable of unspecified number of renewals), began to argue that the *jihad* in the sense of resort to force would be invoked only in the sense of defensive war. In the thirteenth century, when foreign enemies (Crusaders and Mongols) were menacing the gates of Islam, Ibn Taymiya (d. 1328) interpreted the *jihad* to mean waging a defensive war against any community that threatened Islam. Unbelievers who made no attempt to encroach upon Islam, he asserted, were not necessarily enemies of Islam nor should the law and religion of Islam be applied to them. "If the unbelievers were to be killed unless he becomes a Muslim," he went on to explain, "such an action would constitute the greatest compulsion,"[5] a notion which ran contrary to the revelation which states that "no compulsion is prescribed by religion" (Q.II, 257).[6] True, the Ottoman Sultans, in their conquests of European territory often invoked the *jihad*, but they also, at the height of their power, came to terms with European rulers and were prepared to make peace on the basis of equality and mutual interests, as Sultan Sulayman the Magnificent had indeed done in his treaty with Francis I, King of France, in 1535.[7]

In Persia, where the Shi'i creed prevailed from the opening of the sixteenth century, the powers of the Caliph (called Imam and must be a descendant from the Prophet's family), during his absence (the last of the Imams disappeared in the year 874 A.D.) were divided between the Shah and the Mujtahids (scholars in law and theology)—the latter exercised the spiritual power of the Imam and the former his civil power. In the event that the Mujtahids were to assume civil powers and exercise both civil and spiritual powers on behalf of the Imam during his absence, they would be the agent of the Imam, as the present regime in Iran established by the Revolution of 1979 under the leadership of Ayat-Allah Khumayni demonstrated.[8]

STANDARDS OF RESPONSIBILITY IN THE MODERN AGE

Since early modern times, the concept of responsibility for war began to change from a religious to a secular standard, as the sovereignty of

God, no longer contested on the grounds of religion, began to disperse among an increasing number of nations. In Western Christendom, the change began as early as the Renaissance and the Reformation periods, but in Islamdom, younger than Christendom by some six centuries, the change took a much longer time, and the integration of the various Muslim states (which replaced the Islamic empire) into the community of nations did not begin to take place until the latter part of the nineteenth century. Even then certain limitations on the independence of Muslim countries were imposed by the Western powers which prompted them to fall back on Islamic tradition as a measure to protect the dignity and integrity of their territory and their standing as members of the community of nations.

From the time Sultan ʿAbd al-Hamid (1878–1909), head of the Ottoman Empire, was declared Caliph of Islam, which entitled him to invoke the *jihad* against European intervention or pressure, both the Sultan and rulers of the countries that were separated from that Empire after World War I, often sought to use the *jihad* as a weapon against British and French domination in the Middle East and other Asiatic and African countries. Thus when the Ottoman Empire went to war against Britain and France in 1914, the Caliph declared the *jihad* and called upon Muslims in the Middle East and India to rise up against the British and their allies. Sharif Husayn of the Hijaz (an ally of the British) counteracting the Ottoman Caliph's declaration, invoked the *jihad* as an Arab ruler.[9]

During the inter-war years, the Syrian leaders invoked the *jihad* in their struggle against the French in 1920 and 1928. In 1936, the Mufti of Jerusalem invoked the *jihad* against the British. The Libyan tribal struggle against Italian rule in the 1920s, under the leadership of ʿUmar al-Mukhtar, was considered a *jihad*. In Iraq, nationalist opposition to the British in the revolt of 1920 and the military uprising in 1941 were validated by *fatwas* (legal opinions), issued by the Mujtahids as a form of *jihad* in order to provide public support against foreign intervention.

It is in the light of this historic tradition, Iraq and other Arab countries sought to oppose foreign intervention by an Islamic sanction, the *jihad*, in situations which they considered foreign powers should not be involved.

Chapter 15

Arab Responsibilities

The Gulf crisis, leading to the Coalition War, passed through various stages of development. It began as a territorial dispute over the frontiers between Iraq and Kuwait. But when differences on oil prices and overproduction adversely affected Iraq's income from oil, the crisis no longer remained confined to two countries; it first became a problem for Arabs to resolve on the regional plane and later for Western powers on the international plane. A discussion on Arab responsibilities will be dealt with in this chapter, and on Western responsibilities in the pages to follow.

RESPONSIBILITY OF IRAQ

Iraq's responsibility for the Gulf crisis is more complicated and difficult to assess than Kuwait's responsibility on two grounds: one is substantive and the other procedural. On substantive grounds, Iraq's territorial claims began from a modest demand for an access to Gulf waters, such as a port in the Umm Qasr area and the islands of Warba and Bubiyan, to a claim over the sovereignty of Kuwait on historical grounds. As to procedural responsibility, Iraq's method of dealing with Kuwait differed from one regime to another. Iraq often suspended negotiations for a settlement of the dispute, which might have achieved agreement, because the Cabinet that had been conducting the negotiations was suddenly replaced by another that held different views and claims from the previous Cabinet.

Instability in the Iraqi regimes and frequent Cabinet changes made it exceedingly difficult for the Iraqi negotiators to put forth a definitive set of proposals to Kuwait as a basis for an agreement to settle the dispute between the two countries.[1] Kuwait thus often complained that whenever it was seriously considering a set of Iraqi proposals, the new

Iraqi Cabinet that was suddenly formed repudiated the proposals that had just been submitted by the former Cabinet. A case in point, Kuwait stated, is the Agreement of 1963. It was negotiated and signed by an Iraqi delegation, headed by the prime minister, and a Kuwaiti delegation, headed by the foreign minister. A month later, the Iraqi premier resigned and the new Cabinet rejected it. This situation led to differences of opinion on the validity of the agreement. Kuwait, claimed that the agreement, based on an exchange of letters (1932) between the Iraqi prime minister and the Shaykh of Kuwait, was ratified by Kuwait and registered in the United Nations Treaty Series (as it was submitted by Kuwait). Iraq, however, argued that the text of the agreement was signed merely as the draft of an "agreed minutes" by a prime minister who had fallen from power and it was rejected when it came before the Iraqi Cabinet. Nor was it ratified by the president in accordance with Iraq's constitutional procedure in order to be binding.

In these circumstances, it is indeed difficult to assess Iraq's responsibility for the frontier dispute. Some jurists, it is true, argue that once a treaty or an agreement is signed by the two (or more) sides it should be binding, as it is taken for granted that both sides were not unaware of their constitutional limitations. But others insist that it must be ratified in accordance with constitutional procedures, as it would be exceedingly difficult for any government to implement the terms of a treaty or an agreement short of the constitutional requirements to become law of the land.[2] With regard to the Iraq-Kuwait frontier agreement, the Kuwaiti delegation, headed by Shaykh Sabah al-Ahmad—the perennial and well-informed foreign minister—was not unaware that in both Kuwait and Iraq, a treaty or an agreement for frontier, in order to be binding, must be ratified by the two heads of state. Nor was the Iraq delegation unaware that the document it signed—the "agreed minutes," consisting of the draft of an agreement—could not be binding before it had been ratified by the president of Iraq. The Shaykh of Kuwait, considering the "agreed minutes" a sound text of agreement, ratified it, although it was rejected by both the Iraqi Cabinet and president.

As to an access to Gulf waters and, more specifically, to the islands of Warba and Bubiyan, Iraq's claim was based not only on legal grounds. Because its limited coastal areas are unsuitable for a maritime port, Iraq's need for an outlet to sea either at Umm Qasr or in the islands of Warba and Bubiyan is considered very important, as Basra (whose waters now are shared with Iran) has become unsuitable for an expanding trade activities. But Iraq's claims on historical and legal grounds (although the latter is more convincing than the former) have been rejected by Kuwait, as it suspected that Iraq had ulterior political aspirations to play a predominating role in the Arab Gulf coastal area. Iraq, for its part, has been unable to divert its Arab brothers' fears, since it appeared, high-handedly, to expect from a younger brother the traditional Arab respect and deference to the older brother. Thus, when Kuwait rejected Iraq's claims, historical or legal, Iraq resorted to force. Today Iraq and its Arab brother have become equal members in the United Nations which requires the settlement of disputes by peaceful means; thus Iraq's resort to force must be considered a violation of the U.N. Charter as well as the norms of International Law for which Iraq is responsible.

With regard to Iraq's complaint about oil prices and Kuwait's overproduction, Iraq's position was clear—Kuwait's overproduction was a violation of the quota system adopted by OPEC which proved harmful to Iraq's income from the export of oil. As members of an organization to which both Iraq and Kuwait had voluntarily joined, they were under obligation to respect the decisions made by that organization. Arab brothers seem to have been sympathetic with Iraq and urged Kuwait to conform to the OPEC quota.[3]

RESPONSIBILITY OF KUWAIT

Kuwait's responsibility for the Gulf crisis stems partly from the negative attitude it had taken to reject almost all Iraqi proposals, including modest requests, and partly from its dependence on foreign support against Iraq's attempts to persuade its leaders to meet Iraq's essential requirements for trade and security in the Gulf. With regard to the frontier dispute, Kuwait insisted that no proposals for settlement would be accepted unless they were based on the frontiers defined first in an exchange of letters between Sir Percy Cox and the Shaykh of Kuwait (1923), confirmed by another exchange of letters between Iraq and Kuwait in 1932 and finally in the agreement of 1963, although none of these instruments had been approved or ratified by Iraq. Consequently, no compromise agreement had been reached to the satisfaction of both sides. Because Kuwait, unlike Iraq, had a relatively stable regime, it was able to stand firm and submit to Iraq the same proposals for frontier settlement based on the agreements of 1923, 1932, and 1963. By contrast, Iraq's position was considerably weakened by submitting different sets of proposals whenever the two sides met either at the negotiating tables or in confrontation on the battlefield. Even when Kuwait was approached with limited requests, it was hesitant to accept them, mainly because it suspected that Iraq might come back for further territorial demands under more aggressive regimes. Kuwait's refusal to compromise was mainly based on the assumption that any concession would not be the last.

Iraq, on the other hand, considered Kuwait's attitude a rejection of its minimum security requirements. Some of the Iraqi leaders often argued that when Kuwait was under British "protection," it was encouraged by the British to stand firm on its terms in order to protect their own imperial interests in the Gulf. After it achieved independence, Iraq began to realize that Kuwait's diplomacy and firm stand rested on its dependence first on Britain and later on the United States.[4] The Iraqi leaders thus seem to have come to the conclusion that Kuwait would never come to an understanding save by resort to force. As a small country, Kuwait could not possibly defend itself alone in any military confrontation with Iraq. It was accordingly bound to resort to diplomacy by virtue of which it entered into an alliance with a great power for protection. Such an alliance, it will be recalled, was not imposed on it by any foreign power; it was the product of its own historical origins and experiences.

Following the withdrawal of British military presence from the Gulf in 1971, the Shah of Iran, declaring himself the "policeman" of the Gulf, seemed the logical successor to inherent the role of Britain and to stand against foreign (Soviet) intervention. Because of the British withdrawal from the Gulf, Kuwait began to play a more active role in playing one strong Gulf country off against another through the balance of power. To Iran, the principal rival to its leadership was Iraq, with which Iran had a frontier dispute over the Shatt al-Arab waters. Kuwait, maintaining good relationships with Iran, felt that it could resist Iraqi pressure as long as Iran was not on good terms with Iraq. Even when the Shah's regime was overthrown by the Islamic Revolution, Iraq was still considered the rival power to Iran's aspirations to become the leading power in the Gulf.

In 1980, Iraq went to war with Iran, because of increasing frontier frictions and threats of Iranian intervention in Iraqi domestic affairs. Kuwait sided with Iraq, as the Islamic Revolution in Iran sought to "export" the Revolution (based essentially on Shi'i teachings) not only to Iraq but also to Kuwait and other Gulf countries where the Sunni Islamic creed prevailed. But no sooner had the war ended in 1988 than Kuwait quickly moved to normalize its relationships with Iran in pursuit of maintaining the balance of power in the Gulf.

Kuwait's pursuit of dual policies, dependence on the alliance with a great power and on the balance of power, is the privilege of every sovereign state in order to defend itself against any foreign threat or attack, before the matter is brought before the United Nations. As a member of the Arab family, however, Iraq maintained that there were other means and procedures for redress, such as an appeal to the Arab League or the Islamic Conference, which would apply Islamic norms and traditions to protect their common Arab interests.

Kuwait, in reply, might argue that Arab procedures could take a very long time. Long as Arab procedures might take—quarrels within the family always take a long time—Iraq could not possibly have refused to withdraw from Kuwait, as it had already made its intention to withdraw known provided it were not condemned by its Arab brothers. True, Kuwaiti leaders had indeed declared that they were ready to accept Arab mediation, but they also insisted that Iraq must agree to withdraw "immediately and unconditionally" (as stipulated under the U.N. Resolution 660). Iraq, however, complained that under the U.N. resolutions no promise was stipulated that its disputes with Kuwait were to be reconsidered.

Settlement of the crisis by Arab peaceful means would have been much less costly to the Arab world than by foreign intervention. The material and moral cost of the war which all Arab countries, including Kuwait, had to bear in an effort to bring the crisis to an end were enormous.

RESPONSIBILITY OF ARAB REGIONAL ORGANIZATIONS

1) The Islamic Conference Organization

The major Arab regional organizations that existed before the invasion of Kuwait, were the Arab League and two subregional organizations: the Gulf Cooperation Council (GCC) and the Arab Cooperation Council (ACC). The Islamic Conference Organization (ICO) to which we referred earlier, is broader in outlook than a regional organization, since Islam considered all groups and individuals who accepted its teachings were "believers" regardless of ethnic differences or territorial segregation. But as the major members of ICO were in the Arab world, its role in Arab regional affairs was considered so important that its inclusion in a discussion on Arab regional organizations would be unavoidable.

Believers are considered in principle "brothers in religion"; they are accordingly called upon to live permanently in peace with one another. In the event two groups of believers are engaged in a quarrel, all other believers are under obligation to intercede in order to put an end to it in accordance with a Quranic injunction. "If two parties of the believers fight, put things right between them; then if one of them is insolent against the other, fight the insolent one till it revert to God's commandments; if it reverts, set things right between them equitably, and be just" (*Qur'an* XLIX, 9). It follows that: a) it is an obligation on the part of believers to intercede whenever a quarrel or a dispute had arisen among believers; b) the intercession should be to reestablish unity and harmony by all possible peaceful means; and c) settlement of disputes should be on the basis of justice.

The Islamic Conference has been established primarily to deal with the improvement of conditions in the various parts of the Islamic world. For this reason, at the outset it has paid little or no attention to disputes among Islamic states and has left such cases as the Iraq-Kuwait dispute to Arab summits and the Arab League. Since other organizations have already passed Resolutions calling on Iraq to withdraw from Kuwait, the Islamic Conference, in conformity with those organizations, has also called on Iraq to withdraw from Kuwait and to settle their dispute by peaceful means; but it did not intercede to settle the dispute, although its secretary general offered the organization's good offices. It seems that the Islamic Conference felt that the intercession to settle a dispute among states is a "collective duty," which, if fulfilled by some, would relieve others of the duty under Islamic jurisprudence.[5]

The Quranic revelation, however, refer to quarrels and intercessions only among believers, but it made no mention that unbelievers might intercede to settle disputes among believers. For this reason, Muslim scholars were divided on the question of the intervention of the Coalition powers in the case of the Gulf crisis. Some have accepted the Security Council Resolutions demanding Iraq to withdraw "immediately and without conditions" from Kuwait in accordance with Western standards, to settle a dispute between two Muslim states. Iraq, opposed to Western intervention, declared the *jihad* and its action was validated by several Muslim scholars on the grounds that the deployment of foreign forces might lead to the occupation of Islamic lands by the unbelievers.[6] In the meantime, there were other Muslim scholars who rejected Iraq's right to declare the *jihad* on the grounds that Iraq had resorted to force in the first place which prompted Kuwait to invite foreign forces to defend their own lands.[7] There is, indeed, an element of truth in the argument of each side. The scholars who validated Iraq's action argued that the intervention of foreign powers in an essentially Islamic affair deprived the Muslims of the opportunity to resolve their differences by peaceful means in accordance with Islamic standards. The scholars who sided with Kuwait (and other countries in sympathy with it) argued that Iraq's invasion of Kuwait was the immediate cause of foreign intervention in Islamic affairs for which Iraq must be held solely responsible. Thus the Islamic world was divided on the issue of responsibility.

Why did the Muslims, it may be asked, disagree on such a vital issue as the Gulf crisis? In the modern age, when the Islamic countries had become part of the community of nations, Islamic standards could no longer remain immune to foreign standards for the conduct of foreign relations. The norms of International Law and diplomacy have gradually been adopted by Islamic countries ever since the Ottoman Empire, a Muslim power, undertook to uphold the law of Islam and made peace with Christian countries when Sultan Sulayman the Magnificent concluded a treaty of peace with France in 1535. Subsequently, it exchanged diplomatic representatives with European powers and entered into an alliance with some of them. In the nineteenth century, it sought support of some—in particular Britain—in its conflict with Persia and in the settlement of its land frontier under the treaty of Arz al-Rum (Erzerum) in 1876.[8] It even sought the assistance of European powers against some of its own governors who challenged the Sultan's central authority. For example, Muhammed ʿAli, governor of Egypt, who brought under his control Syria and Lebanon for a whole decade, 1831–41, his occupation of the two countries came to an end only after Britain and France intervened to compel Egyptian forces to withdraw from the two other Arab countries. These incidents were justified on the grounds that the Islamic countries have become integral parts of the community of nations and their diplomatic actions have tacitly been accepted by an increasing number of scholars despite occasional protests by some who continued to assert classical Islamic standards.

Small wonder that the Islamic Conference found itself in a difficult position were it to act strictly in accordance with Islam's standard of responsibility. As an Islamic institution, the Islamic Conference was expected to act, in principle, in accordance with Islamic norms, particularly the norms that are clearly prescribed in the *Qur'an* as stated earlier. In accordance with such a standard, the Islamic Conference called upon both Iraq and Kuwait to resolve their differences by peaceful means, but it stopped short of intervention, as the Iraq-Kuwait dispute had already been relegated to the Arab League for resolution. In adopting this procedure, the Islamic Conference had virtually validated a norm pursued by the Arab League representing the state, not religious, authorities, often called the *raison d'état*, subordinating religion to the state, although under Islamic law, the State is subordinate to religion in principle. Muslim scholars who disagreed with the Islamic Conference Resolutions, invoked the classical concept of the *jihad* against foreign intervention. Thus the Islamic world is still divided on the question as to which authority ultimately shall decide on vital Muslim issues: the Islamic religious or the state authorities. The Islamic Conference seems to have felt it was not its responsibility to resolve the Gulf crisis.

2) The Arab League

The Arab League is the regional organization in which all the independent Arab states, including the Palestine Liberation Organization (PLO), are represented, and it is recognized as a "regional arrangement," under the U.N. Charter (Article 52), and represented in the General Assembly by an observer. The Arab League thus is bound to adopt resolutions in accordance with both the norms governing the community of nations and the norms and traditions of the region to which it belongs, although the regional norms may not always be in harmony with the general norms governing the community of nations. The purpose of the Arab League, like other regional organizations, is to resolve disputes which are essentially regional by nature, but disputes which either the regional organization is unable to resolve or are considered a threat to the maintenance of international peace and security would be referred to the United Nations.[9]

The Gulf crisis is a case in point. The Arab League was potentially capable of resolving it, and a considerable number of its members were ready to discuss Iraq's request to resolve the issue in accordance with the norms and traditions ordinarily pursued by the League. Why, therefore, was the League reluctant or unable to resolve the Iraq-Kuwait dispute? Several underlying factors seem to have conspired to prevent the Arab League from dealing with the Gulf crisis before foreign intervention took place. Some were inherent weakness in the League's processes (procedural responsibility), and others were deep differences between Western and regional standards of responsibilities.

The Arab League's procedural responsibilities may be found in the complicated and inflexible processes which had often not only restricted but also prohibited it from action. For instance, before the Arab League Council is usually called to meet for the consideration of any important matter, the foreign ministers of the League's members are expected first to meet and make proposals for possible action. If the matter in question touches high policy, the foreign ministers may suggest the calling of a summit meeting, composed of the heads of state, to discuss the matter and make proposals for the League Council's consideration. Some heads of state may prefer not to attend and a mini-summit may be called instead. This tedious process, potentially leading to differences before the League Council meets, often blocks or renders the issues involved more complicated. During the Gulf Crisis, owing to these intractable procedural difficulties, for which the Arab League was responsible, the Arab countries paid a high price, as the five permanent members of the U.N. Security Council, each concerned about its own national self-interest, were in no mood to wait for a slow-moving regional organization to make up its mind as to how the crisis should be resolved.

The Arab League, however, was not only impeded by procedural but also by even more complicated substantial standards. Whenever the League members met to consider a serious question, they often found themselves widely divided about the kind of standards on the basis of which the question might be resolved. With regard to the Gulf crisis, they were divided into two schools of thought, each advocating a different kind of standard. One school, under the impact of Western norms of International Law and the U.N. Charter, demanded not only the withdrawal of Iraq from Kuwait but also the condemnation of the invasion, as Iraq had violated the independence and sovereignty of Kuwait, which had already been recognized by all the Arab states. The other school, arguing in favor of Arab ideological symbols, proposed to call on Iraq to withdraw in order to uphold Arab brotherhood and solidarity, and warned that dissension in rank might invite foreign intervention. The former school, arguing that condemnation is also a matter of principle, demanded condemnation which rendered agreement between the two schools almost impossible. Thus the Arab League's responsibility may be said to lay in its failure to overcome protracted procedural and substantive obstacles before the impatient Western powers had intervened to resolve the Gulf crisis in accordance with their own standard of responsibility.

3) The Gulf Cooperation Council (GCC) and the Arab Cooperation Council (ACC)

Kuwait is a member of the GCC but not of the ACC. Iraq, on the other hand, is a member of the ACC, but not of the GCC. The absence of Iraq from membership in the GCC and Kuwait from the ACC meant that these two organizations had little or no important direct role to play in resolving the crisis that ensued between the two countries. The Gulf crisis was neither formally brought before the ACC nor to the GCC to adopt a resolution for possible settlement, perhaps mainly because the members of both councils were also members of the Arab League where they had already participated in discussions when the issue was first brought up by Iraq. The GCC, however, had expressed itself under several Resolutions to support Kuwait while the ACC never formally met to discuss the crisis.[10] Had Iraq formally put its dispute with Kuwait before the ACC, it might have had an opportunity to avoid a misunderstanding about its intentions before the question had come before the Arab League. In these circumstances, however, neither of the two subregional organizations had any significant role to play in resolving the Gulf crisis, and consequently neither one of the two organizations could be formally held responsible for the failure to peacefully resolve the crisis.

RESPONSIBILITY OF ARAB LEADERS

In the foregoing pages, we have often referred to a number of personalities who undertook the initiative to persuade the sides concerned to resolve the Gulf crisis by peaceful means. None, it will be recalled, had a chance to succeed. Why, one may well ask, had all such attempts come to naught and who was responsible for failure?

As the Gulf crisis was created by Iraq's invasion of Kuwait, all attempts to resolve it focused on persuading Saddam Husayn to commit himself to withdrawal before settlement of the crisis by peaceful means could be undertaken. At the outset, when the crisis was under discussion among Arab leaders, Saddam seems to have been prepared to withdraw provided Iraq would not be condemned by the Arab League. Saddam's condition was based on the assumption that Iraq's invasion of Kuwait was not just an act of aggression, but the culmination of several failed attempts to settle disputes by direct negotiations. Nevertheless Kuwait refused resolution, save on its own terms. Ever since the United Nations Security Council had passed its first mandatory Resolution—

Resolution 660 (1990)—condemning Iraq's invasion and demanding "an immediate and unconditional withdrawal," Arab leaders have failed to agree on a face-saving formula which would not be humiliating, as Saddam had shown readiness to withdraw. The Arab leaders, however, failed to agree on what the face-saving formula would be.

When several Arab and Western leaders proposed plans for peaceful settlement, Saddam Husayn was encouraged to make a statement on August 12, 1990, in which, it will be recalled, he proposed that Iraq would be prepared to withdraw from Kuwait provided other Arab countries that came under foreign occupation would also be liberated. Saddam's proposals were rejected by Western leaders on the grounds that the linkage of the Kuwait crisis with other cases (such as Israel's occupation of the West Bank) was unacceptable, because the causes and conditions of each situation were different from the other.

Finding that all his offers for a compromise had been rejected, Saddam Husayn felt that Western insistence on withdrawal without regard to his country's claim to equality and justice, a regard that had been granted to other countries of the region in similar situations, was an insult both to his country and to himself. For this reason, he decided to stand firm against threats and pressures, although he was aware that he might not win a contest with the Coalition forces which were ready at any moment to drive him out of Kuwait. Viewing the confrontation with his opponents as a duel, he accepted the challenge as a matter of pride. For, had he turned down the challenge, his name would then go down in history as a "coward" (*jaban*), a word of disdain in Arab culture.[11]

Saddam's firm stand against the Western powers and his declaration of the *jihad* was supported by Muslims in several countries—Algeria, Tunisia, Libya, Sudan, Yaman, and several others—who viewed his attempt at defending Islam as a courageous stand. Muslim realists, however, rejected Saddam's declaration of the *jihad* on the grounds that Iraq had attacked not a foreign but another Muslim country; therefore, they held, it was his own action that led to foreign intervention for which he must be blamed rather than honored.

To Western policymakers, who considered Saddam a secular and realist leader, his stand against withdrawal from Kuwait, despite warnings from friends and allies, came as a surprise. His appeal to Muslims and the declaration of *jihad* were considered hypocritical, intended to create dissension among the Coalition powers and to extract concessions before withdrawal from Kuwait. The views of American policymakers about Iraq and its leaders must have been based on inadequate sources and comprehension of Islamic institutions. For example, Islam has often been narrowly understood to mean merely religious doctrines. As noted earlier, Islam is not only a religion; it is also a political and legal system. The Caliph, although entrusted with the declaration of the *jihad*, is supposed to act in consultation with scholars (*ulama*).

Since the Caliphate had been abolished following World War I, the Caliphial powers have been dispersed among the heads of state of the various countries of the Islamic world. Today, in each Muslim state, whether republican or monarchic, the head of state exercises the Caliphial executive powers. Thus, as head of state, Saddam Husayn declared the *jihad*, validated by the scholars in Iraq and in several other countries that supported Iraq, although it was denounced by the scholars of countries that sided with Kuwait. This situation is not unprecedented, as the declaration of the *jihad* by the Ottoman Sultan-Caliph, an ally of Germany in World War I, was denounced by the Sharif of Makka, who sided with Britain and its allies, declared a counter-*jihad* against the Ottoman Empire.

In his actions, Saddam seemed not only a realist but also an ideological, if not an idealist, leader. To Westerners, such a personage seemed highly hypocritical. But to Muslims, he seemed to have declared the *jihad* as a duty of the head of state in the face of foreign threats and intervention. The fact that he was a leader of the Ba'th, considered a secular party, did not mean that Saddam, also a Ba'thist religious leader, had introduced religion into his party. As a matter of fact, it was 'Aflaq, founding father of the Ba'th and a Christian who admired Islam, who had introduced Islam, in its broader meaning of culture, as one of the basic principles of the Ba'th Party. Thus the Ba'th Party is not completely secular in the sense of the separation between state and religion, because Islam, in the broad cultural sense, is an element of Arab nationalism. Saddam may be considered secular, but not in the sense that Islam is separated from the state.

It is tempting to conclude that in the conduct of state, Saddam has oscillated between the two schools of realism and idealism, combining an element of both in his leadership qualities. For example, in his negotiations with the Shah of Iran concerning the settlement of the Shatt al-Arab frontier dispute, Saddam proved to be a realist, because he knew that to put an end to the Iran- Iraq conflict a measure of flexibility was necessary in order to reach an agreement to the satisfaction of both sides. But in the Iraq-Kuwait frontier dispute, when he was expected to act as a responsible realist, Saddam appeared as the idealist who refused to withdraw from Kuwait because he considered withdrawal under foreign threats was, as a matter of honor, humiliating to his country. For his stand, regardless of the consequences, he was honored by those who shared his views, although the price paid by the sacrifices in blood and property were colossal. Just as Saddam was held in high esteem by a considerable number of Muslims, he has also been blamed and even condemned for undermining the position of the Arab world on both the regional and international planes.[12]

Since Iraq had taken the drastic step to settle its account with Kuwait by resort to force, Kuwait rulers felt that they were bound to defend their country by all possible means at their disposal. Unlike the

Iraqi leaders who invoked idealistic motives, the Kuwaiti rulers opted to act as realists and fled the country the moment they learned that the Iraqi forces had crossed the borders, as it was obvious that a small force could not possibly defend the country against the more powerful and well-equipped Iraqi forces. Well-received by Saudi Arabia, Shaykh Jabir, head of state, accompanied by his premier and foreign minister, became very active as a government in exile, whose legitimacy was not in question, and he began to appeal to Western powers and to the United Nations, of which Kuwait was a member, to compel Iraq to withdraw from his country.[13]

Like Iraq, Kuwait, an independent and sovereign state, and member of the United Nations, felt free to call on all friendly states and allies to come to its defence in accordance with the U.N. Charter (Article 51), in order to restore the independence and territorial integrity that it had just lost. Both Iraq and Kuwait seemed to have left no stone unturned in order that each could defend and justify its stand in accordance with one standard of responsibility or another.

Chapter 16

Western Intervention and Its Rationale

Arab leaders, viewing their differences as "family affairs," looked upon foreign intervention in Arab affairs with suspicion, and often they denounced it as a form of neocolonial or imperial intervention. By contrast, in Western eyes foreign involvement in Asiatic or African affairs before World War I was regarded as a civilizing mission to extend the benefits of progress and development to backward people.[1] During and after the interwar years—in particular since World War II—when the old colonial and imperial ventures came under severe attack and were condemned in international councils, Western involvement in overseas colonies has been reduced; but indirect control and pressures continued during the interwar years, especially in northern Arab countries which were placed under the League of Nations "Mandates" because they were not considered ready for independence. Some of these countries, like Iraq and Egypt, achieved independence before World War II, but other countries like Syria, Lebanon, and Jordan, achieved independence only after the war.

Following World War II, however, some of the Arab countries began to feel that under the guise of such lofty principles as the maintenance of international peace and security, and respect for human rights, they have often been subjected in various degrees to one form of foreign pressure or another, although all have become independent members of the United Nations (with some participating in its establishment). There were several reasons for foreign involvement in Arab affairs; some were regional and others international.

From the regional perspective, the Arab countries were divided on the major issues confronting inter-Arab relationships such as the form of Arab unity and their attitude toward the East-West conflict during the Cold War. The idealist or the pan-Arab school advocated the concepts of Arab brotherhood and Arab solidarity and rejected foreign pressures and intervention in Arab affairs. The realist or the modernist school advocated cooperation with Western democracies and often tolerated Western influence on the grounds that it might speed up development and modernization, although they claimed to honor the principles and values of Arab brotherhood.

From the international perspective, the Arab countries were expecting the United Nations, the custodian of peace and security in the world, to put an end to foreign threats and intervention in domestic affairs. But under the United Nations, global peace and security have been entrusted to the Security Council, a small body of fifteen members dominated by five permanent members who have already been designated in the U.N. Charter by the great powers of World War II and not by the U.N. General Assembly. In all the Resolutions of the Security Council, the five permanent members enjoy the privilege that any Resolution passed by a majority of nine must include the concurring votes of the five permanent members. Consequently if one of them would cast a veto to save an ally or a client, any resolution passed by a majority would be a dead letter. Thus, if Iraq had invaded Kuwait before the Cold War had come to an end, a Soviet veto might have saved it from the Security Council's mandatory sanctions. Following the Cold War, Iraq's invasion of Kuwait became a test-case for the United Nations to demonstrate as to whether it would be decided on the grounds of a clientele relationship or on its merits in accordance with the aims and ideals of the U.N. Charter irrespective of Cold War conditions.

THE GULF CRISIS AND THE UNITED NATIONS RESPONSIBILITIES

The Gulf crisis, for which Iraq was subjected to a set of effective mandatory sanctions by the Security Council, is a unique case in the annals of the United Nations. It is the first case, since the Korean war, when resort to force was used by a Coalition of U.N. members to compel one country to withdraw from another largely because the national self-interest of the five permanent members of the Security Council coincided with the primary purpose of the United Nations to maintain international peace and security. Had Iraq invaded Kuwait before the cold war was over, the Soviet Union would probably have not hesitated to cast a veto. Following the cold war, the protection of Iraq and several other Arab countries—Syria, South Yaman and others—has become far less important to the Soviet Union than cooperation with the United States. The question before the United Nations was whether the Security Council was ready to consider the Gulf crisis as a dispute to be resolved in accordance with the aims specified under the U.N. Charter or merely to punish the side that resorted to force.

Oskar Schachter, in an able article entitled "United Nations Law in the Gulf Conflict,"[2] states that there were in the case of the Gulf crisis some positive and negative aspects of the U.N. collective action. Some, he said, have regarded it as a "vindication of international law and the principle of collective security." Others, he added, viewed it "as still another example of the dominant role of power and national self-interest in international relations." While in each, he opined, a case can be made; he optimistically saw the possibility of a United Nations role "as an instrument of collective responsibility" in the establishment of a new world order based on "the rule of law" to maintain peace and security in the world.

Schacter's call for "the rule of law" as a goal to achieve international peace and security under U.N. collective action, with which we are in agreement, is presumably based on the assumption that U.N. members might be ready to take action against the country that violated "the rule of law" irrespective of their own national self-interest. This is not feasible under the present structure of the United Nations. From its inception the United Nations has been inhibited by certain constraints which have made it exceedingly difficult to meet its responsibilities under the Charter. There are two sets of constraints. One is procedural and the other substantive.

The procedural constraints are inherent in the structure of the Security Council as well as in the voting privileges given to the five permanent members of the Security Council. In structure, the Security Council is composed of fifteen members, one third of which are the five permanent members designated in the Charter by the founding fathers of the United Nations. What makes their influence even more important is the complicated voting process in the Security Council.

In accordance with the Charter (Article 27), decisions of the Security Council on all matters, save procedural matters, are made by the affirmative vote of nine members including the concurring votes of the five permanent members. Thus in the event that one of the five permanent members decided to cast the privilege of veto, regardless whether it is a party to the dispute under vote or not, the decision of the Security Council, even if it were voted by a majority of nine, would remain a dead letter. As the postwar years were dominated by the rivalry between the United States and the Soviet Union (each supported by allies and friends), each camp was not expected to vote against its own national self-interests or the interests of its allies and clients.

Iraq's action, weighed on Schacter's scale, has indeed, by the invasion of Kuwait, violated the "United Nations law"—the Charter—for which Iraq was held responsible. In its defence, however, Iraq's representative to the United Nations, Ambassador al-Anbari, did not defend his country's invasion of Kuwait—he even suggested Iraq's readiness to withdraw from Kuwait—but he objected to the U.N.'s excessive, disproportionate, and swiftly adopted mandatory resolutions made without prior consultation with Iraq's representative. He also indicated some violations of the Charter (Article 51) by individual action, apart from collective action, after the Security Council was apprized of the Kuwait crisis. These were procedural violations of responsibility. There were also substantive violations to which the Iraqi foreign minister, Tariq 'Aziz, referred in his meeting with Secretary James Baker, when he reminded him of the double standard pursued in the U.N. Resolutions concerning Israel's occupation of Arab lands. The substantive violation, to which 'Aziz referred, but Baker dismissed on the ground that no linkage existed between one case and another, is a question of justice, one of the primary aims of the United Nations which ought not to be dismissed as merely a matter of "linkage."[3]

Nor are international peace and security the only primary aims of the United Nations. Under Article 1 of the U.N. Charter, justice and human rights are also stated as primary aims. In his article on United Nations law, Schacter seems to consider the "maintenance of peace and security" to be the primary concern of the United Nations "as an instrument of collective responsibility," although he is not unaware that justice and human rights are also primary aims worthy of consideration.

AMERICAN AND BRITISH RESPONSIBILITIES

Great Britain preceded the United States in its entry into the Gulf region. By virtue of British "protection," Kuwait, a small country among more powerful neighbors, was able to survive. From the moment it entered into British patronage, Kuwait became central to protecting British imperial interests in the Gulf. Because of the intricate and arcane relationships between the two countries, Britain must be held responsible for some of the actions taken by Kuwait (with British tacit approval) leading to a number of crises with Iraq. For example, in 1923 in an exchange of letters between Sir Percy Cox, high commissioner in Iraq, and the Shaykh of Kuwait, Cox decided to include the islands of Warba and Bubiyan within Kuwait's frontiers. Likewise, in 1932, when the premier of Iraq confirmed the frontier between Iraq and Kuwait as it existed in 1923, he was bound to do so in order to obtain British support for Iraq's admission into membership of the League of Nations, although neither the exchange of letters in 1923 nor in 1932 were ratified by the King of Iraq in accordance with Iraq's constitutional process.

After independence, Iraqi leaders often complained about the biased standing of Britain in favor of Kuwait when Iraq was under its control. Had Britain encouraged both sides to reach a compromise border agreement which would provide Iraq with an access to Gulf waters, it could have spared both sides the agony of increasing future frictions. But Britain seems to have decided that its imperial interests in the Gulf, would be better served by dependence on Kuwait rather than on Iraq. After they achieved independence, Iraq and Kuwait, finding themselves poles apart on the unsettled frontier issue, were unable to overcome the difficulties and complications that were bequeathed to them by Britain.

The United States, although aware of the complicated Iraq-Kuwait disputes, was reluctant to assume the responsibilities the British had bequeathed to it. It preferred to protect its own national interests irrespective of internal regional conflicts, leading to further conflicts, into which it was eventually drawn. There were several reasons for the United States to follow essentially the same line of British policy in the Gulf region.

In the first place, the existence of an enormous reserve of oil in the region on which the Western countries were dependent, prompted American policymakers to prevent the fall of Kuwait into the hands of Iraq and to forestall Iraq's resulting power to influence world oil prices single-handed. As the Kuwaiti rulers were committed to pursuing the traditional policy of alliance and friendship with a great power, the United States was bound to follow the same policy of friendship and cooperation with Kuwait. American support of Kuwait was not only made clear during the Iraq-Iran War when the American navy in the Gulf, in pursuit of free navigation escorted Kuwaiti tankers to ward off Iranian attacks, but also, after Iraq had invaded Kuwait, by more aggressive military actions. No sooner had the news about the invasion reached Washington than President Bush, in a statement to the press, declared that the security of the Gulf region and its oil were primary reasons for dispatching the American force to Saudi Arabia. In order to achieve these objectives, the defence of Saudi Arabia and the restoration of the legitimate government of Kuwait were considered necessary to protect American interests in the Gulf region. As one high official in the Bush administration, summing up the American objectives, said:

> The occupation of Kuwait [by Iraq] isn't, in itself, a threat to American interests. The real threat lies in the power Iraq would have in possessing 20 percent of the world's resources of oil, controlling OPEC, dominating the Middle East, threatening Israel and wanting to acquire the atomic bomb.[4]

Second, Britain's decision to withdraw its military presence from the Gulf was likely to invite Soviet intervention despite the offer of the Shah of Iran to play the role of policeman in the Gulf. There was also fear, although proven unfounded, that Iraq, as an ally of the Soviet Union since 1972, might allow Soviet penetration into the Gulf. When the Soviet Union invaded Afghanistan in 1979, it appeared to American policymakers that the Soviet Union was ready to penetrate the Gulf which prompted the American government, under the Carter Doctrine, to warn the Soviet Union against meddling in Gulf affairs.

The security of the Gulf was not the only American responsibility in the region. The security of Israel, to which the United States has been committed, was another one. Ever since Israel was established, the Arab countries have raised objections about the American support of Israel, particularly since the Six-Day War in 1967. But the Arabs were divided as to how the United States might be influenced to reconsider its policy toward Israel. Some, who were friendly to the West, sought to persuade the United States to restrain Israeli attacks and to seek peaceful settlement of the Arab-Israel conflict. Others, like Egypt under the Nasir regime (1952–70), Syria under Asad, and Iraq under the Ba'th leadership, were opposed to American policy. In an alliance with the Soviet Union, they sought to obtain weapons and to settle their accounts with Israel through military confrontations.

Ever since the Ba'th, an ideological party calling for the "liberation of Arab Palestine" achieved power in 1968, Iraq seemed a threat to Israel, although it took no initiative to attack Israel, as no common frontiers between the two countries exist to bring about direct military confrontation. In 1980, when Saddam Husayn became president and Iraq was involved in the war with Iran, it was deemed necessary to embark on a large-scale rearmament program, including chemical, nuclear, and biological weapons, as Iraq was engaged in a conflict with a country three times larger than Iraq in size and richer in human and material resources. Israel was aware that Iraq's disputes were primarily with its Gulf neighbors—Iran and Kuwait—but still its efforts to acquire nuclear weapons was viewed as a challenge to Israel, the only country that sought to possess such weaponry, and considered a threat to its security. For this reason, in a public speech on April 1, 1990, Saddam Husayn threatened to retaliate with equally deadly chemical weapons should Israel again attack Iraq as it did in 1981. Saddam's warning aroused the American Congress and the press, and called for economic sanctions against Iraq for its threat to Israel's security. President Bush, it will be recalled, did not consider it an American responsibility to punish Iraq for Saddam's warning to Israel. But the press campaign against Iraq continued unabated.

Following the war with Iran, Iraq was thus faced with the possibility of a conflict with three countries—Iran, Israel, and Kuwait—each for entirely different reasons. Because of the heavy foreign debt resulting from the costly war with Iran and the purchase of weapons for the rearmament program, Saddam Husayn turned to his Arab brothers for financial support, but Kuwait was not forthcoming. He began to suspect that Kuwait, a small country, but on good terms with Western allies and friends, must have been instigated by Iraq's opponents to enter into an "economic warfare" (in Saddam's words) in order to weaken Iraq and cause the destruction of the regime over which he presided. Saddam also held that the purpose of the Western campaign against Iraq was to create an atmosphere clouded with aversion and detestation favorable for an Israeli action, were it to make another attack on Iraq. When he was assured through Amir Bandar and the Dole mission that neither was Israel planning to attack Iraq nor was the Bush administration intending to apply economic sanctions, Saddam seemed to have been satisfied with those assurances.

There was under the surface, however, a feeling in Baghdad that Saddam Husayn was not *persona grata* to the American public, as the press did not stop its campaign against him and his regime. Nor was there direct contact between the American and Iraqi presidents—only through officials and diplomats—and Saddam had never visited Washington to establish personal rapport with the White House and the Congress or to address the public through the media. Thus Saddam felt he was not treated in the same way as other Middle Eastern heads of state who were often in direct contact with the White House. When President Bush, however, sent a personal letter to President Saddam Husayn on the occasion of Iraq's National Day, Saddam reciprocated on more than one occasion by expressing his own gratification to Bush through official channels. Thus on the surface, it seemed "all was quiet on the Western front," until the beginning of August, 1990.

What appeared to ensure quiet on the surface to Saddam Husayn in the Spring of 1990 is that neither Britain nor the United States were in the mood to enter into a military confrontation with Iraq, as the British Parliament and the American Congress were then opposed to war. On the strength of the evidence provided by a variety of sources, including the advice of his experts on Western democracies, Saddam seems to have made up his mind to settle his accounts with Kuwait by all possible means, including the use of force.[5] But he wanted to be assured that his calculations were correct, especially as to what the American reaction would be. For this reason, Saddam summoned April Glaspie, American ambassador to Iraq, to discuss his differences with Kuwait and other matters and told her that the conversation was a message to President Bush. He obviously wanted to know what Bush's reactions would be to his message. In his conversation with Glaspie, Saddam complained about Kuwait's efforts to undermine Iraq's economy and the support it had received from the United States. "Iraq has its own rights," said Saddam, and he hinted that he might use force to defend them. In reply, Glaspie sought to assure Saddam that Bush's instructions were "to seek better relations with Iraq." "But", she added "we have no opinion on the Arab-Arab conflict, like your border disagreement with Kuwait," although she made it clear that those differences should be settled by peaceful means. As Saddam received no warnings from Washington, despite the fact that Iraq's deployment of three divisions near the Kuwaiti border had already been detected by the Pentagon and Glaspie called Saddam's attention to it, he concluded that the United States was not prepared to be involved in a military confrontation in the Gulf. During the week when he met with the American ambassador, Saddam had already been meeting with his high military commanders and decided not only to use force to occupy the area claimed by Iraq, but also to take control over the whole of Kuwait. A hint to this effect was implied in the instructions he had given to 'Izzat al-Duri, before he attended the Jidda meeting, that in the event the Iraqi demands were rejected by the Kuwaiti premier, then Duri should tell him that Iraq would recognize no other border save that when Kuwait was but a "mud-walled town." Obviously this statement implied that Iraq was ready to use force. While Saddam must be held responsible for resort to force, Bush must also bear the responsibility for not warning Saddam that resort to force would be a matter of concern to the United States.

THE RATIONALE FOR INTERVENTION

As discussed, nder the United Nations Charter (Chap. VII), the enforcement of sanctions, economic or otherwise, against any country is for the purpose of maintaining peace and security in the world. In other words, the United Nations is to act as a world police, one of the functions of an "international government." The United Nations, however, although it could fulfill some functions of an international government, is neither in structure nor in the manner it discharges its responsibilities actually an international government. For instance, all the General Assembly's Resolutions are recommendatory, but the Security Council's Resolutions can be mandatory, provided they were adopted by a majority of nine, including the concurring votes of the five permanent members of the Council. Thus the United Nations is bound to depend on the pleasure of the five permanent members of the Security Council who are not elected by the General Assembly, as are the other ten members, but have already been assigned in the Charter by the founding fathers of the United Nations under the influences of the great powers who won World War II against Germany and its allies. Thus whenever the Security Council has adopted a mandatory Resolution to apply sanctions against any country, it appeared in the eyes of non-Western countries, but little different from the nineteenth-century intervention by Western imperial powers. Small wonder that when the Security Council passed its mandatory Resolutions against Iraq, Saddam Husayn rejected them on the grounds that they were imposed under the influence of the United States and Britain, each for its own reasons. What were those reasons, one may well ask?

AMERICAN AND BRITISH RATIONALE

The intervention of the United States in the Gulf crisis, apart from its obligations as a member of the Security Council, rested on three grounds. First, the United States sought to protect its own national interests in the Gulf region which appeared to have been threatened by Iraq. Second, the United States had certain commitments to a number of countries in the region whose security seemed to have been threatened by Iraq's invasion of Kuwait. Thirdly, as Iraq had declared the *jihad* against Western intervention in Islamic lands, a number of American writers sought to rationalize Western intervention as a form of just war (*justum bellum*), in defence of Western (Christian) values.

With regard to the protection of American interests, President Bush, who sought in vain to influence Saddam Husayn to pursue a policy of peace and moderation, began to hold meetings at the White House and Camp David to define American interests in the Gulf and to determine the steps to be taken to protect them. It was agreed that Saddam Husayn's invasion of Kuwait would put oil prices at his mercy and that this should not be allowed to happen. Discussion then turned to prepare plans to reverse the invasion of Kuwait by the dispatch of a force to Saudi Arabia that might influence Saddam to withdraw. In the meantime, Bush was speaking on the telephone with President Mubarak of Egypt, and King Husayn of Jordan, to seek their support, but they insisted the U.S. should give them first an opportunity to seek an Arab solution. When the Arabs did not act quickly, Bush decided, in agreement with Thatcher, British prime minister, to protect Western interests through the United Nations, presumably on the grounds that Shaykh Jabir, Amir of Kuwait, and Shaykh Saʿd, his premier, had already appealed to him for assistance.

The first initial step taken on the same day when the Iraq invasion had started (August 2, 1990), was a Resolution adopted by the Security Council demanding the immediate and unconditional withdrawal of Iraq from Kuwait. Bush seems to have already been determined that Iraq's invasion of Kuwait should be reversed, but he had not yet made up his mind as to what other steps should be taken. He had already been committed to deliver a speech for the opening of the Aspen Institute Conference on August 2, and he wanted to know what the British prime minister, Margaret Thatcher, had in mind to do. She was also invited to speak and decided to arrive early in order to be present when Bush would give his speech. The strong and militant-minded British premier, after a brief conversation with her ambassador to the United States, had already made up her mind when Bush arrived. After meeting with Bush, as stated in *The Downing Street Years*, she said:

> I told him. . . . First, aggressors must never be appeased. We learned that to our cost in 1930s. Second, if Saddam Hussein were to cross the border

into Saudi Arabia he could go right down the Gulf in a matter of days. He would then control 65 percent of the world's oil reserves and could blackmail us all. . . . [6]

It has been said that Bush was influenced to take a firm stand against Iraq's actions by Margaret Thatcher. Bush seems to have already been mentally prepared to take a firm stand against Saddam, and he was thus encouraged to find Thatcher to his great satisfaction had already made up her mind about Iraq. Both were agreed to cooperate in reversing the invasion by economic sanctions through the United Nations. After his return from Aspen, Bush began to call on other heads of state to cooperate in the implementation of the Security Council's Resolutions, including the use of force, until Iraq not only had to withdraw from Kuwait, but also was disarmed of all weaponry of mass destruction.

As several Muslim scholars began to endorse the declaration of *jihad* by Iraq against Western intervention in the Gulf, a number of Western writers also began to take an interest in the controversy over the meaning of *jihad* and its counterpart in Western society by the concept of just war (*bellum justum*). In earlier pages of this work, the concept of *jihad* is defined as the "just war" of Islam. The expansion of Islam, carried out by the *jihad*, was a religious-legal duty. It was surely as pious and just as *pium* and *justum*, in the ways described by St. Augustine and St. Thomas and later by Hugo Grotius.

Just as the concept of *jihad* had undergone gradual changes from offensive to defensive war, because of changing circumstances, so had the Western concept of the Crusade had changed from the Medieval *bellum justum* to a modern concept of just war which repudiate aggressions and permits the use of force only to reestablish law and order as defined under the United Nations Charter. Today, Western writers consider just war a secular concept based on values which Western society honors. Writers belonging to the realist school of law maintain that the pursuit of national self-interest is the basis of foreign policy. Resort to force in the pursuit of the national interest is a just war, because today the "national interest" is the basis of the modern state.

The idealists, however, argue that the assertion of the national interests by powerful nations may lead to friction among nations, because the national interests of one state may not always coincide with the national interests of another state. The doctrine of national interest might also undermine the world order as defined under the Charter of the United Nations if it came into conflict with one of its aims such as the maintenance of international peace and security, the pursuit of justice, and human rights.

The Gulf crisis is a test-case as to what were the forces behind Western intervention. As it appeared to Iraq and its supporters, the Western powers were prompted to enforce the U.N. sanctions by sheer self-interest. Even other countries that joined the Western powers were motivated by one kind of national self-interest or another. Western idealists and realists were agreed, as Schachter pointed out, that in the Iraq-Kuwait dispute the national self-interests of Western powers coincided with the United Nations primary aims. Small wonder that both Western idealists and realists have come to the conclusion that the Gulf War was a just war.[7]

In view of this overwhelming agreement among nations that took Iraq to task, one may well ask, why did the Iraqi leaders protect the national interests of their own country by refusing the call of so many nations to withdraw from Kuwait? What seduced the Iraqi leadership to persist with its stand that the issue only be settled on the battlefield? Was it because the war was inevitable? An answer to this question will be attempted in the final chapter.

Chapter 17

Conclusion: Was the War Inevitable?

"For every problem there is a solution," Shaykh Jabir, Amir of Kuwait, is reported to have told Saddam Husayn.[1] This saying, often quoted to break a deadlock in negotiations, was made by Shaykh Jabir, when he and King Fahd of Saudi Arabia were on their way to the airport escorted by Saddam Husayn, following the Arab Summit meetings in Baghdad (May 28–30, 1990). In a closed meeting of the summit—to which we have referred earlier—Saddam had bitterly complained about an "economic warfare" which his Arab brothers had waged against Iraq by overproduction of oil resulting in lowering oil prices and reducing Iraq's income from oil. As Kuwait was the leading Arab brother that pursued such a policy, Shaykh Jabir made his statement as a hint that Kuwait was ready to come to an understanding with Iraq to resolve the problems that had arisen between the two countries. But if there is a solution for every problem, as Shaykh Jabir reminded Saddam, why did Saddam resort to force?

Before we answer this question and deal with the subject as to whether the Gulf War was inevitable, a few words about the traditional Islamic theory of free will and predetermination might throw light on the question.

In accordance with Islamic traditions, all human actions—indeed, the whole destiny of mankind—have been predetermined by God, and the human will is hardly more than the shadow of God's will translated into daily human actions. The believers who follow the word of God's will be compensated with eternal life in Heaven and the unbelievers are destined to be in hell and "evil is the destination." The drama of human life on earth, viewed as the unfolding of God's will, is also a Christian doctrine which prevailed during the entire Middle Ages.

In a conversation between Sa'd al-Bazzaz, an Iraqi writer, and Taha

Yasin Ramadan, vice premier and member of the Revolutionary Command Council, Bazzaz inquired as to whether the use of force in the conflict with Kuwait could have been pursued "by means other than war?" In reply, Ramadan said: "History is made by the will of God and the will of man . . . I would have preferred the action to invade Kuwait to take place five years after the war with Iran when Iraq would have achieved further development, but the chain of events have already been determined. . . . [A]t any rate I refuse to say that we could have avoided what had already been [predetermined] for us to do."[2]

At a meeting of the U.N. Security Council (November 29, 1990), when Resolution 678 for the use of force was under consideration to compel Iraq to withdraw from Kuwait, 'Abd al-Amir al-Anbari, Iraq's representative to the United Nations, said that Iraq had already proposed to settle the Gulf crisis by peaceful means, but he added:

> If the United States imposes war on us, then that will be our *destiny* and
> . . . our people will not kneel down and will measure up to its responsibilities.[3] (emphasis added)

In his reference to the imposition of war on Iraq as "our destiny," al-Anbari was, as a matter of fact, echoing what the top leaders and the people throughout the country had been saying that it was ultimately the will of God, expressed in the duty of the *jihad* which the authorities had already declared to defend the country against the attack by the unbelievers. Under Islamic law, the *jihad* is an individual duty, but in the event of a sudden attack, like the Coalition War, it would become a collective duty on all believers, save the elderly and sick, to rise up in arms in defence of the country. If the duty is not fulfilled, the whole community would be in error. These are the views of the school of predestination.[4]

In classical Islam, there was another school of thought, called al-Mu'tazila, which advocated the concept of free will and held that the individual can create his acts. But this school was repudiated by the authorities and most of the *ulama* (scholars) were in favor of the doctrine of predestination. In the modern age, not only the advocates of free will have become more widespread, but also, under the influence of the conspiracy theory, its advocates maintain that human beings can create acts and conditions which would produce the designed goal.[5] In the case of the Gulf crisis, according to this theory, the principal culprits were George Bush and Margaret Thatcher who had from the very beginning of the crisis come to a tacit understanding that Saddam Husayn, an ambitious Arab leader, was not going to stop at Kuwait, but he would go down the Gulf in a matter of few days to control the whole Gulf region. Like Hitler, Thatcher told Bush, he will not stop unless the Western democracies stand together not only to halt him but also to replace him with another leader friendly to the West.

Nor were Bush and Thatcher alone in their suspicion of Saddam's actions. Saddam's surreptitious purchase of high technological instruments from Western countries, which might be used for military purposes against them, gave the media an impetus to criticize the American and British authorities, although these were not slow to stop illegal trade. The advocates of the conspiracy theory held that Bush and Thatcher were moved by personal grudges. Bush, who appeared in the public eyes as a "wimp," sought through the Coalition War to wipe out this stigma. In Thatcher's case, she had called on Saddam through a radio broadcast to release Bazoft—the press reporter to the *London Observer* who was arrested on the grounds of spying—but Saddam ordered his execution anyway, an action seemed to humiliate Thatcher before the British public. Thatcher's opportunity to retaliate came sooner than it was expected. When Saddam invaded Kuwait, Thatcher told Bush at Aspen that it was "No time to go wobbly," as "aggression must never be appeased."[6]

There is an element of truth in each of the two theoretical assumptions. With regard to predestination, there is indeed a widespread tradition in the Islamic world that the human will has very limited role in life. For example, major calamities such as the Mongol invasion and the sack of Baghdad in 1258 were not ascribed merely to the cruelty of conquerors or the failure of the authorities to defend the seat of the Islamic Empire, but to the will of God, predetermined as punishment for widespread sins and immorality in the community of believers.[7] As to the theory of conspiracy, its advocates in the Middle East may be found among elements who had, from Medieval times, invariably upheld the doctrine that ascribed historical events to the personal whims and fancies of rulers.

In the case of the Gulf crisis, the Islamic countries were divided into two camps. Countries that supported Iraq were motivated largely by Islamic standards on the grounds that Iraq was the subject of Western (Christian) intervention in Arab (Islamic) lands and, therefore, was bound to defend itself by the *jihad* against the unbelievers as a matter of duty. The countries which sided with Kuwait argued that since Iraq, an Islamic country, attacked another Islamic country, the declaration of *jihad* against unbelievers was irrelevant. Moreover, as Iraq was governed by the Ba'th Party, considered by opponents a secular political party, its declaration of the *jihad* was questioned, although the Ba'th Party has never officially declared the separation of religion from the state.[8]

From the perspective of the advocates of realism and the conspiracy theory, the United States and Britain have consciously used the United Nations Resolutions presumably for the maintenance of international peace and security—certainly not for justice and human rights as stated in the U.N. Charter (Article 1)—but in reality in pursuit of their vital interests (if not the political ambition of their leaders) which Saddam Husayn had threatened by his invasion of Kuwait. Kuwait was not the central issue—"the occupation of Kuwait isn't, in itself, a threat to American interests," said one of Bush advisers—the central issue was the threat to Western, national, vital self interests.[9] Just as Saddam Husayn, according to the conspiracy theory, had invaded Kuwait in order to possess its oil resources and acquire an access to the sea which would enhance his leadership, so were Bush and Thatcher determined to ensure the availability of oil and enhance their won leadership by preventing him from controlling or blocking free passage of oil through the Gulf.

The purpose of the foregoing theories was essentially to determine the aims and drives of the leaders involved in the Gulf crisis, but not to conceptualize achieving peace and justice in the world. True, there were always a few noble voices calling for peace and justice whether through the United Nations or the instrumentality of law and diplomacy. But neither the advocates of realism nor of the conspiracy theory addressed themselves to the question of peace based on justice, as these two ideals are inseparable. There were on more than one occasion possibilities to achieve peace with justice, but none of those who sought to achieve them had succeeded. Why, one may well ask?

The first and perhaps the most important opportunity to resolve the Gulf crisis was at the Jidda meeting, held under the auspices of the Saudi government on July 31, 1990. As noted earlier, however, neither the Iraqi nor the Kuwaiti delegation was ready to be flexible enough to reach an agreement, as each delegation had been given strict instructions about the fundamental demands that they had been ordered to make firmly. The head of the Kuwaiti delegation, Shaykh Sa'd, claimed that he offered several flexible proposals that might be discussed at the Baghdad meeting, but those proposals seemed to the head of the Iraqi delegation insignificant to warrant holding another meeting in Baghdad, and he left for home when the Iraq Army was ready to march on Kuwait a few hours later.

Had the three Arab leaders—King Fahd of Saudi Arabia, President Husni Mubarak of Egypt, and King Husayn of Jordan—who proposed holding the Jidda meetings in the first place, offered mediation before the Jidda meeting broke down or held an Arab mini-summit and appealed to Iraq and Kuwait to resume negotiations before the crisis had developed, the Western powers could have found no reason to intervene. This was the first and perhaps the most important missed opportunity for an Arab peaceful settlement.

The second opportunity was the personal good offices of two Arab leaders—King Husayn and President Husni Mubarak—who sought, immediately after Iraq's invasion of Kuwait, to persuade Saddam Husayn to withdraw provided negotiations for settlement of the dispute would immediately start. This attempt was important, as it would have met Saddam Husayn's request that any withdrawal would not be preceded by condemnation.

Considering Iraq's invasion of Kuwait a threat to Western vital interests, some members of the Security Council, it will be recalled, moved quickly to adopt the first mandatory resolution demanding the "immediate and unconditional" withdrawal of Iraqi forces on the same day when the invasion of Kuwait started. Four days later, the Security Council adopted another mandatory resolution imposing economic sanctions which signalled that the Gulf crisis had no longer remained a regional issue. When King Husayn and President Mubarak met at Alexandria to discuss ways and means for an Arab solution, they requested President Bush in a telephone conversation to give them enough time to resolve the crisis. Had Bush allowed the two Arab leaders to carry out their proposed plan, the question of the maintenance of international peace and security might not have arisen nor might not the protection of Western interests have needed foreign intervention. Bush, however, insisted that the invasion was a threat to Western interests and even hesitated to give King Husayn and Mubarak forty-eight hours to do their job. He went as far as to disrupt the cooperative efforts of the Arab leaders by persuading Mubarak to issue a condemnation of the invasion and consequently he sided with him, leaving King Husayn to deal with the crisis alone.

Responsibility for this situation might perhaps be equally divided between Western and Arab leaders. As differences among Arab leaders could take quite a while to iron out, Western leaders had taken advantage of this situation without giving the Arabs an opportunity to do their job. When the Arab League finally met in full session to deal with the crisis on August 9–10, 1990, Western intervention had already encouraged several Arab leaders sympathetic with Kuwait to insist on Iraq's withdrawal "immediately and unconditionally," although several other Arab leaders held that a face-saving promise would have encouraged Iraq to withdraw. Moreover, the increasing number of the Security Council Resolutions was overwhelming, which rendered the chances of Arab mediation to achieve peaceful settlement to become almost nil. Several other attempts were made by Western as well as Arab leaders to persuade both Bush to recognize some of Iraq's legitimate security requirements, and Saddam Husayn to withdraw from Kuwait. Neither side was ready to compromise.

Had Saddam Husayn agreed to withdraw from Kuwait, as he was advised by King Husayn, he would have achieved significant advantages to his country and to the Arab world. More specifically, in the words of King Husayn: 1) He would have shown that Iraq's occupation of Kuwait was an "act of self-defence against an inflexible position and not just expansionism"; 2) Iraq's achievement in the development of the infrastructure and industrialization of the country would have been preserved; 3) Attention would have been drawn to address the problem of the growing gap between the rich and the poor Arab countries; 4) Attention would have been called to the need to resolve the Palestine problem as a sequel to Iraq's withdrawal from Kuwait; and 5) The United Nations position in the world would have been enhanced by the resolution of the crisis by peaceful means.

The Gulf War was thus not inevitable. Had Western powers been patient in dealing with Arab leaders, or had the Arab leaders acted more quickly before the wheels of Western intervention rolled, the crisis might have been resolved by peaceful means. The lesson to be drawn from this study is that all those who were involved in the crisis on all sides have indeed paid a high price in varying degrees. Nor is it certain that settlement by the use of force can guarantee peace irrespective of justice.

Epilogue

A s this work was being prepared for the press, suddenly and unexpectedly two members of Saddam's family who occupied high positions in the government defected with their wives and children to Jordan on August 11, 1995. They are Lt. General Husayn Kamil al-Majid, minister of industry and military industrialization, and Lt. Colonel Saddam Kamil al-Majid, head of the presidential guard. Husayn Kamil was also the head of the nuclear, chemical, and biological programs and formerly minister of defence. Both Husayn Kamil and Saddam Kamil are sons-in-law and second cousins of Saddam Husayn. They are thus not only high ranking members of Saddam's regime but also close members of his family. When the news of their defection reached Saddam, he must have been shocked. It has been rumored that for three days, he refused to see anybody, perhaps because he wanted to recover from the shock and to contemplate how he could deal with the situation and its impact on his regime.

This is not the first time that a defection of high ranking officials in the regime had taken place following the Gulf War, as several others had left the country and began to agitate calling for the overthrow of the regime. The defection of Husayn Kamil and his brother, however, is a direct challenge not merely to Saddam's leadership as head of state, but also as head of his own family. For Husayn Kamil and Saddam Kamil are not just distant cousins; they are married to Saddam's daughters—Raghda and Rana—who refused to stay at home and decided to join their husbands not only out of loyalty and love for them and the children, but also because they were disenchanted with a father who paid more attention to the welfare of his two sons, in particular to 'Uday, who had mistreated them, and paid little or no attention to their welfare.

'Uday, a very ambitious young man, has surrounded himself with friends and followers who cultivated his friendship for their own prestige and promotion in government service. 'Uday has also taken advantage of his position as son of the president to enrich himself through a variety of business enterprises, although his official position is only as head of the Iraqi Olympic Society. But he is also the editor and owner of the daily newspaper *Babil* (Babylon) by virtue of which he had often expressed his own views about events and political figures in the country. Naturally he is in favor of his father's policy and he has idealized his leadership. But he has also expressed his own views and remarks about national and foreign affairs, including his critique of men in high authority, like Tariq 'Aziz, deputy premier and former minister of foreign affairs, with whom he seems to have disagreed on certain issues and 'Aziz might have turned down his request for favors. In all activities, 'Uday seems to have an ulterior motive, an ambition to succeed his father as leader and head of state. In this endeavor, he was competing with another member of the family—Husayn Kamil, 'Uday's brother-in-law—who had distinguished himself not only in introducing high technological weaponry into the army but he also in heading its nuclear, chemical, and biological programs.

'Uday's claim to leadership rests on the ground that he is the eldest son of Saddam and on his claim to be the heir apparent. But since Iraq is a republic, 'Uday could not, as under a monarchy, succeed his father as head of State. Under the new Iraqi Constitution, he would have to first be nominated by the National Assembly and elected by the people. Husayn Kamil, on the basis of his record in the service of the state and his high reputation in the army, could present himself to the public as a better candidate than 'Uday. Nor could 'Uday have the support of his family, as he had mistreated his sisters and ignored other members of the family, including his brother Qusay, whose character and dignified way of life could qualify him as a good candidate in the service of the state. Thus 'Uday could not possibly rely on his family for support in his competition for the presidency with Husayn Kamil. Fully preoccupied as head of state and leader of the Ba'th Party, Saddam was not fully informed about 'Uday's activities, although he had known some of Uday's rash actions and had not made up his mind as to whether 'Uday or Qusay would be a better candidate for a public office.

The relationship between Saddam Husayn and Husayn Kamil had always been intimate and cordial ever since Saddam went to school at Takrit; his family and the Kamil family were living in villages close to Takrit and Saddam used to visit the Kamils. When Saddam became president in 1979, some members of his family, like his step brothers Barzan and Wataban, his distant cousins like Husayn Kamil, and others, were appointed first to modest administrative offices and later to higher positions. Husayn Kamil served first as a personal adviser and later minister of defence and minister of military industrialization. Following the Iraq-Iran War, when Husayn Kamil became active in the rearmament programs, the reputation of Husayn Kamil was enhanced. Following the Coalition War and the related deterioration in the economic and health conditions in the country, Saddam's own reputation suffered decline, but his ability to suppress the Shi'i and Kurdish uprisings demonstrated his resolve to remain in power against rival groups inside and outside the country. Saddam's concern about his leadership, however, must have made him highly suspicious not only of hostile elements outside the country, but also of ambitious elements within his own regime.

Husayn Kamil, although he was one of Saddam's top advisers, may have become a focus of Saddam's suspicions owing to Husayn Kamil's high reputation among the army officers which might inspire one of the senior army officers to replace Saddam's regime by another headed by Husayn Kamil. But Kamil had no visible evidence that Saddam was turning against him save that he closed his eyes to 'Uday's interference in his own department.

Owing to his suspicion about Saddam's intentions, real or imaginary, Husayn Kamil began to speculate about his own future career. If Saddam's regime were to survive, he did not think he could achieve any of his political aspirations. If Saddam's regime were ever overthrown by one of the opposition groups inside or outside the country, Kamil's destiny would be no different from others who cooperated with Saddam, as he owed his position to him and continued to serve under his regime. Nor could he secretly cooperate with any opposition group, as those who had already made an attempt to rebel met their demise. He came to the conclusion that the only way to achieve his political aspirations would be to leave the country and seek Western support to replace Saddam's regime by another which would reestablish friendly relationships with Arab and Western countries.

Beforehand, Husayn Kamil made a couple of unannounced visits to Jordan for medical reasons, almost a year before his defection in August 1995. While in Jordan, he was able to send a message through a high authority in Jordan to the American government that he was ready to break with Saddam and cooperate with other opposition groups to replace the Baghdad regime with a democracy based on national elections. Kamil's plan of defection was welcomed by American policymakers at a time when the Iraqi government was engaged in negotiations with the French and the Russian governments for business transactions. Meanwhile, there was an increasing sympathy in Arab and Western countries with the suffering of the Iraqi people which prompted the French and Russian governments to make an attempt to persuade the Security Council to lift at least some of the economic sanctions which the American and British governments were held primarily responsible for perpetuating.

Encouraged by the American authorities to escape from Iraq and given assurances of protection as a refugee by the Jordanian government, Husayn Kamil and his brother and their families left Baghdad for 'Amman on August 11. Upon their arrival, Kamil had an audience with King Husayn who promised that all possible means of protection would be extended to him and his family. As reported in the press, not only the American CIA but also the U.N. Inspection Commission, headed by Rolf Ekeus, were in touch with him. Kamil seems to have provided all the information needed to be learned about Iraq—its leadership, conditions in the country, and its nuclear, chemical, and biological programs. These were considered necessary to reevaluate the attitude of Saddam towards the West and the United Nations.

Iraq's regime, undermined by Kamil's defection and his disclosure of sensitive information, seems to have felt obliged to disclose further evidence about its nuclear, chemical, and biological programs, which it claimed was in the possession of Husayn Kamil who, as chairman of those programs, had withheld such information before he defected. Although the Iraqi regime's claims were not fully convincing, Kamil sought to justify his actions on the grounds that he was fed up with the Iraqi leadership and sought by his desertion to help the Iraqi people; his goal was to relieve them from their sufferings by cooperating with the opposition groups outside the country to replace the regime by another government based on national elections. When, however, he offered to cooperate with those opposition groups, there was no great enthusiasm to respond to his call, as he was one of the pillars of the Iraqi regime and one of the advisers who encouraged Saddam not only to occupy the area of dispute with Kuwait, but also to take control of the whole country. For this reason, when he announced his intention to visit Damascus hoping to recruit supporters from the Iraqi opposition groups, he learned that nobody was ready to cooperate with him. Nor were the opposition groups in London ready to trust him as a leader who could establish a democratic regime to which he had been opposed when he was on good terms with the current regime. Moreover, most Arab countries were not in favor of intervention in domestic affairs and held that the choice of government was the privilege of the Iraqi people.

As Husayn Kamil could not pursuade the Iraqi opposition outside the country to cooperate with him nor to obtain support from the West, he decided to return home. He was counting on American policy makers to pursuade pro-western factions in the Iraq army to overthrow Saddam's regime and turn power to him to establish a democratic government and pursue a pro-Western foreign policy. But the American policy makers were neither ready to assist a leader who was rejected by all opposition groups outside Iraq to cooperate with him nor were Western policy makers impressed by his leadership qualities. Once in the saddle, it was taken for granted by all opposition leaders that Husayn Kamil will govern the country exactly like all other previous regimes, the only form of government he had known.

Nor did Husayn Kamil receive the political support he had expected from Jordan, although he was given all the facilities required for the protection and comfort of his family. King Husayn seems to have taken a negative attitude toward Husayn Kamil when he proposed a form of a federal union for Iraq, composed of three entities, in order to maintain the integrity of the country against centrifugal forces. Husayn Kamil at once denounced the King's proposal, as it may lead to dividing the country into three states and invite foreign intervention in Iraq's domestic affairs.

Finding himself with no prospect of support from Western or Arab governments, Husayn Kamil decided to return home and make peace with Saddam Husayn. Saddam Kamil, Husayn Kamil's younger brother, warned him against gambling with his life, as he was convinced that Saddam Husayn will never forgive him for the defection and he might eventually liquidate him. But Husayn Kamil did not listen to his brother's advice and called Saddam Husayn, pleading forgiveness and requested a guarantee for his life from the Revolutionary Command Council, the highest executive authority in the country, presided over by Saddam Husayn. Convinced that Saddam was not going to kill his son-in-law, at least for the sake of his daughter's own happiness, Husayn Kamil and his wive and children returned home against his brother's advice. He also prevailed over his brother's desire to stay outside Iraq to change his mind and join him, as his wife seems to have wanted to return home. They arrived at Baghdad on February 20, 1996.

Upon their return, the two wives were separated from their husbands, as they chose to live at their father's house while the two husbands were invited to live at the house of Tha'ir 'Abd al-Qadir, one of Husayn Kamil's cousins at Sayidiya, a suburb of Baghdad. The two wives joined their father and stayed in his house rather than joining their husbands, and it was rumored that they did so because they had divorced them. These events have aroused the curiosity of both the Kamil al-Majid family (to which Husayn Kamil belonged) and the Iraqi public as to what Saddam Husayn's attitude toward Husayn Kamil would be.

Saddam Husayn had given Husayn Kamil his word of honor that he will never be harmed, but will Saddam keep his promise? Since Saddam had always presented himself as a man with high sense of honor, he could not possibly go back on his word to Husayn Kamil. But since Husayn Kamil had already betrayed Saddam, to whom he owed his high position in the state, it is likely that Saddam was not quite sure that Husayn Kamil would not try again to intrigue against him. This was one possible danger to Husayn Kamil's life There was another source of danger from some members of his own family, the Kamil al Majid's. On good terms with Saddam Husayn, these felt ashamed that Husayn Kamil had violated the tribal tradition of loyalty and solidarity.

On February 24, 1996, Husayn Kamil was suddenly killed in the house where he was staying at Sayidiya. It was reported in the press that Husayn Kamil was killed as a result of a tribal feud by some members of his family. In an exchange of fire between the two factions, which lasted almost a whole day, Husayn Kamil and his brother were not the only casualties. The press inside the country reported the killing of Husayn Kamil as a family feud, but the press outside the country reported that Saddam must have instigated the attack on Husayn Kamil. These reports prompted Saddam to make a public statement in which he said that had those who killed Husayn Kamil informed him about their intentions, he would have warned them never to resort to killing, as he had promised Husayn Kamil he would never harm him. But the foreign press continued to report that Saddam was responsible for the liquidation of Husayn Kamil, as some of his bodyguards had participated in the battle with those who surrounded the house in Sayidiya resulting in the killing of Husayn Kamil, his brother, and the owner of the house, Tha'ir 'Abd al-Qadir.

Even before Husayn Kamil had returned home, Saddam Husayn decided to refute Western accusations about his regime that it was oppressive and unpopular in the country. For this reason, he declared that he would hold a popular referendum about his presidency.

Early in November, 1995, Saddam declared that he was ready to run for the presidency by direct national elections. He was nominated by the National Assembly and elected as president by a majority of 99.96 percent for a seven-year term in accordance with a draft Constitution which had been prepared by a Constitutional Committee and adopted in 1990 as law of the land by the National Assembly. But it had not been officially proclaimed because of the suddenly developed Gulf crisis.

Since Saddam's election by such a high percentage is unattainable in Western democratic countries, it was dismissed in Western circles and the press (including the Arab press in Western capitals) as unrealistic and manipulated by threats because the names and addresses were required to be reported by the electorate. As a matter of fact, such a high percentage is not uncommon in Middle Eastern elections. In Iraq, for example, when there were elections for Parliament under the monarchy (1921–58), where a democratic system had in principle existed, it was then well-known that the names of candidates in each province were prepared by the ministry of interior (subject to approval by the prime minister) and dispatched to the *Mutasarrifs* (provincial governors) of the provinces who manipulated the elections in such a manner as to ensure that all the candidates proposed by the central government were elected. Only in Baghdad and, to a lesser extent, in Mawsil and Basra, where political parties and groups had existed, did the candidates proposed by political parties participate in the general elections, but rarely could any candidate win unless he was *persona grata* to the government. Nevertheless, even those who were elected by manipulation were, on the whole, accepted by the public as legitimate members of Parliament.

Following the Coalition War, the problem of Iraq vis-à-vis the West, is not because its regime is undemocratic—no Iraqi regime has ever been democratic by Western standards—but because the conduct of its foreign policy came into conflict with Western interests and its head of state—Saddam—Owing to harsh economic sanctions, Saddam was at first expected to fall at any moment, after the crushing defeat of his well-equipped army, either by a popular uprising or overthrown by one of his rival army generals. Saddam's regime, however, has survived as none of the opposition groups friendly to the West were able to replace the Ba'th regime, perhaps mainly because of lack of followings at home. Nor could Husayn Kamil succeed in achieving a military coup whether inside or outside the country. He was able, however, to provide the U.N. Commission headed by Rolf Ekeus and Western intelligence agencies with invaluable information about Iraq's hidden supplies of nuclear and biological weapons which confirmed the suspicion that Saddam was not prepared to meet the demands of all the U.N. sanctions. For this reason, when the French and Russian governments sought to assist Iraq by lifting some of the economic sanctions, they could not possibly succeed in the face of Husayn Kamil's revelations concerning Iraq's hidden weaponry. Thus the economic sanctions were bound to continue in force so long as Saddam's regime remained unwilling to accept all the U.N. resolutions without reservations.

Saddam has argued that some of the U.N. sanctions, especially those relating to Iraq's security and defence requirements, have encroached on the country's sovereignty and independence. He maintains that Iraq has the right to replace the weapons that it had lost during the Coalition War for defence as well as for the integrity of the country and that Western insistence on inspecting all the military programs is considered an interference in the country's domestic affairs. One of Saddam's reasons for survival seems to be his appeal to the people that the Western powers have, through economic sanctions, deliberately been seeking to divide the country, destroy its weapons, and weaken its capacity to defend itself. Thus Saddam has received support by appealing to the pride of his people for allegiance in defence of the country's "honor and independence." These highly sensitive and patriotic slogans may be found on the pages of the press almost every day, particularly in the daily *al-Jumhuriya*, *al-Thawra*, *al-Iraq*, and *Baghdad Observer* (this is now suspended owing to scarcity of paper), and in other media.

As Iraq seems to have continued to acquire weaponry—some are related to nuclear programs—on the grounds that defence and security requirements are the privilege of every sovereign state, the question of lifting the U.N. sanctions might continue indefinitely, although it has become quite clear that most of the economic sanctions have hit hard the Iraqi people with whom the Western powers have no quarrel.

As evidence that the Western Powers did not mean to hurt the Iraqi people, the U.N. Security Council has adopted Resolution 986, which the Iraqi government has accepted, in order to meet the country's immediate needs for food and medicine, but the people are neither prepared nor could possibly act to achieve all United Nations purposes. The economic sanctions did not work in Iraq nor could they possibly work in any other country in the Third World. We suggest that the economic sanctions might be replaced by other political measures in the implementation of which the Arab League might be invited to call on the Iraqi regime to accept them. As Iraq is now keenly feeling its isolation from the Arab family, it would be embarrassing to its regime were it to turn down the Arab League's demand, as its return to the Arab fold is keenly felt by both the rulers and the ruled.

Notes

CHAPTER 1: INTRODUCTION

1. For the tribal structure of Kuwaiti society, see ʿAbd al-ʿAziz Husayn, *Muhadarat ʿAn al-Mujtamaʿ al-ʿArabi Bi al-Kuwait* [Lectures on the Arab Community in Kuwait] (Cairo, 1960), chaps. 3 and 5; and Jacqueline S. Ismael, *Kuwait: Social Change in Historical Perspective* (Syracuse, 1982), chap. 1. For the tribal conditions in the desert area of Iraq and Kuwait, see H. R. P. Dickson, *Kuwait and Her Neighbors* (London, 1956), chaps. 2, 7–9.

2. For brief definitions of *Sabab* and *ʿilla* in Islamic law, see H. Kamali, *Principles of Islamic Jurisprudence* (Cambridge, 1991), 34–37, 206–214.

CHAPTER 2: IRAQ'S HISTORICAL CLAIMS TO KUWAIT

1. For the migration of the ʿAnza tribes and the establishment of Kuwait, see ʿAbd al-ʿAziz al-Rushayd, *Tarikh al-Kuwait* [History of Kuwait] (Bayrut, 1929), vol. I, 29–34; Ahmad Abu Hakima, *Modern History of Kuwait* (London, 1983), 3–4.

2. Al-Rashid, vol. I, 116–117; 121–2; Abu Hakima, *Modern History*, 31ff.

3. Ever since Britain made an agreement with the Arab Gulf Shaykhs in 1820, the British political agent in the Gulf offered his good offices either to settle their differences or to side with one friendly to Britain against others (see Arnold Wilson, *The Persian Gulf* [Oxford, 1928], 171ff.)

4. Conquest with the intention of acquiring territory is an ancient practice that survived until modern times. It was valid under ancient laws as well as Islamic law provided it was ordered by the Caliph and prosecuted in accordance with the rules of the *jihad* (See Shaybani, *The Islamic Law of Nations*, trans. M. Khadduri [Baltimore, 1965], chaps. 1–2).

5. For Ottoman-Kuwait relations under the first three Shaykhs of Kuwait, see Husayn Khalaf Shaykh Khazʿal, *Tarikh al-Kuwait al-Siyasi* [Political History of Kuwait] (Bayrut, 1962), vol. I, 43ff; Alan Rush, *Al-Sabah: Hisotry and Genealogy of Kuwait's Ruling Family, 1752-1987* (London, 1987), 173–217.

6. T. E. Arnold, *The Caliphate* (Oxford, 1924), chap. 10; Sati' al-Husri, *al-Bilad al-'Arabiya wa al-Dawla al-'Uthmaniya* (Bayrut, 1960), 42–46.

7. For the proclamation of Sultan 'Abd al-Hamid (Abdul Hamid) as Caliph, see Robert Devereux, *The First Ottoman Constitutional Period.* (Baltimore, 1963), chap. 3 (section on the Sultan), 63–66.

8. For the text of the treaty of Kuchuk Kaynarja (July 21, 774), which refers to the Sultan as "the Grand Caliph of Mahometism" (Article 3), see J. C. Hurewitz, *The Middle East and North Africa in World Politics: A Documentary Record* (New Haven, 1975), vol. I, 94.

9. For text of the Treaty of Paris, see Hurewitz, *The Middle East*, vol. I, 320.

10. For text of the first treaty that the Arab Shaykhs concluded with Britain, see C. U. Aitchison, *A Collection of Treaties, Engagements and Sanads* (Delhi, 1933), vol. XI, 245–49; Hurewitz, *The Middle East*, vol. I, 217–19.

11. For the life of Midhat Pasha, see Ali Haydar Midhat, *Midhat Pacha: sa Vie—Son Ouevre* (Paris, 1908), 19–20; Khaz'al, *Tarikh*, vol. I, 136–38; Abu Hakima, *Modern History*, 83–92.

12. For the life of Shaykh Mubarak, see Khaz'al, *Tarikh*, vol. II (the whole volume, 350 pages, is devoted to the career of Shaykh Mubarak).

13. Khaz'al, *Tarikh*, vol. III, 187–98; Briton C. Busch, "Britain and the Status of Kuwait," *Middle East Journal*, vol. XXI (spring 1987), 187–98.

14. Aitchison, *A Collection of Treaties*, vol. XI, 262; Hurewitz, *op cit*, vol. I, 476.

15. Hurewitz, *The Middle East*, vol. I, 476–77.

16. For Shaykh Mubarak's dealings with the Ottoman authorities, see Khaz'al, *Tarikh*, vol. II, 74–90; Sayf Marzuq al-Shamlan, *Min Tarikh al-Kuwait* [From the History of Kuwait] (Cairo, 1959), 264–70. For an account of the Anglo-Ottoman controversy over the status of Kuwait following the agreement of 1898, see Richard Schofield, *Kuwait and Iraq: Historical Claims and Territorial Disputes* (London, 1991), 14–24, 27–28.

17. Aitchison, *A Collection of Treaties*, vol. XI, 262–63. For full text, see G. P. Gooch and Harold Temperly, eds., *British Documents and the Origins of War, 1898–1914* (London, 1938), part 2, 191–93. For English translation, see Hurewitz, *The Middle East*, vol. II, 567–68.

18. V. A. O'Rourke, *The Juristic Status of Egypt and the Sudan*, (Baltimore, 1953), chap. 1.

19. Philip Graves, *The Life of Sir Percy Cox* (London and Melbourne, 1941), 168–70.

20. For text of the declaration of *jihad*, see Ahmed Emin, *Turkey in the World War* (New Haven, 1930), 175–77.

21. In his *Political History of Kuwait*, Husayn Khalaf Shaykh Khaz'al maintains that the smuggling of foodstuff through Kuwait to the Ottoman Empire was beyond the control of Shaykh Salim partly under pressure of Ottoman coreligionists and partly for his own sympathy with the Ottoman Caliphate (See Khaz'al, *Tarikh*, vol. IV, 106ff. For an account of Shaykh Salim's attitude towards the British, see Rush, *Al-Sabah*, 79–82.

22. See W. E. Hall, *A Treatise on the Foreign Power and Jurisdiction of the British Crown* (Oxford, 1894), 204–207; James Lorimer, *Institutes of the Law of Nations* (Edinburgh, 1884), 160–61.

23. For the termination of the British Mandate over Iraq, see L. H. Evans,

"The Emancipation of Iraq From the Mandate System," *American Political Science Review*, vol. XXVI (1932), 1024–29.

CHAPTER 3: DISPUTES OVER STATUS, TERRITORY, AND FRONTIERS

1. The governor of Baghdad was given more extensive powers than the governors of Mawsil and Basra. For the position of the governor of Baghdad and his relationship with other governors, see S. H. Langrigg, *Four Centuries of Modern Iraq* (Oxford, 1925), chaps. 4, 9, 12, 19.

2. For text of General Maude's speech, see Edmund Candler, *The Long Road to Baghdad* (Boston and New York, 1919), vol. II, 114–116.

3. For Western accounts of the Iraqi revolt of 1920, see P. W. Ireland, *Iraq: A Study in Political Development* (London, 1937), chaps. 8–18; Lt. Gen. Sir Aylmer L. Haldane, *The Insurrection in Mesopotamia, 1920* (London, 1922); Gertrude Bell, *Review of the Civil Administration of Mesopotamia* (London, 1920); Sir Arnold Wilson, *Loyalties: Mesopotamia* (Oxford, 1920), vol. II. For accounts by Iraqi writers, see Faruq Salih al-ʿUmar, *Hawl al-Siyasa al-Baritaniya fi al-Iraq* [British Policy in Iraq] (Baghdad, 1978); ʿAbd-Allah Fayyad, *al-Thawra al-Iraqiya al-Kubra* [The Great Iraqi Revolt] (Baghdad, 1973); Wamidh Nazmi, *al-Thawra al-Iraqiya* [The Iraqi Revolt] (Baghdad, 1987).

4. For British policy in Iraq under the Mandates system, see Sir Percy Cox's essay in Lady Bell, ed., *The Letters of Gertrude Bell* (London, 1927), vol. II, 526ff. For an account of the discussion in London on the future policy in the Middle East, see Aaron Klieman, *Foundations of British Policy in the Arab World: The Cairo Conference of 1921* (Baltimore, 1970), chap. 5.

5. Philip Graves, *The Life of Sir Percy Cox* (London, 1941), chap. 21.

6. For text of the Treaty of Lausanne, see *Treaty of Peace with Turkey and Other Instruments*, signed at Lausanne, July 24, 1923 (London, His Majesty's Stationery Office, 1923), CMD 1929.

7. For full text of Article 22 of the Covenant of the League of Nations, see Great Britain, *Treaty Series* (192), No. 11,CMD 964, 11–12. See also, J. C. Hurewitz, *The Middle East and North Africa in World Politics: A Documentary Record* (New Haven and London, 1979), vol. II, 179–80.

8. For text of the San Remo Acts, see E. Lauterpacht, et al., *The Kuwait Crisis: Basic Documents* (Cambridge, 1991), 38.

9. For Amin al-Rihani's conversation with King Faysal during a visit to Baghdad, see Amin al-Rihani, *Muluk al-Arab* [Arab Kings] (Bayrut, 1920), vol. II, 275–76. Behind the scenes, there were long and intense conversations between Faysal and Cox on the question of the relevance of the Mandate in the proposed treaty between Iraq and Britain during which Cox sought to reconcile Faysal's views with Churchill's proposals, but it is clear that Churchill had pressured Faysal to accept the terms of the League Mandate, although reference to it was not made in the treaty. For a summary of the dispatches between Churchill and Cox, see Klieman, *Foundations*, 163–167. See also Cox's account on the treaty negotiations in Bell's *Letters*, vol. II, 535–37.

10. For the text of the Anglo-Iraq treaty, see *Treaty of Alliance Between Great Britain and Iraq*, October 10, 1922 (London: His Majesty's Stationery Office, 1925), CMD 2370. For Cox's brief account, supplemented by Sir Henry Dobb's

further negotiations (Dobbs succeeded Cox as British high commissioner in Baghdad); see the essays of both Cox and Dobbs in Bell's *Letters*, vol. II, 535–37, 546–48.

11. For the careers and personalities of the three Shaykhs who succeeded Shaykh Mubarak, see ʿAbd al-ʿAziz al-Rushayd, *Tarikh al-Kuwait* [History of Kuwait] (Bayrut, 1929), 2 vols.; Husayn Khalaf al-Shaykh Khazʿal, 1962), vols. 3 and 4; and Alan Rush, *Al-Sabah: History and Genealogy of Kuwait's Ruling Family, 1952-1987* (London, 1987) 51–97. For a brief account, see Ahmad M. Abu Hakima, *The Modern History of Kuwait* (London, 1983), chap. 11.

12. For the status of Kuwait, see Richard Schofield, *Kuwait and Iraq: Historical Claims and Territorial Disputes* (London, 1921), 54–57, 60–61, 62–67.

13. Schofield, *Kuwait and Iraq*, 21–22.

14. In his book, *Shifting Lines in the Sand*, David H. Finnie states that "Majid Khadduri's suggestion that the 'capitulations' applicable to Europeans in the Ottoman Empire extended to foreign consulates in Kuwait is puzzling; there were no consulates in Kuwait until 1950" (D. H. Finnie, *Shifting Lines in the Sand* [Cambridge, Mass.], 1992, 182–83, n. 27. In Khadduri's article, however, there is nothing indicating that there were foreign consulates in Kuwait, whether before or after World War I. For this reason, Britain formally assumed judicial jurisdiction over foreigners in Kuwait; see Khadduri, "Iraq's Claim to the Sovereignty of Kuwait," *Journal of International Law and Politics*, vol. 23, no. 1 (Fall 1990), 17.

15. Cox's essay in Bell's *Letters*, vol. II, 506–07, 534–35; Jacqueline S. Ismael, *Kuwait: Social Change in Historical Perspective* (Syracuse, 1982), 17ff.

16. Amin al-Rihani, *Tarikh Najd al-Hadith wa Mulhaqatuh* [The History of Modern Najd and its Dependencies] (Bayrut, 1928), 281.

17. For Dickson's account of the Uqayr Conference, see H. R. P. Dickson, *Kuwait and its Neighbors* (London, 1956), 270–78; Philip Graves, *Sir Percy Cox*, 322–323.

18. For text of the Uqayr Protocol, see Foreign Ministry (Saudi Arabia), *Majmuʿat al-Muʿahadat* [Collection of Treaties] (Jidda, 1375/1955), 5–7.

19. Dickson, *Kuwait and its Neighbors*, 279.

20. For a summary of dispatches between Cox and the Colonial Office, see Schofield, *Kuwait and Iraq*, 60–61. For a discussion on the subject, see Daniel Silverfarb, *The Twilight of British Ascendancy in the Middle East: A Case Study of Iraq, 1941–1950* (New York, 1944), Chap 5.

21. For text, see C. U. Aitchison, *A Collection of Treaties, Engagements and Sanads*, (Delhi, 1933) vol. XI, 266.

22. E. Lauterpacht, et al., *The Kuwait Crisis*, 48–49; Schofield, *Kuwait and Iraq*, 61. It is interesting to note that while the ʿUqayr Protocol concerning the Iraq-Najd frontier was ratified by King Faysal, the exchange of notes concerning Iraq-Kuwait frontier was not ratified by King Faysal, although Cox had informed the British Colonial Office that Faysal would "almost certainly" not object to them.

23. Cox's essay in Bell's *Letters*, vol. II, 506.

24. The advisory function of the British high commissioner, as stated in Article 22 of the League Covenant, which Britain as a mandatory power over Iraq had accepted, was reiterated in the Treaty of Alliance with Iraq (October 10, 1922), which defined the British high commissioner's standing vis-à-vis Iraq, namely to advise the King of Iraq "on all important matters affecting the in-

ternational and financial obligations" of the British Government. It is puzzling that David Finnie, *Shifting Lines*, in his statement about the British high commissioner's functions, as defined in the Anglo-Iraq treaty, 1922, states that the treaty was not ratified to be binding until 1924 (a year after the exchange of letters in 1923). The functions of the mandatory power, however, had already been defined in the League of Nations Covenant (Article 22) which Britain had accepted, and the Anglo-Iraq treaty merely reiterated an already binding commitment by the British Government irrespective of the treaty with Iraq.

25. For texts of the exchange of notes between Britain and Kuwait, see H. M. Albaharna, *The Arabian Gulf States* (London, 2nd ed., 1975), 374–75; Lauterpacht, *The Kuwait Crisis*, 49.

26. Schofield, *Kuwait and Iraq*, 65.

27. League of Nations, *Minutes of the Permanent Mandates Commission* (Geneva, 1931), 20th Session, 56–79, 86–131; 156–59, 168–80, 195–99, 221–25. See also Walter H. Ritsher, *Criteria of Capacity for Independence* (Jerusalem, 1934), 15–40.

28. See C. A. Hooper, *The Constitutional Law of Iraq* (Baghdad, 1928), 69–70; M. Khadduri, *Independent Iraq* (London, 2nd. ed., 1960), 23.

29. For treaty-making power under Islamic law, see Muhammad Bin al-Hasan al-Shaybani, *The Islamic Law of Nations: Shaybani's Siyar*, trans. Khadduri (Baltimore, 1965), 154–157; Khadduri, *War and Peace in the Law of Islam* (Baltimore, 1955–69), 202–22.

CHAPTER 4: KUWAIT'S ATTEMPT AT UNITY WITH IRAQ

1. For general conditions in Kuwait following World War I, see Jacqueline S. Ismael, *Kuwait: Social Change in Historical Perspective* (Syracuse, 1982), part II, 81ff.

2. For Shaykh Ahmad's promise of consultation and the establishment of a Consultative Council (Majlis al-Shura), see Sayf Marzuq al-Shamlan, *Min Tarikh al-Kuwait* [From the History of Kuwait] (Cairo, 1959), 199–200; Rashid ʿAbd-Allah al-Farhan, *Mukhtasar Tarikh al-Kuwait* [Short History of Kuwait] (Cairo, 1960), 93–94.

3. For the life of Shaykh Ahmad al-Jabir, see al-Shamlan, *Min Tarikh*, 198–208; al-Farhan, *Mukhtasar Tarikh*, 92–100; Alan Rush, *Al-Sabah: History and Genealogy of Kuwait's Ruling Family, 1752–1987* (London, 1987), 51–59.

4. Kamal O. Salih, "The 1938 Kuwait Legislative Council," *Middle Eastern Studies* vol. 28 (January 1992), 70; J. E. Peterson, *The Arab Gulf States* (New York, 1988), 29ff.

5. Rush, *Al-Sabah*, 52.

6. For full text, see Rush, *Al-Sabah*, 71–72. *Al-Istiqlal*, edited by ʿAbd al-Gafur al-Badri, an Iraqi pan-Arab, who was well-known in other Arab countries, started his career in the last days of Ottoman rule in Arab lands (Rafael Butti, *al-Sahafa Fi al-Iraq* [The Press in Iraq] [Cairo, 1955], 58–79.

7. Lutfi Jaʿfar Faraj, *al-Malik Ghazi* [King Ghazi] (Baghdad, 1987), 218ff.

8. Muhammad Husayn al-Zubaydi, *al-Malik Ghazi* [King Ghazi] (Baghdad, 1989), 102–105.

9. See Naseer H. ʿAruri, "Kuwait: A Political Study," *The Muslim World*, vol. LX (October 1970), 321–343; al-Farhan, *Mukhtasar Tarikh*, 96.

10. For an account of the activities of the merchant movement, see Jill Crystal, *Oil and Politics in the Gulf* (New York, 1990), 47–55; J. E. Peterson, *The Arab Gulf States* (New York, 1988), 29–35; Salih, "The 1938 Kuwait Legislative Council", 76ff; Richard Schofield, *Kuwait and Iraq: Historical Claims and Territorial Disputes* (London, 1991), pp. 74–77.

11. Taha al-Hashimi, *Mudhakkirat Taha al-Hashimi* [Taha al-Hashimi's Memoirs] (Bayrut, 1967), 300. Hashimi's "memoirs" are brief daily entries about events and personalities.

12. Naji Shawkat, *Sira Wa Dhikrayat Thamanin ʿAman* [Autobiography and Memoirs of Eighty Years] 2nd ed., (Bayrut, 1975), 341–42.

13. Shawkat, *Sira*, 342.

14. Shawkat, *Sira*, 345–47.

15. For King Ghazi's pan-Arab activities in Kuwait and his relationship with the Axis powers, see Faraj, *Al-Malik Ghazi* [King Ghazi] 218–39. Faraj points out that Ghazi was not sympathetic with Nazi Germany, he only sought to obtain weapons denied to him by the British. For summary of the British documents on these matters, see Richard Schofield, *Kuwait and Iraq: Historical Claims and Territorial Disputes* (London, 1991), chap. 4, 68ff. Also, see D. H. Finne, *Shifting Lines in the Sand* (Cambridge, Mass., 1992), 106–13.

16. See Faraj, *Al-Malik Ghazi*, 266–68.

17. Faraj, *Al-Malik Ghazi*, 258–64; Gerald de Gaury, *Three Kings in Baghdad* (London, 1961), 105–06, 111–12.

18. For text of the official communiqué, see *Iraq Times* (Baghdad), April 6, 1939.

19. *Iraq Times* April 6, 1939.

20. Faraj, *Al-Malik Ghazi*, 268–76; Cf. Shawkat's "Memoirs," *Sira*, 356–58. The most important works by Iraqi writers who maintain that Premier Nuri, under British influence, was responsible for the killing of King Ghazi are Faraj and al-Zubaydi, noted earlier, but there were others, especially Salah al-Din al-Sabbagh, *Mudhakirat* [Memoirs], 2nd ed. (Baghdad, 1983), 103–108, who had earlier accused Nuri of killing Ghazi.

21. Khayri Amin al-ʿUmari, *al-Khilaf Bayn al-Bilat wa Nuri al-Saʿid* [Conflict Between the Court and Nuri al-Saʿid] (Baghdad, 1979), 39–64.

22. For a brief summary of Suwaydi's aide-memoire, see his *Mudhakkirati* [My Memoirs] (Bayrut, 1969), 583–85.

23. For text of Suwaydi's aide-memoire, see F. O. 371/21858, dated September 28, 1938.

24. For the minutes of Suwaydi's meetings with Lord Halifax and his meetings with the Foreign Office experts, see F. O. 371/21859, dated October 4, 1938.

25. Suwaydi, *Mudhakkirati*, 300.

26. For a summary of British good offices, see Schofield, *Kuwait and Iraq*, 87–100.

CHAPTER 5: PROPOSALS FOR UNITY BY MEANS SHORT OF WAR

1. For background on the Arab opposition to the Baghdad Pact, see J. Gallman Waldemar, *Iraq Under General Nuri* (Baltimore, 1964), chaps. 4–5; Lord

Birdwood, *Nuri al-Sa'id* (London, 1959), chap. 16. Birdwood's book is based on extensive interviews with Nuri.

2. For Nasir's drive to achieve pan-Arab unity, see Nejla M. Abu Izzeddin, *Nasser of the Arabs* (Bayrut, 1975), chaps. 14–15; R, Hrair Dekemejian, *Egypt Under Nasir* Albany, 1971), chaps. 7–8.

3. For Nuri's conversation in London (1958), see Birdwood, *Nuri al-Sa'id,* chap. 18.

4. For the views of Hashimi rulers in Jordan and Iraq on Arab unity, see King Hussein of Jordan's autobiography, *Uneasy Lies the Head* (London, 1962), chap. 12; Birdwood, *Nuri al-Sa'id,* chap. 18.

5. 'Abd al-Karim al-Uzri, *Tarikh Fi Dhikrayat al-Iraq* [History of Iraq from Memory] (Bayrut, 1982), vol. I, 600–03. This book is the only source in print that deals with the inside story of the Arab Federal Union.

6. Shaykh 'Abd-Allah's plan to visit Cairo and meet Nasir aroused concerns in Baghdad, as he might fall under Nasir's influence. The British advised against visiting Egypt and Shaykh 'Abd-Allah changed his mind about the matter. See FO. 372775 (May 11, 1958), No. 765; FO. 372775 (May 12, 1958), No. 783; FO. 372775 (May 13, 1958) No. 1244.

7. Uzri, *Tarikh Fi Dhikrayat,* 605–06.

8. Uzri, *Tarikh Fi Dhikrayat,* 607.

9. Uzri, *Tarikh Fi Dhikrayat,* 608 (translation of Wright's statement, as reported by Uzri in Arabic). In his dispatch to the Foreign Office, Wright reported only the tenor of Nuri's full statement (see FO. 371/1322776, No. 1002 [June 9, 1959]).

10. For text of the AFU memorandum, see the dispatch from Baghdad to the Foreign Office (June 6, 1958), FO. 371/132776, No. 977. 'Abd-Allah Bakr, chief of the royal court in 1958 and a protégé of Premier Nuri, told Khadduri during one of his visits to Bayrut in 1966 (where Bakr had resided following the July Revolution of 1958) that Nuri once said that his "memorandum about Kuwait might well be the cause of the destruction of the Hashimi family." What Nuri really meant was that the British government had to make a choice either to side with the Iraqi royal house or the Kuwaiti royal house in the contest for survival.

11. FO. 371/132776, No. 2141 (July 5, 1958).

12. FO. 371/132776, No. 1599 (July 10, 1958).

13. FO. 371/132776, No. 406 (July 7, 1958).

14. Uzri, *Tarikh Fi Dhikrayat,* 626.

15. Khadduri, *Republican Iraq* (London, 1969), 55.

16. Khadduri, *Republican Iraq,* 56. See also Gerald de Gaury, *Three Kings of Baghdad, 1921–1958,* (London, 1961), chap. 6.

17. Kamil Muruwa learned about Nuri's negotiations with Britain from Uzri who had fled Iraq shortly after Qasim seized power (see Uzri, *Tarikh Fi Dhikrayat,* 626–28). Uzri tells about how he fled the country through the assistance of the American Embassy, where he stayed in disguise for a couple of days, see Gallman, 202–03 (Uzri's name is mentioned as "our guest" but Gallman told Khadduri that the "guest" was 'Abd al-Karim al-Uzri).

18. For the text of the frontier agreements between Saudi Arabia and Kuwait, see E. Lauterpacht, et al., *The Kuwait Crisis: Basic Documents* (Cambridge, 1991), 57–60. For Kuwait's foreign relations, see Richard Schofield, *Kuwait and Iraq: Historical Claims and Territorial Disputes* (London, 1921), chap. 5.

19. Richard Gott, "Kuwait Incident," *Royal Institute of International Affairs Survey (R.I.I.A.) 1961*, 526.

20. Qasim's *Speeches* (Baghdad 1961), 226. Mahmud 'Ali al-Dawud, Qasim's adviser on Gulf affairs, told Khadduri (Dawud was a former student of Khadduri) that Qasim began at that time to ask for information on Kuwait's historical connections with Iraq (Khadduri, *Republican Iraq*, 169). See also 'Abdul Reda Assiri, *Kuwait's Foreign Policy* (Boulder, Colo., 1990), 19ff.

21. Humphry Trevelyan, *The Middle East in Revolution* (London, 1970), 184.

22. For the text of the exchange of letters between Kuwait and Britain (June 19, 1961), see CMD 1409 and R. I. I. A., *Documents, 1961*, 771–72; Husain M. Albaharma, *The Arabian Gulf States*, 2nd. ed. (Bayrut, 1975), 384–85.

23. For the full text of Qasim's statement at a press conference on June 25, 1961, see Ahmad Fawzi, *Qasim wa al-Kuwait* (Cairo, 1961), 45–51.

24. Trevelyan, *The Middle East*, 187–89. Prime Minister MacMillan, in a statement in Parliament about the landing of a British force on July 1, 1961, said there was: "evidence accumulated from a number of sources that reinforcements, especially reinforcement of armor, were moving towards Basra" (House of Commons Debates, vol. 643, Col. 1006).

25. It was upon Trevelyan's suggestion that the British force was sent in advance to Kuwait before Qasim's attack (see Trevelyan's *The Middle East*, 190).

26. For extracts of the speeches by the British and Iraqi representative at the Security Council, see Lauterpacht, *The Kuwait Crisis*, 51–55. For full texts, see U.N., S/4844, S. 4845, and S/4847, SCOR, 16th year, supplement, July, August, and September, 1961, pp. 1ff.

27. Arab League, *Proceedings of the Council*, 35th Session (1961), 45ff. For the role of Hassuna, secretary of the Arab League, and his account of the Kuwait affair, see Hussein A. Hassouna, *The League of Arab States and Regional Disputes* (New York, 1975), chap. 6.

28. For the constitutive and declaratory recognition as well as acts leading to the recognition of a new state, see E. Lauterpacht, *Recognition in International Law* (Cambridge, 1948), 38–51.

29. For the admission of Israel to membership of the United Nations before making peace with Arab states, see M. Khadduri, "Some Legal Aspects of the Arab-Israeli Conflict of 1967," in Albert Lepawsky, et al., eds., *The Search for World Order* (New York, 1971), 238ff.

30. As no record has yet been published about the negotiations between Iraq and Kuwait save the text of the agreement of 1963, we relied on the unpublished memoires of Shukri S. Zaki, minister of economics (later minister of finance and petroleum) and a member of the Iraqi delegation who participated in the negotiations with Kuwait in 1963 (courtesy of Zaki, who was a former student of Khadduri in Baghdad).

31. As Zaki, minister of economics, had already resigned from the Cabinet, the information in his *Memoirs* came from another member of the delegation who represented the Iraqi Foreign Office.

32. Zaki, *Memoirs* (unpublished text).

33. For text of the agreement, see *United Nations Treaty Series*, vol. 485 (1964), 321–29.

34. Government of Iraq (Ministry of Information), *al-Minhaj al-Marhali li al-Majlis al-Watani li-Qiyadat al-Thawra* [Transitional Program of the National Council of the Revolution] (Baghdad, 1963), 8–9.

35. For material in this section, we have drawn freely from the chapter concerning Iraq's relations with Kuwait in Khadduri, *Socialist Iraq*, (Washington, D.C., 1978) 153–50, based essentially on unpublished Kuwaiti and Iraqi documents as well as interviews with men in high authorities in both countries. Cf. Schofield, *Kuwait and Iraq* chap. 5; D. H. Finne, *Shifting Lines in the Sand* (Cambridge, Mass, 1992), chap. 10.

36. For Khadduri's interview with Sa'dun Hamadi, see *Socialist Iraq*, 158.

CHAPTER 6: IMPACT OF THE IRAQ-IRAN WAR ON IRAQ'S RELATIONSHIP WITH ARAB GULF COUNTRIES

1. Following the war with Iran, the Iraqi leadership declared that all projects for economic developments would be implemented; but later, when the war did not end as soon as it was expected, only some of the projects that were absolutely necessary were implemented.

2. Before 1975, the Iraq-Iran water-border was the eastern bank of the Shatt al-Arab, but under the frontier Accord of 1975, the *thalweg* (median line) of the Shatt was established as the water-border between the two countries. See Khalid al-'Izzi, *The Shatt al-Arab Dispute* (London, 1981); Jasim M. 'Abdul-Ghani, *Iran and Iraq: The Year of Crisis* (London, 1984). For the text of the Algerian Accord, see Khalid al-'Izzi, 230–31.

3. See Muhammad 'Aziz Shukri, *The Question of the Arab Gulf Islands and International Law*, (Damascus, 1972) (Arabic text).

4. For Iran's aspiration to play a hegemonic role in the Gulf, see M. Khadduri, *The Gulf War: The Origins and Implications of the Iraq-Iran Conflict*, (New York, 1988), chap. 11.

5. For American concerns about Iraq's rearmament programs, see the views of military experts on the subject in S. C. Pelletereau, et al., *Iraq's Power and U. S. Security in the Middle East*. (U. S. Army War College, Carlisle Barracks, Penn., 1990), chaps. 5 and 7.

6. For a record of the debate among Iraqi leaders on the proposals for a new political system, see Saddam Husayn, *al-Dimuqratiya wa al-Ta'addudiya al-Hizbiya* [Democracy and the Multiple Party System] (Baghdad, 1989).

7. Today, the senior members of the National Democratic Party are: Muhammad Hadid, Husayn Jamil, Khadduri Khadduri, Yusuf al-Hajj Iliyas, Mazhar al-'Azzawi. Numbers 1, 3, and 4 consider themselves retired and preoccupied in their own private business. Numbers 2 and 5 are prepared to reenter politics as they argue that perhaps more freedom might be granted than if they did not take a negative attitude. As to the Istiqlal (Independent) Party, most of the distinguished members, like Mahdi Kubba and the popular Fa'iq al-Samarra'i, have passed away. Siddiq Shanshal, former secretary of the party, maintains that as an Arab nationalist he would be prepared to cooperate with the Ba'th Party. Shanshal has passed away, but his cousin, a high ranking army officer who served as chief of staff and minister of defence (now an adviser to Saddam Husayn) is prepared to cooperate with the Ba'th Party. 'Abd al-Rahman al-Bazzaz, once a member of the Jawal Group (pan-Arab) was a supporter of the Istiqlal Party and served as premier (1963–68) under the 'Arif regime. He was arrested and thrown into prison in 1968 and died two years later. The only

remaining Arab nationalists are young men; some have already joined the Ba'th Party; others who came into conflict with the regime have left the country.

8. See 'Abdul-Reda Assiri, *Kuwait's Foreign Policy* (Boulder, Colo., 1990), chap. 4.

9. For Kuwait's contact with Iran to reestablish friendly relations with Iran, see M. H. Haykal, *Harb al-Khalij* [Gulf War] (Cairo, 1922), 298–99. (Arabic text)

10. There are several studies on Saudi foreign policy in Arabic, the most extensive analysis is in Ghassan Salama, *al-Siyassa al-Kharijiya al-Sa'udiya* [Foreign Policy of Saudi Arabia] (Bayrut, 1980); M. A. Hamid, *Arabia Imperilled: The Security Imperatives of the Arab Gulf States* (Washington, D. C., 1980); Adeed Dawisha, *Saudi Arabia's Search for Security* (London, 1980). See also James F. Aiken, *Oil and Security in the Arabian Gulf* (New York, 1981); 'Abdul Kasim Mansur (pseud.), ''The Military Balance in the Persian Gulf: Who Will Guard the Gulf States from the Guardians,'' *Armed Forces Journal International* (November, 1980); Robert R. Sullivan, ''Saudi Arabia in International Politics,'' *Review of Politics*, vol. 32, (October, 1970), 436–60.

11. For Shaykh Jabir's state visit to Iraq, see Sa'd al-Bazzaz, *Harb Talid Harb* [War Leads to War] (Amman, Jordan, 1992), 38–40; Haykal, *Harb al-Khalij*, 302–304.

12. Bazzaz, *Harb Talid Harb*, 39–40; Haykal, *Harb al-Khalij*, 302–303.

13. For an account on the OPEC meetings and the controversy of oil prices and overproduction of oil, see Charles K. Zhinger and John P. Banks, ''OPEC in 1990: The Failure of Oil Diplomacy,'' in David P. Newsom, ed., *The Diplomatic Record, 1990–1991* (Boulder, Colo., 1992), 109–32; Bazzaz, *Harb Talid Harb*, 50–51.

14. As no summit meeting had been held in Iraq since 1978 (the meeting in which Egypt was suspended from membership in the Arab League owing to Sadat's separate peace with Israel), it was decided to hold another summit in Baghdad in 1990.

15. Margaret Thatcher, *The Downing Street Years* (London, 1994), 816ff; Bazzaz, *Harb Talid Harb*, 51–42, 53–55.

16. Captain (later Admiral) Alfred T. Mahan, who wrote several works on ''the influence of sea power on history,'' became interested in the Middle East (the first to use the term) and contributed an article on ''The Persian Gulf and International Relations'' (published in the September issue of the *National Review* of London) in which he discussed the significance of the Gulf to the security of Britain's position in the Indian subcontinent and the Indian Ocean (see Roderic H. Davison, ''Where is the Middle East?,'' *Foreign Affairs* (July 1960), 665–75.

17. For the controversy over ''piracy'' in the Gulf as to whether it was a reaction to foreign intervention or for private gain which prompted Britain to suppress it, see Sultan Muhammad al-Qasimi, *The Myth of Arab Piracy in the Gulf* (London, 1986); Muhammad M. 'Abdullah, *The United Arab Amirates* (London, 1978).

18. For the Iraq-Iran war, see Khadduri, *The Gulf War*, chap. 8.

19. For an account of the origins and collapse of the Baghdad Pact as an American strategic plan for the Middle East, see Waldemar J. Gallman, *Iraq Under General Nuri* (Baltimore, 1964), chap. 5 (Gallman was the American Ambassador to Iraq from 1954 to 1958).

20. For an account of how the Ba'th Party achieved power and the role of Saddam Husayn in its activities, see Fouad Matar, *Saddam Husayn* (Bayrut, 1980); M. Khadduri, *Socialist Iraq* (Washington, D. C., 1978), 17–24.

21. The minister of planning, Jawad Hashim, held that the Soviet technology was not the best in the world and he urged the Iraqi government to purchase American technology as the Soviet government itself imported American technology (Khadduri's interview with Hashim in 1977).

22. For American commitments to the Shah of Iran in an effort to keep the Gulf region out of Soviet reach, see R. K. Ramazani, *Iran's Foreign Policy, 1941–1973* (Charlottesville, Va, 1975), and his *The United States and Iran* (New York, 1982); Shahram Chubin and Sepehr Zabih, *The Foreign Relations of Iran* (Berkeley and London, 1974).

23. For an account of the Carter Doctrine and its relevance to the Gulf region, see Zbigniew Brzezinski, *Power and Principle*, rev. ed., (New York, 1985), 444ff.

24. Alexander Haig, *Caveat, Realism, Reagan and Foreign Policy*, (New York, 1984), 190.

CHAPTER 7: DRIVES AND EVENTS LEADING TO THE INVASION OF KUWAIT

1. As the official American papers dealing with the Gulf crisis have not yet been made open to the public, a brief account of the conversations of President Bush with his advisers may be found in 1. James A. Baker, III, *The Politics of Diplomacy* (New York, 1995); 2. Colin Powell, *My American Journey* (New York, 1995); 3. Pierre Salinger and Eric Laurent, *Secret Dossier: The Hidden Agenda Behind the Gulf War* (New York, 1991); 4. Bob Woodward, *The Commanders* (New York, 1991).

2. In his *The Politics of Diplomacy*, Baker gives a summary of his conversation with 'Aziz in which he said: "'Aziz accused the United States of interfering in Iraq's internal affairs," although Iraq's complaints were made specifically against "certain circles", especially the CIA, and not against the President or his Secretary of State. 'Aziz also complained about the press campaign against Iraq, but Baker made no reference to the press or to the Bush administration's having nothing to do with that campaign. Saddam Husayn held that perhaps the American president had tacitly approved of it (pp. 264–67). Cf. Sa'd Bazzaz, *Harb Talid Harb* [War Leads to War] (Amman, 1992), 151–53.

3. For Kelly's meeting with Saddam only a short paragraph is devoted to it in Baker's *Politics of Diplomacy*, but a more detailed account may be found in an article by Don Oberdorfer based on an interview with Kelly, see Don Oberdorfer, "Missed Signals in the Middle East," *Washington Post Magazine*, March 17, 1991, 19ff. When Kelly met with Saddam, Ambassador Glaspie was not with him, as Baker states in his book.

4. Baker, *The Politics of Diplomacy*, 267.

5. For Bazoft's visit to Iraq, his arrest and execution, see *al-Thawra* (Baghdad) (March 5, 1990), 6–7. Saddam Husayn's view of Bazoft as an Israeli spy was intimated to Amir Bandar, Saudi Ambassador to the United States, as reported in Woodward's *The Commanders*, 203.

6. For an account of Gerald Bull's relations with Iraq, see Kelvin Toolis,

"The Man Behind Supergun," *New York Magazine*, August 26, 1990, 46–50, 76–77; Lawrence Freedman and Efraim Karsh, *The Gulf Conflict*, 1990–1991 (Princeton, 1993), 34–35.

7. For the text of Saddam's speech on April 1, 1990, see *al-Thawra* (Baghdad), April 2, 1990. The speech was made to a group of army officers on the occasion of honoring them for their military accomplishments in the war with Iran.

8. For Israel's reaction in statements made by General Barak and Premier Shamir, see Haykal, *Harb al-Khalij*, 192–96.

9. The statement was made public by Margaret Thatcher at the instance of the Secretary of State. See Baker, *The Politics of Diplomacy*, 268.

10. For an account of Amir Bandar's mission, see Woodward, *The Commanders*, 199–204.

11. For the text of the Dole mission, see Iraq [Ministry of Foreign Affairs], *Message of Peace*. The text of President Saddam Hussein's meeting with U. S. senators (Led by Senator Bob Dole), April 12, 1990 (Baghdad, 1990). For the official Arabic text, see Fouad Matar, *Mawsu'at Harb al-Khalij* [Gul f War Panorama] (London, 1994), vol. II, 482–92, reproduced from the Iraqi press.

12. In his work, *The Politics of Diplomacy*, Baker states that Senator Dole "announced that Saddam was a leader with whom the United States could work" (Baker, 269).

13. Saddam's Husayn's speech on his country's differences with Kuwait in the closed meeting of the Arab summit has not been published, but some passages have been quoted in some of the Arab published works (see Matar, *Mawsu'at Harb al-Khalij*, vol. II, 15–16; Bazzaz, *Harb Talid Harb*, 43).

14. Haykal, *Harb al-Khalij*, 309–11.

15. For Sa'dun Hamadi's visit to Kuwait and his conversation with its leaders, see *al-Thawra* (Baghdad), June 27, 1990. See also Bazzaz, *Harb Talid Harb*, 44–45.

16. For text, see *al-Thawra* (Baghdad), June 27, 1990; Matar, *Mawsu'at Harb al-Khalij*, vol. II, 7–11.

17. For text, see Matar, *Mawsu'at Harb al-Khalij*, vol. II, 11–15.

18. *Mawsu'at Harb al-Khalij*, vol. II, 16–18.

19. *Mawsu'at Harb al-Khalij*, vol. II, 18–19.

20. *Mawsu'at Harb al-Khalij*, vol. II, 19–22.

21. Baker, *The Politics of Diplomacy*, 271.

22. For statements by Saddam and Mubarak as to what each had meant about Saddam's intentions, see Matar, *Mawsu'at Harb al-Khalij*, vol. II, 593–613; Bazzaz, *Harb Talid Harb*, 58–59; Haykal, *Harb al-Khalij*, 329.

23. No official text of the Saddam-Glaspie conversation has yet been published. For an unofficial text of the Iraqi Foreign Ministry, see Matar, *Mawsu'at Harb al-Khalij*, vol. II, 30–35. For translation of excerpts from the document, see the *New York Times*, September 23, 1990, 19.

24. For excerpts of the letters Glaspie had received from the State Department, see the *Washington Post*, October 21, 1992. See also Baker, *The Politics of Diplomacy*, 272.

25. Haykal, *Harb al-Khalij*, 331 (English ed., 181).

26. Haykal, *Harb al-Khalij*, 332.

27. Matar, *Mawsu'at Harb al-Khalij*, vol. II, 316ff.

28. Matar, *Mawsu'at Harb al-Khalij*, vol. II, 60ff.

29. Bazzaz, *Harb Talid Harb*, 79–85.

30. Bazzaz, *Harb Talid Harb*, 82.

CHAPTER 8: THE INVASION OF KUWAIT

1. Sa'd al-Bazzaz, *Harb Talid Harb* [War Leads to War] (Amman, 1992–93), 23–24; Cf. Ofra Bengio, "Iraq," *Middle East Contemporary Survey*, vol. XIV (1990) who maintains that Saddam had decided to invade Kuwait several months before August, 1990.

2. Sa'd al-Bazzaz, "Ramad al-Hurub," [Ashes of War] *al-Sharq al-Awsat* (London), May 20, 1995, 8.

3. As the official American documents dealing with the Gulf crisis have not yet been made open to the public, a brief account on the conversations of President Bush with his advisers may be found in (A) James A. Baker, III, *The Politics of Diplomacy* (New York, 1995); (B) Colin Powell, *My American Journey* (New York, 1995); (C) Pierre Salinger and Eric Laurent, *Secret Dossier: The Hidden Agenda Behind the Gulf War* (New York, 1991); (D) Bob Woodward, *The Commanders* (New York, 1991).

4. For a statement to this effect made by Saddam Husayn in his conversation with April Glaspie, American ambassador to Iraq, see chapter VII.

5. Muhammad H. Haykal, *Harb al-Khalij* [Gulf War] (Cairo, 1992), 357–58.

6. Woodward, *The Commanders*, 215.

7. Woodward, *The Commanders*, 237.

8. For an account of President Bush's conversation with Prime Minister Margaret Thatcher at Aspen, see Margaret Thatcher, *The Downing Street Years* (New York, 1993), 817–18; 820–21. For Bush's conversation with King Fahd, see Woodward, *The Commanders*, 231–32; 254–56.

9. For Turkey's role in the Gulf crisis, see Sa'd al-Bazzaz, *Harb Talid Ikhra* [War Leading to Another War] (Amman, 1992–93), 271–89; Baker, *The Politics of Diplomacy*, 283–85.

10. For American-Soviet negotiations on the Gulf crisis, see Baker, *The Politics of Diplomacy*, 281–83, 285–87, 305–13.

11. For the attitude of the American public toward the Gulf War from its various perspectives, see John Mueller, *Policy and Opinion in the Gulf War* (Chicago, 1994).

12. The government of the Hashimite Kingdom of Jordan, *White Paper* (Amman, 1991), p. 3.

13. For Saddam's statement in reply to Mubarak, see Fouad Matar, *Mawsu'at Harb al-Khalij* [Gulf War Panorama] (London, 1994), vol. II, 597.

14. Haykal's interview with King Husayn, (April 28, 1991); see Haykal, *Harb al-Khalij*, 381.

15. Haykal, *Harb al-Khalij*, 382–83; Cf. Government of Jordan, *White Paper*, 3–4.

16. Government of Jordan, *White Paper*, 4–5. President Mubarak's justification that he was under pressure which prompted him to issue the condemnation of Iraq's invasion of Kuwait derived partly from the influence of President Bush and partly from his concern as to what role Egypt should play

in the Gulf crisis. According to Haykal, the experts at the Egyptian Foreign Ministry suggested that Egypt should pursue an independent role and assert its leadership in cooperation with the rich Arab Gulf countries (for text of the Memorandum, see Haykal, *Harb al-Khalij*, 374).

17. *White Paper*, 9–10. For text of King Husayn's letter to Saddam Husayn, see *White Paper*, 32–36.

18. Woodward, *The Commanders*, 241.

19. Woodward, *The Commanders*, 239ff. On his way to Saudi Arabia, Prince Bandar stopped in Morocco, where his father, Prince Sultan (Saudi minister of defence) was recuperating from surgery, to acquaint him with the purpose of his visit to meet with King Fahd before the Cheney mission had arrived in Saudi Arabia.

20. In his *Politics of Diplomacy*, Baker refers to his trip to Saudi Arabia in early September 1990, where he met with King Fahd and Shaykh Jabir, Amir of Kuwait, when he was reassured of Saudi contribution of 15 billion dollars as part of the Coalition War efforts. Shaykh Jabir also promised a contribution of another $15 billion. Baker also visited Cairo and talked with President Mubarak, who told him that he ''believed Saddam's ability to threaten his neighbors must be destroyed. '' He also told him that ''he was delighted to learn that the United States was prepared to forgive his $7. 1 billion in debt.'' (pp. 289–91).

CHAPTER 9: THE ROLE OF THE UNITED NATIONS

1. Readers who wish to see the full text of the Security Council's consideration of the resolutions concerning the Iraq-Kuwait crisis may be referred to the minutes of the Security Council sessions published by the United Nations. Excerpts of the speeches by the principal members who participated in the discussion over the Security Council resolutions may be found in E. Lauterpacht, et al., *The Kuwait Crisis: Basic Documents* (Cambridge, 1991). For Abu al-Hasan's statement, see 99–100.

2. Lauterpacht, *The Kuwait Crisis*, 100.

3. Lauterpacht, *The Kuwait Crisis*, 100.

4. Article 52 (Chapter VIII) provides for the establishment of regional ''arrangements or agencies'' dealing with the maintenance of peace and security ''provided that such arrangements or agencies and their activities are consistent with the purposes and principles of the United Nations. ''

5. Lauterpacht, *The Kuwait Crisis*, 102–03.

6. Lauterpacht, *The Kuwait Crisis*, 103.

7. Lauterpacht, *The Kuwait Crisis*, 103.

8. Lauterpacht, *The Kuwait Crisis*, 103.

9. Lauterpacht, *The Kuwait Crisis*, 103.

10. Lauterpacht, *The Kuwait Crisis*, 105.

11. Lauterpacht, *The Kuwait Crisis*, 104–05.

12. For an account of the Kuwait Provisional government and the role of its head, 'Ala Husayn al-Khafaji, see *al-Majalla* (London), No. 698 (July 30, 1993), 27–33. See also Lauterpacht, *The Kuwait Crisis*, 108–09.

13. For the composition and functions of the U.N. Committee for imple-

mentation of sanctions, see SC/5203 (August 9, 1990); Lauterpacht, *The Kuwait Crisis*, 197–98.

14. Lauterpacht, *The Kuwait Crisis*, 224ff.

15. For text of Jordan's letter to the president of the Security Council (August 20, 1990), see Lauterpacht, *The Kuwait Crisis*, 238–40.

16. For the Security Council's report on the economic problems of Jordan arising from carrying out the measures of economic sanctions under Resolution 661 (1991), September 18, 1990, see Lauterpacht, *The Kuwait Crisis*, 241–43.

17. SC/21498 (August 13, 1990); Lauterpacht, *The Kuwait Crisis*, 245.

18. For Libya's letter, see SC/21529 (August 15, 1990); Lauterpacht, *The Kuwait Crisis*, 246–247.

19. See SC/21564 (August 20, 1990) and SC/21568 (August 20, 1990); Lauterpacht, *The Kuwait Crisis,* pp. 248 and 251–53.

20. Lauterpacht, *The Kuwait Crisis*, 245, 248.

21. For Tariq ʿAziz's statement to press reporters, see the *Washington Post*, September 1, 1990.

22. *New York Times*, September 3, 1990.

23. For Mitterand's speech, see Lauterpacht, *The Kuwait Crisis*, 287–88.

24. For the text in Arabic of Shaykh Jabir's speech before the UN General Assembly, see Fouad Matar, *Harb al-Khalij*, vol. I, *Gulf War Panorama* (London, 1994), vol. II, 97–99; English text in A/45/PV. 10 (October 3, 1990).

25. Lauterpacht, *The Kuwait Crisis*, 190–91.

26. *Washington Post*, October 4–5, 1990; *New York Times*, October 5, 1990.

27. Lauterpacht, *The Kuwait Crisis*, 123–24.

28. Lauterpacht, *The Kuwait Crisis*, 125–26.

29. Lauterpacht, *The Kuwait Crisis*, 134–35.

30. John Norton Moore, *Crisis in the Gulf* (New York, 1992), 152–56. For a critique of Moore's book, see M. Khadduri, "Perspectives on the Gulf War," *Michigan Journal of International Law*, vol. 15 (Spring 1994), 847–61.

31. Lauterpacht, *The Kuwait Crisis*, 159–60.

32. Lauterpacht, *The Kuwait Crisis*, 160–61.

33. Lauterpacht, *The Kuwait Crisis*, 161–63.

34. Lauterpacht, *The Kuwait Crisis*, 166–67.

35. Lauterpacht, *The Kuwait Crisis*, 170–76.

36. Records of the Geneva meeting were published in the Iraqi press early in January 1991. See *Baghdad Observer*, January 9–22, 1992; for the Arabic text, see Matar, *Mawsuʿat Harb al-Khalij*, vol. II, 321–34. As the official American text has not been published, a summary of the essential parts may be found in James A. Baker, III *Politics of Diplomacy*, (New York, 1995), 351–65. Baker's and ʿAziz's accounts seem to agree.

37. President Bush's letter seems to have been picked up by officers of the Intercontinental Hotel and perhaps it remains there (see Haykal, *Harb al-Khalij*, 579). In his *Politics of Diplomacy*, Baker also states that another Arabic translation of the letter was sent to President Saddam through the Iraqi ambassador in Washington (Baker, 158).

38. Pierre Salinger and Eric Laurent, *Secret Dossier* (New York, 1991), 214. Baker complained at the press conference that ʿAziz moved not even an inch on withdrawal (Baker, *The Politics of Diplomacy*, 363–64).

39. Salinger, *Secret Dossier*, 217. A detailed account of the de Cuellar mission was reported in the Iraqi press. For a summary of the Arabic account, see

Sa'd al-Bazzaz, *Harb Talid Harb* (War Leads to War], (Amman, Jordan, 1992–93), 351–68.

40. Salinger, *Secret Dossier*, 217–18.

41. For Gorbachev's exchange cables with Iraq, see Matar, *Mawsuʿat Harb al-Khalij*, vol. II, 381–82.

42. For the establishment and functions of the Arab League, see Robert W. MacDonald, *The League of Arab States* (Princeton, 1965); Ahmed M. Gomaa, *The Foundation of the League of Arab States* (London, 1977); M. Khadduri, "Towards an Arab Union," *The American Political Science Review*, vol. 40 (February 1946), 90–100; Khadduri, "The Arab League as a Regional Arrangement," *American Journal of International Law*, vol. XL (October 1946), 756–77.

43. For an informal Arab summit meeting preceding the Arab League Council meeting, see Tariq ʿAziz's account in Matar, *Mawsuʿat Harb al-Khalij*, vol. II, 89–92.

44. Haykal, *Harb al-Khalij* [Gulf War] (Cairo, 1992), 432.

45. Haykal, *Harb al-Khalij*, 434.

46. Haykal, *Harb al-Khalij*, 434

47. For text of the resolution, see Matar, *Mawsuʿat Harb al-Khalij*, vol. II, 85–88.

48. For a discussion of pan-Arabism and Arab unity and the controversy over the unitary and federal schemes, see Amir Shakib Arslan, *al-Wahda al-ʿArabiya* [Arab Unity], (Damascus, 1937); Satiʿ al-Husri, Akram Zuʿaytar, and Kamil Muruwa, *Risala fi al-Ittihad* [A Treatise on Unity] (Bayrut, 1954); Muhammad ʿIzzat Darwaza, *al-Wahda al-ʿArabiya* [Arab Unity] (Bayrut, 1958).

49. For Saudi Arabian foreign policy and King Faysal's views on Islamic cooperation, see Ghassan Salama, *al-Siyasa al-Kharijiya al-Saudiya* [Saudi Foreign Policy] (Bayrut, 1980), 641ff. For an analysis by a Saudi scholar, see ʿAbd-Allah Saʿud al-Qabbaʿ, *al-Siyassa al-Kharijiya al-Saudiya* [Saudi Foreign Policy]. See also Nadav Safran, *Saudi Arabia* (Cambridge, Mass., 1985); Robert R. Sullivan, "Saudi Arabia in International Politics," *Review of Politics*, vol. 32 (1970), 436–60; Adeed Dawisha, *Saudi Arabia's Search for Security* (London, 1979); James P. Piscatori, "Ideological Politics in Saudi Arabia," in J. P. Piscatori, ed., *Islam in the Political Process* (London, 1983), 56–72. For an evaluation of King Faysal's contribution to Saudi development in domestic and foreign affairs, see Willard A. Beling, ed., *King Faisal* (London, 1980).

50. For resolutions of the Islamic Conference, see the *Secretariat of the Arab Gulf Cooperation Council* (Riyad, Saudi Arabia, 1992), vol. IV, 85–88.

CHAPTER 10: THE COALITION WAR

1. *Washington Post*, January 17, 1991; Cf. Saddam Husayn's speech in Fouad Matar, *Mawsuʿat Harb al-Khalij* [Panorama of the Gulf War] (London, 1994), vol. II, 371–72.

2. Jeffrey McCausland, "The Gulf Conflict: A Military Analysis," *Adelphi Papers: 28* (London, 1993), 24. See also General Khalid Bin Sultan, *Desert Warrior* (New York, 1995), 341ff.

3. For use of Scud missiles, see Colin Powell, *My American Journey* (New York, 1995), 511–12. See also *Los Angeles Times*, January 20, 1991; *Washington Post*, November 18, 1991.

4. For the impact of the Scuds on Israel and the use of the Patriots, see

James A. Baker, III, *The Politics of Diplomacy* (New York, 1995), 385–90; Powell, *My American Journey*, 512–13; Cf. Iraq Military Command Proclamation in Matar, *Mawsu'at Harb al-Khalij*, vol. II, 372–73.

5. *Los Angeles Times*, February 26, 1991; *al-Hayat* and *al-Sharq Al-Awsat*, February 26 and 27, 1991.

6. Simon Li, et al., *Witness to War: Images from the Persian Gulf War from the Staff of the Los Angeles Times*, (Los Angeles, 1991), 31.

7. Powell, *My American Journey*, 507–10; McCausland, *The Gulf Conflict*, 27.

8. Powell, *My American Journey*, 109–10; Los *Angeles Times*, January 14–15, 1991.

9. James Ridgeway, *The March to War: From Day One to War End and Beyond* (New York, 1991), 175.

10. *New York Times*, February 6, 1991; *Los Angeles Times*, February 6, 1991.

11. Powell, *My American Journey*, 513; *Los Angeles Times*, February 14–15, 1991; Dilip Hiro, *Desert Shield to Desert Storm* (New York, 1992), 359–62.

12. *Al Nahar*, February 14–18, 1991.

13. Ridgeway, *The March to War*, 177.

14. Khalid Bin Sultan, *Desert Warrior* 361ff; Li, et al, *Witness to War*, 45.

15. Hiro, *Desert Shield*, 344–45; *Al Nahar*, January 31, 1991; *al-Safir*, February 1–3, 1991.

16. *Los Angeles Times*, January 31, 1991.

17. Lee Hackstader, "Battered Baghdad Struggles On," *Washington Post* (February 28, 1991); Hiro, *Desert Shield*, 345.

18. *International Herald Tribune*, February 4, 1991; Hiro, *Desert Shield*, 345.

19. *Los Angeles Times*, February 20 and 23, 1991; Hiro, *Desert Shield*, 367–371.

20. *Los Angeles Times*, February 23, 1991.

21. *Al-Safir* (Bayrut), February 18–19, 1991; *Independent*, (London) February 18, 1991, cited in Hiro, *Desert Shield*, 366–67.

22. *Al-Nahar*, (Bayrut) February 22–23, 1991; *Washington Post*, February 22 and 24, 1991.

23. *Washington Post*, February 23, 1991.

24. For an account of the military and political developments, see "*Azamat al-Khalij wa-Ta'diyatuha 'Ala al-Watan al-Arabi*" [The Gulf Crisis and its Impact on the Arab Homeland], proceedings of a conference organized by the Center for Arab Studies (Bayrut, 1991); Ramsey Clark, *The Fire This Time*, (New York, 1992); Anthony Cordesman, *Iran and Iraq: The Threat From the Northern Gulf* (Mimeo, 1993); Department of Defense, *Conduct of the Persian Gulf War: Final Report to Congress*, vols. 1–3, (Washington, D. C. : Department of Defense, 1992); James F. Dunningham and Austin Bay, *From Shield to Storm* (New York, 1991); Lawrence Freedman and Efraim Karsh, *The Gulf Conflict* (Princeton, 1993); Norman Friedman, *Desert Victory*, (Annapolis, 1991); Jeffrey McCausland, "The Gulf Conflict: A Military Analysis," *Adelphi Paper: 282*, (London, 1993); John Pimlott and Stephen Badsey, *The Gulf War Assessed* (London, 1992); James Ridgeway, ed., *The March to War: From Day One to War's End and Beyond*, (New York, 1991); Bruce W. Watson, *Military Lessons of the gulf War*, (London, 1991); Martin Yant, *Desert Mirage*, (New York, 1991).

25. Powell, *My American Journey*, 518–21.

26. For an account of these events see: *Al-Nahar* and *Al-Hayat*, February 27–March 3, 1991; *Los Angeles Times*, *New York Times*, and *Washington Post*, Feburary 27–28; Hiro, *Desert Shield*, 381-96.

27. Yant, *Desert Mirage*, 143–50.

28. *Boston Globe*, March 14, 1991. A Kuwaiti was quoted as having witnessed Iraqi troops retreating from Kuwait 36 hours before allied forces; President Bush and some of his advisers, however, had invested much of their reputation and much capital and wanted to deliver a knockout blow to the Iraqis. Powell, *My American Journey*, 515. Some advisors also wanted to be rid of the Vietnam Syndrome and were determined to make a show of American power in the post cold war period.

29. Baker, *The Politics of Diplomacy*, 410.; Powell, *My American Journey*, 521-22.

30. *Boston Globe*, March 14, 1991; Yant, *Desert Mirage*, 143-50; *Los Angeles Times*, February 28 1991.

31. André Gunder Frank, "A Third World War, A Political Economy of the Persian Gulf and the New World Order," in H. Mowlana, et. al, *Triumph of the Image* (Boulder, Colo., 1992), 11–12.

32. Powell, *My American Journey*, 527.

33. *Washington Post*, February 28, 1991.

CHAPTER 11: IRAQ UNDER THE AEGIS OF THE UNITED NATIONS

1. Eric Rouleau, "Iraq's Human Plight," *Foreign Affairs* (January–February 1955), 64.

2. Harvard Study Team Report, *Public Health in Iraq After the Gulf War* (May 1991), 103 (mimeograph).

3. A Pentagon official said that American Commanders "did not distinguish between military and civilian use of electricity, communications and oil centers," David Zucchine, "The Iraqi who Stay Face a Slow Death," *Philadelphia Inquirer*, 1.

4. For further details, see Ahmad Hashim, "Iraq the Pariah State," *Current History* (January, 1992), 13–14.

5. The Iraqi army was "decimated" according to a staff study, titled "The Civil War in Iraq," released by Senator Claiborne Pell, chairman of the Senate Foreign Relations Committee, prepared by his aide Peter Galbraith. The report stated that 100,000 Iraqi soldiers died during the Coalition War. Other figures state 158,000 soldiers were killed.

6. See The Report of the Iraq Advisory Committee on the Political and Economic Changes in Iraq (September, 1995) (Arabic); ʿAbbas al-Nasrawi, *The Economy of Iraq* (Westport, 1994).

CHAPTER 12: SHIʿI AND KURDISH UPRISINGS

1. For details on the Islamic and other opposition groups, see a series of articles published in *al Shiraʿ* Magazine, Bayrut, under the title of "Milaf al-Harakat al-Islamiya" [File on Islamic Movements], *al-Shiraʿ* (Bayrut), March 11–25, 1991; Saʿd al-Din Ibrahim, ed., *Hummum al-Aqaliyyat* [Concerns of the Minorities] (Cairo, 1993), 217–87; "Iraqi Opposition Adrift", *Issues* (Paris) vol. I, no. G. (March, 1992), 1–4; Amazia Baram, "From Radicalism to Radical Pragmatism: The Shiʿite Fundamentalist Opposition Movements in Iraq", in James

Piscatori, ed., *Islamic Fundamentalisms and the Gulf Crisis* (Chicago, 1991); Ofra Bengio, "Shi'is and Politics in Ba'thi Iraq," *Middle Eastern Studies* (January, 1985); Edmund Ghareeb, "Domestic Politics and Development in Iraq" in Z. Michael Szaz, ed., *Domestic and Foreign Policy Issues in Iraq.* (Washington, D.C.); Majid Khadduri, *The Gulf War* (New York, 1988); Yitzhak Nakash, *The Shi'is of Iraq* (Princeton, 1994); Joyce Wiley, *The Islamic Movement of Iraqi Shi'as* (Boulder, Colo., 1992); Antoine Jalkh, "L'opposition Irakienne Dans Tous les Etats," *Arabies* (Paris), no. 51 (March 1991); Laurie Mylroie, *The Future of Iraq* (Washington, D.C. 1991), 34–46; Peter Galbraith, *Civil War in Iraq*, Staff Report to the Committee on Foreign Relations, U.S. Senate, May 2, 1991.

2. For details about the uprising in the South, see Ahmad Hashim, "Iraq the Pariah State," *Current History*, vol. 91, no. 561 (January 1991), 11–16; D. Hiro, *Desert Shield* pp. 400–409. Kana'n Makiya, *Cruelty and Silence: War, Tyranny, Uprising and the Arab World* (New York, 1993); Pierre Martin, "Les Chiites d'Irak Sur la Scene Politique," *Maghreb-Machrek* (Paris), no. 132, (Avril-Juin 1991); Milton Viorst, "Report From Baghdad," *New Yorker*, June 29, 1991, 55–73; Nora Boustany, "Refugees Tell of Turmoil in Iraq: Troops Recall Allied Onslaught," *Washington Post*, March 4, 1991; Galbraith, *Civil War in Iraq*, 1–9.

3. *Washington Post*, February 16, 1991.

4. Ghareeb's interviews with Najm al-Din Karim of the Kurdish Congress of North America and Barham Salih of the PUK, August 9, 1991. See also *al-Shira'* (Bayrut), March 18, 1991, 23–28; Galbraith, *Civil War in Iraq*, 22; Mylroie, *The Future of Iraq*; Omar'Ali, *Crisis in the Arabian Gulf* (Westport, 1993), 94–96.

5. *Sawt al-Kuwait al-Arabi* (London), March 1, 1991.

6. *Sawt al-Iraq al-Hurr* [Voice of Free Iraq], February 24, 1991, cited in an opposition leaflet distributed in early March 1991.

7. 'Abd-Allah Fahd al-Nafisi, *Dawr al-Shi'a Fi Tattawur al-Iraq al-Siyasi al-Hadith* [The Shi'i Role in the Political Development of Modern Iraq], 2nd ed. (Bayrut, 1986), 69ff.

8. For these and other events, see Makiya, *Cruelty and Silence*, 62–78.

9. *al-Shira'*, 26.

10. "Opposition Seeking New Political System", *Al-Ahram al-Dawli* (Cairo) February 22, 1991), 1, 3; "Baqir al-Hakim Interviewed on Future Government," *Profil* (Vienna; in German), March 18, 1991, 49. See also *al-Bilad* interview with *al-Hakim* (Bayrut), March 23, 1991.

11. Makiya, *Cruelty and Silence*, p 75; Viorst, "Report from Baghdad," 73.

12. Viorst, "Report from Baghdad," 72.

13. Hashim, "*Iraq the Pariah State*," 12.

14. *Al-Iraq* (Baghdad), March 7, 1991.

15. *Al-Qadisiya* (Baghdad), March 8, 1991.

16. *Al-Thawra* (Baghdad), March 17, 1991; Hashim, "*Iraq: The Pariah State*," 12.

17. For further information on the Shi'is and other religious and ethnic groups, see Naji Nu'man, ed., "*Al-Majmu'at al-'Irqiya wa al-Madhhabiya Fi al-'Alam al-'Arabi* [Ethnic Groups and Religious Groups in the Arab World] (Bayrut, 1990); Sa'd al-Din Ibrahim, ed., *Hummum al-Aqalliyat*; Yitzhak Nakash, *The Shi'is of Iraq*; Edmund Ghareeb, *Al-Haraka al-Qawmiya al-Kurdiya* [The Kurdish National Movement] (Bayrut, 1972); 'Abd al-Razzaq al-Hasani, *Tarikh al-Wazarat al-'Iraqiya*, [History of Iraqi Cabinets] 4th expanded ed. (Bayrut, 1974) vols. 1–10; Hanna Batatu, *The Old Social Classes and the Revolutionary Movements in Iraq* (Princeton, 1978), 818; Joyce Wiley, *The Islamic Movement of Iraqi Shi'as* (Boulder,

Colo., 1992); Ofra Bengio, "Shi'is and Politics in Ba'thi Iraq," *Middle Eastern Studies*, vol. 25. (1985), 6; Hanna Batatu, "Shi'i Organizations in Iraq: al-Duwal al-Islamiya and al-Mujahidin," in Juan Cole and Nikkie Keddie, eds., *Shi'ism and Social Protest* (New Haven, 1986).

18. For details on this period, see Majid Khadduri's *The Gulf War* (New York, 1988); Edmund Ghareeb, "The Roots of the Crisis" in Christopher Joyner, ed., *The Iraq-Iran War* (Connecticut, 1990); *Business Week*, March 22, 1982), 54; Edmund Ghareeb, "Domestic Politics and Development in Iraq," in M. Szaz, ed., *Sources of Domestic and Foreign Policy in Iraq* (Washington, DC, 1986), 17–27.

19. Ghareeb's interview with Jalal Talabani, May 6, 1988.

20. Edmund Ghareeb, *The Kurdish Question in Iraq* (Syracuse, 1981), 6–7; 'Ubayd-Allah al-Nahri, Shaykh Mahmud of Sulaimaniya, the Shaykhs of Barzan, the Sayids of Shamdinan, the Khanaqa Sayids, and the Naqshabandi Shaykhs north of Mawsil.

21. Ghareeb, *The Kurdish Question*, 6–7.

22. For details, see Ghareeb, *The Kurdish Question*, 1–27.

23. Ghareeb, *The Kurdish Question*, 31–32. See also Ghareeb, *Al-Haraka al-Qawmiya al-Kurdiya* [The Kurdish National Movement] (Bayrut, 1973).

24. Ghareeb, *Al-Haraka*, 37–44; Sa'd Jawad, *Iraq and the Kurdish Question* (London, 1981), 63–95.

25. Ghareeb, "Domestic Politics and Development in Iraq," 10–11.

26. For the full text of the Manifesto, see *al-Thawra* (Baghdad), March 11, 1970. For further elaboration on the contents and significance of the Manifesto, see Ghareeb, *The Kurdish Question in Iraq*, 87–89.

27. For details on Iranian, U.S., and Israeli roles, see Ghareeb, *The Kurdish Question in Iraq*, 131–46.

28. Ghareeb, *The Kurdish Question in Iraq*, 171–74.

29. For information on Iraqi government policies and Kurdish activities during this period, see Ghareeb, *The Kurdish Question in Iraq*, 176–93.

30. Donald Neff, "The U.S., Iraq, Israel and Iran: Backdrop to War," *Journal of Palestine Studies*, vol. XX, no. 4 (Summer 1991), 23–41. See also the *Washington Post*, May 3, 1990.

31. Stephen Pelletière, Douglas Johnson, and Leif Rozenberger, *Iraqi Power and U.S. Security in the Middle East* (Carlisle Barracks, 1991), 52.

32. U.S. Congress, *Senate Foreign Relations Committee Report on Chemical Weapons Use in Kurdistan: Iraq's Final Offensive, Committee Print 100–148*. (Washington, DC, 1988), 32; Neff "The U.S., Iraq, Israel and Iran," 32; *Financial Times*, September 10, 1988. Western journalists interviewed one Kurdish *peshmerga* who said that his unit was hit by an Iraqi gas attack.

33. Hanna Frayj, "Al-Masala al-Kurdiya fi al-Iraq wa al-Tadakhul al-Ajnabi, [The Kurdish Question in Iraq and Foreign Intervention] *Qira'at Siyasiya*, vol 3, no. 1 (1993), 22.; *The Middle East* (London), February 1991, 19.

34. Frayj, 1993, 22; *The Middle East*, 1991, 19.

35. "The War We Left Behind," *Frontline*, reported by Andrew and Leslie Cockburn. Most Kurdish leaders interviewed by Ghareeb denied receiving weapons during this period. One Kurdish official who wished to remain anonymous said weapons were provided to Iraqi Kurds in Turkey. A State Department official interviewed by Ghareeb on November 11, 1991, also denied this report, but admitted that he was unaware of all that was going on.

36. *Washington Post,* April 9, 1991.

37. Dilip Hiro gives a figure of 100,000 while Ghareeb's interviews with Dr. Najm al-Din Karim, a Kurdish National Congress leader, and Dr. Barham Salih of the Patriotic Union of Kurdistan provided the higher figures.

38. Ghareeb's interviews with a number of anti-regime figures, who wish to remain anonymous, in August and September, 1991, Cf. Hiro, *Desert Shield,* 4–5.

39. Ghareeb's interviews with Talabani and Hushiyar Zibari, Oct. 6, 1991.

40. Ghareeb's interviews (Oct. 6, 1991); Michael Gunter, *The Kurds of Iraq* (New York, 1992), 51–52.

41. For details about the Kirkuk controversy in the 1970's, see Ghareeb, *The Kurdish Question in Iraq,* 1981, 119–125, 154–156.

42. Ghareeb's interview with Talabani.

43. Ghareeb's interview with Zibari.

44. J. Bulloch and H. Morris, *No Friends but the Mountains,* (Oxford, 1992), 12–13.

45. *Washington Post,* March 27, 1991, cited in Gunter, 50.

46. In Ghareeb's interview, Talabani denied that the Kurds surrendered these prisoners to Iran, as they were executed according to the Mujahidin. Talabani claimed that the Kurds sought to win them over and that they were a formidable force, but they participated in the fighting between Kifri and Tuz Khurmatu. See Galbraith, *Civil War in Iraq,* 5–6; Makiya, *Cruelty and Silence,* 82–84; *Middle East International,* April 5, 1991, 2–3, and April 19, 1991, 8.

47. IRNA, April 19, 1991, cited in an Iraq opposition leaflet (September 1992).

48. Viorst, "Report from Baghdad," 70. Viorst interviewed Kurds who claimed that their leaders promised "an independent Kurdistan" after the revolution.

49. Robert Parry, *Fooling America* (New York, 1992) 152. Parry states that President Bush and the CIA urged the Kurds to rise against the government; Ghareeb's interview with Zibari.

50. Ghareeb's interview with a Kurdish leader (June 8, 1991).

51. Ghareeb's interview with Mulla Mustafa Barzani, September 13, 1976; Ghareeb, *The Kurdish Question,* 179.

52. Ghareeb's interview with Mus'ud Barzani.

53. *Washington Post* February 16, 1991.

54. Federal News Service, Washington, March 16, 1991.

55. "Civil War In Iraq," Staff Report to Senate Relations Committee.

56. Ghareeb's interviews with Talabani, Zibari, and Sami Mahumud 'Abd al-Rahman, February 28, 1991; "Civil War in Iraq", 23–24.

57. Ghareeb's interview with Heino Kopietz who served as a go-between during this and later periods and helped to arrange the interviews, May 1989.

58. Ghareeb's interview with Talabani, May 6, 1988.

59. Interview with Kopietz.

60. *Washington Post,* February 16, 1991.

61. *Civil War in Iraq,* 28.

62. *New York Times,* March 29, 1991.

63. *Washington Post,* April 14, 1991; *Middle East International,* April 19, 1991.

64. *al-Thawra* (Baghdad), April 7, 1991.

65. Baghdad Domestic Service in FBIS, April 12, 1991.

66. See *Civil War in Iraq*, U.S. Senate Staff Report.

67. *Al-Thawra.* (Baghdad), April 19, 1991.

68. *Washington Post*, May 10, 1991; *al-Hayat* (London); *al-Nahar* (Bayrut) May 10–15, 1991.

69. Ghareeb's interviews with Talabani and Zibari; Talabani said that Saddam Husayn joked with him as soon as he entered into his office about his wearing glasses and his getting grayer in order to break the ice. Talabani responded by saying: "You have made us grayer, Mr. President," and the two embraced.

70. Ghareeb's interview with Talabani who was willing to go, but who wanted an authorization from Barzani saying he was speaking on his behalf.

71. Ghareeb's interviews with Barzani and Hushiyar Zibari, October 6, 1991; Cf. Gunter, 61

72. Interviews with Barham Salih and Jalal Talabani, September, 1991. The papers discussed include *Mashru' al-Jabha al-Kurdistaniya al-'Iraqiya lil Hukm al-Dhati* [The Iraqi Kurdistan Front's Program for Autonomy], *Tatbi' al-Awdha' fi Kurdistan bi inha al-zuruf al-Istithna'iya* [The Normalization of the Situation in Kurdistan by ending the Exceptional Conditions and Situations], *Mulahazat Hawl al-Dimuqratiya fi al-Iraq* [Observations on Democracy in Iraq], and *Qanun al-Hukm al-Dhati li Mantiqat Kurdistan* [The Self-Rule Law for the Kurdish Region].

73. Gunter, 60,

74. Gunter 62; *Al-Hayat* (London) and *Al-Nahar* (Bayrut), April 26–27, 1991.

75. Gunter, 63; *Al-Sharq al-Awsat* (London), May 1 and May 10, 1995.

76. Gunter 70–71; *Al-Hayat* (London), June 29–30, 1995.

77. Ghareeb's interviews with Barzani, Talabani, and Zibari. See also *Issues*, (Paris), (March, 1992), 1–4.

78. *Ibid.*

79. *Al-Thawra.* (Baghdad), April 3–9, 1995. For Saddam Husayn's bitter criticizm of the behavior of party officials during the uprising, see FBIS-NES, (May 3 and June 27, 1995), 13–14, 14–17.

CHAPTER 13: DEMARCATION OF THE FRONTIERS

1. The text of Security Council Resolution 687; see Richard Schofield, *Kuwait and Iraq: Historical Claims and Territorial Disputes* (London, 1994), 150-1951.

2. See *al-Sharq al-Awsat* (London) Aug. 28, 1991; *Washington Post*, Aug. 29, 1991. For a more detailed account, see Schoefield, *Kuwait and Iraq*, 158–61.

3. Secretary General's final report titled, *Final Report on the Demarcation of the International Boundary Between the Republic of Iraq and the State of Kuwait by the United Nations Iraq-Kuwait Boundary Demarcation Commission*, IKDBC/Rep. 8, 13ff.

4. Secretary General's final report, 15.

5. Secretary General's final report, 14ff.

6. Secretary General's final report, 16.

7. See Tawfiq al-Suwaydi, *Mudhakirati* [My Memoirs] (Bayrut 1969), 299–300. Suwaydi, Iraq's Foreign Minister in 1938–39 and 1958, always held that the two islands of Warba and Bubiyan were Iraqi territory.

8. Secretary General's final report, IKDBC/Rep. 8, 22ff.

9. For Iraq's rejection of the U.N. demarcation report, see *The Baghdad Observer*, June 2–10, 1992.

10. For Kuwait's position on the demarcation of the boundary, see a study on the subject by eight Kuwaiti experts, including Tariq Razzuqi (Kuwait's representative in the IKBDC) titled *Tarsim al-Hudud al-Kuwaitiya al-Iraqiya* [Demarcation of the Kuwaiti-Iraqi boundaries] (Kuwait, 1992), 69ff; Schofield, *Kuwait and Iraq*, 170–72.

11. Lauterpacht, *Recognition in International Law*, chaps. 4 and 5, 38ff.

12. J. L. Brierly, *The Law of Nations*, ed. H. Waldock (Oxford, 1963), chap. 7, 317ff; Lord MacNair, *Law of Treaties* (London, 1938). For the controversy over ratification, see Research in International Law, part III, *Law of Treaties* (James W. Garner, reporter), supplement to *American Journal of International Law*, vol. 29 (1935), 778–87.

13. For Kuwait's position on the validity of the demarcation, based on the Security Council resolutions, see an interview by Huda al-Husayni, a press reporter, with ʿAbd-Allah Bishara, former secretary of the Arab Gulf Cooperation Council, in *al-Sharq al-Awsat* (London) Aug. 13, 1993.

14. For the views of the Iraqi opposition leaders and the Kuwaiti men in official and unofficial capacities, see *al-Majalla* (London), Aug. 13, 1993.

15. *al-Majalla* (London), Aug. 13, 1993, 27–28.

16. For boundaries as possible cause of trouble between neighbors, see Richard Schofield, ed., *Territorial Foundation of the Gulf States* (New York, 1994), 3ff.

CHAPTER 14: STANDARDS OF RESPONSIBILITY

1. See *The Politics of Aristotle*, trans. Ernest Barker (Oxford: Clarendon Press, 1946, rev. 1952), 3, 388. Hans Kelsen, "Aristotle's Doctrine of Justice," in *What is Justice?* (Berkeley and Los Angeles, 1960), 110–36. For the Greek distinction between Hellenes and Barbarians, see T. A. Walker, *A History of the Law of Nations* (Cambridge: University Press, 1899), vol. I, 38–39.

2. T. A. Walker, *A History*, 58–59.

3. For an exposition of the *jihad* in classical works, see Muhammad Bin al-Hasan al-Shaybani, *Kitab al-Siyar*, trans. M. Khadduri, *The Islamic Law of Nations* (Baltimore, 1965), 10–17, 130–141.

4. Edward Gibbon, *The History of the Decline and Fall of the Roman Empire* (London, 1876), vol. V, 435.

5. Taqi al-Din Ibn Taymiya, "Qaʿida fi Qital al-Kuffar," in H. H. al-Fiqqi, ed., *Majmuʿat Rasaʾil*, (Cairo, 1949), 115–46.

6. For an interpretation of this Quranic Revelation, see Muhammad Bin Jarir al-Tabari, Shakir, ed., *Tafsir* (Cairo, n.d.), vol. V, 407ff.

7. For a discussion of Sultan Sulayman the Magnificent treaty with King Francis of Frances, see Nasim Sousa, *The Capitulatory Regime in Turkey* (Baltimore, 1935), chap. 4; H. H. Liebesny, "The Development of Western Judicial Privileges," in Khadduri and Liebesny, ed., *Law in the Middle East*, (Washington, D. C. 1955), vol. I, 309–33.

8. Imam Khomeini, *Islam and Government*, trans. Hamid Algar (Berkeley, 1981), 27ff.

9. For the Sultan's declaration of the *jihad* as "holy war," see Ahmed

Emin, *Turkey In the World War*, (New Haven, 1930), chap. 14; A. J. Toynbee, *Survey of International Affairs*, 1925, vol. I: *The Islamic World Since the Peace Settlement* (London, 1925), 43, 44; for Sharif Husayn's declarations of a counter-*jihad*, see "Proclamation to the Muslim World" in Muhammad Tahir al-'Umari, *Muqaddarat al-Iraq al-Siyasiya* [Political Destinies of Iraq] (Mawsil, 1924), vol. I, 257–68 (original text), 269–74 (edited text published in Cairo). See also Sulayman Musa, *al-Husayn Bin Ali* (Amman, 1957), 100–07. The British authorities in Cairo had reservations about Sharif Husayn's appeal to the Islamic world, as they wanted his revolt to be confined to the Hijaz and Syria, but not to be an appeal to Muslims in India and Egypt which might adversely affect the British standing in those countries (see Sulayman Musa, *al-Haraka al-'Arabiya, 1908–1924* (Bayrut, 1970) chap. 5.

CHAPTER 15: ARAB RESPONSIBILITIES

1. The average life of a Cabinet in Iraq under the monarchy (1921–58) was eight months, and the Cabinet changes following the Revolution of 1958 were at the pleasure of the top military leaders. For a discussion of the frequent changes of Cabinets and instability of the Iraqi regimes, see M. Khadduri, *Independent Iraq* (London, 2nd ed., 1960), chap. XIV, 270–72.

2. For the controversy over the necessity of the ratification of treaties and agreements from the constitutional and international law viewpoints, see Quincy Wright, *The Control of American Foreign Relations* (New York, 1922), in which the American constitutional process is discussed; Arnold McNair, *Law of Treaties* (London, 1938), in which the international law viewpoints are discussed.

3. See the reply of the United Arab Amirate to the memorandum of Iraq to the Arab League (July 15, 1990), in Fouad Matar, *Mawsu't Harb al-Khalij*, vol. II, 18–19 (Arabic text).

4. Iraq maintained that Kuwait's firm stand was the result of its dependence on foreign support leading to foreign intervention in Arab affairs. During the Iraq-Kuwait crisis in 1990, some Kuwaiti leaders complained to Bush that Saddam Husayn had taken a threatening and arrogant attitude toward Kuwaiti leaders. For Iraq's accusation of Kuwait's dependence on foreign support, see Tawfiq al-Suwaydi, *Mudhakkirati* [My Memoirs] (Bayrut, 1969), 584–85. For Kuwaiti complaints about Saddam's threats and arrogance, see an interview by four Arab news reporters with George Bush in *al-Sharq al-Awsat* (London), March 10, 1991, 6–7.

5. For the distinction between individual and collective duties in Islamic jurisprudence, see *Islamic Jurisprudence: Shafi'i's Risala*, trans. Khadduri (Baltimore, 1961), 84–86.

6. Matar, *Mawsu'at Harb al-Khalij*, vol. II, 46–47, 167–68.

7. Matar, *Mawsu'at Harb al-Khalij*, vol. II, 342–45.

8. In the negotiation of the Treaty of Erzerum (Arz al-Rum) between the Ottoman Empire and Persia (Iran) by virtue of which the frontier dispute between the two Muslim countries were settled, Great Britain and Russia were instrumental in bringing an understanding between the Ottoman and Persian delegations. For the historical background and settlement of the dispute, see Khalid al-'Izzi, *The Shatt al-Arab Dispute* (London and Baghdad, 1981), 27ff.

9. For a background on the structure and working of the Arab League, see Robert W. MacDonald, *The League of Arab States* (Princeton, 1965); Ahmed

M. Gomaa, *The Foundation of the League of Arab States* (London, 1977); M. Khadduri, "The Arab League as a Regional Arrangement," *American Journal of International Law* vol. XL, (1946), 756–77.

10. For the GCC's resolution concerning the Gulf crisis, see Matar, *Mawsuʿat Harb al-Khalij*, vol. II, 52–53.

11. In a tradition from the Prophet Muhammad, any person who is "*jaban*" is described as the one who is deprived of good qualities. For text of the Prophet's tradition, see Abu Dawud, *Sunan* (Cairo, 1935), vol. III, 12.

12. Both in the press and in the media, Saddam Husayn was often maligned, but he was also praised in high political circles in Arab and some Western countries (see Matar, *Mawsuʿat Harb al-Khalij*, vol. II, 49–50; 104–05; 108–12; 137–38; 166–67.

13. For statements by Amir Jabir and Shaykh Saʿd, the Amir and premier of Kuwait, about their actions following the invasion of their country, see Matar, *Mawsuʿat Harb al-Khalij*, vol. II, 59–60; 212–213; 213–217.

CHAPTER 16: WESTERN INTERVENTION AND ITS RATIONALE

1. For the significance of imperialism as a civilizing mission, see John R. Seeley, *The Expansion of England* (London, 1883); Leonard S. Wolf, *Civilization and Colonization* (London, 1933).

2. Oscar Schachter, "United Nations Law in the Gulf Conflict," *American Journal of International Law*, vol. 85 (July 1991), 452ff.

3. For the meanings of linkage in the Arab-Israel conflict, see Ibrahim Abu-Lughud, "The Politics of Linkage: The Arab-Israeli Conflict in the Gulf War," in Phyllis Bennis and Michael Mushabeck, eds., *Beyond the Storm* (New York, 1991), 183ff.

4. Salinger, *Secret Dossier* 130; Woodward, *The Commanders* chaps. 17–18.

5. For advisers in high authority who gave Saddam conflicting views about Western democracies, see Saʿd al-Bazzaz, "*Ramad al-Hurub*" [Ashes of War], *al-Sharq al-Awsat* (London), May 20, 22, 1995.

6. Thatcher, *The Downing Street Years*, 817, 819–20.

7. Cf. James T. Johnson and George Weigel, *Just War and Gulf War* (Washington, D. C., 1994); John Kelsay, *Islam and War* (Louisville, Kentucky, 1993); James Piscatori, *Islamic Fundamentalists and the Gulf Crisis* (Chicago, 1991); David E. Decosse, ed., *But Was it Just?*, Reflections on the Morality of the Persian Gulf War (New York, 1991).

CHAPTER 17: CONCLUSION: WAS THE WAR INEVITABLE?

1. "For every problem there is a solution," is a well-known saying in the Middle East intended to encourage all parties to a dispute to find a solution. Cited by Shaykh Jabir in his conversation with Saddam Husayn, in the presence of King Fahd, it was an indication that both sides should continue negotiations seeking a solution to the satisfaction of both sides. See Haykal, *Harb al-Khalij*, 310–311.

2. Bazzaz, *Harb Talid Harb*, 3–34.

3. For Ambassador al-Anbari's statement, see *Role of United Nations in the Gulf Crisis*, chapter IX, 158.

4. For the text of the proclamation of *jihad* by Muslim scholars in Iraq, see Matar, *Mawsu'at Harb al-Khalij*, vol. II, 167–68.

5. For al-Mu'tazila's ideas about free will and voluntary acts, see W. M. Watts, *Free Will and Predestination in Early Islam* (London, 1953), 58–82.

6. Thatcher, *The Downing Street Years*, 816ff.

7. For the belief in the doctrine of predestination by the rank and file in Iraq, see 'Ali al-Wardi, *Dirasa Fi Tabi'at al-Mujtama 'al-Iraqi* [A Study in the Nature of the Iraqi Society] (Baghdad, 1965), 304–05.

8. For the Ba'th Party's idea that Islam is a cultural element in Arab nationalism and not separate from the state, see Michel Aflaq, *Fi Sabil al-Ba'th* 2nd, ed. (Bayrut, 1963), 122–36.

9. Salinger, *Secret Dossier*, 130.

Index